BOY SCOUT HANDBOOK

BOY SCOUT
HANDBOOK
TENTH EDITION

BOY SCOUTS OF AMERICA

Dedicated to the American Scoutmaster
who makes Scouting possible

In appreciation

This handbook, the official BSA manual, is based
on the experience of the Boy Scouts of America
in the United States since its founding in 1910,
and is administered under the leadership of

Norman R. Augustine, *President*

Jere B. Ratcliffe, *Chief Scout Executive*

The manuscript for this new edition of the
Boy Scout Handbook was written by Robert C. Birkby, Eagle Scout,
mountaineer, and former director of Conservation
at Philmont Scout Ranch.

Copyright © 1990
Boy Scouts of America
Irving, Texas
Printed in U.S.A.   300M296
No. 33229

Tenth Edition • SixthPrinting
Total copies of Tenth Edition—2,800,000
Total printing since 1910—35,660,000

Library of Congress Cataloging-in-Publication Data

Boy Scouts of America.
    Boy Scout handbook.

    "Manuscript . . . was written by Robert Birkby"—T.p. verso.

    1. Boy Scouts of America—Handbooks, manuals, etc.
2. Boy Scouts—United States—Handbooks, manuals, etc.
I. Birkby, Robert.   II. Title.
HS3313.B69   1990   369.43   89-81626

ISBN 0-8395-3229-6

CONTENTS

v

FROM THE CHIEF SCOUT EXECUTIVE . . .

There's nothing better than a well-used Boy Scout Handbook. *The copy you are holding may be new right now, but it won't stay that way for long. Bursting with challenging adventures, it's a book built for rugged use. Stuff it in your pack and take it to troop meetings. Read it at home and in camp. Carry it with you as you master the best ways to have fun in the outdoors and learn how to care for the land. Camping, hiking, canoeing, observing nature—the* Boy Scout Handbook *will introduce you to dozens of terrific activities.*

Of course, Scouting is much more than enjoying the outdoors. The handbook will also help you learn about your community and nation and discover ways to make them better places. With your Scouting know-how, you can do a lot for your family and neighbors. Handbook information shows you how to keep yourself strong and healthy and make the most of school. With hard work and dedication, you might serve as a leader in your Scout troop and advance in rank along the trail to Eagle.

This Boy Scout Handbook *is your guide to all that Scouting has to offer. Don't let it gather dust on a shelf. Use it regularly. Study it. Make it uniquely yours. The pages may become tattered, but the skills and wisdom you gain from them will remain with you for the rest of your life.*

Good luck and good Scouting!

Jere B. Ratcliffe

Chief Scout Executive

THE ADVENTURE BEGINS

Be a Scout! That's the dream of many boys just like you. Maybe you have seen Scouts hiking, camping, and enjoying lots of other terrific activities. Perhaps friends who are in a troop have been telling you about the skills they are learning as they work toward becoming First Class Scouts.

Don't wait a minute longer to get in on all the fun Scouts have. The following pages explain how easy it is to join. If you are the right age, you'll be setting out on one of the best adventures of your life — being a member of the Boy Scouts of America.

CHAPTER 1

WELCOME TO THE ADVENTURE OF SCOUTING!

ADVENTURE! That's what Scouting is. You are standing at the doorway to the most exciting adventures you can imagine. Step into the world of Scouting, and you'll find yourself hiking along trails, canoeing across misty lakes, and camping under the open sky. Smell fresh rain in the woods and fill your mouth with the taste of wild strawberries. At the end of a patrol bike-hike, plunge into a cool mountain lake. Cook your meals over a camping stove. Travel the backcountry without leaving a trace, and live well with only what you carry in your pockets and pack. Sound inviting? As a Scout, you can do all of this and more.

Scouting is also a doorway to friendship. Boys you know might be joining your troop, and you'll meet lots of other Scouts along the way. Scouting is a worldwide brotherhood many millions strong. Almost anywhere you go, you will find Scouts excited about the same things you are.

Want to learn the skills that are used outdoors? Scouts know how to find their way with a map and compass, to stay warm and dry in stormy weather, and to give proper first aid. They observe wildlife close up and study nature all around them. There are plenty of important Scouting skills for you to master. You can also teach others what you know. Everyone helping everyone else—that is part of Scouting, too.

People have always relied on Scouts to be prepared in time of need. Your troop leaders will show you meaningful ways to help your family, community, nation, and world. The small acts of kindness you perform every day will improve the lives of others. In an emergency, you will be ready to do whatever the situation requires.

Outdoor adventures, service projects, leadership in your patrol and troop — Scouting will give you experiences and responsibilities that will help you mature. The Scout Oath and the Scout Law provide the guidelines you need to grow into a strong, confident adult. The knowledge and attitudes you develop as a Scout will spill over into the rest of your life.

Finally, Scouting is fun. You can look around during Scouting activities and notice a smile on every face. Everyone is sharing, learning, and living the Scout life.

Are you ready to get in on all the fun that Scouts have? Do you want to enjoy the adventures and friendship of a troop and patrol? This handbook will tell you all you need to know. The rest is up to you.

BECOMING A SCOUT

In order to become a Boy Scout, you must:

☆ Be a boy who has completed the fifth grade, or who has earned the Arrow of Light Award, or be 11 years of age but not yet 18.

☆ Find a Scout troop near your home.

☆ Complete the Boy Scout joining requirements.

Your Age

You can become a Boy Scout right away if you are the right age. If you are not yet old enough, you can join Cub Scouting, the branch of Scouting for younger boys. Cub Scouts have a great time with other guys their own age. As you enter the fourth grade, you may move into your Cub Scout pack's Webelos den. There you will learn all you must know to become a Boy Scout. You don't need to have been a Cub Scout or Webelos Scout to become a Boy Scout. Your leaders will teach you the skills you need to be a successful Scout.

Finding a Troop

If you don't know where a Scout troop meets, ask Scouts in your neighborhood or school. They will invite you to their next meeting. You can also call the Boy Scouts of America in your area. If their number isn't listed in your phone book, write to the national office at the following address:

Boy Scouts of America
1325 West Walnut Hill Lane
P.O. Box 152079
Irving, TX 75015-2079

The national office will put you in touch with a nearby troop. Even if you live where there is no troop, you can take part in the Boy Scout program by becoming a Lone Scout. There are people at the national office who can tell you how this works.

Joining Requirements

At your first troop meeting, your Scoutmaster will explain the following joining requirements of the Boy Scouts of America:

☆ Submit a completed Boy Scout application and health history signed by your parent or guardian.

☆ Repeat the Pledge of Allegiance (page 468).

☆ Demonstrate the Scout salute, sign, and handclasp (pages 564–565).

☆ Show how to tie the square knot (also known as the joining knot) (pages 132–133, 141).

☆ Understand and agree to live by the Scout Oath (pages 549–551), the Scout Law (pages 553–561), the Scout motto (page 562), the Scout slogan (page 563), and the Outdoor Code (pages 55–59).

☆ Describe the Scout badge (page 565).

☆ With your parent or guardian, complete the exercises in the pamphlet *How to Protect Your Children from Child Abuse: A Parent's Guide.*

☆ Participate in a Scoutmaster conference (pages 589–590).

When you have completed these, welcome! You are a Scout! Your Scoutmaster will give you a certificate of membership, and you can proudly wear the Boy Scout badge and uniform. You may also subscribe to *Boys' Life,* the monthly magazine that is full of exciting articles for and about Scouts.

Became a Boy Scout on _____ 19 _____

_____
Scoutmaster's signature

SCOUT OATH

On my honor I will do my best
To do my duty to God and my country
and to obey the Scout Law;
To help other people at all times;
To keep myself physically strong,
mentally awake, and morally straight.

A Scout is TRUSTWORTHY. *A Scout tells the truth. He keeps his promises. Honesty is a part of his code of conduct. People can always depend on him.*

A Scout is LOYAL. *A Scout is true to his family, friends, Scout leaders, school, nation, and world community.*

A Scout is HELPFUL. *A Scout is concerned about other people. He willingly volunteers to help others without expecting payment or reward.*

A Scout is FRIENDLY. *A Scout is a friend to all. He is a brother to other Scouts. He seeks to understand others. He respects those with ideas and customs that are different from his own.*

A Scout is COURTEOUS. *A Scout is polite to everyone regardless of age or position. He knows that good manners make it easier for people to get along together.*

A Scout is KIND. *A Scout understands there is strength in being gentle. He treats others as he wants to be treated. He does not harm or kill anything without reason.*

A Scout is OBEDIENT. *A Scout follows the rules of his family, school, and troop. He obeys the laws of his community and country. If he thinks these rules and laws are unfair, he tries to have them changed in an orderly manner rather than disobey them.*

A Scout is CHEERFUL. *A Scout looks for the bright side of life. He cheerfully does tasks that come his way. He tries to make others happy.*

A Scout is THRIFTY. *A Scout works to pay his way and to help others. He saves for the future. He protects and conserves natural resources. He carefully uses time and property.*

A Scout is BRAVE. *A Scout can face danger even if he is afraid. He has the courage to stand for what he thinks is right even if others laugh at him or threaten him.*

A Scout is CLEAN. *A Scout keeps his body and mind fit and clean. He goes around with those who believe in living by these same ideals. He helps keep his home and community clean.*

A Scout is REVERENT. *A Scout is reverent toward God. He is faithful in his religious duties. He respects the beliefs of others.*

The Scout Motto

The Scout motto is BE PREPARED. A Scout prepares for whatever comes his way by learning all he can. He keeps himself strong, healthy, and ready to meet the challenges of life.

The Scout Slogan

The Scout slogan is DO A GOOD TURN DAILY. Good Turns are helpful acts of kindness done quietly, without boasting, and without expecting reward or pay. Doing at least one Good Turn every day is a normal part of a Scout's life.

YOUR PATROL

As soon as you join the Boy Scouts, you will become a member of a patrol, which is a group of three to eight boys who enjoy Scouting together. A patrol leader will help you plan exciting things to do with some of your best friends — hikes, campouts, projects, and plenty of other activities. Your patrol will work to bring those plans to life.

Your first patrol may be made up of boys your age who are also just starting out. This new Scout patrol will be your home in the troop until you earn your First Class badge or enter the seventh grade, whichever comes first.

You and the other members of the new Scout patrol will elect your own patrol leader. Leaders of new Scout patrols change every few months, so you may soon have a chance to be the head of your patrol.

A very important person in your new Scout patrol is the troop guide. He's an older, experienced Scout appointed by the Scoutmaster to make sure everyone in your patrol gets the most out of Scouting. He will help you learn the skills that lead to the ranks of Tenderfoot, Second Class, and First Class. You can think of the troop guide as a big brother — a wise, older Scout who wants you to have a terrific time in the troop.

An assistant Scoutmaster will work closely with your troop guide to make the patrol a good one. He also may meet with your parents or guardians to keep them informed of troop activities and ways that your family can support your efforts as a Scout.

The goal of the new Scout patrol is to help you become:

☆ A good outdoorsman

☆ Active in your troop and patrol

☆ Physically fit

☆ A knowledgeable, participating citizen

☆ A young man who lives by the Scout Oath and Law

Once you have earned the First Class badge or have entered the seventh grade, you will have learned all you can from your new Scout patrol. You will be ready to join one of your troop's experienced Scout patrols.

A patrol is just the right size for outdoor adventures. On camping trips, a few tents will provide shelter for all of you. You can cook tasty meals over a couple of backpacking stoves or a small fire. You will all become good observers of nature; you will be able to track animals and study their habits. Along with many other Scouting skills, you will learn how to roam the outdoors without leaving any signs that you were there.

Your patrol is a strong, active unit. All of you win when every member pitches in and does his best. At patrol meetings, on the trail, and in camp, you will share many of Scouting's finest times.

YOUR TROOP

Your Scout troop you join is made up of all the patrol members, Venture crew members, and troop leaders. There is great strength in a full troop. The energy of so many Scouts lets a troop tackle big projects in the community and the backcountry. At troop meetings, patrols may compete in games that test their Scouting skills. Expect your troop to get outdoors often. Hikes, camp-outs, camporees with other troops, and a yearly trip to summer camp are a few of your troop's adventures.

Every troop has quiet times, too. Near the end of a meeting, your Scout-master may share some worthwhile thoughts with all of you. At special troop ceremonies called courts of honor, your family will see you receive awards for the hard work you have done as a Scout. Around a campfire, you can join your troop in singing songs, telling stories, and enjoying the fellowship of Scouting.

Your patrol and troop bring you together with others who share your interests and excitement about the outdoors. Patrol and troop leaders provide the guidance you need. Then it's up to you and the rest of your patrol to make the most of what Scouting has to offer.

You will find more information about patrols and troops starting on page 535.

ADVANCEMENT

The Scouting program provides many opportunities for you to learn skills and take part in terrific adventures. It also recognizes your achievements by awarding badges of rank. The first three are Tenderfoot, Second Class, and First Class. Next come Star and Life. The highest rank is that of Eagle Scout.

Each rank is more challenging than the one before it. Each prepares you to be a better camper, hiker, and Scout. As you complete the requirements for a rank on patrol and troop outings, you will find that you can use your new knowledge immediately. You will also have the background you need for achieving even more as you set out toward the next rank.

Active Scout participation and advancement go together. So, if you want to advance, first and foremost, take part in all the activities of your patrol and troop.

When you do, you will pick up most of the Scoutcraft skills you need for your advancement. Work with the other Scouts of your troop on service projects. Help other Scouts. As you do, your leadership abilities will develop. Your troop guide will help you learn the skills you need to advance from Tenderfoot to First Class.

Then when you have completed the tests for the award you are aiming for, tell your Scoutmaster. He will sit down with you for a Scoutmaster conference. After this, he will arrange for a board of review. When this review is over, your Scoutmaster will order the badge you have earned. It will be presented to you at a ceremony.

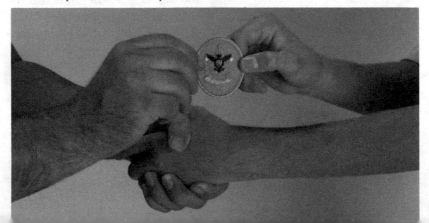

Tenderfoot

3/20 MM 1. Present yourself to your leader, properly dressed, before going on an overnight camping trip. Show the camping gear you will use. Show the right way to pack and carry it (pages 27–39).

3/20 MM 2. Spend at least 1 night on a patrol or troop campout. Sleep in a tent you have helped pitch on a ground bed you have prepared (pages 42-43, 33–34).

5/31 Rm 3a. Demonstrate how to whip and fuse the ends of a rope (pages 129–130).

5/8 Rm 3b. Demonstrate you know how to tie the following knots and tell what their uses are: two half hitches and the tautline hitch (pages 137–138, 43).

3/20 MM 4. Explain the rules of safe hiking, both on the highway and crosscountry, during the day and at night. Explain what to do if you are lost (pages 175–177, 209–211).

5/8 Rm 5. Demonstrate how to display, raise, lower, and fold the American flag (pages 473–475, 477–478).

5/8 Rm 6. Repeat from memory and explain in your own words the Scout Oath, Law, motto, and slogan (pages 5–9).

3/20 mm 7. Know your patrol name, give the patrol yell, and describe your patrol flag.

3/20 Mm 8. Explain why we use the buddy system in Scouting (pages 229–230, 598).

3/20 Rm 9a. Record your best in the following tests:
Pushups __6__   Pullups _____   Situps __24__
Standing long jump __4__ ft. __1__ in.
Run/walk 500 yards _____ (pages 393–395)

5/31 Rm 9b. Show improvement in the activities listed above after practicing for 30 days.

5/8 Rm 10. Identify local poisonous plants; tell how to treat for exposure to them (pages 428–429).

3/20 Mm 11a. Demonstrate the Heimlich maneuver and tell when it is used (pages 416–417).

3/20 Mm 11b. Show first aid for the following:
- Simple cuts and scratches (page 419)
- Blisters on the hand and foot (page 422)
- Minor burns or scalds (first degree) (page 420)
- Bites or stings of insects and ticks (pages 423–424)
- Poisonous snakebite (pages 426–427)
- Nosebleed (page 420)
- Frostbite and sunburn (pages 430–431, 420–421)

5/31 Rm 12. Participate in a Scoutmaster conference.

5/31 13. Board of review completed ___5-31-97___
(date)

Second Class

Date/Leader's
Initials

__8-5__ __Rm__ 1a. Demonstrate how a compass works and how to orient a map. Explain what map symbols mean (pages 187–192, 181–185).

__7-15__ __Rm__ 1b. Using a compass and a map you've drawn, take a 5-mile hike (or 10 miles by bike) approved by your adult leader and your parent or guardian (pages 193–195).*

__7-15__ __Rm__ 2a. Since joining, have participated in five separate troop/patrol activities (other than troop/patrol meetings), two of which included camping overnight.

__7-15__ __Rm__ 2b. On one campout, demonstrate proper care, sharpening, and use of knife, saw, and ax (pages 63–76).

__7-15__ __Rm__ 2c. Use the tools listed above to prepare tinder, kindling, and fuel for a cooking fire (pages 83–88).

__7-15__ __Rm__ 2d. Light the cooking fire. Assist with the meal preparation and cleanup (pages 89–92).

__7-15__ __Rm__ 2e. On one of these campouts, select your patrol site and sleep in a tent that you pitched (pages 42–49).

__7-15__ __Rm__ 3. Participate in a flag ceremony for your school, religious institution, chartered organization, community, or troop activity.

__7-15__ __Rm__ 4. Participate in an approved (minimum of 1 hour) service project.

__8-5__ __Rm__ 5. Identify or show evidence of at least 10 kinds of wild animals (birds, mammals, reptiles, fish, mollusks) found in your community (pages 291–312).

__8-5__ __Rm__ 6a. Show what to do for "hurry" cases of stopped breathing, serious bleeding, and internal poisoning (pages 405–417).

__8-5__ __Rm__ 6b. Prepare a personal first aid kit to take with you on a hike (pages 28–29).

__8-5__ __Rm__ 6c. Demonstrate first aid for the following:
- Object in the eye (page 427)
- Bite of a suspected rabid animal (page 425)
- Puncture wounds from a splinter, nail, and fish hook (page 428)
- Serious burns (second degree) (pages 420–421)
- Heat exhaustion (page 429)
- Shock (page 418)
- Heat stroke, dehydration, hypothermia, and hyperventilation (pages 429–430, 431)

__7-15__ __Rm__ 7. Tell what precautions must be taken for a safe swim. Demonstrate your ability to swim 50 yards using two different strokes (pages 229–236).†

__7-26__ __Rm__ 8. Participate in a school, community, or troop program on the dangers of using drugs, alcohol, and tobacco, and other practices that could be harmful to your health. Discuss your participation in the program with your family (pages 388–392).

__8-5__ __Rm__ 9. Demonstrate Scout spirit by living the Scout Oath (Promise) and Scout Law in your everyday life.

__8-9__ __Rm__ 10. Participate in a Scoutmaster conference.

__8-14__ 11. Board of review completed ___8-14-97___
(date)

*If you use a wheelchair or crutches, or if it is difficult for you to get around, you may substitute "trip" for "hike."
†This requirement may be waived by the troop committee for medical or safety reasons.

WELCOME TO THE ADVENTURE OF SCOUTING!

8-14-97 Mark Milner

8-14-97 Mark Neubauer

First Class

8 6   Rm   1. Demonstrate how to find directions during the day and at night without using a compass (pages 206–209).

8-6   Rm   2. Using a compass, complete an orienteering course that covers at least 1 mile and requires measuring the height and/or width of designated items (tree, tower, canyon, ditch, etc.) (pages 196–197, 203–205).

8-5   Rm   3. Since joining, have participated in ten separate troop/patrol activities (other than troop/patrol meetings), three of which included camping overnight.

8-7   Rm   4. On one campout, serve as your patrol's cook. Prepare a breakfast, lunch, and dinner menu that requires cooking; secure ingredients; supervise your assistants in fire building; and prepare the meals. Lead your patrol in saying grace at the meals, and supervise cleanup (pages 98–125, 84–92).

8 5   Rm   5. Visit and discuss with a selected individual approved by your leader (elected official, judge, attorney, civil servant, principal, teacher) your constitutional rights and obligations as a U.S. citizen (pages 457–462, 483–485).

8-7   Rm   6. Identify or show evidence of at least 10 kinds of native plants found in your community (pages 318–345).

6-6   Rm   7a. Demonstrate tying the timber hitch and clove hitch and their use in square, shear, and diagonal lashings by joining two or more poles or staves together (pages 139–140, 149–152).

8-7   Rm   7b. Use lashing to make a useful camp gadget (pages 152–155).

8-7   Rm   8a. Demonstrate tying the bowline (rescue) knot and how it's used in rescues (pages 134–136).

8-7   Rm   8b. Demonstrate bandages for injuries on the head, the upper arm, and collarbone, and for a sprained ankle (pages 423, 434–436).

8-7   Rm   8c. Show how to transport by yourself, and with one other person, a person:
- from a smoke-filled room
- with a broken leg, for at least 25 yards (pages 437–439)

8-7   Rm   8d. Tell the five most common signs of a heart attack. Explain the steps (procedures) in cardiopulmonary resuscitation (CPR) (pages 407–413).

8-7   Rm   9. Demonstrate your ability to swim 100 yards using one resting stroke and two other strokes, and to float (rest) as motionless as possible for 1 minute (pages 231–236).*

8-9   Rm   10. Demonstrate Scout spirit by living the Scout Oath (Promise) and Scout Law in your everyday life.

8-9   Rm   11. Participate in a Scoutmaster conference.

8-14   Rm   12. Board of review completed   8-14-97   _____
                                                            (date)

*This requirement may be waived by the troop committee for medical or safety reasons.

Mark Neubauer   8-14-97

You may pass any of the requirements for Tenderfoot, Second Class, and First Class at any time. For example, if you fulfill a First Class requirement before you are a Second Class Scout, you may go ahead and check off the First Class requirement as complete. However, you must still earn the ranks in their proper order.

Earning badges can be very satisfying. However, badges are not the most important part of Scouting. Of greater value is what the badges represent. The skills you master, the wisdom you gain, and the experiences you enjoy are what really count. Those are what truly make you a Scout.

How to Use This Boy Scout Handbook

The *Boy Scout Handbook* is divided into six sections.

☆ The Adventure Begins

☆ Outdoor Adventures

☆ Growing from Boy to Man

☆ Your Life as a Scout

☆ Trail to Eagle

☆ High Adventure and Sports

By some headings are color-coded squares for reference to information you need in order to complete the requirements for each rank.

Besides helping you with advancement, the *Boy Scout Handbook* is a fine guide to outdoor adventures and to living a good life. It is written for members of the Boy Scouts of America, but its message can be shared by every reader.

Welcome to the Boy Scouts of America. You are beginning a journey that will bring you years of excitement, satisfaction, and plenty of good fun. Scouting is *your* doorway to adventure. To walk through it, just turn this page.

The colored squares by headings in this book show that information under that heading deals with requirements for Tenderfoot through First Class ranks. The colors are

T Tenderfoot

2 Second Class

1 First Class

WELCOME TO THE ADVENTURE OF SCOUTING!

OUTDOOR ADVENTURES

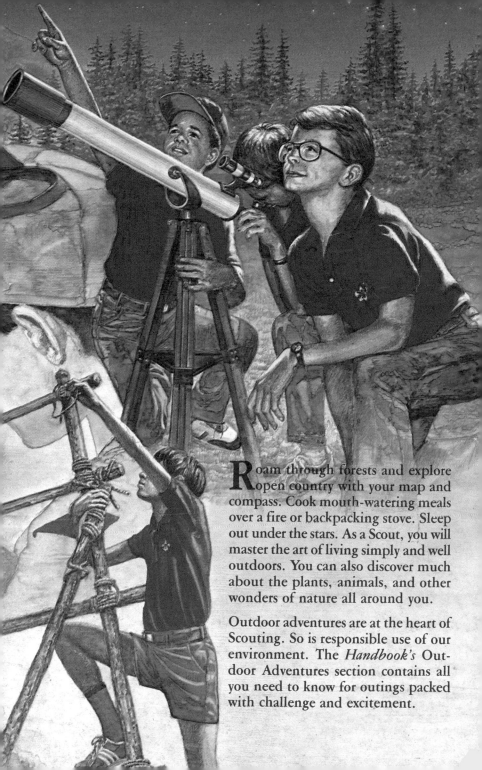

Roam through forests and explore open country with your map and compass. Cook mouth-watering meals over a fire or backpacking stove. Sleep out under the stars. As a Scout, you will master the art of living simply and well outdoors. You can also discover much about the plants, animals, and other wonders of nature all around you.

Outdoor adventures are at the heart of Scouting. So is responsible use of our environment. The *Handbook's* Outdoor Adventures section contains all you need to know for outings packed with challenge and excitement.

LET'S GO CAMPING!

PULL on your Scout shirt and lace up your hiking boots. Grab your grub and gear. You're a Scout now, and that means you're going camping! You can bet there's nothing better than swinging a pack on your shoulders and spending a night in the great outdoors.

What will you find on a campout? Just about the finest adventures you could ever want. You can use your Scouting skills to follow hiking trails deep into forests and across rugged land. Keep your eyes peeled for deer, beaver, and maybe even a bear. Climb to the windy top of a real mountain. Swim in sparkling lakes and catch fish from cold, rushing streams.

Late in the day you'll make camp and cook your dinner. How about fixing a tasty pot of stew, or spaghetti with your own special sauce? Campfire smoke mixes with the rich smell of hot biscuits dripping with jam. Later you can bake a peach cobbler for dessert.

After dark, gather around the fire with your friends. As the flames die down, you'll sing songs and laugh at each other's stories. Firelight dancing in the embers will spark your imagination, just as it has for every Scout sitting by a campfire in years gone by.

Then crawl into your warm sleeping bag. You're tired from a day full of fun, but before you fall asleep, gaze awhile at the sky. Have you ever seen so many stars? Listen for the hoot of an owl and the long, distant wail of a coyote. The next thing you know, the first rays of sunlight will be breaking through the trees.

Scouting *is* camping. And it's hiking, canoeing, bicycling, reading a map and compass, practicing first aid, and plenty of other exciting challenges. Scouting is outdoor adventure at its best, and it's all yours for the taking.

The *Boy Scout Handbook* will show you how to become a good camper. Your Scoutmaster and other Scouts will help you learn, too. Add your own energy and willingness to try, and nothing can stand in your way.

So stop dreaming and start packing. The greatest adventures of your life begin the moment you take your first step down a trail.

MEET THE LOW-IMPACT/NO-TRACE CAMPING CHALLENGE

In the early days of our country, you could have camped almost anywhere. Most of the land was a wilderness of vast forests, rivers, mountains, and plains. There were few towns and not many roads.

The needs of a growing nation have turned much of that open land into farms and cities. Dams have tamed many rivers. Trees have become lumber for buildings.

The wild country that remains is home to a rich variety of animals and plants. It supplies clean water for you to drink and freshens the air you breathe. Wilderness reminds us of how the land once looked. When you want to get away from the city, you have the freedom to enjoy parks, forests, and Scout camps across the nation.

With that freedom comes your duty to care for the land. That means enjoying the outdoors, learning from it, and then leaving it just as you found it. Scouts call this *low-impact camping*. On outings with your troop, you will discover how to hike and camp without leaving a trace.

Millions of Scouts before you have hiked and camped in the American outdoors. In the years to come, many more will visit the backcountry you have enjoyed. Do all you can to leave them an outdoors as wonderful as the one you are about to find. (For more information on low-impact and no-trace methods, see pages 366–370.)

TRY THESE DIFFERENT KINDS
OF CAMPING

Short-term camping includes overnight campouts and weekend trips. Most troops go camping at least once a month in nearby county and state parks or in Scout campgrounds. By camping as often as you can, you will have plenty of chances to master good outdoor skills.

Long-term camping takes you on outings of more than a few days. Spend a week with your troop at Scout camp, or plan an expedition that includes hiking, boating, and other Scouting know-how. Longer trips usually take place in the summer when you are out of school, but don't pass up opportunities for winter trips in the backcountry.

Venture camping combines camping with backpacking, orienteering, canoeing, snow travel, long-distance bicycling, wilderness conservation projects, and dozens of other challenging activities. Older Scouts may join a Venture crew whose planning and practice lead to ultimate adventures deep in the backcountry, on rivers and lakes, in wilderness areas, and over the open road.

High-adventure camping takes you to adventure bases run by the Boy Scouts of America. On wilderness treks of a week or longer, you can push yourself toward a mountaintop, wrestle a canoe through thundering rapids, sail a ship on the open sea, try scuba diving, and experience many other exciting adventures.

CHAPTER 2

PLAN YOUR CAMP

If you are like most Scouts, you can hardly wait to get outdoors. But before your troop or patrol takes off, you need to ask the following questions. Your answers will help you prepare for a safe, exciting adventure. You will also have the fun of thinking about the good times to come.

☆ Where do you want to go? Every part of the United States has fine camping areas. Your Scoutmaster will know of some, and so will the people in charge of parks and forests. Look in the phone book for the numbers of federal, state, and local land management agencies. If you obtain permission, private lands may also offer good camping. Many Scout camps can be used year-round.

☆ Is there water for drinking, cooking, and washing? Developed campgrounds usually have public water systems. In more primitive areas, plan to gather your water from streams, springs, or lakes, and then purify it before use.

☆ Are campfires allowed? Campfires are prohibited in many areas. Dry weather raises the risk of sparks starting a forest fire. Fire rings and ashes can spoil backcountry campsites. Fragile plant life can be damaged by heat. There might not be enough firewood. If fires are banned, you can do your cooking over a small camping stove.

Where fires are allowed, you may need to get a permit from park or forest managers. They issue permits in order to educate people about the dangers of fires and to control where they are built.

☆ Is group size limited? Scout camps and many developed sites in public campgrounds are large enough to handle an entire troop of Scouts. The reasonable noise and activity of so large a group will not bother other campers.

However, a big group can be hard on the land. All those feet trample vegetation. All those tents require space for the night. To ease impact on regulated forests and parks, travel and camp in the backcountry with groups no larger than a Scout patrol.

☆ What do you want to do? Hiking, swimming, cooking, trail repair, bird watching, photography, tree planting, star study—the possibilities are endless. Your Scoutmaster and park or forest rangers can suggest many

A successful outing takes planning. Prepare well for your adventures to make them safe and exciting.

activities just right for the places where you will be camping. They can also help you understand why some activities are not appropriate in certain areas.

☆ How about the weather? The long, warm days of summer are perfect for camping. But don't put away your boots just because autumn has arrived. Learn to use the right clothing and equipment so that you can be in the backcountry any time of the year and in any weather.

In southern states, cool winter months clear the woods of mosquitoes and heavy brush. Farther north, snow turns familiar fields and forests into a wintry wilderness. Conditions may be perfect for snow shoeing, skiing, building igloos, and tracking animals. Remember that night comes early in winter. When the days are short, plan to make camp early.

☆ How will you reach camp? Hike or bike to campgrounds that are close to home. For more distant destinations, your Scoutmaster will see that you have a ride to the campsite or the beginning of a trail.

☆ How much will it cost? Camping should be simple, inexpensive, and fun. You will need some camping gear, but most of it can be made from things around the house or purchased at surplus stores, garage sales, and the Boy Scouts of America national Supply Division. Clothing for the outdoors is probably in your closet right now. Your troop will have tents, pots and pans, and other group equipment.

You may be asked to cover your share of meal costs. If you don't have enough money, there might be ways you can earn a few dollars for camp. Ask your Scoutmaster. No Scout should ever be left behind because of lack of money.

☆ Do you have permission? Tell your parents or guardians where you are going. Explain what you will be doing and when you will return. Your Scoutmaster should also contact them to be sure it is all right for you to go.

☆ How will you protect the land? Take pride in leaving the outdoors so clean that it looks as if you were never there. Pick up litter left by campers less considerate than you. Learn low-impact and no-trace methods and use them on every hike and camping trip.

WHAT GEAR DO YOU NEED? T

In 1803, the explorers Lewis and Clark set out on a 3-year journey that took them across America. They hoped they could get the food they needed by hunting and trading with native Americans. But they had to carry everything else with them — tools, blankets, and pots and pans. There were no stores where they were going.

You will take gear and clothing on your camping trips, too. Since you may be carrying everything on your back, you will want a light load that allows you to move easily over the trails. Pack just what you need to keep yourself safe and to make good camp, then leave everything else at home. Like those explorers of old, you will quickly learn the joys of living simply and well.

SCOUT OUTDOOR ESSENTIALS

_____ *Pocketknife*

_____ *First aid kit*

_____ *Extra clothing*

_____ *Rain gear*

_____ *Canteen or water bottle*

_____ *Flashlight*

_____ *Trail food*

_____ *Matches and fire starters*

_____ *Sun protection*

_____ *Map and compass*

The Scout Outdoor Essentials T 2

The Scout Outdoor Essentials listed below are the basic tools and supplies you should carry on every Scout outing. *Always* have them with you in your pockets or pack. They often make a pleasant journey even better. In an emergency, they could even help you save a life.

Pocketknife. A pocketknife is the most useful tool you can own. Keep yours clean and sharp. (For more on pocketknives, see pages 63–67.)

First aid kit. In addition to the complete first aid kit carried by your patrol, bring along your own first aid supplies to treat minor injuries. Include the following:

★ moleskin for blisters

★ a few adhesive bandages

★ a small roll of adhesive tape

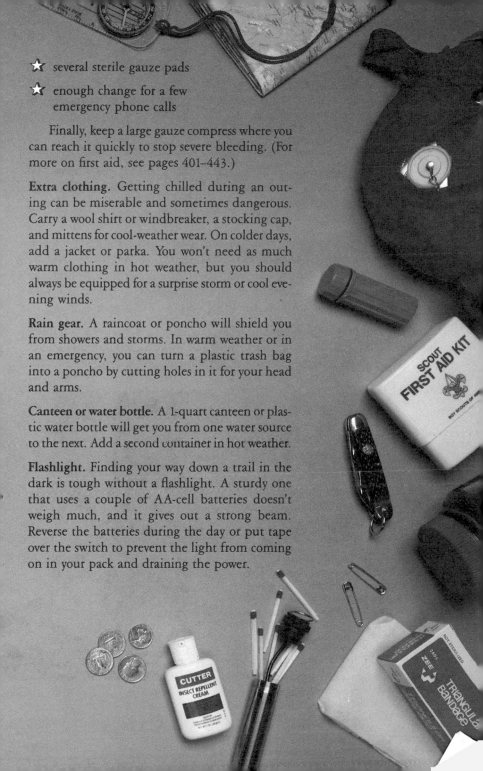

- ★ several sterile gauze pads
- ★ enough change for a few emergency phone calls

Finally, keep a large gauze compress where you can reach it quickly to stop severe bleeding. (For more on first aid, see pages 401–443.)

Extra clothing. Getting chilled during an outing can be miserable and sometimes dangerous. Carry a wool shirt or windbreaker, a stocking cap, and mittens for cool-weather wear. On colder days, add a jacket or parka. You won't need as much warm clothing in hot weather, but you should always be equipped for a surprise storm or cool evening winds.

Rain gear. A raincoat or poncho will shield you from showers and storms. In warm weather or in an emergency, you can turn a plastic trash bag into a poncho by cutting holes in it for your head and arms.

Canteen or water bottle. A 1-quart canteen or plastic water bottle will get you from one water source to the next. Add a second container in hot weather.

Flashlight. Finding your way down a trail in the dark is tough without a flashlight. A sturdy one that uses a couple of AA-cell batteries doesn't weigh much, and it gives out a strong beam. Reverse the batteries during the day or put tape over the switch to prevent the light from coming on in your pack and draining the power.

Trail food. Your body burns a lot of energy during outdoor adventures. Patrol or crew cooks will prepare tasty camp feasts that will satisfy your hunger. In addition, include a piece of fruit, a small bag of granola, or some raisins and nuts in your Scout Outdoor Essentials. Snack on them if you need an energy boost between meals.

Matches and fire starters. Wooden strike-anywhere matches can be made waterproof by painting them with clear fingernail polish or dipping them in melted paraffin. Or you can store your matches in an empty plastic aspirin bottle with a tight cap. Fire starters help you get a blaze going when the weather is windy or wet. (For instructions on making fire starters, see pages 86–87.)

Sun protection. Doctors warn that too much exposure to sun can be harmful, especially if you have fair skin. A broad-brimmed hat will shade your face. Lip balm helps keep the wind and sun from chapping your lips. At high elevations or on snow, protect your eyes with sunglasses. Guard your skin with a sunscreen with a sun protection factor (SPF) of 15 or higher.

Map and compass. A compass and a map are essentials whenever you travel in areas unfamiliar to you. Of course, they aren't much good unless you know how to use them. (For more on map and compass, see pages 178–199.)

Overnight Gear

Your Scout Outdoor Essentials go with you on every Scout outing. They are the most important part of your equipment. When you want to spend a night under the stars, just add some overnight gear to your Scout Outdoor Essentials. You will be ready to roam anywhere in the backcountry, making camp wherever darkness finds you.

Sleeping bag. At home, your mattress beneath you and the blankets on top trap your body heat and keep you warm. Outdoors, a couple of blankets will do the same thing on summer campouts in mild weather.

Blanket sleeping bag is made from two blankets. Fold first blanket in three layers. Pin down free edge with blanket pins. Place on half of second blanket. Bring bottom up and pin. Fold other half of second blanket over first blanket. Pin edges. Fold bottom under.

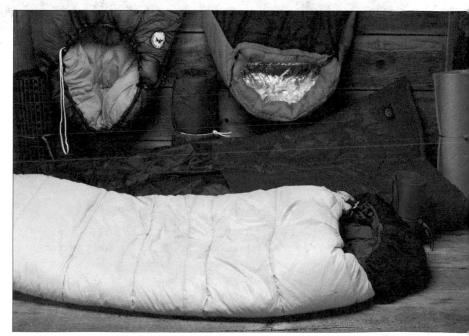

Sleeping bags are warmer than blankets and easier to pack.

Extra clothing stuffed into a duffel bag makes a comfortable pillow.

Fold the blankets into the shape of an envelope and hold the edges together with big safety pins.

If you have a choice, though, use a sleeping bag. Because you can crawl right into it, a bag will keep you warmer than blankets. It is also easier to pack and carry to and from camp.

The cloth part of a sleeping bag is called the *shell*. Inside the shell is fluffy *fill* of artificial fibers or the fine down or feathers of ducks and geese. This fill traps the heat from your body and holds it close to you. For more warmth, zip the bag closed and pull the drawstring snug around your face.

Air mattress or sleeping pad. Either one of these will increase your comfort and warmth by giving you a soft surface on which to sleep and protecting you from the cold ground which draws away your body heat. The pad is a thin piece of foam that goes beneath your blankets or bag. You can find one at a camping supply store or a Scouting equipment distributor.

Ground cloth. Use this to keep ground moisture away from your bedding. You can use a plastic sheet 3 feet wide and 6 feet long or two plastic trash can liners taped end to end.

Make Your Camp Bed

You've reached camp and eaten supper. Now you're getting settled for the evening. What's the best way to arrange your sleeping gear for a comfortable night outdoors?

Start by finding a fairly level spot. If it's under a tree, less dew will form on your blankets or bag. Out in the open, though, you can see the stars. Boulders and bushes can act as windbreaks. Toss aside stones and sticks that might poke you, but don't rake away pine needles or leaves. They will cushion your bed and lessen your impact on the campsite.

Spread out your ground cloth and lay the sleeping pad on top of it. Arrange your sleeping bag or blankets on the pad. Want a pillow? Stuff extra clothing inside a sweater or sleeping bag sack and tuck it under your head. In damp weather, some Scouts leave their bags and blankets rolled up until they are ready to sleep so that their bedding won't absorb moisture from the air.

When you crawl into bed, keep your shoes or hiking boots close. Store your watch, glasses, and other small items in one of them. Drop your flashlight in the other so you can find it in the dark. Have a water bottle nearby, too, in case you get thirsty before dawn. Shake out your boots in the morning before you put them on. Small animals sometimes creep inside in search of shelter and warmth.

Use the same methods to make a bed in a tent. In a tent with a floor you won't need a ground cloth. You will probably be warmer inside a tent because it blocks the wind. Wearing a stocking cap to bed also helps prevent heat loss. It's all right to pull on a warm shirt during the night, and a sweater, extra socks, and even mittens if they will keep you from getting chilled. Finally, don't go to bed hungry. Your body will put out plenty of heat, but only if it has calories to burn.

Utensils for Eating

Camp meals are hearty, and most can be eaten with simple utensils. Take an unbreakable plate, bowl (an empty margarine tub is perfect), and a sturdy drinking cup. A cup marked with measurements will be helpful when you are cooking. Round out your eating gear with a spoon and fork. Use your pocketknife for cutting and spreading.

On winter trips, an insulated plastic mug keeps cocoa and soup warm, and you won't burn your lips on the rim. Loop a piece of cord through the handle and hang the cup on your pack for use on the trail, or tuck it in an outside pocket where you can easily reach it.

Try whittling some eating utensils in camp. Perhaps you can carve a dining tool with a fork on one end and a spoon on the other. Chopsticks are easy to make and fun to use. Just skin the bark from two straight, slender sticks.

Take Care of Yourself

Part of the joy of camping is not worrying about getting dirty. But at the end of the day, you'll want to clean up. You will feel better, and your sleeping bag will stay fresher. Bring the following items with you. As long as you have them, don't forget to use them.

Soap. You won't need much. A bar that's nearly used up is plenty. Store it in a plastic bag.

Small towel and washcloth. Soil won't show up on these quite so soon if they are dark in color.

Toothbrush and toothpaste. A little toothpaste goes a long way. Get the smallest tube you can find, or save a family tube when it's almost empty.

Dental floss. Flossing every day helps keep your gums and teeth in good shape. Floss is also a strong sewing thread for emergency repairs.

Extras

A few extra items can make a camping trip even better. You may want to bring along some of the following:

- ☆ Watch
- ☆ Camera and film (keep them dry in a plastic bag)
- ☆ Notebook and pencil
- ☆ Insect repellent
- ☆ Swimsuit
- ☆ Sunglasses
- ☆ Binoculars
- ☆ Magnifying glass
- ☆ Bird and plant identification books
- ☆ Harmonica, penny whistle, or other small musical instrument
- ☆ Prayer book or Bible

LET'S GO CAMPING!

What Kind of Pack?

Packs are really just canvas or nylon bags with carrying straps sewn to them. A pack gives you a place to stow your food and gear. It lightens your load and frees your hands.

Day packs are the smallest. You may already use one for carrying your books to school. They are just the right size to hold the Scout Outdoor Essentials you need on a day hike. (For ways to make a day pack, see page 38.)

On campouts, though, you will want to carry more than you can fit into a day pack. In the early days of Scouting, boys made *bedroll packs* by rolling their equipment and supplies inside their blankets. They bent the loaded blankets into a horseshoe shape, tied the ends together, and slung the bundle over one shoulder. Bedroll packs weren't very comfortable, but they got the job done.

A better idea is a pack that is like a day pack, only larger. These are called *rucksacks, haversacks,* or *ranger packs.* One of them will hold just what you need for a summer night in camp.

Hitting the trail for more than a night or two? Carrying cold-weather clothing or a bulky sleeping bag? Then a *backpack* is what you need. A backpack is bigger than most overnight packs. It may have outside pockets to hold maps, fuel bottles, and small gear. The pack is usually attached to a stiff frame that fits against your back. A hip belt shifts the weight of the load from your shoulders to the strong muscles of your legs.

Packing Up

You may have dresser drawers at home where you keep your things. On a campout, your pack is like a dresser. Instead of drawers, you can use small bags to keep clothing and gear sorted and safe from the rain. Bread wrappers are just the right size; so are the stuff sacks you can buy at camping supply stores or make from the legs of old pants.

MAKE YOUR OWN STUFF SACKS

Start by cutting a leg off worn-out trousers or jeans. Stitch the bottom shut with a sewing machine or a needle and strong thread. Fold over the top inch of the open end and sew it down for a collar. Snip a small hole in the collar. To easily thread a drawstring through, first pin a safety pin in one end of a shoestring or a 24-inch length of cord. Push the closed safety pin through the hole, then work it down the length of the collar. Turn the bag right side out, and it's ready to be filled with clothing or gear.

CHAPTER 2

Sort similar clothing and equipment into separate sacks. Put socks and underwear in one, eating utensils in another, and so on. Pull the drawstring tight or use a rubber band or a loose overhand knot in the top of each sack to keep it closed.

Stow everything into your pack. In addition to your own gear, you may carry some patrol or crew equipment. Your share might include pots and pans, part of a tent, and some food. Arrange soft items in your pack so they will cushion your back. Keep your rain gear, flashlight, first aid kit, and water bottle near the top or in pockets on the outside of your pack where you can reach them quickly without digging through the entire load.

Put your blankets or sleeping bag inside your pack if there is room. Otherwise, wrap your bedroll inside your ground cloth or stuff it in a trash can liner to protect it from the elements. Tuck it right under the pack's top flap or tie it to the frame above or below the pack. If you have a pot that's too big to fit inside your pack, try slipping it over one end of your sleeping bag before you lash the bedroll to the frame.

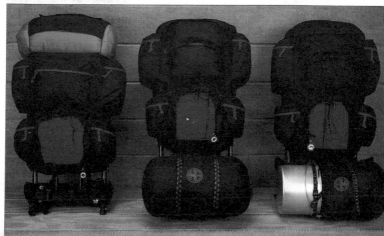

Camp Shelters

Years ago, campers cut down trees and green branches to build lean-to shelters. It was hard work and took a long time. Of course, the campers could not return the branches to the trees when they no longer needed the shelters. They did not yet know about low-impact camping.

Today, a tarp or tent gives you a shelter you can take anywhere. It will protect you from bad weather, keep away insects, and give you privacy. You can roll up your tent and carry it with you when you break camp. Unlike a lean-to, it is a shelter that leaves no trace.

Tarps

The simplest camp shelter is a large waterproof sheet of cloth called a *tarp*. It is often used on Scout camping trips as a dining fly to cover the camp kitchen.

Many tarps are made of nylon or canvas. You can make a light, inexpensive tarp from a sheet of *polyethylene plastic* such as used by carpenters to shield lumber from the rain. The best thickness for camp use is *4-mil*, which means four one-thousandths of an inch. It is sold in hardware stores in rolls that are 10 or 12 feet wide. Ask a clerk to cut a piece for you that is as long as it is wide. Clear plastic will let the sun shine through.

NO FIRES IN TENTS

No tent is fireproof. All of them can burn or melt when exposed to heat. Keep all flames away from tents. Never use candles, matches, stoves, heaters, or lanterns in or near tents. Flashlights only!

Tarp corner with grommet

Tarp corner with stone and cord

CHAPTER 2

Some tarps have metal rings called *grommets* at the corners so you can tie cords through them. If not, you can still attach lines without harming the cloth or plastic. Start with plenty of ⅛-inch cord and a handful of small, smooth stones (small pinecones work just as well).

Tie a double half hitch in the end of a 10-foot piece of cord. Hold a stone under the corner of the sheet, and then work the knot's loop over the plastic and the stone. Draw the knot tight. The stone will keep the tarp from slipping out of the knot, and that will hold the cord to the tarp. Repeat for the remaining corners of the sheet. (To tie a double half hitch, see page 137.)

One way to set up a tarp as a dining fly is to toss a long cord over a tree branch above your camp kitchen. Tie an end to the center of the tarp with a stone and double half hitch, then hoist the tarp's center 8 feet or more off the ground. Spread open the tarp and use taut-line hitches to tie the corner cords around trees or tent stakes. Corner ropes that tighten a tarp or tent are called *guy lines*. If rain blows in, simply lower the center of the tarp and adjust the guy lines. (To tie a taut-line hitch, see page 138.)

Another dining fly design begins with a rope stretched between two trees and tied 8 feet above the ground with taut-line hitches. Drape the tarp over the rope, then pull out the corners and tie the guy lines to trees or stakes. You'll have a shelter shaped like the pitched roof of a house.

Set the tarp closer to the ground if you want to sleep under it. Lowering the edges of the tarp will give you extra protection from the wind.

Tents

Tents used to be made of canvas, a fabric similar to that of your blue jeans. Keeping rain from dripping through the cloth was a real challenge. Scouts waterproofed canvas tents by boiling them in mixtures of paraffin, turpentine, and beeswax.

A modern nylon tent requires no boiling. It is also lighter than a canvas tent. Most camping tents today have an A-frame or a dome shape and are roomy enough for two to four Scouts. The tents are usually dyed green, brown, or blue so that they will blend in with their surroundings.

Those old-time Scouts who waterproofed their tents also had to make their own stakes and poles. With a knife or an ax they shaped pieces of wood to hold up their shelters and pin down the corners.

Philmont Backpacker tent

Dome tent

Free Spirit II tent

free-standing expedition tent

lightweight backpacking tent   **Aurora 2 tent with vestibule**

The tent you use should have its own metal or plastic stakes and light, strong poles made of aluminum or fiberglass. The poles come apart into sections just the right size to fit into your pack. One Scout can take the main tent and poles while another carries the rain fly and stakes.

Begin setting up your shelter (Scouts call it *pitching* a tent) by choosing a level site. Remove stones and sticks, but don't disturb pine needles or grasses. If you have a ground cloth, spread it out to protect the tent floor from dirt and sharp objects. Unfold the tent on top of the ground cloth. Pull out the corners of the floor and stake them to the ground. Assemble the poles and put them in place.

There may be guy lines that stretch the tent into shape. Tie each line through a tent grommet with a bowline knot or a double half hitch. Use taut-line hitches to tie the free ends around stakes in the ground, and pull the lines tight. (To tie a bowline knot, see page 134.)

Shake off debris before rolling up your tent.

Dry a tent you had to pack wet as soon as you get home.

Finish by putting the rain fly over the tent and staking it down. Never dig a ditch around a tent. Ditches can leave scars on the ground that take a long time to heal. You will stay just as dry without disturbing the land.

Keep the inside of your tent clean by slipping off your boots before you go inside. Brush dirt out of a tent with your hand or with a dirty sock or T-shirt.

Take down, or *strike,* a tent by reversing the steps you used to pitch it. Remove the stakes and poles. Shake out any dirt, pine needles, or leaves, then roll up the tent.

Whenever you can, let your tent dry in the sun before you strike it. Sometimes this is not possible and you have to pack a wet tent. As soon as you get home, set it up in your yard or hang it indoors and let it dry completely before putting it away. That will prevent mildew from ruining the fabric.

WHERE CAN YOU CAMP?

The success of a campout depends a lot on the campsite you choose. A good site is safe and fun, and there is plenty to see and do. Your campsite will probably be one of three kinds.

◀ **Public and private campgrounds.** These are usually in parks, forests, and Scout camps, and can be reached by road. They may be near an inviting hiking trail, a good fishing hole, or a scenic view. To limit the impact of the many people who wish to enjoy the area, sites have been designed for camping. They may have picnic tables, fire rings, running water, and outhouses. Special sites are sometimes set aside for large groups.

Backcountry sites. You'll hike to ▶ backcountry sites over trails rather than roads. The sites are seldom as developed as those in campgrounds. In fact, many backcountry sites evolved simply because campers so often used the same place.

Wilderness sites. Wilderness is ◀ remote country little changed from the time humans first saw it. It can be reached only by trails. No motorized vehicles are allowed and campfire use is limited. Wilderness campsites should lie lightly on the land, disturbing the area as little as possible.

45

HOW TO CHOOSE A CAMPSITE

Whenever you go camping, you will need to find a place to spend the night. Here are some things to consider in selecting a campsite:

Environmental impact. Use established campsites whenever possible. If fires are allowed, build them in existing fire rings. Try not to put fresh marks on the land.

Safety. Avoid hazards. Don't pitch your tent under dead trees or limbs that might fall in a storm. Stay out of gullies that could channel flash floods. Camp away from lone trees, mountaintops, and high ridges, the most frequent targets of lightning. Camp away from game trails, especially in bear country.

Size. A site should be large enough for all of your tents and your cooking area. Where there is little open land, it may not be appropriate for your entire troop to camp together. Save small campsites for outings with your patrol or a Venture crew.

Shelter. Look for shade from the sun and protection from the wind. At night, damp air and insects tend to settle toward valley floors. A campsite partway up a hillside may be breezier, drier, and have fewer mosquitoes. Tops of hills are inviting, but they can catch the force of bad weather.

Too many tents crowd a small campsite. Use small campsites for patrol and crew outings.

Build fires in existing fire rings.

Purify water taken from streams, rivers, or lakes.

Water. You must have water for drinking, cooking, and cleanup. That amounts to several gallons a day for each Scout. Public water supplies are safest. Water taken from streams, rivers, or lakes must be purified before use. In high mountains and during the winter, you can get water by melting snow. Camping in dry areas is possible if you are willing to carry water to your site.

Ground. Does the site slope gently for good drainage? Leaves, pine needles, and other natural cover help keep campsites from becoming muddy.

Firewood. If fires are permitted, look for a supply of dead twigs and fallen branches. Consider bringing wood from home to roadside campsites, or use charcoal. In the backcountry where wood is scarce or fires are not allowed, use a backpacking stove to heat your water and cook your meals.

Privacy. Camping is a popular activity. Your group may not be the only one using an area, so you'll want to respect the privacy of other people. Trees, bushes, and terrain can screen your camp from trails and neighboring campsites. When other campers are near, keep the noise down.

Permission. Find out who owns private land and get permission from them before camping on it. On public lands, check ahead with rangers. In addition to issuing the maps and permits you need, they will have suggestions of ways you can enjoy a terrific adventure.

BE EASY ON THE LAND!

Several types of terrain demand special care in campsite selection.

Meadows. Whenever possible, camp in the forest away from meadows and the trees at their edge. These are important feeding areas for animals that may be frightened away by your activities. Deeper in the forest, you will be sheltered from sun and wind, and your camp will blend into its surroundings. You are also less likely to beat down meadow grasses and create erosion.

Lakes and streams. Like meadows, shorelines are heavily used by wildlife. Pitch your tents several hundred feet back from the edges of streams and lakes. This will allow the animals to reach the water and also reduce human impact along fragile shores.

Alpine areas. Winters in the high mountains are long and harsh. Plants have just a few warm months in which to grow. Camping on top of them can cause them serious injury. For that reason, try to make your high mountain camps only in established campsites, on bare ground, or on snowfields.

Keeping Clean

Hard work and play can leave you dusty. Always wash your hands with soap and water before handling food. On an overnight campout, you won't need to do much more than brush and floss your teeth before bed. You can clean up when you get home.

On longer adventures, you and those around you will be much happier if you take a bath once in a while. Doing it the right way will prevent any harm to the environment.

Many kinds of soap contain chemicals harmful to aquatic plants and animals. *Biodegradable* soaps are safer, but keep *all* soap at least 200 feet (75 steps) from any stream, lake, or spring.

Fill a basin or pot with water, carry it away from the source, and use it to bathe. Scatter the water when you are done, or pour it in a sump hole.

Take the same precautions if you do laundry. Carry water 200 feet or more from streams, lakes, and springs. Stir a little biodegradable soap into a pot of water and soak soiled clothing in it to loosen the dirt. Then scrub your laundry, rinse it, and hang it on bushes or a clothesline strung between two trees.

Dig a narrow trench for your latrine. Protect the turfs so that you can replace them later.

Make a trash "basket" by draping the top of a trash can liner over three upright stakes.

Latrines

Disposing of human waste outdoors requires special care. In campgrounds that have rest rooms or outhouses, be sure to use them. Where those don't exist, dig a cat hole or latrine.

Cat hole. Find a secluded spot at least 200 feet (75 steps or more) from water, camp, and trails. Use your heel or a camp shovel to dig a shallow hole no more than 6 inches deep. Organisms in the top layers of earth will break down human waste and small amounts of toilet paper.

After you have used it, fill the cat hole with soil and replace any ground cover. Push a stick into the ground to warn others against digging in the same spot.

Latrine. Dig a latrine if you camp more than a night or two in the same place or are out with a large group. With a shovel, make a shallow trench 1 foot wide and 3 or 4 feet long. Remove and save sod or ground cover. As with the cat hole, go no deeper than the topsoil. You want waste to stay in organic earth where tiny creatures can turn it into soil nutrients.

Sprinkle a layer of dirt in the latrine after each use to keep away flies and hold down odors. Lengthen the trench if it becomes full. Whether you use a cat hole or a latrine, always wash your hands when you are done.

CHECKLIST FOR SCOUT CAMPOUTS

Scout Outdoor Essentials

_____ Pocketknife

_____ First aid kit

_____ Extra clothing

_____ Rain gear

_____ Canteen or water bottle

_____ Flashlight

_____ Trail food

_____ Matches and fire starters

_____ Sun protection

_____ Map and compass

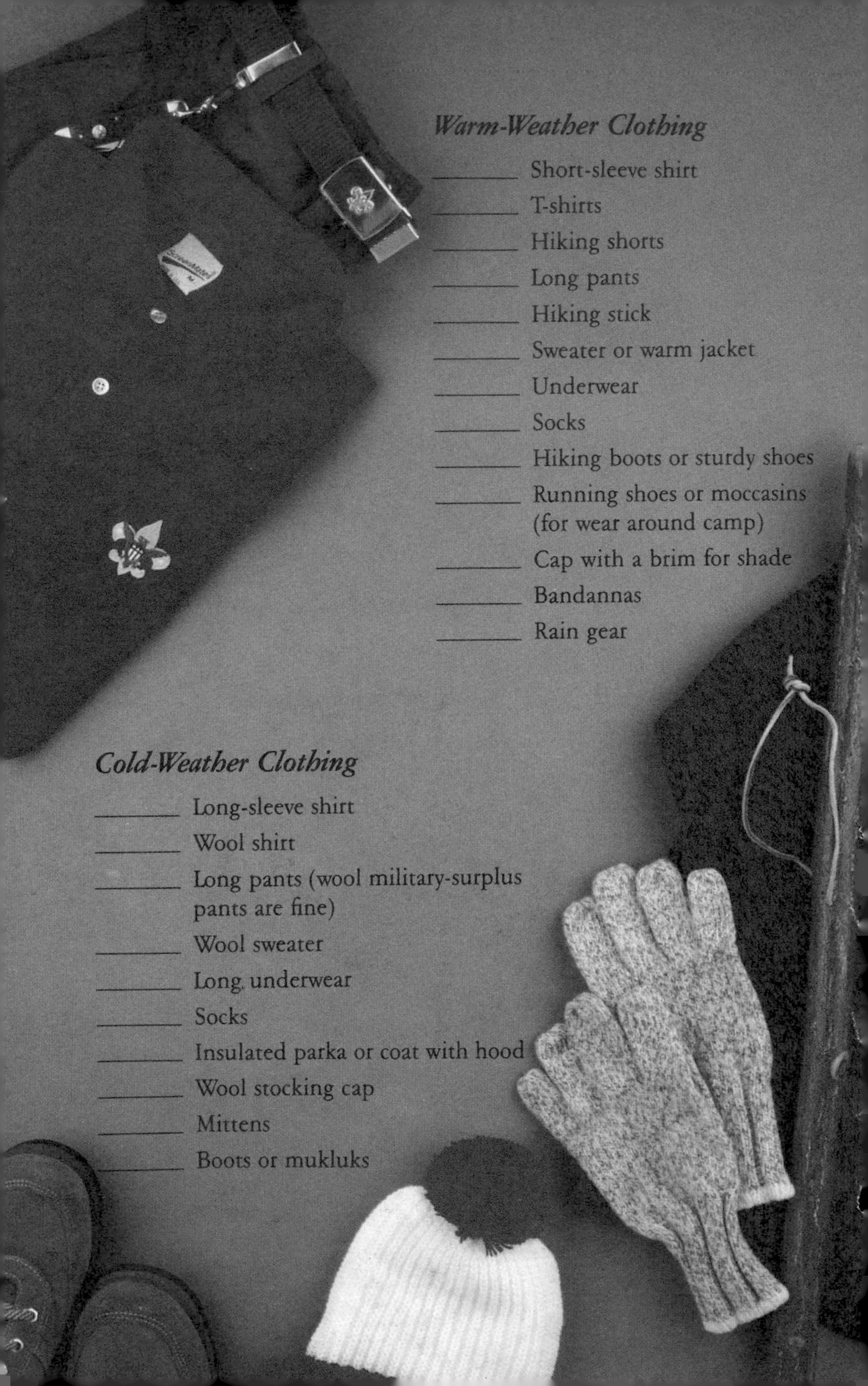

Warm-Weather Clothing

_____ Short-sleeve shirt
_____ T-shirts
_____ Hiking shorts
_____ Long pants
_____ Hiking stick
_____ Sweater or warm jacket
_____ Underwear
_____ Socks
_____ Hiking boots or sturdy shoes
_____ Running shoes or moccasins
          (for wear around camp)
_____ Cap with a brim for shade
_____ Bandannas
_____ Rain gear

Cold-Weather Clothing

_____ Long-sleeve shirt
_____ Wool shirt
_____ Long pants (wool military-surplus
          pants are fine)
_____ Wool sweater
_____ Long underwear
_____ Socks
_____ Insulated parka or coat with hood
_____ Wool stocking cap
_____ Mittens
_____ Boots or mukluks

Personal Overnight Camping Gear

_____ Scout Outdoor Essentials

_____ Clothing for the season

_____ Pack

_____ Sleeping bag **or** 2 or 3 blankets

_____ Foam sleeping pad **or** air mattress

_____ Ground cloth

_____ Eating kit:

    _____ Spoon

    _____ Fork

    _____ Plate

    _____ Bowl

    _____ Cup

_____ Cleanup kit:

    _____ Soap

    _____ Toothbrush

    _____ Toothpaste

    _____ Dental floss

    _____ Comb

    _____ Washcloth

    _____ Towel

_____ Personal extras you may want to take:

    _____ Watch

    _____ Camera and film

    _____ Notebook and pencil or pen

    _____ Insect repellent

    _____ Sunglasses

    _____ Magnifying glass

    _____ Binoculars

    _____ Bird and plant identification books

    _____ Musical instrument

    _____ Swimsuit

    _____ Prayer book or Bible

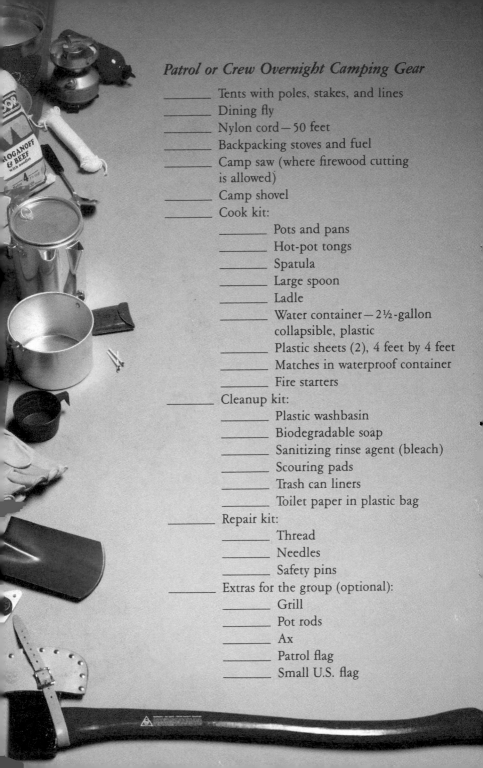

Patrol or Crew Overnight Camping Gear

_____ Tents with poles, stakes, and lines
_____ Dining fly
_____ Nylon cord—50 feet
_____ Backpacking stoves and fuel
_____ Camp saw (where firewood cutting
is allowed)
_____ Camp shovel
_____ Cook kit:
  _____ Pots and pans
  _____ Hot-pot tongs
  _____ Spatula
  _____ Large spoon
  _____ Ladle
  _____ Water container—2½-gallon
  collapsible, plastic
  _____ Plastic sheets (2), 4 feet by 4 feet
  _____ Matches in waterproof container
  _____ Fire starters
_____ Cleanup kit:
  _____ Plastic washbasin
  _____ Biodegradable soap
  _____ Sanitizing rinse agent (bleach)
  _____ Scouring pads
  _____ Trash can liners
  _____ Toilet paper in plastic bag
_____ Repair kit:
  _____ Thread
  _____ Needles
  _____ Safety pins
_____ Extras for the group (optional):
  _____ Grill
  _____ Pot rods
  _____ Ax
  _____ Patrol flag
  _____ Small U.S. flag

OUTDOOR CODE

As an American, I will do my best to —
Be clean in my outdoor manners,
Be careful with fire,
Be considerate in the outdoors,
     and
Be conservation-minded.

MEANING OF THE OUTDOOR CODE

Whenever you are outdoors, use the Outdoor Code as your guide. It has four important points.

As an American, I Will Do My Best to:

Be clean in my outdoor manners. *I will treat the outdoors as a heritage. I will take care of it for myself and others. I will keep my trash and garbage out of lakes, streams, fields, woods, and roadways.*

A heritage is a gift given by one generation to those that follow. For thousands of years, the land of America has been the heritage of all people living on the continent. Today, that gift is yours. One day you will pass the land on to your children and to all future generations. Do everything you can now to take care of the land, both for your own enjoyment and for use by people hundreds of years from now.

Be careful with fire. *I will prevent wildfire. I will build my fires only where they are appropriate. When I have finished using a fire, I will make sure it is cold-out. I will leave a clean fire ring, or remove all evidence of my fire.*

In the right setting, an open fire is a wonderful part of an outdoor adventure. However, not every outdoor spot can withstand the impact of a campfire. Sometimes there is not enough firewood. Dry weather may create a danger of wildfire. The ashes and blackened stones left by open fires can spoil the beauty of an area.

Build a campfire only if you are sure its impact on the land will be small. Use established fire rings whenever you can. Make your fire no larger than necessary. Watch a fire at all times to prevent sparks or flames from spreading into surrounding grass and trees. Where fires are not appropriate, cook your meals over backpacking stoves.

What you do after you douse a fire is as important as getting it cold-out. Properly dispose of ashes. Follow low-impact methods to erase every sign of your fire.

Be considerate in the outdoors. *I will treat public and private property with respect. I will use low-impact methods of hiking and camping.*

Public lands belong to every one of us. You are one of millions of owners of all national parks and forests, state lands, and even a small city park near your home. Ownership carries with it a great responsibility to look after your possession.

Begin by learning all you can about nature and the outdoors. The more you understand, the easier it will be for you to make wise choices. Leave no trace of your outdoor adventures. That may mean keeping your groups small, camping only in designated sites, and maintaining reasonable levels of noise. Respect the rights of others by doing nothing that would spoil their backcountry experiences.

Be conservation-minded. *I will learn how to practice good conservation of soil, waters, forests, minerals, grasslands, wildlife, and energy. I will urge others to do the same.*

Throughout America, Scouts like you enjoy outdoor adventures. Many also take pride in rebuilding trails, repairing damaged meadows, and restoring eroded hillsides and shorelines. By volunteering to help forest and park managers, you can give something back to the land that has given so much to you.

Of course, you need not limit your efforts just to the backcountry. In cities and towns, along highways, and in farmlands, you will find many opportunities to protect the environment.

When it comes to conservation, the efforts of a single Scout are of great value. The combined energy of millions of Scouts across the nation is making a tremendous improvement in the quality of America's parks and forests. Many Scouts are being recognized for knowing how to use the land wisely and how to lend a helping hand for the environment. Strive to be one of them.

LET'S GO CAMPING!

SEVEN KEYS TO LOW-IMPACT
AND NO-TRACE CAMPING

a. Wear a uniform or other clothing that will blend into your surroundings.

b. Stow food in containers you will carry home at the end of a trip.

c. Take along trash bags and use them.

d. Plan 12 or fewer in your group or patrol.

e. Select areas that are right for your activities.

a. Stay on the trail.

b. Avoid cutting across switchbacks.

c. Select hard ground or snow for cross-country travel.

a. Choose sites free of fragile plants.

b. Camp out of sight of trails, streams, and lakes.

c. Do not ditch tents.

a. Build fires only where appropriate. Otherwise, use back-packing stoves.

b. Use existing fire rings rather than making new ones.

c. Burn small wood gathered from the ground.

d. Make sure your fire is cold-out.

e. Replace sod or ground cover to erase burn scars.

Sanitation

a. Use all soap and detergent at least 75 steps away from streams, lakes, and springs.

b. Pour wash and dish water into a sump hole.

c. Dig latrines at least 75 steps from camps, trails, and any source of water.

d. Bury sump holes and latrines when you are through with them, and restore ground cover.

e. Pack out all garbage and trash you have not burned.

Horses

a. Keep number to a minimum.

b. Tie to sturdy trees or rope.

c. Hobble or picket in dry areas.

d. Scatter manure.

Courtesy

a. Hikers step off a trail to let horses pass.

b. Do not pick wildflowers. Enjoy them where they are, then leave them for others to see.

c. Keep noise down when you are around other campers and hikers. Leave radios and tape players at home.

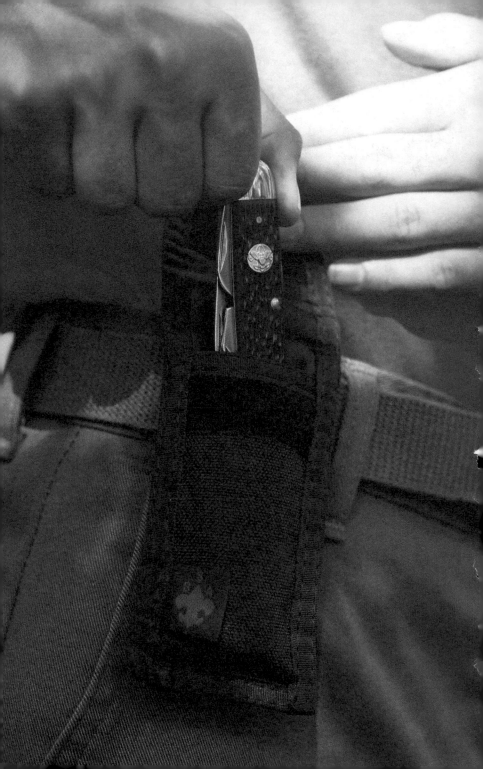

CHAPTER **3**

USING
WOODS TOOLS

H AVE you ever needed to cut a rope? Open a can of food? Whittle a
tent stake, slice a fresh loaf of bread, or punch a hole in a belt? Want
to tighten a screw on a stove or pack frame, trim a bandage, or make wood
shavings to start a fire? A pocketknife can help you with all those tasks, and
a thousand more. In fact, a knife has so many uses that it is hard to imagine
going camping without one.

The pocketknife, saw, and ax you use as a Scout are the same woods tools
used by park rangers, trail builders, and rustic carpenters. Whether you are
splitting firewood, repairing equipment, or clearing a fallen log from across
a trail, woods tools make your work easier and more enjoyable. Take pride in
learning the right way to use each one.

Just as important as handling tools well is knowing what *not* to do with
them. Carving or chopping on live trees may kill them. Hacking at dead
trees can leave ugly scars. Don't cut any trees without guidance from a ranger
or landowner.

USING YOUR POCKETKNIFE

The best knife for outdoor use has one or two folding blades for cutting,
and special blades for opening cans, driving screws, and punching holes.
Always follow these rules for safe knife use:

DO:

☆ Keep the blades closed except when you are using them.

☆ Cut away from yourself.

☆ Keep your knife sharp and clean. A sharp blade is easier to control than a dull one; a clean blade will last longer.

☆ Close the blades before you pass a knife to someone else.

DON'T:

☆ Carry a knife with the blade open.

☆ Cut toward yourself. If the blade slips, you may be injured.

☆ Pound on a knife handle or blade with another tool. The knife may bend or break.

☆ Throw a knife.

☆ Pry with the point of a cutting blade. It can snap off.

☆ Put a knife in a fire. New knife blades are hardened, or *tempered*, with just the right amount of heat. Reheating them may ruin the temper and weaken the knife.

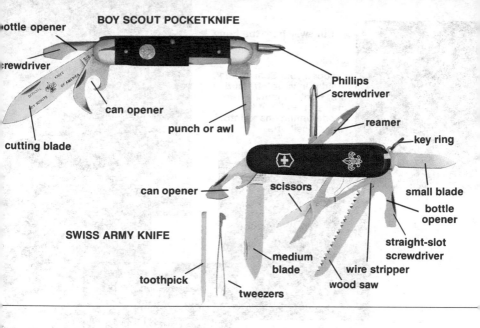

BOY SCOUT POCKETKNIFE

bottle opener

screwdriver

cutting blade

can opener

punch or awl

Phillips screwdriver

reamer

key ring

can opener

scissors

SWISS ARMY KNIFE

small blade

bottle opener

straight-slot screwdriver

medium blade

wire stripper

wood saw

toothpick

tweezers

Caring for Your Pocketknife

Most pocketknives are made of a strong steel alloy that won't rust. However, dirt and lint can collect inside, and ordinary use will dull the blades.

Cleaning a pocketknife. Open all of the blades, taking care not to nick your fingers. Twirl a small bit of cloth or paper towel onto the end of a toothpick. Moisten it with oil and wipe the inside of the knife. Be sure to clean the joint at the base of each blade. Swab out excess oil with a clean cloth. If you have used your pocketknife to cut food or spread peanut butter and jam, wash it in hot, soapy water along with your dishes.

Cut away from the body. ▶

◀

To open your Scout knife, hold it in your left hand. Put right thumbnail into nail slot. Pull out the blade until it snaps into open position.

To close knife, hold handle with left hand. Keep fingers safely on sides. Push against back of blade with fingers of right hand. Let knife snap shut.

Sharpening. Sharpen your knife with a *whetstone.* Most whetstones are made from granite and other materials harder than knife metal. Some are covered with diamond dust. Stones are used dry or with a few drops of water or honing oil.

Hold the blade against the stone at an angle of about 30 degrees. That means the back of the blade is tilted off the stone one-third of the way to vertical.

Push the blade along the stone as though you were slicing a layer off the top. The stone's gritty surface will sharpen, or *hone,* the blade much the same way sandpaper smooths wood. To sharpen the other side, turn the blade over and pull it along the stone toward you. Clean tiny bits of metal off the stone by slapping it on your hand or pants leg.

Work the blade back and forth across the stone several more times. Wipe the knife with a clean cloth and look directly down at the edge of the blade in the sun or under a bright light. A dull cutting edge reflects light and looks shiny. A sharp edge is so thin that it has no shine at all.

About the worst thing that happens to pocketknives is that they get lost. Keep track of yours by using a bowline knot to tie a 3-foot length of cord to the ring in the handle. Use another bowline to tie the other end to a belt loop of your pants. Your knife will always be within easy reach. Or you can thread a brightly colored shoestring through the ring and tie the ends in a square knot. That splash of color will help you find your knife if you drop it in grass, leaves, or snow.

CAMP SAW

A camp saw is the right tool for most outdoor woodcutting. The blades of *folding saws* close into their handles, much like the blades of pocketknives. *Bow saws* have curved metal frames that hold their blades in place.

Saw Safety

Saw teeth are needle-sharp. Treat every saw with the same respect you give your pocketknife. Close folding saws when they aren't in use and store them in a tent or under the dining fly. Protect the blade of a bow saw with a sheath made from a piece of old garden hose the length of the blade. Slit the hose down one side, slip it over the blade, and hold it in place with duct tape or cord.

You can carry a folded camp saw inside your pack. With its sheath covering the blade, tie a bow saw flat against the outside of your pack.

Using a Camp Saw

Brace the wood to be cut against a solid support. Use long, smooth strokes that let the weight of the saw pull the blade into the wood.

When sawing a dead branch from a tree, make an *undercut* first, then saw from the top down. The undercut prevents the falling branch from stripping bark and wood from the trunk. Make a clean cut close to the trunk so you don't leave an unsightly "hat rack." Cut saplings level with the ground so there are no stumps for someone to trip over.

Saw Sharpening

Touch up the teeth of your saw with a small triangle file or ignition file. Put on leather gloves to protect your hands, and then stroke the file upward, following the shape of each tooth. Sharpen one side of the saw, then the other.

The teeth on saw blades are *set*—bent so that they cut two thin grooves in the wood and then rake out the shavings between the grooves. Even with the best care, the teeth will slowly lose their set. A saw without set binds in the wood, making cutting difficult. Fortunately, bow saw and folding saw blades are replaceable and are not very expensive. Take along a spare blade if you will have a lot of cutting to do.

▲ Protect the saw blade with a
garden hose sheath.

Start with an undercut, then ▶
saw from the top down.

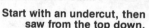

Place the wood you are cutting so that
the cut end falls free of the support.

When sharpening the saw, ▶
stroke the file upward.

▼ Don't leave "hat racks."

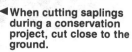

◀ When cutting saplings
during a conservation
project, cut close to the
ground.

AX

American pioneers used axes to cut trails through the wilderness. Axes bit into towering trees as settlers cleared forests to make way for gardens and fields. Loggers used axes to hew timber into boards and beams. With their axes, frontier craftsmen shaped the notches that held their buildings together.

Today's Scouts are more interested in preserving trees than cutting them down. The ax is a tool with a long and colorful history, but of limited use today. Most hikers and campers find that a pocketknife and camp saw are the only woods tools they ever need. Still, there is a satisfaction in knowing how to handle an ax well and when one can be used. That knowledge will also prepare you for using an ax to complete approved conservation and trail repair projects.

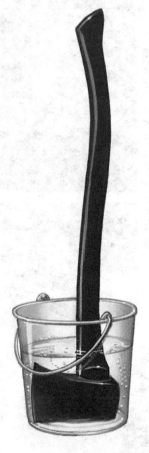

Ax Safety

2

Because of its size and the way in which it is used, an ax can be more dangerous than other woods tools. Remove the sheath only when you are prepared to use your ax correctly. Give it your full attention.

Safe tool. An ax must be sharp and in top condition. If the head is loose, soak the ax for a few hours in a stream or a bucket of water. The wood in the head will swell, and the handle will be tight for a while. When you get home, drive a wedge into the wood in the head, or replace the worn handle with a new one.

Safe shoes. Always wear sturdy leather boots when you are chopping with an ax. Leather won't stop a blade from hitting your foot, but good boots may limit the extent of an injury.

CHAPTER 3

Safe cutting requires ▶ clearance of at least an ax length all around.

Wear long pants and sturdy leather boots for protection when using an ax.

When chopping and ▶ splitting, keep ax and wood together—in contact.

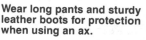

Safe working area. You must have plenty of room in which to swing an ax. Check your clearance by holding your ax by the head. Slowly swing the handle at arm's length all around you and over your head. Remove any brush or branches that the handle touches. While you are cutting, be certain other people stay at least 10 feet away.

In a long-term camp using lots of firewood, rope off an ax yard large enough to provide the clearance you need to work. Enter the yard only to chop and saw wood. Allow just one person at a time in the ax yard. Clean up the chips, bark, and other debris of cutting.

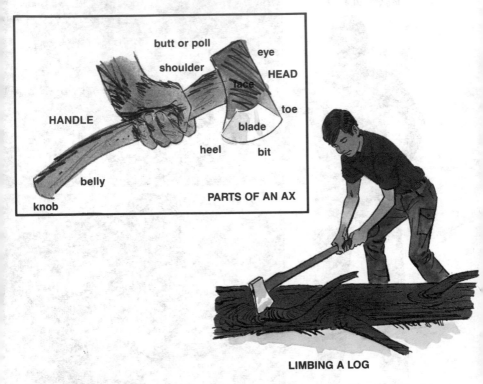

PARTS OF AN AX

butt or poll
shoulder
eye
HEAD
face
toe
HANDLE
blade
heel
bit
belly
knob

LIMBING A LOG

Safe technique. Chopping branches off a downed log is called *limbing*. Stand on the side of the log opposite a branch. Chop close to the base of the branch, driving the ax into the underside of the limb. Keep the log between you and your cuts. If the ax misses a branch, the blade will hit the log rather than your leg.

Bucking a log means cutting through it. Stand beside the log with your feet shoulders-width apart. Hold the ax with one hand near the head and the other close to the knob of the handle. Lift the head above your shoulder, then slide your hands together as you swing the bit into the log. Let the falling weight of the ax do most of the work. Slide your hand back down the handle to the head. Lift it and swing again. Aim your strokes so that you cut a V-shaped notch twice as wide at the top as the log is thick.

Learn to *switch-hit* with your ax. As you cut on the right side of a notch, let your right hand slide on the ax handle. Switch your grip and slide your left hand up the handle as you work the left side of a notch. Develop a relaxed, easy rhythm, switching hands after each blow.

CHAPTER 3

Cutting small sticks and splitting large chunks of wood known as *rounds* are best done on a chopping block, which is a thick piece of a log that has been sawed and turned upright to provide a flat surface. It should be about 2 feet high so that you won't have to lean down much as you work. A chopping block is important for safety, too. If you swing your ax badly, the bit will probably hit the block instead of flying on toward your feet.

To split a large round of wood, stand it upright on a chopping block. Swing the ax as you would to buck a log, driving the bit into the end of the round. If the wood doesn't split, remove the ax before swinging it again. Do not swing an ax with a piece of wood wedged on the bit.

◀ Use a chopping block to split a large round of wood. Always remove the ax after driving it into the end of the round until the wood splits.

Safe carrying. Place a sheath over an ax blade whenever it is not in use. Carry an ax at your side with one hand, the blade turned out from your body. If you stumble, toss the ax away from you as you fall. Never carry an ax on your shoulder.

Safe storage. Sheathe your ax and store it under the dining fly or in a tent. On the trail, a sheathed ax can be tied or strapped to the outside of your pack.

Safe handling. To pass an ax to another person, hold the handle near the knob with the head down. Pass the ax with the bit facing out at right angles between you and the other person. When your partner has a grip on the handle, he should say "Thank you." That's your signal to release your hold.

Sharpening an Ax

2

Keep your ax sharp with a *mill bastard file* 8 or 10 inches long. The lines across the face of the file are the teeth. They angle away from the point, or *tang*. A sharp file will be a drab gray color. A silvery shine means a file has broken teeth that won't sharpen very well.

Whenever you sharpen with a file, wear leather gloves to protect your hands. Also, make a *knuckle guard* from a 3-inch square of leather, plywood, or an old inner tube. Cut a small hole in the center of the guard. Slip it over the tang and hold it in place with a *file handle.* Buy a handle at a hardware store or make one from a piece of wood or a corn cob.

Brace the ax head on the ground between a small log and two wooden pegs or tent stakes. Another Scout can help hold the ax handle steady. Place the file on the edge of the blade and push it into the bit. Use enough pressure so that you feel the file cutting the ax metal.

Lift the file as you draw it back for another stroke. A file sharpens only when you push it away from the tang. Dragging the file across the blade on the return will break off the teeth and ruin the file.

Sharpen with firm, even strokes. After you have filed one side of the bit from heel to toe, turn the ax around and do the other side. Under bright light, a dull edge reflects light. Continue to file until the edge seems to disappear.

Filing can leave a tiny curl of metal called a *burr* on the edge of the bit. Remove the burr by honing the bit with a whetstone, just as you would the blade of a pocketknife.

TOTIN' CHIP

1. Read and understand the *Boy Scout Handbook* information on safe use of woods tools.

2. Demonstrate proper handling, care, and use of the pocketknife, ax, and saw.

3. Knives, axes, and saws are serious tools. Use them only when you are willing to give them your full attention.

4. Respect property. Cut living and dead trees only with permission and with good reason.

5. Use woods tools in such a way that you leave no trace.

I realize that my "totin' rights" can be taken from me if I fail to follow these requirements.

SHOVEL

A small camp shovel or garden trowel can be used to remove and save the grassy turf from the top of a latrine hole or fire lay. You can use a shovel to move hot coals when you are cooking with aluminum foil or a dutch oven. However, do not use your shovel to dig ditches around your tents. Ditches are unnecessary, and they may start erosion.

A camp shovel is useful for making low-impact fire lays and latrines.

CHAPTER **4**

CAMPFIRES AND CAMPING STOVES

C AMPFIRES have always been an important part of Scout camping. A fire can warm you, cook your meals, and dry your clothes. Bright flames lift your spirits on a rainy morning. On a starry night, glowing embers stir your imagination. The smell of campfire smoke and the crackle of burning wood are among the best memories of adventures gone by.

A good Scout knows how to build a fire. He also knows when he should not build one. Campfires can char the ground. Fires consume dead branches, bark, and other organic material that would have provided shelter and food for animals and plants. In the days when not many people went camping, there weren't enough fires to cause problems. But today, hiking and camping are popular activities. Hundreds of fires can have a serious impact on the well-being of the backcountry.

Before a campout, learn whether campfires are allowed in the area you plan to visit. Find out if there will be enough firewood. You may need permits to build fires in public parks and forests. Your Scoutmaster will help you get the permission you need.

If fires are not allowed, you can still go camping. Backpacking stoves are lightweight, easy to use, and clean. Properly handled, they are a good alternative to campfires.

CAMPING STOVES

Almost every Scout crew going into the backcountry at Philmont Scout Ranch carries a stove. Like those Philmont Scouts, you will find that a camping stove gives you a fast, easy way to do your cooking. In a few moments it produces a flame just right for warming a single cup of soup or cooking a big pot of stew. A stove won't blacken rocks or cooking gear, and it won't scorch the soil. With a stove, you can camp where there is no firewood or where campfires are not allowed. A stove works well in deserts, mountains, and deep forests. It is ideal for use in storms and on snow.

Many camping stoves burn *kerosene* or *white gas.* Store these fuels in special metal bottles with lids that screw on tightly. Choose bright red bottles or mark them with colorful tape so there is no chance of mixing them up with your water bottles.

Butane and *propane* stoves burn gases from small cans called *cartridges.* Cartridges and fuel bottles should be stowed in plastic bags and carried in outside pockets of your pack. That way, gas fumes can't get near your food.

Some backpacking stoves have padded carrying sacks to protect them as they bounce around in backpacks. If you don't have such a sack, roll your stove in a piece of foam and hold it in place with rubber bands.

When you are ready to cook, place your stove on a flat surface. A patch of bare ground or a flat rock is all you need. In winter, put your stove on a 6-inch square of plywood. The wood will hold your stove on top of the snow and prevent the cold ground from chilling the stove.

Larger kerosene and white gas stoves are too heavy to carry in a pack, but they are fine for use in camps that can be reached by road. Two or three burners give you all the room you need to cook meals for an entire patrol.

Different kinds of stoves operate in different ways. Read your stove's instructions carefully and do exactly what they say. In addition, *always* follow these stove safety rules:

Use camping stoves only where allowed and only with adult supervision.

Never use a stove inside a tent or cabin. There is a danger of fire and of poisoning by odorless gas fumes. Refuel and light stoves outdoors where there is plenty of fresh air.

Before lighting the burner, tighten the caps on the stove and on any fuel containers. Do not loosen the fuel cap of a hot stove.

Stoves sometimes flare up. Keep your head and hands to one side of a stove as you light and adjust it.

Don't overload a stove with a heavy pot. Instead, set up a grill over the stove to bear the weight of the pot.

Never leave a lighted stove unattended.

Let hot stoves cool before refilling fuel tanks. Refill stoves and store extra fuel well away from open flames such as other stoves, candles, campfires, and lanterns.

Carry home all empty fuel containers. Do not place them in or near fires. If heated, they may explode.

CAMPFIRES

Make a Safe Fire Site

Every year, wildfires destroy large areas of grasslands and timber. Many of these blazes are caused by people who are careless with campfires. From the moment you light a fire or stove until it is completely out, it is your responsibility to keep it under control.

A safe fire site is one on which nothing will burn except the fuel you feed your fire. It's a spot from which flames cannot spread. Parks and Scout camps may have large metal rings, grills, or stone fireplaces. Use these existing fire sites whenever you can.

Otherwise, select a spot on gravel, sand, or bare soil well away from trees, bushes, dry grasses, and anything else that might burn. Look overhead for branches that sparks could ignite. Stay clear of boulders that may be blackened by smoke, or large tree roots that might be harmed by too much heat.

Clean the fire site down to bare soil, then remove all burnable material from the ground around it. The cleared circle should be about 10 feet across. Rake away pine needles, leaves, twigs, and anything else that might catch fire from a flying ember. Save the ground cover so you can put it back when you are done with your fire. Keep a pot of water close to the fire site for emergency use.

If the site is grassy, use your camp shovel to cut around and under a 2-foot-wide square of sod. Lift out the loosened sod, lay it right side up in the shade, and sprinkle it with water. The grass should stay fresh until you replace it as you break camp.

Archaeologists uncovering the remains of ancient civilizations find rocks still smudged by fires that burned thousands of years ago. Before building a fire on bare rock, put down a 2-inch layer of sand or soil. Otherwise, your fire may leave a permanent black stain. Scatter the protective layer when you are done, and the stone should be unmarked.

Preparing Materials   2

The flame of a match is just large enough to burn a matchstick. To light a campfire, you have to give the match some help. You'll need *tinder, kindling,* and *fuelwood.*

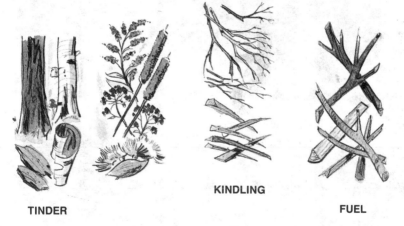

KINDLING

TINDER   FUEL

Tinder. Tinder catches fire easily and burns fast. Wood shavings, pine needles, dry grasses, shredded bark, and the fluff from some seed pods all make good tinder. Gather a double handful or enough to fill your hat once.

Kindling. Dry, dead twigs no thicker than a pencil are called kindling. Find enough to fill your hat twice.

Fuel. Fuelwood can be as thin as your finger or as thick as your arm. Use dead, dry, sticks you find on the ground. Live wood is a poor fuel because it is full of moisture.

Build small fires you can get close to rather than roaring blazes that drive you back. A quick fire to boil a pot of water takes just a few handfuls of sticks. You may need several armloads of wood to cook a large meal. Gather all the fuel before you light the fire so that you won't have to run off and find more wood while you are fixing dinner or enjoying an evening campfire with your friends.

Softwoods such as pine, fir, and aspen burn rapidly with lots of flames. Oak, maple, hickory, and other hardwoods burn more slowly and produce long-lasting beds of coals. Break or saw fuelwood into pieces about a foot long. Stack your firewood under the dining fly if you expect rain, or cover it with a plastic ground cloth or trash can liner.

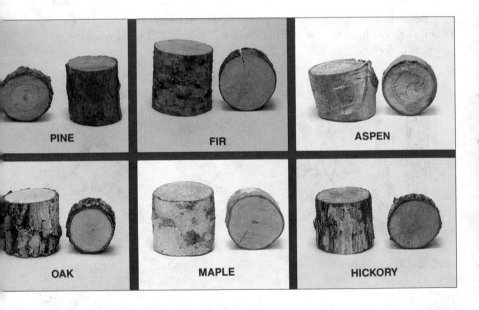

PINE   FIR   ASPEN

OAK   MAPLE   HICKORY

Building the Fire

Now you are ready to arrange tinder, kindling, and fuel so that the heat of a single match can grow into the flames of a campfire. A tepee fire lay is a good way to start.

Tepee fire lay. Place a big, loose handful of tinder in the middle of your fire ring. Lean plenty of small kindling around it. Let the tops of the kindling sticks touch like the poles of a tepee.

A fallen branch makes a handy "rake" to clear a fire site. Save the ground cover and place it back over the fire site before you leave.

Build your fire on bare soil and keep your fire lay small. ►

TEPEE FIRE LAY

Arrange larger sticks of fuel around the kindling. Leave an opening in the tepee on the side against which the wind is blowing. This "door" will let air reach the middle of the fire.

To light the fire, crouch in front of this door and strike a match. When the match is burning brightly, ease it under the tinder.

The flame should spread through the tinder and crackle up into the kindling. As the smaller sticks burn, larger fuel above them will become hot enough to ignite, too. Feed the growing fire with kindling and fuelwood.

Study the photographs of two other fire lays on page 86. They all have plenty of tinder and kindling. Light each fire low and let the wind blow the flames into the wood.

CAMPFIRES AND CAMPING STOVES

LEAN-TO FIRE LAY

CRISSCROSS FIRE LAY

FIRE STARTERS

Fuzz sticks are the true woods-man's fire starters. And whittling fuzz sticks is an excellent test for proving your skill with a knife.

Use dry sticks, thumb-thick, and a handspan long. Point one end. Hold the pointed end and fuzz the stick.

With kindling piled around the fuzz stick, fire building is simple. Fuzz sticks are especially good to make when wood is damp or wet, as the inside of the stick is always drier than the outside.

For "fire bugs," roll up four newspaper sheets. Tie strings 2" apart. Cut between.

Melt paraffin in tin can placed in boiling water. Soak "bugs." Cool.

Make a Fireplace 2 1

A fireplace holds your pots above the flames and allows air to reach the fire. Try to avoid using rocks in your fireplaces. Smoke and flames will stain them. Also, heat acting on the dampness in sandstone, shale, and stones from streams may cause them to explode.

Three-point fireplace. This is the ▶ simplest fireplace for a single pot or pan. Make a three-point base by sticking three metal tent stakes into the embers.

Hunter's fireplace. Place two logs close enough together that your pots will rest on them. Lay your fire between the logs. The fire will slowly burn through the logs, so keep an eye on the pots.

Trench fireplace. A trench fireplace allows you to cook in open, windy country. In almost any terrain, it lets you break camp with no trace of your blaze.

Use your camp shovel to remove a strip of sod about 6 inches wide and 2 feet long. Moisten the sod and store it in the shade. Dig a trench a foot deep and save the dirt by piling it on a ground cloth nearby. Build your fire in the bottom of the trench and do your cooking.

After the fire is cold out, return the dirt to the trench. Put the sod back on top, tamp it into place, and water it again. The site will heal quickly.

Pot Rods and Grills

Make your own pot rods with a couple of old metal tent pole sections or some foot-long pieces of iron reinforcing bar like those used in building construction. Just place them across the top of your fireplace for a solid base on which to rest your pots.

A small grill or oven grate can be used in the same way. If the grill has folding legs, you won't need a fireplace at all. Just set the grill over your fire.

Wet-Weather Fire Tips

The following tips will help you be prepared for rainy weather:

☆ Before the rain begins, gather tinder and kindling for several fires and store it under your dining fly.

☆ Keep a supply of dry tinder in a plastic bag.

☆ Split open wet sticks and logs. The dry wood inside will burn.

☆ If the fire in damp tinder is slow to ignite, blow gently on it. The extra air may help it burst into flame.

☆ Waterproof your matches before going camping. Dip each "strike-anywhere" match in melted paraffin or paint it with clear fingernail polish. An empty plastic aspirin bottle with a watertight lid makes a good match carrier.

☆ A butane lighter will give you a flame in even the wettest weather. Store it away from heat and flame.

☆ Use fire starters. Fire starters won't take the place of tinder and kindling, but they can give your matchflame a boost to get a blaze going. Make your own fire starters at home or carry a candle stub. In some parts of the country, you can find *pitch wood* — a piece of dead pine heavy with dried sap. The ease with which it burns makes it the perfect natural fire starter.

Making Fires Without Matches

Before the invention of matches, people knew many clever ways to make fire. Mastering those methods today can be fun, and you'll have a skill that may be very useful in an emergency.

Flint and steel. *Flint* is a hard, gray rock with smooth faces and sharp edges. Native Americans fashioned it into arrowheads. They also used it to start fires. So can you.

You'll need a piece of *steel* such as a small file or the back of a closed pocketknife blade. You may find bits of flint in road gravel. Other kinds of stone can also produce sparks. Test them by striking them with the steel.

Make a *spark catcher* from a 3-inch square of cotton or linen cloth. Put it in an empty coffee can and light it with a match. When the cloth is burning, place a lid on the can to smother the flame. The cloth should only be charred, not turned to ash. A bit of lint from the screen of a clothes dryer makes a good spark catcher, too.

▲ SPARK CATCHER

After you have laid a fire, gather a handful of very fine, dry tinder. Lay it on the ground and nest a bit of spark catcher in the center. Hold the flint over the tinder. With the steel, strike a glancing blow against the flint, knocking sparks into the spark catcher. It may take a number of tries before a good spark lands on the charred cloth. Lift the smoking tinder and blow on it very gently. When it bursts into flame, slide it under your fire lay just as you would a burning match. Take care not to burn your fingers.

Fire by friction. Rub your hands together and feel the friction warming your palms. Rub two sticks together in just the right way, and the heat can start a fire.

Begin by making a fire-by-friction set. The *spindle* is 1 foot long and about ¾ inch thick. Round both ends of it. The *fireboard* is about 4 inches wide,

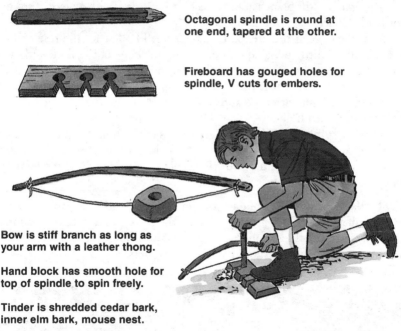

Octagonal spindle is round at one end, tapered at the other.

Fireboard has gouged holes for spindle, V cuts for embers.

Bow is stiff branch as long as your arm with a leather thong.

Hand block has smooth hole for top of spindle to spin freely.

Tinder is shredded cedar bark, inner elm bark, mouse nest.

½ inch thick, and 1 foot long. Make both the spindle and fireboard from a softwood such as aspen, poplar, balsam, willow, yucca, basswood, or cottonwood. The wood must be dead and very dry.

Carve a *hand piece* from softwood or hardwood. Whittle a smooth hole partway through it to fit over one end of the spindle. Rub a little bar soap into the hole to help the spindle turn more easily.

The *bow* is a stiff branch about 2 feet long. String it with a piece of strong cord, a leather thong, or a bootlace.

Near the edge of the fireboard, carve a small hollow for the free end of the spindle. Whittle a V-shaped notch from the edge of the fireboard into the hollow. Put some very fine tinder under the fireboard notch, then kneel with one foot on the board. Twist the bowstring around the spindle and hold the spindle upright with the hand piece. Press down on the spindle to keep it in the fireboard hollow.

Turn the spindle with long, steady strokes of the bow. Keep going until heavy smoke pours from the notch. Lift the fireboard and tinder together and blow on the ember in the notch until it ignites the tinder. Slide the flaming tinder under your fire lay.

Fire by glass. On a very bright day, you can start a fire with a magnifying glass or a lens of a pair of thick eyeglasses. Move the glass until it focuses the sun's rays into a small, brilliant point of light on your tinder or charred cloth. In a few moments, the fuel should begin to smolder.

Putting out a Fire

Extinguish every fire when it is no longer needed. Make sure it is **COLD OUT**, not just out. That means the ashes are so cool you can touch any part of the fire lay with your hands.

With water. Splash water on the embers. Stir the damp ashes with a stick and splash them again. Turn smoldering sticks and wet them on all sides. Use plenty of water. Repeat until you can touch every part of the fire lay.

Without water. When water is scarce, work sand or dirt into the coals. Keep stirring soil through the fire until it is out. Rub burned sticks against the ground to extinguish embers. Give the fire the **COLD-OUT** test by touching the dirt and dead ashes with your hands.

Cleaning a Fire Ring

After you have extinguished a fire in an old fire ring, pick out all bits of paper, foil, and unburned food, then pack them home in a trash bag. Bury the ashes in your latrine or grease pit. Leave the fire ring clean for other campers to use.

Erasing a Fire Ring

If you made a new fire ring, it's best to take it apart and erase all evidence of your fire. Scatter any rocks, turning their blackened sides to the ground. Bury cold ashes in your latrine pit. Replace ground cover and sod, and toss away extra firewood. When you're done, the site should look just as it did when you found it.

CHARCOAL

Where wood fires are not allowed, charcoal may give you the heat you need for cooking. Follow the same fire-making safety rules as you would for any camping stove or open flame.

Charcoal Stoves

Charcoal burns best when it is contained in a stove. The stove directs the heat where you want it. A stove may help protect the soil from being scorched.

Make a small charcoal stove from a large coffee can or No. 10 can, which holds 100 ounces. Remove the lid of the can, but not the bottom. Use a triangle-shaped can opener to cut air holes every 2 inches around the sides of the can near the base and the top. With pliers, bend sharp edges safely out of the way.

Punch the can lid full of holes with a hammer and nail. Rest the lid on a couple of wires pushed through more nail holes halfway down the can. The perforated lid will serve as a grate to hold the charcoal the right distance from the food. Punch a ½-inch hole in the side of the can just above the grate. You can slide a lighted match through it to ignite the charcoal.

To cook for more than a couple of Scouts, you may want several tin can stoves, or you can make a larger charcoal burner by cutting open a thoroughly cleaned 5-gallon oil can. Fold back the sides so that the can rests firmly on the ground.

CHARCOAL STOVE FROM #10 CAN

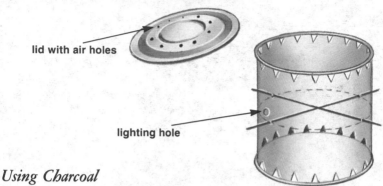

lid with air holes

lighting hole

Using Charcoal

A tin can stove will use 6 or 7 charcoal briquettes. Larger stoves burn 15 to 20 at a time.

Charcoal fires take awhile to reach cooking heat. Light the briquettes at least 15 minutes before you need them.

The safest way to start briquettes is with tinder and kindling, much as you would any campfire. Pile enough briquettes to cook an entire meal on top of a double handful of wood shavings and twigs. Light the base of the tinder with a match. Fan the flame with a pot lid or plate to speed the burning.

In larger stoves, use a stick to spread out glowing coals for a slow fire just right for frying and broiling. For boiling, push coals together to concentrate the heat. Cool a charcoal fire by sprinkling it with a little water.

Dump hot briquettes into a pot of water to extinguish them. Immediately drain them and spread them on the ground. Their own heat will dry them. Use the same briquettes to cook your next meal, or carry them home for proper disposal.

COOKING
IN CAMP

C AMP COOKING! At the end of a long day on the trail, it's a hearty helping of stew, a couple of biscuits, and perhaps pudding with fresh mountain blueberries you've just picked. On a snowy winter day, it's a steaming cup of soup or a mug of rich cocoa that warms you down to your toes.

As dawn breaks over the mountains, camp cooking is the sound of bacon and eggs sizzling over a backpacking stove. At night under a dining fly rattling with rain, it's the yeasty smell of baking bread.

Food in the outdoors is more than just a way to cut your hunger. It powers your body through days packed with action. It helps you stay warm at night. When the sky turns stormy or when you are tired and feeling low, a good meal restores your energy and helps you enjoy everything about hiking and camping.

Becoming a good backcountry cook begins with what you do at home. Help prepare family meals whenever you can. You will get a feel for using pots, pans, and utensils. Learn to cook in your own kitchen, and you will find that it is easy to cook on the trail.

The planning you do before an outing is also important. At home, you can reach into a cupboard for ingredients, or run down to the store. But when you go camping, everything you'll need for cooking and cleanup must be in your pack.

Start cooking outdoors by fixing tasty, simple meals. As you gain confidence, you can try new recipes and experiment with different ways of cooking. You will find that camp cooking is an outdoor adventure full of excitement and fun—and you can always eat the results when you are done.

WATER

Your body needs plenty of fluids to keep you cool, digest your food, and maintain your health. Drink at least 2 quarts of fluid (six to eight glasses) each day, in cold weather as well as warm.

On Scout outings, you will also need water for cooking and washing. Count on using several gallons a day. A gallon of water weighs more than 8 pounds, so you probably won't want to carry more than a quart or two with you. Draw the rest from water sources in camp and along the trail.

Public supplies. Water from faucets and drinking fountains in campgrounds and Scout camps usually has been tested by public health officials. You can use it just as it is.

Snow. Get the water you need on winter trips and in high mountains by melting clean snow. Each time you sip from your water bottle, replenish it with a handful of loose snow. Water remaining in the bottle will help melt the snow.

In camp, gently heat a pot of snow over a stove or fire. A few cups of water in the bottom of the pot will speed the process.

Open water. Even the clearest water taken from streams and lakes may contain bacteria, viruses, and parasites too small for you to see. Drinking impure water can make you very ill. *Always* disinfect any water that does not come from a tested source.

Methods of Disinfecting Water

Boiling. Heat kills organisms. Bringing water to a rolling boil is the surest way to disinfect it. Boiled water can taste flat. Freshen it after it has cooled by pouring it back and forth between two pots.

Iodine. Water can also be disinfected with iodine tablets, which are sold in small bottles just the right size for hikers and campers. The label usually instructs you to drop one or two tablets into a quart of water and then wait 30 minutes before drinking.

CHAPTER 5

◄ boiling

▼ using a filter system

iodine tablets

Iodine tablets rapidly lose their effectiveness after a bottle has been opened. Within 2 or 3 months, tablets may be useless. Find the date on the label and use only fresh tablets.

Iodine leaves a chemical flavor in the water. You might want to add some drink mix to improve the taste, but wait until the iodine has had a full 30 minutes to do its work.

Filters. Camping stores and catalogues offer water purification filters. Some pump the water through pores small enough to strain out bacteria. Others contain iodine or other chemicals. Like iodine tablets, they may lose strength over time. Carefully follow the instructions that come with any filter.

Treating muddy water. Sometimes the only water you can find is clouded with silt. Strain the water through a neckerchief or bandanna into a pot, and let it stand for an hour. Most of the mud should settle to the bottom. Use a cup to dip the clear water into another pot. Then boil it, treat it with iodine tablets, or run it through a filter.

FOOD FOR CAMP

Every Scout wants to eat well. Careful planning allows you to take the right amount of food so that everyone in your patrol gets enough, but there's not much left over.

Some ideas for a balanced diet include:

Meat, poultry, fish, and eggs. Protein is one of the body's building blocks. In addition to fresh fish, poultry, and meat, you can use canned meat and small tins of chicken or tuna. Eggs must be carried with care. Some camping stores sell dried eggs.

Protein also comes from mixing grains and legumes. Combinations of beans, corn, rice, lentils, barley, wheat, and bulgur (parched cracked wheat) are nutritious and tasty.

Milk and cheese. Dried milk requires no refrigeration. Stir a few spoonfuls of the powder into puddings, stews, and egg dishes for extra richness. Mix it with water for drinking.

Cheese stored in the shade keeps well on trips of a week or more. Cheddar, jack, and other hard cheeses hold up better than softer varieties. Serve slices of cheese on sandwiches or crackers. Stir small bits into scrambled eggs, sauces, stews, and soups.

Vegetables and fruits. Many kinds of vegetables and fruits can be packed into camp fresh, canned, or dried. The choice depends on how much weight you are willing to carry. Good vegetables for camp cooking are carrots, cabbage, potatoes, cucumbers, celery, radishes, and green peppers. A few tasty fruits are apples, peaches, apricots, raisins, bananas and figs.

Bread and flour. You can tie a loaf of bread on the outside of your pack where it won't be squashed, or stow it inside a pot or an empty cardboard oatmeal box. Crackers are easier to carry than bread and stay fresh longer. Noodles, macaroni, spaghetti, and other pastas serve as bases of many main dishes.

Baking is a highlight of any camp kitchen. Preparing biscuits, corn bread, cobblers, and cakes requires practice, but the good eating is worth the effort.

Grains and nuts. Brown or white rice, barley, oats, and other grains can be served alone or mixed into stews and soups. Peanuts, almonds, and sunflower seeds are rich in nutrients. Snack on them during the day, and include them in your recipes.

Spice kit. Spices bring out the flavor in your cooking. Store spices in empty 35-millimeter film canisters or small, clean plastic aspirin bottles, then stow all the containers in a stuff sack or plastic bag. Use spices sparingly. Sprinkle in a little and see how it tastes. You can always add more, but you can't take out a spice if you use too much.

Good spices for camp cooking include salt, pepper, chili powder, thyme, oregano, garlic flakes, bay leaves, and cinnamon.

Spices add flavor to food on the trail. Make your own spice kits using film canisters or small bottles.

KEEP A COOKING NOTEBOOK

Camp cooking is a skill you can master by doing a lot of it. Write your food lists and recipes in a notebook every time you prepare for a campout. At the end of each trip, make notes about what worked well and what didn't. Perhaps you took too much cocoa. Maybe you needed a larger fry pan or more oatmeal. As you plan your next outing, your notebook will remind you of changes you want to make.

PLANNING YOUR MEALS

You need to know the following before you plan your outdoor meals:

☆ *How long will you be out?* For short outings, fresh foods are fine. For trips of more than a day or two, carry supplies that won't spoil.

☆ *How many people are going?* Then you can decide how much food to take for each meal.

☆ *What are you going to do?* Estimate how much time you want to spend cooking. For days packed with action, choose recipes that won't take long to prepare. However, cooking may be your major camp activity. Take the ingredients and gear you'll need to cook up a real feast.

☆ *How will you reach camp?* Are you traveling by car? Then you can take griddles, dutch ovens, and plenty of utensils. If you'll be packing everything on your back, keep your menus and your load basic and light.

☆ *What kind of weather do you expect?* Winter menus should contain more of the fats your body burns for heat. Include soup mixes and hot drinks. Summer meals may be lighter and include more cold fluids.

Now you have the information you need to follow these steps for purchasing food wisely:

Menus. Once you know how many meals will be needed, write down what you want to prepare and eat for each of those meals. The recipes in this chapter will give you some ideas. Stick with good, healthy foods.

Shopping list. After making a menu, list every ingredient for each dish. Use the chart on page 105 to determine the amounts you will need for the number of people in your patrol. Don't forget items such as margarine, honey or sugar, and spices.

Pricing. Take your shopping list to a grocery store and write down the prices of the ingredients you plan to buy. The store manager may be able to help.

Cost per person. When you have priced each item, add up the costs. Divide the sum by the number of Scouts. This will give you each Scout's share of the expense.

Buying the food. When all of the Scouts have paid their shares, return to the store and purchase your supplies.

SIZE OF SERVINGS

Food packages often list suggested amounts for one or more servings. You can also use this chart to help you decide how much of each food you will need.

MEAT, POULTRY, FISH, AND EGGS

(One Serving)

Steak . . . . 6–8 oz.

Chops . . . . 4 oz.

Stew meat . . . . 4 oz.

Hamburger . . . . . . 4 oz. (1 patty)

Hot dogs . . . . 4 oz. (2 hot dogs)

Chicken, fresh . . . . 12 oz.

Ham,
precooked . . . . 3 oz.

Bacon . . . . 2 oz. (3–4 slices)

Beef, canned . . . . . 3 oz.

Chicken,
canned . . . . 3 oz.

Fish, canned . . . . . 3 oz.

Eggs, fresh 2

Eggs, dried . . . . . . ½ oz.

MILK AND CHEESE

Milk, fresh . . . . 1 pt.

Milk, powdered . . . 2 oz.

Cocoa, instant . . . . 1 individual packet

Cheese . . . . 2 oz.

VEGETABLES AND FRUITS

Orange 1

Apple 1

Tomato 1

Juice, canned . . . . 4 oz.

Cabbage, raw . . . . ¼ head

Carrot, raw 1

Vegetables,
canned . . . . 4 oz.

Vegetables,
dehydrated . . . . . . ½ oz.

Potatoes, raw . . . . 2 medium

Potatoes,
instant . . . . 2 oz.

Corn, raw . . . . 2 ears

Onion, raw . . . . . . 1 medium

Soup, canned . . . . 5 oz.

Soup mix . . . . 1 individual packet

Fruit, fresh . . . . . . 1–2 pieces

Fruit, canned . . . . 5–6 oz.

Fruit, dried . . . . . . 2 oz.

BREAD, FLOUR, AND PASTA

Bread . . . . 2–4 slices

Cookies . . . . 2 oz.

Cakes . . . . 2 oz.

Cereal—
oatmeal . . . . 2 oz.

Cereal—cold . . . . . 2 oz.

Pancake mix . . . . . 3 oz.

Brown rice . . . . . . ½ cup uncooked

White rice . . . . ½ cup uncooked

Instant rice . . . . . . ½ cup precooked

Spaghetti . . . . 3 oz.

Macaroni . . . . 3 oz.

Noodles . . . . 3 oz.

Ramen noodles . . . 1 packet (3 oz.)

Pudding mix . . . . . 1½ oz.

Other Items to Consider: Salt, pepper, catsup, mustard, relishes, salad dressing, flour, honey or sugar, butter, margarine, cooking oil, shortening, jam, jelly, syrup, and peanut butter.

Repackaging Food

Avoid carrying excess weight and clutter by taking some of the foods out of the original packages. Measure only as much of each ingredient as you will need for one meal and put it in a plastic bag. Carry peanut butter, jam, and margarine in wide-mouth plastic jars with screw-on lids. Tape a label on each bag or jar, and write on it the name and amount of the ingredient inside.

Stow all the repackaged ingredients for each meal in a larger bag, along with the recipes for that meal's dishes. Label the big bag with the name of the meal. When you reach camp, you will have in one place all of the ingredients and instructions for every meal.

BREAKFAST IN CAMP

Get your day off to a fine start with a real stick-to-your-ribs breakfast. Healthy foods won't take long to prepare. Here are some suggestions. *All of the recipes are for one serving.*

Fruit

Fresh fruit. Apples, oranges, grapefruit, and bananas are available all year. Fresh peaches, melons, and berries are in the stores in the summer and fall.

Canned fruit. Many kinds of fruit are available in cans. Plan on about 6 ounces per serving.

Dried fruit. Dried fruits, raisins, and banana chips are delicious just as they are. Many dried fruits can be soaked overnight and used in recipes in place of fresh fruit.

COOKING IN CAMP

Cereal

A steaming pot of hot cereal tastes great on chilly mornings. In the summer, you may prefer cold cereal or granola with milk.

Hot oatmeal. For each serving, bring 1 cup of water to a boil. Add a pinch of salt. Stir in ½ cup quick-cooking rolled oats. Let it simmer a few minutes, stirring often so the cereal doesn't stick to the bottom of the pot. For extra flavor, drop some raisins or chopped fruit into the boiling water. Serve oatmeal with milk, brown sugar, butter, cinnamon, or even a spoonful of jam.

Granola. Granola, a cereal made of toasted oats, is terrific for outdoor breakfasts. Different brands come mixed with nuts, raisins, and other tasty ingredients. Try a bowl of granola with milk. Hot granola is very good on cold mornings — cook it just as you would hot oatmeal. During the day, a handful of granola makes a tasty trail snack.

Eggs

Boiled eggs. Boiling is the easiest way to cook eggs. Use a spoon to lower each one into a pot of boiling water. Boil about 5 minutes for soft-boiled eggs, 10 minutes for hard-boiled. Cool hard-boiled eggs in cold water to make them easy to peel.

Fried eggs. Heat 1 teaspoon of butter, margarine, or bacon fat in a pan. Crack in 2 eggs, taking care not to break the yolks. Fry over low heat until the white becomes firm. Flip them if you like your eggs "over easy," or serve them "sunny-side up."

Scrambled eggs. With a fork, beat 2 eggs in a bowl. Add ½ cup of milk and a pinch of salt and pepper. Heat butter or margarine in a pan, then pour in the eggs and cook over low heat. Stir occasionally, scraping the bottom of the pan with a spatula or fork. For variety, add finely chopped onions, tomato, green pepper, mushrooms, or shredded cheese to the eggs before you cook them.

One-eyed jacks. Use an upside-down cup to cut a hole out of the center of a slice of bread. Lay the bread in a hot, greased pan and crack an egg into the hole. Fry it a few minutes until the egg sets, then flip the bread and egg with a spatula and cook the other side. You'll have an egg and toast all in one.

Bacon and Ham

Fried bacon. Put 3 or 4 slices of bacon in a pan and cook over low heat. Turn the slices when half done. Pour bacon grease into an empty tin can and save it for frying eggs and other breakfast foods.

Fried ham. Heat a little butter or margarine in a pan. Put in a slice of precooked ham and fry over low heat until the meat is lightly browned. Turn it and fry the other side.

You do it with a smooth, looping-the-loop motion, not with a violent toss.

From the Griddle

Pancakes. Flapjacks are a real camp treat. They are best cooked in a heavy fry pan or on a griddle.

Follow the instructions on a box of pancake mix to make batter. (If you have no prepared mix, make your own before you leave home by mixing together ½ cup white flour, ½ teaspoon baking powder, a pinch of salt, and ½ teaspoon sugar. In camp, make the batter by stirring in 1 egg and ¼ to ½ cup of milk.) If you have them, you can add fresh berries, chopped fruit, or nuts to the batter.

Heat the pan and grease it with a little butter, margarine, or bacon fat. Carefully pour batter into small cakes. Fry over low heat. When bubbles burst in the center of the cakes and the edges begin to brown, turn each flapjack and fry the other side. Serve with butter and syrup, or jam.

French toast. Beat together 1 egg, a pinch of salt, and a cup of milk. Add a sprinkle of cinnamon. Dip both sides of a slice of bread in the egg mixture and fry the bread as if it were a pancake. The mixture from 1 egg is enough for 3 or 4 slices of french toast. Serve with butter and syrup or jam.

Breakfast Drinks

Milk, cocoa, and fruit juices all go well with breakfast. Use fresh drinks, dried milk, cocoa mixes, or fruit juice powder.

LUNCH

After a busy morning, you will be more than ready for lunch. You can make lunch right after breakfast and take it with you, or if you'll be near camp in the middle of the day, you may want to cook a hot, nutritious meal.

Sandwiches. An easy way to serve sandwiches is to lay out all the makings on a sheet of plastic and let each Scout build his own. Use whole wheat or enriched breads. For fillings, choose from peanut butter and jelly, cheese, luncheon meats, canned tuna or salmon, sardines, sliced tomatoes, hard-boiled eggs, pickles, and lettuce. Round out the meal with a glass of milk, a piece of fruit, and a few cookies.

Hot dishes. Light a stove and fry a hamburger or boil some hot dogs. Toast a cheese sandwich by frying it on both sides in a little butter or margarine. A cup of soup will warm you on a chilly day. Make it from a can or an instant mix by following the instructions on the label.

SUPPER

Starved at the end of the day? The evening meal gives you a chance to satisfy your hunger and show your cooking skill. You can go easy with a quick one-pot stew. Or, if time permits, go all out by preparing a main dish with meat, poultry, or fish. Fix some vegetables, bake bread or biscuits, and add a dessert and something to drink. You'll have an outdoor feast to remember.

Cooking Meat

There are many ways to cook meat. Grilling and frying are the quickest, stewing the slowest. Keep preparation times in mind as you plan your menu.

Grilled meat. Kindle a fire and let the flames die down. Place a wire grill above the coals. Lay the meat on the grill and adjust it to hold the meat close enough to the coals for moderate cooking (test the heat with the hand thermometer method). Grill hamburgers 3 to 4 minutes on each side. An inch-thick steak requires about 8 to 10 minutes on a side. Cut into the center to see if the meat is done the way you like it.

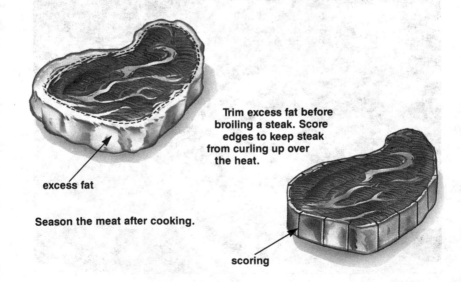

Trim excess fat before broiling a steak. Score edges to keep steak from curling up over the heat.

excess fat

Season the meat after cooking.

scoring

Fried meat. Heat a spoonful of cooking oil in a fry pan. Drop in hamburger patties, pork chops, or steaks. Cook over coals or a stove turned low. Hamburgers take just a couple of minutes on each side; steaks, 6 to 8 minutes on a side; lamb chops, 8 to 10 minutes on each side; pork chops, 12 to 15 minutes. Pork must always be very well done.

Stewed meat. For one serving: ¼ pound of beef or lamb cut into ¾-inch cubes. Rub flour into them and fry in a pot with a few spoonfuls of oil until brown. Add enough water to cover them. Bring the water to a boil, then lower the fire under the pot. Let the meat simmer for an hour. With 30 minutes to go, add a chopped onion, carrot, and potato. Season with salt and pepper. Simmer until done.

Broiled chicken. Lay pieces of chicken on a wire grill. Cook over coals 15 minutes on each side. While it's broiling, keep the chicken moist by brushing it with butter, margarine, or barbecue sauce.

Fried chicken. Cut a half chicken into 2 or 3 pieces and roll them in flour. Fry in 2 tablespoons of butter or margarine, turning the chicken now and then until pieces are golden brown. Add ½ cup of water, cover with a lid, and steam over low heat for about 20 minutes.

Cooking Fish

When you've had some luck with your fishing pole, there are plenty of good ways to turn your catch into dinner. First, clean the fish. Slit open the belly and pull out the guts. If the fish has scales, remove them by scraping with a knife from the tail toward the head. Burn the entrails or carry them home in a trash bag. Rinse the fish with water inside and out.

Fried fish. Roll the fish in flour or cornmeal. Fry in a few spoonfuls of butter or oil until golden brown, turning the fish once. It won't take long.

Poached fish. Drop fish into salted, boiling water. Simmer gently until the flesh can be picked from the bones.

HAND THERMOMETER

Hold your palm where the food will be cooking: over the coals for broiling, in front of a reflector oven for baking. Count "one-and-one, two-and-two . . .," and so on, for as many seconds as you can hold your hand still. Move your hand around to find the spot with the temperature you want.

Seconds Counted	Heat	Temperature
6 – 8	Slow	250° – 350°F
4 or 5	Moderate	350° – 400°F
2 or 3	Hot	400° – 450°F
1 or less	Very hot	450° – 500°F

Vegetables

Boiled potatoes. Wash and quarter a couple of medium-size potatoes. Put them in a pot and cover with water. Boil gently for about 20 minutes. Test with a fork. If it goes in easily, the potatoes are done. Season with salt and pepper. Serve with a little butter or margarine. (Many people leave the skins on potatoes for the nutritious vitamins and minerals they contain.)

Fried potatoes. Boil several potatoes. Let them cool. Slice the cold potatoes and fry in hot oil until they are brown. For extra flavor, fry a chopped onion with the potatoes. Season with salt and pepper.

Mashed potatoes. Boil 2 or 3 potatoes. Drain off the water and mash the potatoes with a fork. Add butter or margarine and a dash of salt. For smoother potatoes, stir in 2 tablespoons of milk.

Boiled vegetables. Choose from among these single servings: 1 or 2 medium carrots, 2 ears of corn, ¼ head of cabbage, or ½ cup of string beans or shelled peas. Cover with a little water and simmer over low heat. Carrots cook in 25 minutes, corn on the cob in 6 to 10 minutes, cabbage in 7 minutes, string

CHAPTER 5

beans in 30 minutes, and peas in 10 to 15 minutes. At high elevations, add a few minutes to the cooking time. Pour canned vegetables into a pan and heat them in their own liquid.

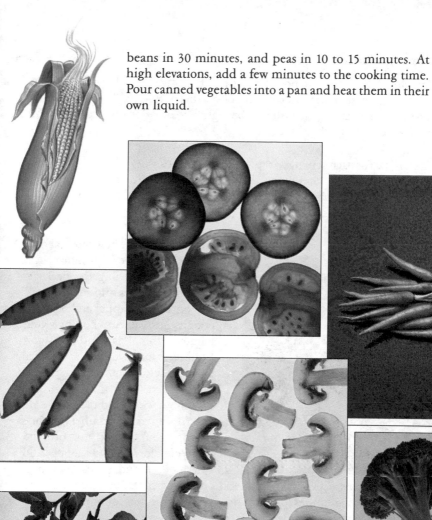

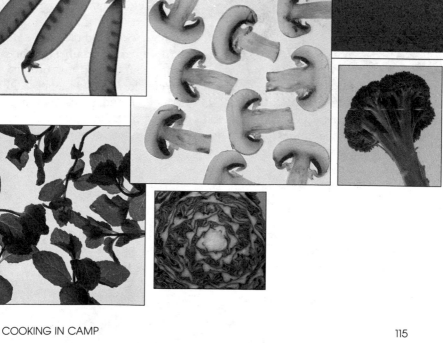

Pasta and Rice

Spaghetti. Bring a large pot of water to a boil. Add 1 tablespoon of butter or margarine, then drop in 4 ounces of spaghetti. Boil hard for 5 to 10 minutes until tender. Spaghetti should be slightly chewy; don't overcook it. Drain and serve with spaghetti sauce.

Macaroni. For each serving, drop 4 ounces of macaroni into a pot of boiling water. Boil for 10 to 15 minutes, then drain the water. Stir 2 ounces of cut-up cheese and 1 teaspoon of powdered milk into the cooked macaroni to make macaroni and cheese. Salt to taste.

Ramen noodles. These oriental noodles usually come in 3-ounce packages. Before opening the package, crush the noodles into small pieces. Tear open the wrapper and pour the noodles into 1½ cups boiling water. Remove from heat and let stand 5 minutes until done. A 3-ounce package yields a solid single serving.

Rice. Both white and brown rice are rich in minerals and fiber. For one serving, pour ½ cup raw rice and 1 cup of cold water into a pot. Add a dash of salt and ½ teaspoon butter or margarine. Cover with a lid and bring to a boil. Let it simmer until done—about 10 minutes for white rice, 20 to 30 minutes for brown rice. You don't need to stir rice while it is cooking.

One-Pot Camp Stew

It's hard to beat the one-pot stew for quick and easy outdoor dining. With a few ingredients and a little imagination, you can make dozens of different kinds of stew. Just combine one item from each of the following lists:

All amounts are for one serving.

116

3–4 ounces cooked:	3–4 ounces:	1 packet:	1 handful:
spaghetti	canned tuna fish	gravy mix (chicken, mushroom, onion)	cooked vegetables
macaroni	canned chicken		chopped cheese
noodles	tofu or textured vegetable protein	spaghetti sauce	chopped nuts
ramen noodles		stroganoff sauce	

Serve vegetables separately from the stew, or drain them and stir right into the pot. Season to taste. Add a beverage, some bread, and a dessert to round out this hearty meal.

Bread

Biscuits. Follow the package directions to make dough from ½ cup of biscuit mix. Divide the dough and shape into 3 or 4 biscuits about ½ inch thick. Place them on the greased pan of a reflector oven and bake in front of a steady fire for about 15 minutes. Test by pushing a matchstick or wood shaving into a biscuit. The biscuits are done when the wood comes out clean.

If you don't have biscuit mix, prepare your own by stirring together 1 cup flour, ¼ teaspoon salt, and 1 teaspoon baking powder. To make biscuits, add 2 tablespoons oil, margarine, or butter and just enough water or milk to keep the dough together but not too sticky.)

Dutch oven bread. A dutch oven is a heavy iron pot with deep sides and a tight, flat lid. The oven must be "seasoned" before its first use. Warm the oven and drop in a dab of butter or grease. Spread it all over the inside of the oven and lid with a paper towel. Bake at 450° for 30 minutes. The metal will be protected from rust, and foods you prepare in the oven will be less likely to stick. Soap strips away the grease, so it's best to wash a dutch oven in hot water only. Reseason your oven whenever it has been scrubbed with soap.

For a quick bread, mix up enough dough for 8 biscuits. Use a shovel to move one scoop of coals to the side of a fire. Place the empty oven on them and let it warm. Arrange the unbaked biscuits in the bottom. Put on the lid and shovel coals on top — three times as many coals on the lid as underneath the oven. The lip of the lid will help hold the coals in place. In about 10 minutes, the biscuits will be ready. It's a good idea to wear gloves and use hot-pot tongs whenever you handle a hot oven.

Dutch ovens and reflector ovens are also fine for baking pies, cobblers, cakes, cookies, and brownies. The same is true of most backpacking ovens.

Stove-top ovens. Ovens for use with backpacking stoves are available at camp supply stores. Like reflector ovens, they are light in weight and fold flat to slip into your pack. Use them as you would an oven at home, keeping your stove flame low to allow gentle baking.

Frying pan bread. Almost any bread or biscuit recipe can be cooked in a greased fry pan. Flatten the dough into a large pancake and fry it over the fire. Turn it with a spatula to allow both sides to brown. The trick is to cook the dough slowly enough for the center to become done before the crust is too brown.

Dumplings. Another speedy way to fix bread is to drop small spoonfuls of biscuit dough right on top of a one-pot stew. Cover and let steam for about 10 minutes. The dumplings will be moist and just right to eat with the stew.

Desserts

Fruit or cookies finish off a meal nicely. Pudding mixes are available in many flavors, and instant pudding requires no cooking. Baked desserts are always a special camp treat.

COOKING IN ALUMINUM FOIL

Want to leave the pots and pans at home? Wouldn't you like to have nothing to wash but your knife and spoon? Then give aluminum foil cooking a try. Simply wrap food in a piece of heavy-duty foil. Join the edges and fold them over so that steam cannot escape. Place the foil package on a bed of hot coals and turn it several times during the cooking. When you unwrap your dinner, you can eat right out of the foil.

Foil cooking is possible because aluminum doesn't burn. That also means you will want to carry used foil home for recycling or disposal.

Time the placing of the food so that everything will be ready at the same time.

Hamburger. Shape 4 ounces of hamburger into a patty. Cut a medium-size potato and carrot into thin strips. Peel and slice a small onion. Arrange all of the ingredients on a square of foil and sprinkle lightly with salt. Fold the foil into a tight package. Lay it on the coals and cook for about 15 minutes.

Foil stew. Cut 4 ounces of beef or lamb into cubes. Slice a potato, carrot, and small onion. Sprinkle with salt. Add several tablespoons of water and fold up the foil. Cook on the coals for about 20 minutes.

Chicken. Smear chicken pieces with butter or margarine. Salt lightly and wrap each one in a separate piece of foil. Turn them several times as they cook over the coals for 20 minutes.

Baked potato. Poke through the skin of a potato several times with a fork, then wrap the potato in foil. Bury it in the coals and wait 30 to 40 minutes or more.

Corn on the cob. Dab butter or margarine on an ear of corn. Wrap it in foil and roast for 10 minutes on the coals.

Baked fish. Fresh fish is so moist that you can bake it in foil with just a bit of butter or margarine. For extra flavor, add finely chopped onions and carrots. Wrap the fish in foil and bake on coals — 3 minutes on each side for a small fish, 10 minutes or more per side for a whopper.

Biscuits. Follow the usual recipe to make biscuit dough. Grease a 12-inch square of foil. Shape the dough into a 2-inch ball and drop it onto the center of the foil. Fold the foil loosely around the dough and seal the edges. The biscuit will expand as it cooks, so leave plenty of space inside the foil. Bake 6 to 10 minutes, turning often to brown all sides.

Baked fruit. For a special dessert, cut out the core of a raw apple and replace it with a pat of butter, a few raisins, some cinnamon, and a teaspoon of brown sugar. Wrap in foil and bake for 30 minutes. A banana still in its skin can be baked in foil in 10 minutes or less.

COOKING WITHOUT UTENSILS

Cook a meal without pots, pans, *or* foil? You'll be surprised how easy it can be. The secret is a good bed of hot coals.

Cooking in Coals

Roast potatoes. Coat each potato with a thick layer of mud and bury it in the hot coals. Bake 30 to 40 minutes. The mud will become caked and hard, but the potato inside should come out just right.

Cooking on Coals

Caveman steak. Level a bed of wood coals with a stick. Place a steak right on top of the coals. Broil 3 to 5 minutes, then turn it and broil the other side.

Roast corn. Open the husks and remove the thread-like silk. Reclose the husks. Dip the ears in water, then place them on the coals. Roast 8 minutes, turning them often as they cook.

Cooking over Coals

Broiled steak. Find a long, green, forked stick. Trim off any leaves and twigs. Bend the two branches of the fork into the shape of a tennis racquet and twist the branches around each other to hold them in place. That's the frame of your broiler.

Place straight green sticks across the broiler frame. Lay a steak on them and hold it down with more sticks anchored to the broiler. You can also use the broiler to toast slices of bread.

Kabob. Start with 1-inch cubes of beef, lamb, or ham. Add mushroom caps, chunks of tomato, onion, green pepper, pineapple, or slices of zucchini. Slide the pieces onto a thin green stick and broil them a few inches above the coals for 10 to 15 minutes.

Fish. Run a sharp kabob stick into the flesh along the length of the spine of a small trout, or tie the fish to the stick with several wraps of string. Hold it over the coals and cook for a few minutes. Fins and skin will pull off, leaving the tender meat beneath.

Chicken. Skewer a small whole chicken onto a sturdy green stick about 3 feet long. Tie the legs together with cord and rub the bird with butter or margarine. Rest the ends of the stick on logs placed on either side of the coals. Turn the stick occasionally so that all sides of the chicken will brown. Allow about an hour of cooking time.

Twist. Roll stiff biscuit dough into a long sausage shape. Find a clean stick as thick as an ax handle and twist the dough around it. Lean the stick over a bed of coals. Turn occasionally and bake until the bread is done.

Bread cup. Instead of twisting the dough, mold it onto the end of the stick and bake it over the coals. Slip it off for a bread cup you can stuff with sandwich fillings.

SHARING KITCHEN DUTIES

When you cook on your own, you have only yourself to please. Protect your food and cooking gear from dirt by laying a plastic sheet on the ground and using it as a table. Make yourself comfortable, then see how well you can prepare a meal and clean up afterward.

When there are two of you, both of you can pitch in and help with all the cooking and cleanup. Or one can act as cook while the other cares for the stove or fire, brings in water, and washes the pots. Switch jobs at the next meal so you each have a chance to do everything.

In larger groups, make up a duty roster. A third of the group cooks, a third gathers water and firewood or tends to the stoves, and the others do the cleanup. During an overnight campout, each Scout can have the same job for all the meals and then move to a new spot on the roster for the next outing.

KEEPING YOUR CAMP CLEAN

You know that keeping yourself clean is important for your health. Did you also know that keeping your camp clean is important for the health of the environment? Some ways of doing dishes and disposing of trash can cause harm to plants and animals. Stick with the following plan and you will be practicing the best *low impact* cleanup methods.

Dishwashing

Whether you cook with a stove or over an open fire, start heating a pot of water before you serve a meal. The water will be hot by the time you have finished eating.

Proper cleanup requires three pots—a warm wash, a cold rinse, and a hot rinse. The first pot contains warm water (about 100°F) and a few drops of biodegradable soap. The second holds cold water to which you've added a few drops of bleach or a sanitizing tablet. The third contains clear, boiling-hot water.

Each Scout can wash his own eating utensils. If everyone also does one pot, pan, or cooking utensil, all the work will be finished in no time at all. Food stuck to the bottom of a pan can be scoured with wet sand carried some distance away from open water. Use hot-pot tongs to dip plates and spoons in the hot rinse. Lay clean utensils on a plastic groundsheet and let them air dry.

WASH   **COLD RINSE**   **HOT RINSE**

Don't bury extra food or scatter it in the woods. Animals will almost always find it, and it is seldom healthy for them to eat. Food scraps can also draw animals close to campsites where they may lose their fear of man. That can be dangerous for them and for you.

Leftover food should be carried home in a trash bag or destroyed in a hot campfire. Burn it by pushing a little at a time into the flames—not too much or you'll smother the fire. You can burn waste paper, too, but don't put plastic bags in a fire. Burning plastic releases toxic gases into the air.

Wash out jars and put them in your trash bags. Wash cans, cut out both ends, flatten them, and carry them home for recycling.

SOAPING A PAN

For quick pot- and pan-washing, smear soap powder paste, softened soap, or liquid dish soap on the outside of the pot before using it over an open fire. After use, soot will wash off easily.

Dishwater Disposal

On an overnight campout, strain any food bits out of your dishwater and burn them or put them in a trash bag. Then take both the wash and rinse water away from camp and at least 75 steps from any streams or lakes. Give it a good fling to spread it over a wide area.

For longer stays at one site, dig a *sump hole* at the edge of camp. It should be about 8 inches across and 2 feet deep. Place a piece of window screen across it.

Keep the sod cool in the shade until you are ready to replace it.

Pour wash and rinse water through the screen into the sump. The screen will catch food particles which must be burned or put in a trash bag. Fill the sump hole when you break camp, and replace the ground cover.

Food Storage

Protect your food from mice, chipmunks, raccoons, and even bears by hanging it from a tree. Toss a rope over a high tree branch. Put your food in a stuff sack or clean trash bag, tie it to one end of the rope, then hoist it above the reach of animals. In bear country, bags should be at least 10 feet off the ground and 6 feet or more away from the trunks of trees.

MAKING A BEAR BAG

SETTING UP A BEAR BAG

CHAPTER 5

Using two cords, toss the end of one over a high branch and tie it to a tree trunk, then toss the other end over a branch of equal height on a tree some distance away. Pull the cord tight and tie that end, too. Next, tie one end of the second line to the food bag and throw the free end over the center of the line between the trees. Pull the bag into the air and secure the line to the tree, suspending your bear bag far from the reach of prowling animals.

Another way is to divide your provisions into two bags. Using a bear rope tossed over a branch, raise one bag in the usual way, then tie the free end of the cord to the second bag. Lift it overhead and use a stick or hiking staff to shove it out of reach. The bags will counterbalance one another, and your food will be safe. To retrieve the bags, use the stick to push one bag even higher, causing the other to come down within your grasp.

KEEP SOAP AND DETERGENT AWAY FROM OPEN WATER

You may have heard that you should keep all soap, shampoo, and detergent out of streams and lakes. Here are some reasons why:

☆ *Detergents and shampoos contain chemicals that encourage algae to grow. Algae can crowd out the native plants, making it harder for fish and other animals to survive.*

☆ *Soap, shampoo, and detergent leave an oily film in the water that can harm tiny aquatic life.*

Never put anything into the water that you aren't willing to drink as it floats away.

'PACK IT IN, PACK IT OUT'

That's an important backcountry saying. Whatever you take to camp must be carried back home. Don't leave anything behind — no litter, no cans, nothing buried, and nothing thrown in the woods, lakes, or streams.

CHAPTER 6

ROPES, KNOTS, AND SPLICES

ROPE is one of man's oldest and most important tools. The knots Scouts tie today have been around for hundreds of years. Most were developed by sailors for use on sailing ships. You'll find many ways to use them every day.

You probably know how to tie a few knots. At home, you tie your shoes and necktie, and bind packages. On camping trips, you will use knots to hold gear on your pack, set up tents and dining flies, and secure canoes and boats. In emergencies, knots can hold bandages in place and help you make rescues on the water and in the mountains.

ROPES

Over the centuries, ropes have been made of plants called manila, hemp, and sisal. Long, tough stem fibers are wound into *yarn* which is then twisted into *strands*. The strands are wrapped around one another to produce the rope. Today, many ropes are made of nylon, plastic, and other man-made materials.

Care of Rope

Rope strands sometimes begin coming apart, causing the ends of the rope to turn into fuzz. Unless you do something about it, the fraying will continue until the rope is destroyed.

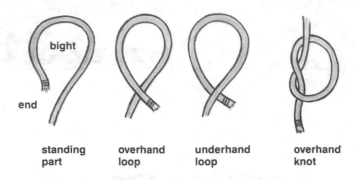

bight

end

standing
part

overhand
loop

underhand
loop

overhand
knot

The parts of a rope are called end and standing part. All knots are made by combining bights, loops, or overhand knots in different ways.

Two quick ways to protect the end of a rope are to tie a knot in it or wrap it with tape. For a permanent solution, *whip* the ends of your ropes or put in a *back splice. Fuse* each end of a rope constructed of man-made materials.

Whipping. Cut off any of the rope that has already unraveled. Take a piece of strong string or twine at least 2 feet long. Form a loop in it and lay the loop near the end of the rope. Tightly wrap, or *whip,* the string around the rope. When the whipping is as wide as the rope is thick, pull hard on the free ends to tighten the string. Trim off extra string, then whip the other end.

Fusing. Ropes and cords made of plastic and nylon melt when exposed to high heat. Hold each end a few inches above a lighted match or candle. It takes only a moment for the strands to fuse together. Use caution—melted plastic is very hot and sticky. *Do not* try to fuse ropes made of manila, sisal, hemp, or cotton. They will burn rather than melt.

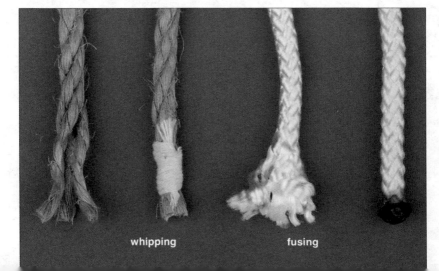

whipping   fusing

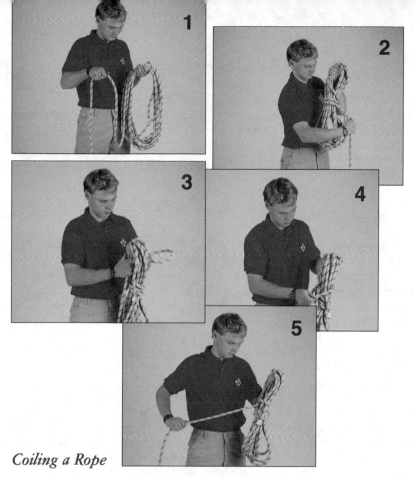

Coiling a Rope

Coil your rope when it is not in use to prevent it from tangling. A coiled rope is easy to carry and simple to loosen the next time you need it.

1. Hold one end of the rope in your left hand. With your right hand, lay coils of rope on your left palm. Make all the coils the same size. Keep the rope from twisting by turning it as you form the coils.

2. Grasp the last few feet of line in your right hand and wrap it neatly around the middle of the coils.

3. Pass a loop of the running end of the rope through the coil.

4. Pull the loop over the top of the coil.

5. Draw the loop snug. Use the free end of the line to carry the coil.

LEARNING KNOTS

Knot tying is a lot of fun, but there is also a serious side to it. Tying the right knot at the right time will make your outdoor adventures safer and easier. Someday a knot you tie may even save a life.

There are three tests of a good knot.

☆ It should be easy to tie.

☆ It should stay tied.

☆ It should be easy to untie.

You will have to practice if you expect to become good with knots. Even after you've learned to tie one, review it often to keep it fresh in your mind. Carry a piece of cord in your pocket. Pull it out when you have a few spare moments and tie the knots you know. Keep at it until you can tie each one with your eyes closed. When you can tie the knots automatically, you are ready to use them in any situation.

Knots for Joining

Joining knots are used to tie together the ends of two ropes.

Square knot. Sailors call this a *reef knot.* They use it to tie ropes around rolled, or *reefed,* sails. The square knot is fine also for tying packages and first aid bandages. However, it may be hard to untie if it has been under strain. Because it sometimes slips, the square knot is not as good as the sheet bend for joining two ropes.

To tie the square knot, hold one rope end in each hand. Tie an *overhand knot* by putting the right end over and under the left rope. Tie a second overhand knot, but this time put the left end over and under the right rope. "Right over left and under, left over right and under." That saying will help you remember where the ends should go.

▼

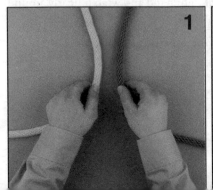 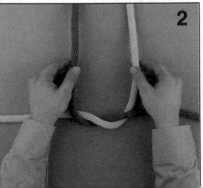

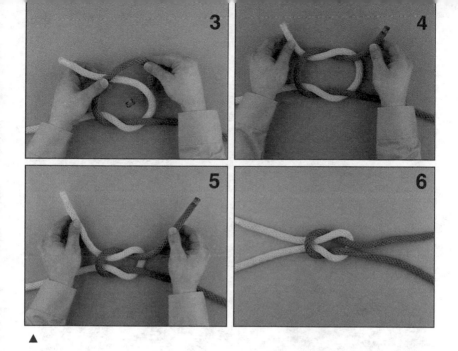

You may be surprised to learn that you probably tie your shoestrings with a type of square knot. Pull the loops the rest of the way out of a shoestring knot and you will see a regular square knot.

Sheet bend. The *sheet bend* gets its name from *bending* (tying) a *sheet* (that's a rope on a sail). It is a very good knot for tying together two ropes, especially if they are of different thicknesses. The sheet bend is a strong knot that is easy to untie.

Put a loop in the end of the thicker rope and hold it with one hand. Pass the end of the other rope up through the loop. Take that end on around behind the loop. Bring the end back across the top of the loop, and tuck the end under its own standing part. Tighten the knot by pulling the standing part of the smaller line.

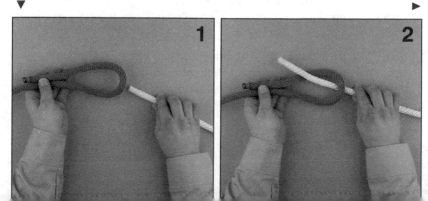

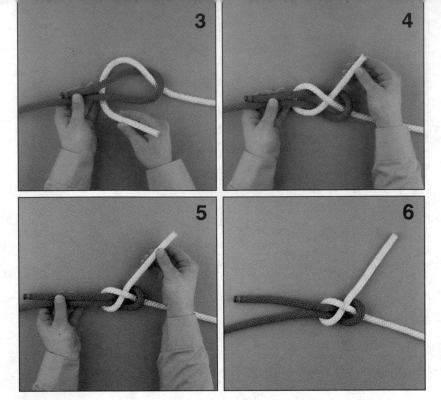

Loop Knots

The knot most often used in the backcountry is a loop knot called the *bowline*.

Bowline

1

The bowline forms a loop that will not close. Because it doesn't slip, the bowline is the most reliable knot for tying a rope around your waist. That makes it an important knot for lifesaving and mountain climbing. Learn to tie it around yourself, around a post, and in the free end of a rope. With practice, you can even tie it with one hand.

Try each of the following ways of tying a bowline and see which is easier for you:

1. Make a small overhand loop in the standing part of a rope. Bring the rope end up through the loop, around behind the standing part, and back down into the loop. Tighten the bowline by pulling the standing part away from the loop.

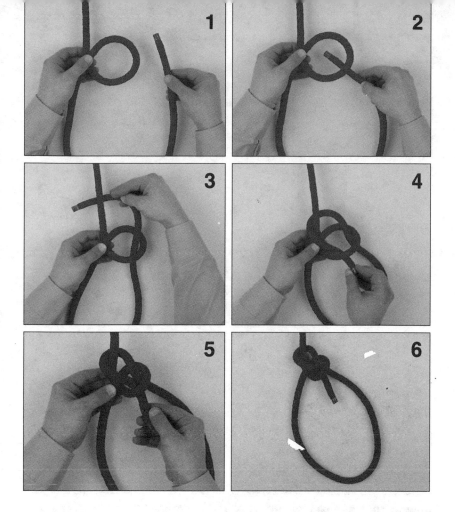

2. A faster method, shown on page 136, is also easier to tie in the dark. Hold the rope end in your right hand and the standing part in your left. Lay a few inches of the end across the standing part. With your right hand, grasp the point where the rope crosses. With your left hand, lift the standing part up and around the rope end, forming a small loop with the rope end inside of it. Now pass the rope end around behind the standing part and bring the end down through the small loop. Tighten the knot.

Notice the collar-shaped bend of rope in the bowline. To untie the knot, push the collar away from the loop as if you were opening the top on a soda can. That will break the knot and allow you to loosen the rope.

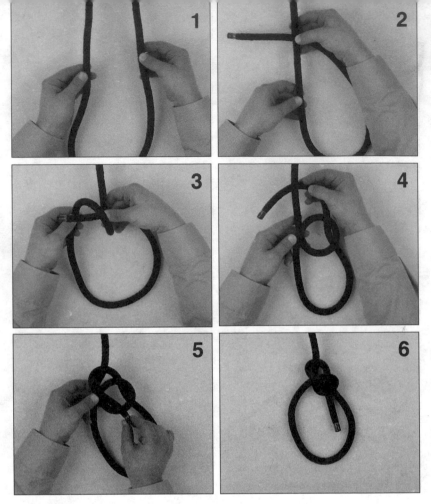

HOW TO TIE A BOWLINE IN THE DARK ▲

Bowlines for Joining

You can use bowlines to join two ropes together. Tie a bowline in the end of each rope so that their loops interlock like the links of a chain. ▼

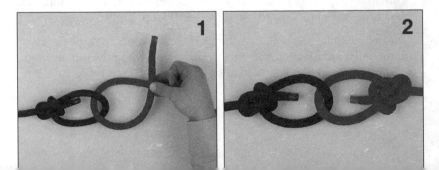

Hitches

A *hitch* is a knot that ties a rope to an object. Friction caused by the wraps of the rope holds the knot in place.

Two half hitches. Use two half hitches to tie a rope around a post or through T a ring or a tent grommet. Unlike the bowline, it forms a loop that will close.

Pass the end of the rope around a post. Bring the end over and under its own standing part, and back through the loop you've formed. That makes a *half hitch*. Take the end around the standing part a second time and tie another half hitch. Pull the knot snug.

▼

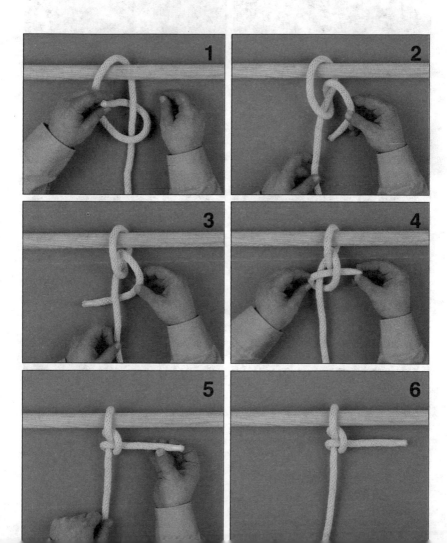

Taut-line hitch. The taut-line hitch is tied on a line that is tight, or *taut*. Use it on a tent guy line and you can tighten or loosen that line by pushing the hitch up or down the standing part. Here's how.

Pass the rope around a tent stake. Bring the end under and over the standing part and twice through the loop you've formed. Again bring the rope end under, over, and through a loop, but this time farther up the standing part. Work any slack out of the knot. Slide the hitch to adjust the tension on the rope.

▼

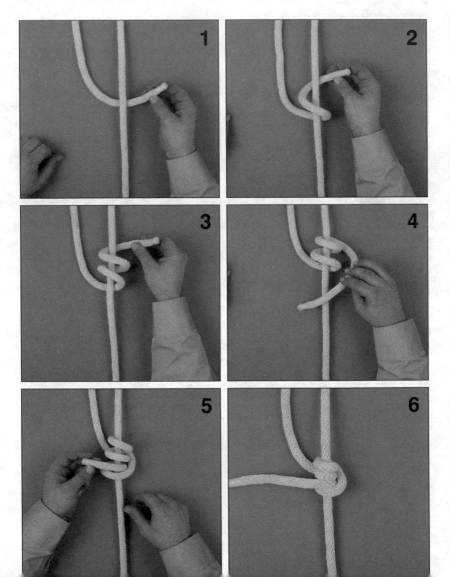

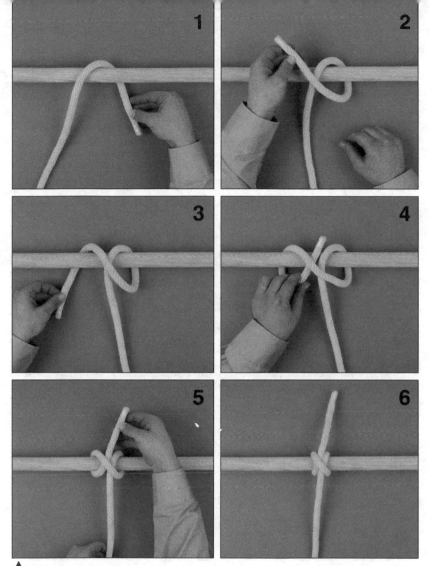

 Clove hitch. *Clove* comes from the word *cleave*, meaning "to hold fast." The clove hitch holds well when the standing part of the rope is pulled straight out from a pole or post. It is the knot used to start and finish most lashings.

Bring the rope end over and under the post. Take it around a second time, crossing over the first wrap to form an X on the post. Bring the rope end around a third time, then tuck it under the center of the X. Tighten the knot by pulling the end and the standing part.

Timber hitch. When you want to use a rope to drag a log, tie it with a timber hitch. Begin by passing the end of the rope around the log. Bend the end around the standing part of the rope, then twist the end around itself three or more times. Tighten the knot against the log.

An additional half hitch thrown near the end of a log will increase the rope's grip on slippery timber and help you keep the end from digging into the earth as you haul it along.

▼

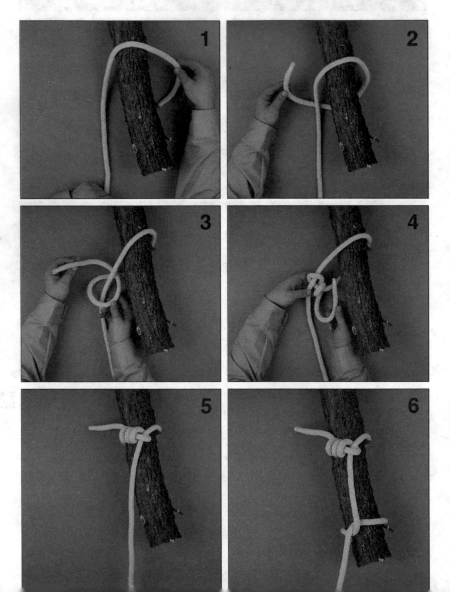

USES FOR KNOTS

SQUARE KNOT is a binding knot. It is used for tying up bundles and packages. Its most important use is in first aid, where it is used for tying bandages.

Hold one rope or bandage end in one hand, the other end in the other. Twist left-hand end over, under, and over the right-hand end, and pull taut. Once more twist the same rope end over, under, and over, and pull taut. When tied correctly, the rope ends both lie on the same side of the knot.

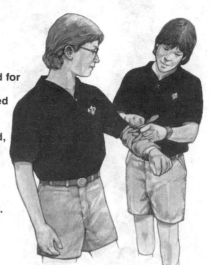

SHEET BEND gets its name from "bending" (tying) a "sheet" (rope on a sail). It is the best knot for tying two ropes together, especially if of different thicknesses.

Hold heavier rope in left hand, lighter rope in right hand. Cross end of lighter rope under heavier rope.

BOWLINE forms a loop that will not close up. It has many uses on the trail, in camp, and during rescues.

Make an overhand loop in the rope's standing part. Bring the rope end up through that loop, around behind the standing part, and back down through the loop. Tighten by grasping the bend in the rope and tugging on the standing part.

TWO HALF HITCHES are used for tying a rope—such as a clothesline or the rope of a boat—to a post or a ring. It forms a loop that can be pulled tight.

Pass the end of the rope around the post. Bring the rope end over and under its own standing part and through the loop thus formed. Do the same once more in front of this first half hitch.

TAUT-LINE HITCH can be tied on a line that is taut. Tighten or loosen a tent guy line by pushing the hitch up or down the standing part.

Pass rope around tent stake. Bring end under and over standing part, then twice through the loop it forms. Further up the standing part, pass rope end under and over, then once through the newly formed loop.

ROPES, KNOTS, AND SPLICES

CLOVE HITCH (from cleave, to hold fast) is used for starting and finishing most lashings.

Bring the rope end around the pole and in front of its own standing part. Bring the rope end once more around the pole. Finish by pushing the end under the rope itself. Then tighten as much as possible.

TIMBER HITCH is used for raising logs, for dragging them ▶ over the ground or pulling them through water. In pioneering it is used to force two timbers together.

Pass the end of the rope around the log. Then under and over its own standing part a few times and through the loop thus formed. Push the hitch firmly up against the log. Make it taut by pulling the standing part. To better guide an object, add a simple hitch near the front end.

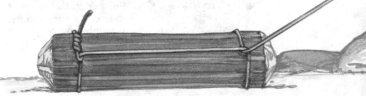

End Knots

End knots keep the end of a rope from being pulled through a hole or pulley. They become very tight under tension, and can be difficult to untie.

Overhand. The simplest knot of all, the overhand is the beginning of many other knots.

▼

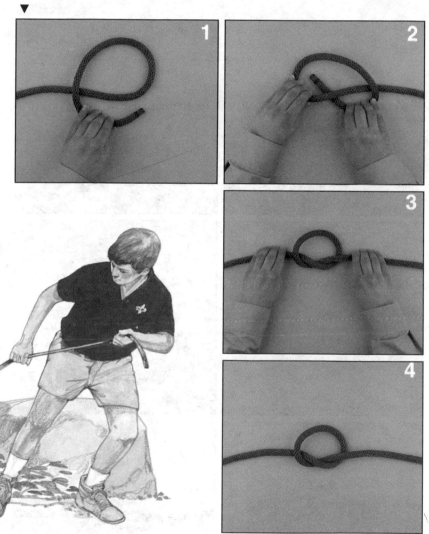

Figure-eight. The figure eight looks like the number for which it is named. Start by making a bend in the end of the rope. Twist the bend twice, forming a small loop. Pass the rope end down through the loop.

Tie a *figure eight on a bight* and it will form a very reliable end loop.

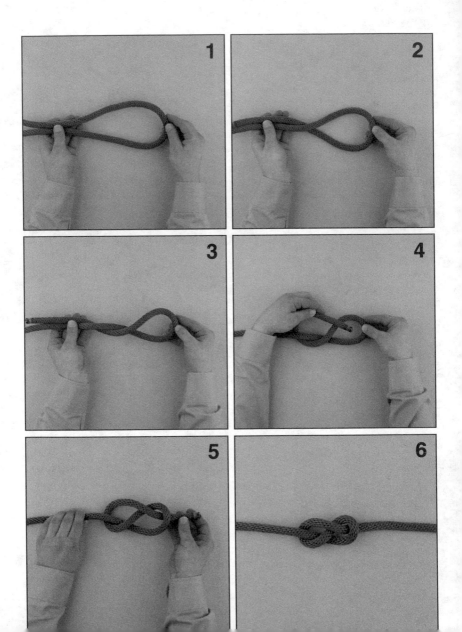

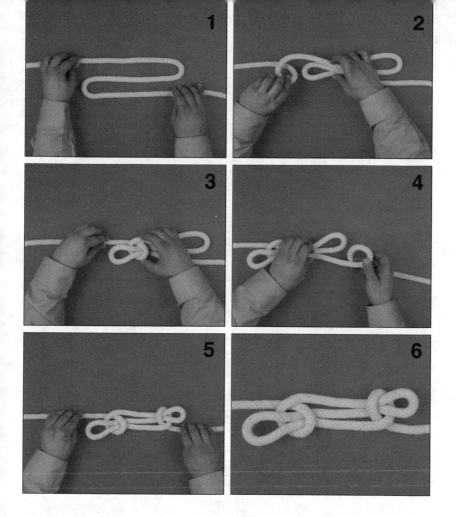

A Knot for Shortening a Rope

The *sheepshank* lets you shorten a rope without cutting it. You can also use it to bypass a damaged section of a rope. The name comes from its similarity in shape to the leg of a sheep.

Start by doubling up the slack. Put a half hitch over each bend in the slack. Tighten the knot by pulling the standing parts of the rope away from the sheepshank. The knot will hold as long as there is tension on the rope. The sheepshank is not completely dependable; don't trust it where safety is a concern.

END KNOTS

stopper knot   shoestring knot

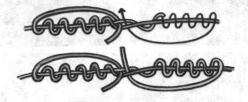

blood knot

JOINING KNOTS

fisherman's knot   surgeon's knot

SHORTENING KNOT

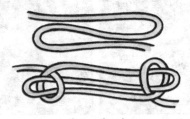

sheepshank

HITCHES

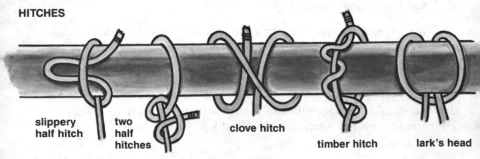

slippery
half hitch   two
half
hitches   clove hitch   timber hitch   lark's head

Lashings

Native Americans had no nails or screws with which to make their tools. Settlers moving into the American frontier built homes with only the materials they found in the forests. In Indian camps and pioneer settlements, craftsmen used lashings to bind together structures and gear.

You probably will not have the time or the need to build structures on your campouts and backpacking trips. During longer stays, a few structures in camps where they are appropriate can make you more comfortable. A table will lift meal preparation off the ground. A tripod will hold a washbasin. A raft can carry you onto a lake. At your council Scout camp, you may even have a chance to lash together a tower or a bridge.

Obtain permission before building any camp structures. They are prohibited in many backcountry areas as a way of encouraging no-trace camping. Where structures are allowed, use only those materials approved for the project. Scout staves make excellent poles for lashing. Take everything apart when you are done and stack the poles if they are to be used again. If not, scatter them. Coil your ropes and take them home. Leave no evidence in your campsite that you were ever there.

A trestle

X trestle

TRIANGLE PRINCIPLE IN LASHINGS

All pioneering projects that use lashings must be safe and steady. To ensure this, they should have triangles built into their design. A square will wobble in all directions. Triangles make a structure sturdy.

H trestle

TIGHTENING STICK

Use a tightening stick *to draw your lashings extra snug. As you lay in your wraps and fraps, twist the standing part of the rope around a sturdy, foot-long stick. The stick gives you a handle on which to pull.*

Square lashing. The square lashing is used to bind together two poles that already touch one another.

Place the poles on the ground in the shape of a cross. Tie a clove hitch around the bottom pole near the crosspiece. Twist the free end of the rope around its own standing part and tuck it out of the way. Now make three wraps around both poles. Keep the rope very tight. As you form the wraps, lay the rope on the outside of each previous turn around the crosspiece, and on the inside of each previous turn around the bottom pole. Then wind two fraps around the wraps to tighten the lashing as much as you can. Finish with a clove hitch around the crosspiece. Remember: Start with a clove hitch. *Wrap* the poles three times. *Frap* them twice. End with a clove hitch.

Diagonal lashing. To bind two poles that do not touch, use a diagonal lashing. Start by tying a timber hitch around both poles and pulling it snug. Make three tight wraps around the poles, laying each wrap neatly alongside the timber hitch. Make three more wraps across the first three. Finally, cinch down the wraps with two fraps between the poles. Tie off the rope end with a clove hitch.

Tripod lashing. If you put up a tepee, the first three poles will form a tripod. You can also use a tripod to hold a washbasin or a water bag.

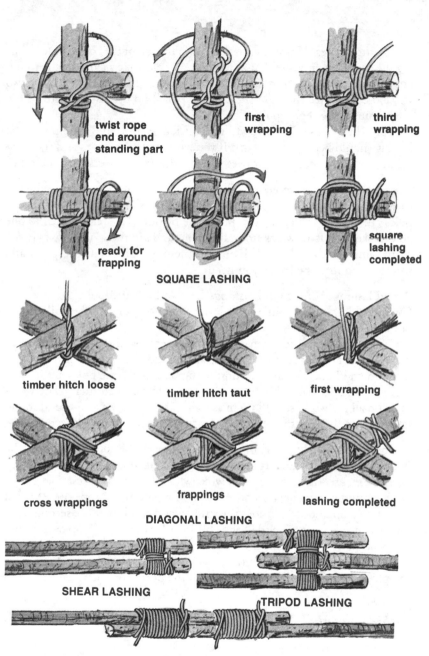

twist rope
end around
standing part

first
wrapping

third
wrapping

ready for
frapping

square
lashing
completed

SQUARE LASHING

timber hitch loose

timber hitch taut

first wrapping

cross wrappings

frappings

lashing completed

DIAGONAL LASHING

SHEAR LASHING

TRIPOD LASHING

ROUND LASHING

Lay three poles alongside each other with the top of the center pole pointing the direction opposite that of the outside poles. Tie a clove hitch around one outside pole. Loosely wrap the poles five to eight times, then make two very loose fraps on either side of the center pole. End the lashing with a clove hitch around the center pole.

Spread the legs of the tripod into position. As you move the poles, the lashing should become very tight. If you have made the wraps and fraps too secure, you may need to start over again and leave more slack in the rope.

Shear lashing. Tie two poles together with a shear lashing and you can raise them as an A-frame. Think of the shear lashing as a tripod lashing for two poles rather than three. Lay two poles side by side. Tie a clove hitch to one pole. Make three loose wraps around the poles and put two loose fraps between them. Finish with a clove hitch around the other pole. Lift the poles and spread them into the shape you need.

Round lashing. With round lashings you can bind two poles side by side. Use round lashings to join a few short poles into a long bridge railing or a tall flagpole.

Place two poles beside each other and tie them together with a clove hitch. Make seven or eight very tight, neat wraps around the poles. Finish the lashing with another clove hitch around both poles. Since the poles are so close together, you won't be able to work any fraps in between them. The wraps must do all the work, so pull them as tight as you can. Make a second round lashing near the first to keep the poles from twisting out of line.

Floor lashing. The floor lashing will hold in place the top of a table or the floor of a signal tower, a raft, or a bridge. Lay your poles side by side on top of the *stringers* — the two poles on which your platform will rest. Tie a clove hitch around one stringer. Bend the standing part of the rope over the first pole. Pull a bight of rope under the stringer and cast it over the second pole. You may need to lift the end of the pole in order to get the loop over it. Pull the rope tight, then bend it over the next pole. Repeat the process until all the poles are bound to the stringer. Finish with a clove hitch, then repeat the procedure to lash down the poles on the other stringer.

Lashing Together Models   [1]

Opportunities for building big projects like bridges and signal towers don't come along very often. However, with straight sticks and strong string, you can lash together models of any rustic structure. Use a pocketknife to cut sticks the right length. A replica signal tower may be only 2 feet high. A bridge might have a span of just 12 inches.

Make your models as authentic as you can. Use the correct knots and lashings. If you ever need to make the real thing, you will know just what to do.

THINGS TO MAKE FOR SCOUT CAMP

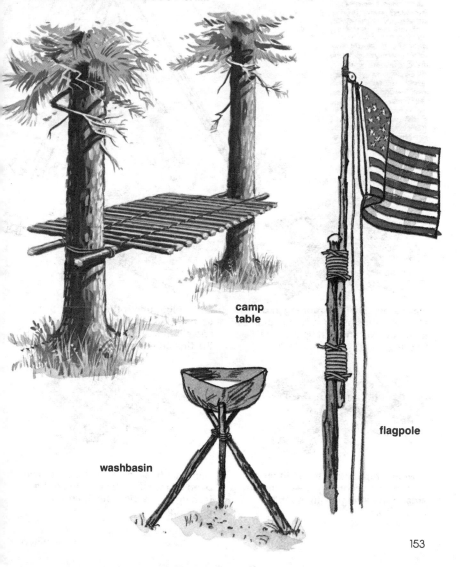

camp
table

washbasin

flagpole

monkey bridge

HOW TO BUILD A RAFT

Make a pigtail of the running and standing ends of the rope and pull it snugly over the first spar of the flooring.

Pull a bight under the stringer and up between the first two spars and slip the bight over the end of the first spar.

Now pull rope under the stringer and up over the second spar—on the outside of the stringer—then repeat third step.

Continue this way until all spars have been laid firmly in place. Finish the lashing with a clove hitch around the stringer.

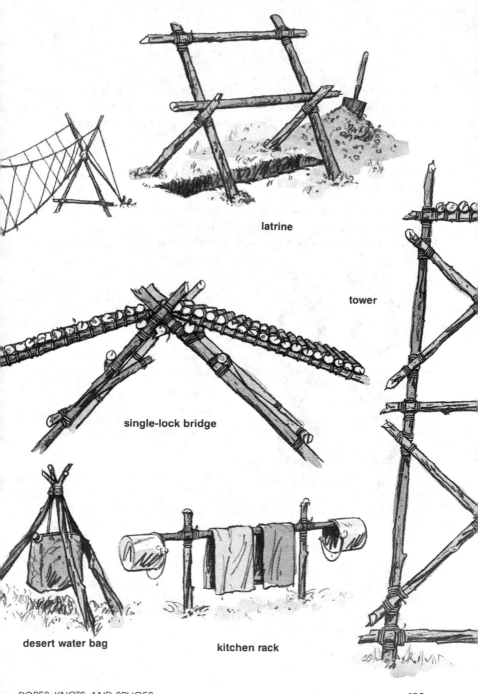

latrine

tower

single-lock bridge

desert water bag

kitchen rack

SPLICES

Splicing is the weaving together of rope strands to protect a rope from fraying, to join two ropes together, or to create an eye in a rope end. As with many knots, splices come to us from the days when sailing ships were rigged with hundreds of feet of rope.

Manila rope of about ⅜-inch diameter is easy to work with. Put tape or temporary whipping around the ends of strands to keep them from unraveling as you make a splice.

Eye splice. An eye splice forms a permanent loop, or *eye,* in the end of a rope. Begin by untwisting, or *unlaying,* about a foot of the rope end. Use string or tape around the rope to prevent further unraveling.

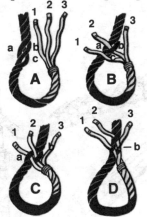

A. Twist open the standing part of the rope, and tuck strand 2 over c and under b. Bring it out between strands b and a.

B. Bring strand 1 *over* strand b and tuck it *under* strand a.

C. Tuck strand 3 under strand c.

D. Make two or more tucks with each strand. Take the end of the strand *over* the closest strand and *under* the next strand.

E. Smooth the splice by rolling it under your foot on the floor, then trim off what remains of each strand.

Another way to end the splice is called *tapering.* After making three tucks with each strand, trim away just half of each one. Tuck the smaller strands again, then trim them a second time. Make a final tuck. Roll the splice underfoot and cut away what is left of the strands. The finished splice will taper neatly into the body of the rope.

Back splice. Like whipping and fusing, a back splice protects a rope end from unraveling. Unlay about 10 inches of rope end. Wrap a piece of tape or a temporary whipping around each strand to prevent it from fuzzing.

Follow drawings A, B, and C to tie a *crown knot.* Bend the center strand (1) back between strands 2 and 3. Take the strand on the right (2) and wrap it *behind* the loop of strand 1, but *in front* of strand 3. Now bend strand 3 over 2 and through the loop of strand 1.

Draw down the crown knot by gently pulling the strands snug. When you are finished, the positions of all the strands will be identical, and the top of the knot will be flat. Now you are ready to begin the splice itself.

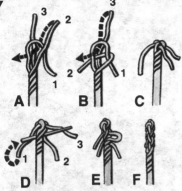

A. Pass any strand over the strand next to it, then tuck the end under the strand beside that, just as you did in making an eye splice. You will need to twist the rope open a little to get under the second strand.

B. Do the same with the end of the second strand, and then with the end of the third. If everything comes out right, the position of each strand should again be identical to that of the other strands.

C. Repeat the cycle several more times, then roll the splice under your foot and trim off the ends.

Short splice. A short splice joins two ropes of equal diameter. It is commonly used to repair a rope when a frayed section has been cut away. Unlike most knots, it does not weaken the rope at all.

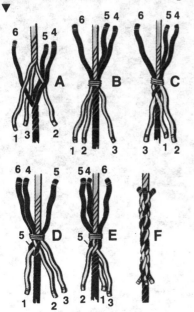

A. Unlay 12 inches of each rope end. Push the ends into each other, alternating the strands.

B. Tie down or tape the strands to prevent more unlaying.

C. Bring strand 1 over the opposing strand and under the next. This is similar to the tucking of strands done in the eye splice and back splice.

D. Bring strand 2 over strand 5 and under the next one.

E. Bring strand 3 over strand 6 and under the next one. The three strand ends should be in positions identical to one another.

F. Remove the string or tape and repeat steps C, D, and E with the other rope end.

G. Make a few more tucks with each strand.

H. Roll the splice to smooth it, then trim the strand ends.

LET'S GO HIKING!

HAVE you ever been hiking in the spring? Did you walk past freshly plowed farm fields or take a trail into the woods? The air along forest paths is sweet with the smell of wildflowers. A spider web shines in the sun, and dew sparkles on new grass. The outdoors is full of small wonders, and you can be there.

Did you ever escape the heat of summer by hiking with your patrol along city streets at dawn? Perhaps you've mapped a route that takes you through interesting neighborhoods and through small parks. By the time the sun is high, you're in the cool shade of a museum or zoo, or you may have ended your hike at a local swimming pool. Cities are full of adventure, and you can be there.

Your boots crunch through the dry leaves of autumn. The morning is cool, and the trees are splashed with red and gold. Overhead, flocks of geese honk noisily as they migrate south. With a map and compass you can roam far into the backcountry. Hiking is freedom, and you can be there.

Winter finds you tromping through snowdrifts toward a frozen waterfall. Maybe you're wearing snowshoes or skis. Your breath hangs in the cold air like a cloud. Snow turns forests and fields into a frosty wilderness, and you can be there.

Every season is special when you are hiking, and so is every trail. You can hardly wait to see what's over the next hill and around the next bend. You are free from the noise of traffic, and away from the blare of TV and radio.

Hiking is good for your body. It firms your muscles and strengthens your heart and lungs. And it's good for your mind. It fills you with confidence, energy, and respect for the outdoors.

You won't always have fair weather. Sometimes rain will fall, or snow and wind will chill you. The trails may be rocky and steep, and there will be times when you are weary to the bone. But facing hardships is part of hiking, too. Overcoming them helps you become a seasoned outdoor traveler. Hiking is adventure at its best.

MAKING A TRIP PLAN

A trip plan is a kind of insurance policy. Thinking about a hike ahead of time prepares you to meet challenges along the way. The plan is also a form of trust with your family and Scoutmaster. They expect you to stick to your route and return when you say you will. Honor their trust by following your plan and returning home on time.

Write down the five *W*'s of your trip plan, as follows:

☆ **WHERE** are you hiking? Decide on your destination and the route you will use to reach it. If you will come back a different way, put that in your plan, too. For backcountry hiking, leave a copy of your map with your route marked in pencil. Get permission if crossing private land.

☆ **WHEN** will you return? Your family and Scoutmaster will assume you have run into difficulty if you have not arrived home reasonably close to the hour you list on your trip plan. They can take steps to locate you and, if necessary, provide help.

☆ **WHO** is going with you? List the names of your hiking partners. Do you need a ride to or from the trail? Write down who will do the driving.

☆ **WHY** are you going? To fish in a lake? To reach a mountaintop? Explore a new trail? Or simply to see the colors of autumn leaves? Write a sentence or two about the *why* of your hike.

☆ **WHAT** are you taking? You'll always want to carry the Scout Outdoor Essentials with you (see page 28). How about some extras, such as a fishing rod and a swimsuit? Binoculars or a telescope? A jar for collecting insects? A mirror for sending signals?

Add one more item to the list:

☆ **HOW** you will respect the land by using low-impact and no-trace methods as you hike.

FOOTGEAR

If your feet feel good while you are hiking, chances are you'll have a great time. But it is pretty hard to get excited about walking when your feet are hot, sore, and blistered. Foot care starts when you choose your hiking boots and socks.

Almost any shoes will do for wear in camp and on short walks on smooth ground. But for longer hikes, trips with backpacks, or journeys over rough terrain, hiking boots are better. Higher tops, or *uppers*, support your ankles. Thick *soles* guard your feet against sharp stones and roots. The *tread* on the soles grips the ground so you won't slip.

Lightweight boots with uppers made of nylon look a little like overgrown running shoes. They are good for most hiking. Some are designed to keep your feet dry in the rain. That's something to think about if you do much hiking in foul weather.

Boots with leather uppers may last longer than nylon models. Leather is stiffer than fabric, giving your feet and ankles added protection. Good leather boots will keep snow and rain from soaking your socks. They will serve you well on easy hikes as well as cross-country trips in rugged country.

Leather boots are heavier than nylon ones, but don't get boots that weigh *too* much. Boots made for serious mountain climbing or the worst winter travel are probably more than you need. Boots for hiking should weigh no more than 3 or 4 pounds a pair. The soles should bend as you walk.

Try on new boots with the same socks you will use on the trail. The boots must fit very comfortably. Your heels should not slip much when you walk, and your toes should have a little room to wiggle.

New boots may feel stiff. Before using them on a hike, wear them around home for a few days until they adjust to the shape of your feet.

Caring for Your Boots

Both nylon and leather boots will last a long time if you take care of them. When they become wet, dry them in the sun. Excessive heat can melt nylon and cause leather to shrivel, so don't put your boots too close to a fire or radiator.

After a hike, use your pocketknife or a stiff brush to remove mud and dirt from your boots. Rub boot dressing into the leather. Oils and waxes in the dressing will keep the leather flexible and help the boots repel water.

Socks

Hiking socks draw perspiration away from your feet and keep them dry. Socks made of wool, polypropylene, or a wool/nylon blend also cushion your feet as you walk. For more comfort, wear a pair of thin cotton or wool socks underneath your hiking socks. The thin socks will slide against the heavier ones, reducing friction on the skin of your feet and lessening your chances of getting blisters. Carry spare socks on your hikes. Late in the day when your feet begin to tire, change into clean, dry socks. They will refresh you from the soles up.

CLOTHING FOR THE SEASON

Since there is no outdoor climate control knob to regulate the warmth of the woods, you must be prepared to adjust your clothing to suit the conditions. Not only will your clothing keep you comfortable, it will also protect you from the sun and wind, and from the bites of insects and scratches of branches.

The secret to dressing for the outdoors is wearing *layers*. Imagine hiking on a snowy trail. The sky is clear as you start out, and there is no wind. You're wearing your Scout uniform, a wool shirt, and a sweater. Because the day is chilly, you also have on a scarf, mittens, and a stocking cap. Hiking burns energy, and soon you are too warm. You stop for a moment to peel off your sweater, scarf, and mittens, and stuff them into your pack.

As the miles pass, clouds fill the sky and the air becomes colder. You put your sweater back on, then your scarf and mittens. The wind begins to blow, so you take your parka from your pack and pull it on, too.

Since you have lots of layers, you can wear as much or as little clothing as you need at any moment. That's much better than wearing one heavy coat the entire time.

In addition to layering, choose clothes made of materials that are best suited for the weather you expect.

Wool. The tight weave of wool helps keep out the wind. Wool keeps you warm even when it is damp from rain. If a wool shirt feels scratchy against your skin, wear a T-shirt underneath it.

Cotton. Cotton is fine for warm-weather wear. It absorbs moisture, cooling you as it draws sweat away from your body. Once wet, though, it is slow to dry. Wet cotton will not keep you warm, and that makes it almost useless in storms or on winter outings.

Synthetic fibers. *Polypropylene* is a synthetic fabric with the comfort of cotton and the warmth of wool. Clothing made of polypropylene and many other modern materials keeps you warm whether it is wet or dry. Look for these fabrics in long underwear, sweaters, vests, parkas, mittens, socks, and hats.

Rain Gear

A *poncho* is a waterproof cape with a hood. Large enough to fit over a pack on your back, a poncho lets summer rains drip off you and your gear. In the wind, you may need to strap it around your waist with your belt or a piece of cord.

Because a poncho is so loose, it isn't your best choice for severe weather. It flaps in strong winds and does little to keep out snow. When your hiking adventures begin taking you farther from home and deeper into the wilderness, consider some of the following special rain gear:

Rain parka. A parka is a long, hooded jacket that repels rain.

Rain pants. Rain pants extend the protection of a poncho or parka, from your waist down to your ankles.

Rain chaps. Lighter than rain pants, chaps are waterproof leggings that allow you easy access to your pants pockets. Keep them up by tying them to your belt.

Gaiters. Gaiters shield your feet and lower legs from the rain. They'll keep snow out of your boots during winter hikes.

Umbrella. If you've ever hiked in a downpour, you know how tiring it is to feel the rain beating on your hat or parka hood. A small, inexpensive umbrella fits right inside your pack. An umbrella makes a great sunshade, too.

Baseball cap. A cap with a visor is just the thing to shield your face from sun and storm. If you wear eyeglasses, a cap will help keep them clear of rain.

EQUIPMENT FOR HIKING

No matter how short a hike or how close you will be to your home, always carry these Scout Outdoor Essentials:

_____ Pocketknife

_____ First aid kit

_____ Extra clothing

_____ Rain gear

_____ Canteen or water bottle

_____ Flashlight

_____ Trail food

_____ Matches and fire starters

_____ Sun protection

_____ Map and compass

Day pack. A small pack will hold everything you need for a day hike. If you don't have a pack, make one from a parka or a pair of pants.

Pants pack. Close the snap and zipper of a pair of pants. Tie a 1-foot piece of cord around the cuff of the right pant leg. Fold the leg in half at the knee and tie the cord to the belt loop just to the right of the zipper. With another piece of cord, tie the left cuff to the first belt loop left of the zipper. Make a drawstring by threading a third cord, about 3 feet long, through all the belt loops. Put your gear and lunch inside the pants pack and close the top with the drawstring. Slip your arms behind the pant legs as if they were the straps of a pack.

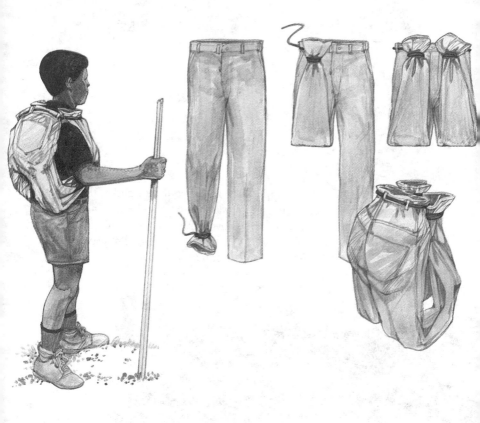

▲

Parka fanny pack. Close the zipper or snaps of your rain parka, then spread it out on the ground. Lay your lunch, water bottle, and equipment on the chest of the parka. Fold the hood down over your gear, then fold the bottom hem of the parka upward. Gently lift the parka to the small of your back and tie the sleeves around your waist with a square knot.

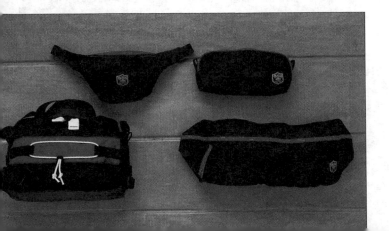

Hiking stick. In Baden-Powell's first drawing of a Scout, the founder of the Scouting movement showed a boy with a staff in his hand. The hiking stick has long been a symbol of travel. Carry one with you, and you will find that it helps the miles glide by. It swings comfortably in your hand, giving balance and rhythm to your pace.

Use your stick to push back branches and brush, to flick sticks and stones off the trail, and to poke behind rocks and in holes. A staff is especially useful when you are wading a stream. Added to your own two legs, a stick gives you the stability of a tripod.

One of the oldest uses of a stick is to keep records. Decorated with feathers, the coup sticks carried by some native Americans marked victories in battle.

You can record your own adventures by whittling a small notch on your hiking stick for every 5 miles you walk. Elsewhere on the staff, cut a notch for each night you spend under the stars.

The best hiking sticks are those you find in the woods and keep through many trips. Dry hardwoods such as ash, oak, and maple are good choices, as are aspen and birch. If the bark is smooth and tight, leave it on. Otherwise, scrape it away, at least in the place where you grip the stick.

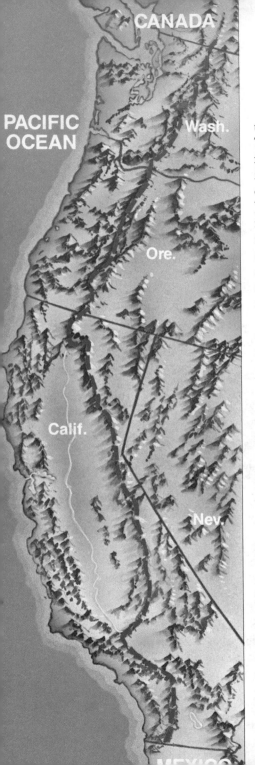

CANADA

PACIFIC
OCEAN

Wash.

Ore.

Calif.

Nev.

MEXICO

WHAT IS A TRAIL?

One of the best-known hiking trails in the world is the Appalachian Trail, stretching over 2,000 miles from Maine to Georgia. Even longer is the Pacific Crest Trail, winding over the mountain ranges of the far West from Canada to Mexico. These famous trails allow walkers to travel from one part of the country to another. But like the thousands of shorter trails all over America, they are much more than just a way to reach a destination.

Scenery, closeness to nature, the chance to see wild animals — every foot of a trail carries you into fresh experiences. Over every horizon is

something you've never seen before. The air is full of new sounds and scents.

A good trail blends into the backcountry so well you will hardly notice it beneath your feet. Look closely, though, and you may see rock walls, bridges, and other structures built to make the pathway smooth and safe.

A well-made trail also protects the land it crosses. The path may lead you around meadows or away from fragile lakeshores. Since water from rain and melting snow can rush down a steep path and turn it into a gully, a good route switches back and forth as it goes up the side of a hill. That gentle grade is easier on the land, and easier on you.

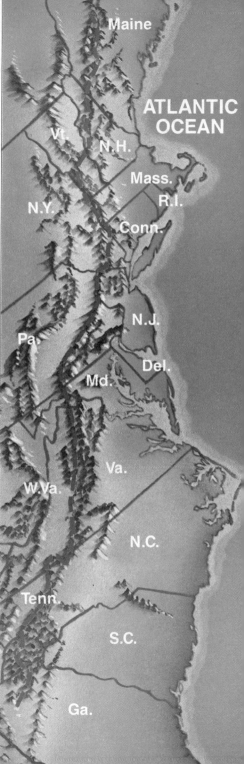

FOOD AND WATER

The most important meal for hiking is the breakfast you eat before you hit the trail. Whether in camp or at home, a hearty breakfast starts the day right.

Carry a lunch in your pack. Sandwiches, fruit, nuts, and raisins are tasty. Or, instead of sandwiches, try crackers with peanut butter, sardines, or cheese.

You may want to take a bag of energy food to munch on while you are walking. Granola is the choice of many hikers. You also can shake up a handful of nuts and raisins in a small bag. For variety, try different kinds of nuts or add some coconut and chopped dried fruit. Apples, oranges, and bananas are good trail snacks, too.

Fill your canteen or water bottle before you start out, and sip from it whenever you are thirsty. In hot weather, you may need to carry several water containers. Remember to purify any water taken from streams, lakes, or springs before you drink it. (See page 98 for ways to disinfect water.)

LOW-IMPACT HIKING

You already know that when you pack up after a night in camp, you don't want to leave any sign that you were there. Practice the same low-impact ethic when you are on the trail. It's easy to hike in such a way that you leave nothing behind but a few footprints. That shows you care about the backcountry and know how to travel through it wisely.

Stay on the trail as you hike. Walkers cutting across switchbacks can trample down vegetation that holds topsoil in place. As the loosened earth washes away, an ugly ditch will form. Sometimes the erosion caused by such shortcuts ruins large areas of land.

Help keep trails clean by picking up litter. Kick off small stones and sticks. Pull away fallen branches. A good trail lies lightly on the land. Hike lightly, too, and leave no trace.

LET'S GO HIKING!

SETTING A PACE

Walking fast is usually not very important during a hike. Take time to see the sights around you, examine plants, listen to birds, and study wildlife.

On open trails across rolling ground, an average hiker can stroll along at 2 or 3 miles an hour. As the land becomes more rugged, speed decreases. In the mountains, add an hour's hiking time for every thousand feet of elevation you must gain.

Travel no faster than a pace comfortable for the slowest member of your patrol. Even though you may feel as though you could race along forever, the safety of the whole group is more important than speed. Also, you can have a better time sticking with your patrol than going off by yourself. Others will point out things you miss. Let slower hikers take the lead and set the pace.

Resting

When you're taking it easy on a hike and stopping often to look at plants and animals, you may not need any rest stops at all. However, if you are pushing steadily down the trail, a 5-minute break every half hour or so is a good idea. It will give you a chance to adjust your clothing, doctor your feet, take a drink of water, and have a bite of food.

CHAPTER 7

HIKING SAFETY

Safety on trails. Travel single file on most trails. Leave some space between you and the Scout ahead of you. You can see where you are going, and you won't run into him if he suddenly stops.

Horses and mules may be spooked by hikers. If you meet people on horseback, stop where you are. A rider will probably ask you to step four or five paces downhill from the trail and stand quietly while the animals pass.

Safety hiking cross-country. Cross-country hiking lets you get away from everything man-made, including trails. Of course, you must be able to find your way so that you don't become lost. That may mean using a map and compass.

Staying with your patrol is as important in cross-country hiking as for any other outdoor adventure. You can share the fun, and you will be available if your patrol needs your help.

Away from the smooth tread of a trail, footing can be uncertain. Underbrush and rugged terrain make for slow going. When you are scrambling on rocks, guard against snakebites and insect stings by watching where you put your hands. Take care also not to pull a stone down onto yourself or onto Scouts climbing behind you.

Logs across your route may be slippery. Instead of jumping over a log and risking a twisted ankle, carefully step over it. Sit down on large logs and swing your legs across.

Chart your course on a map before you start a cross-country hike so you won't be surprised by rivers, cliffs, and other barriers. If you do run into terrain that you aren't sure you can cross safely, go around it or go back the way you came. A smart hiker always knows when to turn his back on a dangerous route.

Crossing streams safely. As adventures take you farther into the backcountry, your trails may lead across streams that have no bridges. Study a stream before trying to cross. How wide is it? How deep? Wading is very difficult in rushing water, especially when the water is cold. Look downstream. Is there any chance you will be swept into rocks or rapids if you lose your footing? Don't wade into water that worries you. Find a better place to cross or don't cross at all.

If you do decide to walk into a stream, wear shoes for traction and to protect your feet from sharp stones. Change into the shoes you wear around camp and keep your boots dry by stowing them in your pack. Otherwise, take off your socks and pull your boots over your bare feet.

Always unfasten the hip belt of your backpack and loosen the shoulder straps before you enter the water. If you do fall, you will be able to slip easily out of your pack before it drags you under the water.

A hiking stick will give you added support as you ford a stream, or you can form a human tripod with two other hikers. Facing inward, form a circle and put your arms around each other's shoulders. Lean on your buddies for balance as you cross.

Safety on roads. Quiet backroads are wonderful for hiking. However, try to avoid walking on busy streets and highways. Use extra care whenever your route takes you along any road.

Walk single file on the left side of the road, facing the traffic. You will be able to see vehicles coming toward you. Wear light-colored clothing so that drivers notice you, too. Even better are the bright orange vests worn by hunters and highway workers. If you must hike along a road at night, tie strips of white cloth or fluorescent ribbon around your right arm and leg. Use flashlights to light your way and make your presence known.

Finally, don't hitchhike. It can be dangerous, it may be illegal, and it always spoils the spirit of a hike.

LET'S GO HIKING!

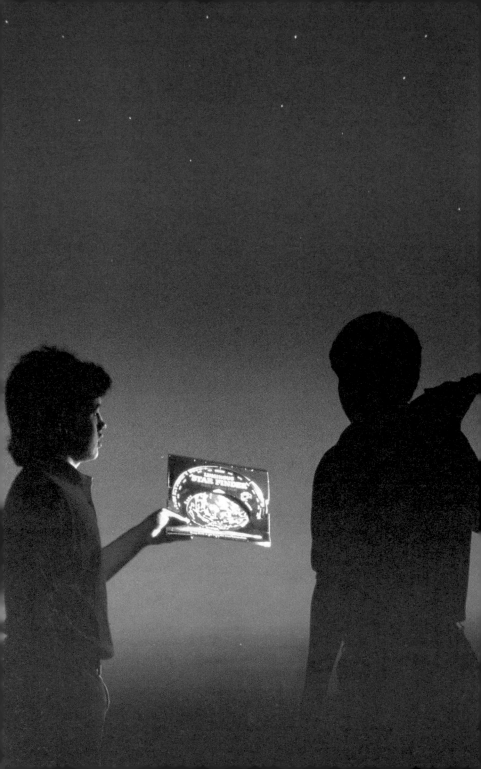

FINDING
YOUR WAY

O VER the centuries, native Americans have often traveled long distances. By studying the landscape, feeling the wind, watching constellations of stars, and noting the location of the sun, they could tell which direction they should go.

You probably have a strong sense of direction, too, at least when you are in familiar surroundings. For instance, you can travel around your city or town without much difficulty. The grid of streets provides points of reference you may use to find houses and stores. Perhaps you look in the distance for a tall building, a water tower, or a radio antenna to give you an idea of where you are.

Many of your Scout hikes will lead you to destinations you know well. But you may also want to take off for places you've never been before. When your desire to travel exceeds your natural sense of direction, you can still find your way if you have mastered the use of two important tools — a map and a compass.

MAP

A map is a picture of a piece of land as it would look from the air. The maps showing the largest areas of all are globes of the world. You have probably also seen maps of North America, and those representing all of the United States. Road maps often cover a single state, and your library has county, township, and city maps.

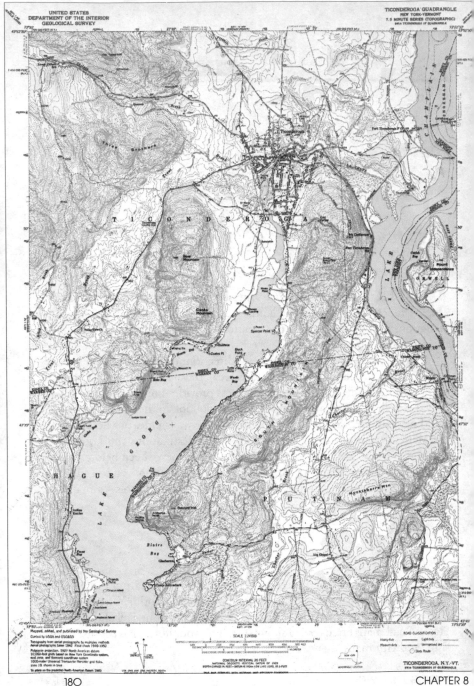

SCALE 1:24000

CONTOUR INTERVAL 20 FEET

TICONDEROGA, N.Y.-VT.

The most useful maps for hikers are made by the United States Geological Survey (USGS). They are called *topographic* maps—from the Greek *topos* (place) and *graphein* (to write). Because they enclose a four-sided area, you may hear them called *quadrangle* maps.

Camping and sporting goods stores often sell topographic maps of nearby recreation areas. You can also order maps by sending a postcard to:

U.S. Geological Survey
Distribution Branch
Box 25286 / MS 306
Federal Center
Denver, CO 80225

Ask for an order form and a map index for your state. The index is a state map divided into sections called *quadrangles*. Locate the quadrangle covering your hiking area, then order the map by giving the name of the quadrangle and sending a money order or check for payment.

Topographic maps come in several sizes. The most detailed is the *7.5-minute series*. The area of a 7.5-minute map is about 7 miles long and 7 miles wide. A *15-minute series* map represents a region about 15 miles on each side. Maps taking in even larger areas can give you a general feel for the land, but not enough detail to be of much use on the trail.

Reading a Map 2

Reading a map is easy and fun. Here is some of the information a map will give you:

Description. Degrees of longitude ▶ and latitude shown in numbers at the edges of a topographic map pinpoint the area's location on the globe. The name of a map is given in its margin. You will also find the names of the maps that border the edges and corners of your map.

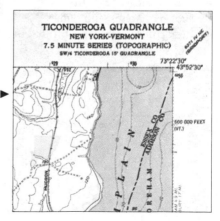

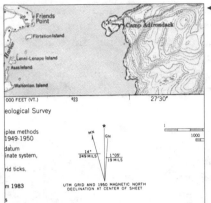

◀ **Directions.** An arrow drawn on the map points north. On most maps, *north* is toward the top. The bottom is *south,* the left side is *west,* and the right side is *east.*

Distances. Bar scales in the bottom margin give you the means for measuring distances on the map.

▼

Scale. The *scale* of a map compares its size with the size of the area it represents. Topographic maps usually have a scale of 1:24,000 or 1:62,500. That means 1 inch on your map equals 24,000 or 62,500 inches on the ground. One foot equals 24,000 or 62,500 feet, and so on.

Details. Landscape features are shown on maps with symbols and colors. Names are printed in several sizes and styles of type, each with its own meaning. ▶

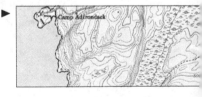

◀

Date. A map's date tells when it was drawn or last revised. An older map will not show recent buildings, roads, trails, and other changes on the land.

CHAPTER 8

If you flew over an area, you could look down and see roads, rivers, fields, forests, cities, and towns. On a map, many of those features are represented by symbols. The most obvious symbols are colors.

Green. Solid green indicates forests, woodlands, orchards, and other areas of heavy vegetation.

White. White portions of the map are mostly clear of trees. They may be fields, meadows, rocky slopes, or other open country.

Blue. The color blue always means water. A large patch of blue is usually a pond or a lake. A blue band is a river, and a blue line is a stream. If the line is broken, the stream it represents doesn't flow all of the time. Marshes and swamps are drawn with broken blue lines and tufts of grass. Symbols for glaciers look like marshes without the grass. Names of all water features are written in *italic type*.

Black. Everything that is printed in black on a map is the work of humans: rail lines, bridges, buildings, boundaries, names. Roads are shown as parallel black lines. The lines are solid for paved and gravel roads, broken for dirt roads. A single broken line is a hiking trail.

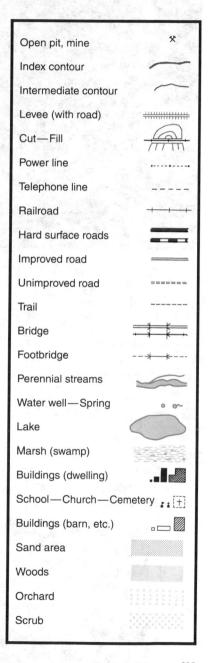

Open pit, mine

Index contour

Intermediate contour

Levee (with road)

Cut—Fill

Power line

Telephone line

Railroad

Hard surface roads

Improved road

Unimproved road

Trail

Bridge

Footbridge

Perennial streams

Water well—Spring

Lake

Marsh (swamp)

Buildings (dwelling)

School—Church—Cemetery

Buildings (barn, etc.)

Sand area

Woods

Orchard

Scrub

Black squares and rectangles are buildings. Those that are completely black are inhabited — houses, schools, churches. Black just around the sides means barns, sheds, and other outbuildings.

Brown. Dark brown contour lines, called *index lines,* are marked with the elevation above sea level. For instance, every point on a line marked *100* is a hundred feet above sea level.

Understanding Contour Lines

2

Maps are flat, but the areas they represent are full of hills, valleys, mountains, and plains. Brown *contour lines* represent points of equal elevation. The lines allow mapmakers to show the lay of the land very clearly.

To understand how contour lines work, make a fist with one hand. A fist has *width, length,* and *height,* just like the land. With a pen, draw a level

circle around your highest knuckle. Draw a second circle just below that one. Start a third line a little lower. Notice that to stay on the level, the pen may trace around another knuckle before the third circle is closed. Continue to draw circles, each one beneath the last. Lines will wander in and out of the valleys between your fingers, over the broad slope on the back of your hand, and across the steep cliffs above your thumb.

After all the lines are drawn, spread your hand flat. Now it has only *width* and *length,* just like a map. But by looking at the contour lines, you can still imagine the shape of your fist. Small circles show the tops of your knuckles. Lines that are close together indicate steep areas. Lines farther apart show the more gentle slopes of your hand.

The *contour lines* of a map represent terrain in the same way. Small circles are the tops of hills. Where the lines are far apart, the ground slopes gently. Where they are close together, a hillside is steep.

Chart a Course

You already understand enough about maps to draw the route for a hike. Plan to start from a point you know, such as a road crossing, and find it on the map. Next, find the symbol for your destination—a hilltop, for example. Using a pencil, lightly draw the best route to walk to your goal. Where will you cross streams? How will you get around lakes? What will you see along the way? The map symbols will help you decide. Study the contour lines showing how the hill rises so that you can climb it with the least effort.

Measure Your Route

After you have drawn a route, you will want to know how far you are going to hike. Take a piece of string and put one end on the map at the starting point of your hike—in this case, the crossroads. Lay out the string so it rests right on top of the line marking your entire route. Pinch the string where it touches your destination and pick it up. Now stretch it out on the bar scale at the bottom of the map and measure the string up to the point where you are pinching it. That's the same length as your route.

Visually Orienting a Map

2

Hundreds of years ago, European explorers were trying to reach those regions of the Far East called the Orient. Many of the maps they drew had the Orient at the top. Today, most maps are drawn with north at the top, but the act of turning a map to match the landscape is still called *orienting*.

Go to the starting point of the route you drew on your map. Can you see some landscape features—a building, a bridge, and perhaps the top of a hill? On your map, find the symbols for those features. Turn the map until the symbols line up with the landscape they represent. The top of your map should now be aimed to the north.

You can use a visually oriented map to show you the way to your destination. Reorient your map often as you walk along your route, and identify on it as many land features as you can.

To orient a map by sight, you must be able to see and recognize some landscape features. In unfamiliar territory, heavy forests, or poor light, that may not be possible. That is when you need a compass.

COMPASS

The first compasses appeared in China a thousand years ago, and in Europe two hundred years later. Travelers noticed that a magnetized needle floating on a chip of wood always swung around to point north. Many people thought the needle moved by magic.

Today we know that the earth itself acts as a huge bar magnet. A pole of that global magnet—magnetic north—is in northern Canada. One end of every compass needle is drawn toward it. That end is painted red or stamped with the letter *N*.

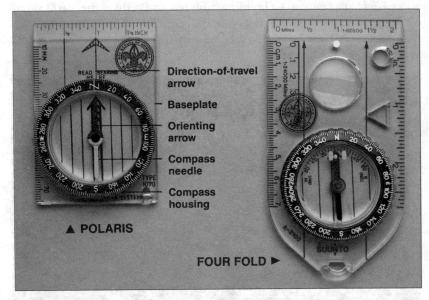

Each official Boy Scout compass has a compass housing attached to a baseplate. The compass acts as a direction pointer, a tool for taking bearings, and a ruler for measuring map distances.

Taking a Compass Bearing

Look at the compass housing. It is a full circle marked off in 360 equal parts called *degrees*. Zero is also marked with an *N* for north. There is an *E* at 90 degrees for east, an *S* at 180 degrees for south, and a *W* at 270 degrees for west. The top of the circle, 360 degrees, is also the zero point marked *N* for north.

CHAPTER 8

THE COMPASS POINTS. When you know from the compass needle where north is, you can find the eight main points of the compass: Face north. South is then right behind you. West is on your left. East is on your right. Halfway between north and east is northeast. Halfway between east and south is southeast. Halfway between south and west is southwest. Halfway between north and west is northwest. Or, starting from north and going clockwise: north, northeast, east, southeast, south, southwest, west, northwest, and back to north.

A *bearing* is the number of degrees between an object in the field and north on your compass. For instance, the bearing of straight east is 90 degrees. A tree directly south of you has a bearing of 180 degrees.

To find a bearing, hold your compass in the palm of your hand at waist height. Point the *direction-of-travel arrow* at a landmark. Now twist the *compass housing* until the compass needle lies right over the *orienting arrow*. Be sure the north end of the needle points to the letter *N* at the top of the housing. Read the number on the rim of the housing at the spot where it touches the direction-of-travel arrow. That's the *bearing* of the landmark—the number of degrees it is from magnetic north.

Taking a bearing

Two Norths

A topographic map is drawn with *true north* at the top. Extend the side lines of a map far enough, and those lines will touch the North Pole. You could say that maps speak the language of *true north*.

Compasses, however, do not point at true north. Instead, they are drawn to magnetic north, the region in Canada more than a thousand miles away from the North Pole. Compasses speak *magnetic north,* a different language than that used by maps.

Two arrows in the bottom margin of a map show the difference between the two languages. The true-north arrow points to the North Pole. The magnetic-north arrow points toward magnetic north. The angle between them, measured in degrees, is called *declination.*

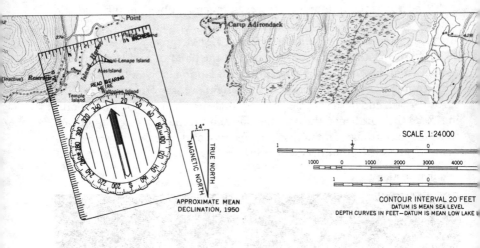

To orient a map with a compass, set the compass bearing at *N* (360°). Place the compass on the map with one edge alongside the magnetic-north line in the margin. Turn the map and compass together until the needle lies over the orienting arrow with the north part pointing to *N*. The map is oriented.

Look at the map on page 191 and you will see that declination differs for various parts of the country. When you use a map and compass together, declination can cause large errors as you take bearings and try to follow routes.

To avoid problems caused by declination, make your compass and map speak the same language. There are several ways to do this:

CHAPTER 8

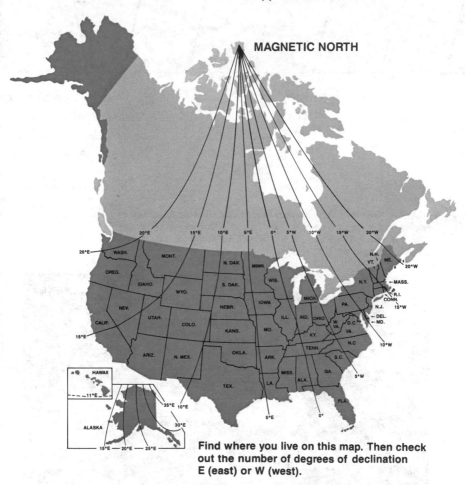

★ **NORTH POLE**

MAGNETIC NORTH

Find where you live on this map. Then check out the number of degrees of declination E (east) or W (west).

Change the map. With a pencil and a long ruler, extend the magnetic-north arrow up through the map. Then draw other lines a ruler's-width apart and parallel to the first line. Your compass needle naturally points to magnetic north. Now, so does each of these lines.

Change the compass. Some compasses can be adjusted to point toward true north, just like your map. The change is made by turning a small screw that shifts the position of the numbers on the compass housing. Compasses that adjust cost a few dollars more than those that do not, but they are so easy to use that they are often worth the extra expense.

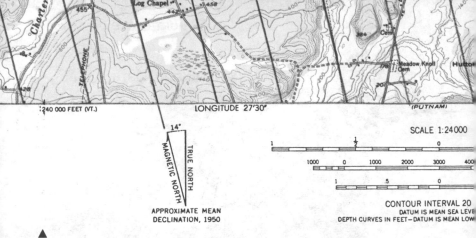

14°

MAGNETIC NORTH

TRUE NORTH

APPROXIMATE MEAN
DECLINATION, 1950

LONGITUDE 27'30"

(PUTNAM)

240 000 FEET (VT.)

SCALE 1:24000

1 $\frac{1}{2}$ 0

1000 0 1000 2000 3000 400

1 .5 0

CONTOUR INTERVAL 20
DATUM IS MEAN SEA LEVEl
DEPTH CURVES IN FEET—DATUM IS MEAN LOW

▲
CHANGE THE MAP. Draw magnetic north lines on the map by
extending the magnetic north arrow found in the margin. That way,
both the map and a compass that is not adjusted for declination
speak the same language—magnetic north.

CHANGE THE COMPASS. Shift the declination on an adjustable compass by turning a small screw. That way, both map and compass speak the same language—
true north.

USING A MAP AND COMPASS TOGETHER

By using a map and compass together, you can travel cross-country to destinations hidden from view. You can also identify features you see on the land.

Following a Route

Step 1. On the map, line up the edge of the compass with your route. Locate the map symbols for the starting and ending points of your hike. Place the compass on the map with the edge of the *baseplate* touching both the starting and ending points. The direction-of-travel arrow should be pointing in the direction you want to go.

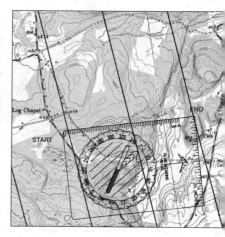

Step 2. To set the compass bearing, start by holding the baseplate firmly on the map. Paying no attention to the needle, turn the compass housing until the *meridian lines* on the floor of the compass housing are parallel with any magnetic-north line drawn on your map. The *N* on the compass housing should point toward the top of the map. (If you have adjusted the declination on your compass, turn the housing until the meridian lines parallel any true-north map lines.)

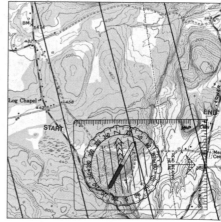

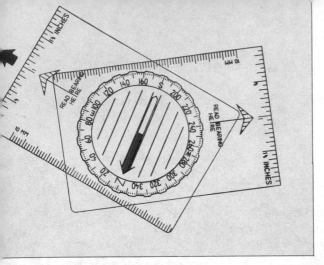

Step 3. In the field, follow the compass bearing. Standing at the starting point of your hike, hold your compass in front of you with the direction-of-travel arrow pointing straight ahead. Turn your entire body until the north part of the compass needle covers the orienting arrow on the bottom of the compass housing. The direction-of-travel arrow now points to your destination. Pick a tree, rock, or bush in line with the direction-of-travel arrow and walk to it. Orient your compass again, walking from one feature to another until you reach your goal.

COMPASS PRACTICE

Here's a good three-step exercise for taking compass bearings and following a route:

1. *Push a stick into the ground beside your foot. Turn the compass housing to any bearing — 15 degrees, for example. Orient the compass and sight along the direction-of-travel arrow to a landmark. Walk 50 steps toward it.*

2. *Add 120 degrees to your first bearing, and set your compass again (in this example, 120° + 15° = 135°). Walk 50 steps on the new heading.*

3. *Finally, add 120 degrees to that second bearing (120° + 135° = 255°). Take a bearing and walk 50 steps.*

If you have done everything right, you will be standing beside the stick where you started.

Identifying Features

Step 1. In the field, take a bearing on a landmark. Hold the compass in your hand and aim the direction-of-travel arrow at the point you want to identify. Turn the compass housing until the needle lines up over the orienting arrow. The north end of the needle should be pointing at *N* on the compass housing. ▶

Step 2. On the map, locate your position. Find the symbol that represents the place where you are standing. ◀

Step 3. Identify the landmark. Place your compass on the map with one edge of the baseplate touching your location. Move the entire compass around until the meridian lines in the housing are parallel with the magnetic north-south lines on the map. (Use true-north lines if your compass is adjusted for declination.) The *N* on the compass housing should be pointing toward the top of the map.

Draw a line along the baseplate starting at your location and going in the direction of travel. Look at the symbols under that line. One of them should represent the landmark you want to identify. ◀

Take an Orienteering Trip

The best way to master map and compass is to go outdoors and use them as much as you can. A map-and-compass trip of a few hours could use a topography map like the one on page 180.

Let's say you want to start at the crossroads marked 442 just to the south of Log Chapel. A day hike might take you to the road intersection marked 179 north of Meadow Knoll Cemetery, then to the farm house at road bend 149. From there you could walk to the crossroads at 432 north of Log Chapel and then back to your starting point at 442.

Before you set out, study the map and select a hiking route. Look for roads and trails. They offer the easiest walking, but not necessarily the quickest or most interesting way to go. For instance, you can reach intersection 179 by walking along the roads from 442 down to Meadow Knoll Cemetery and then turning left.

If you want to stay off most of the roads, you could instead walk south of 442 until you come to the stream. Turn left and follow its bank in an easterly direction. Where it spills into the second stream, you may be able to see point 179. If not, you can take a compass bearing and follow your direction-of-travel arrow to the road intersection.

A third route could lead you over the tops of some of the big hills indicated on the map by their contour lines. You may need to take compass bearings from your starting point and from each summit in order to stay on course.

You might even want to do a "bee-line" hike. Set your compass so that the direction-of-travel arrow is aimed from your starting point (crossroads 442) to your first destination (intersection 179). Follow that bearing as carefully as you can, and see how close you come to your goal.

Once you reach 179, how will you travel to intersection 149? The most obvious route is right up the road. However, you may want to go cross-country to the lake and then follow the shoreline back around to the road.

Whatever you decide to do, use a pencil to draw your route on the map *before you leave home*. Let your Scoutmaster and parents know where you

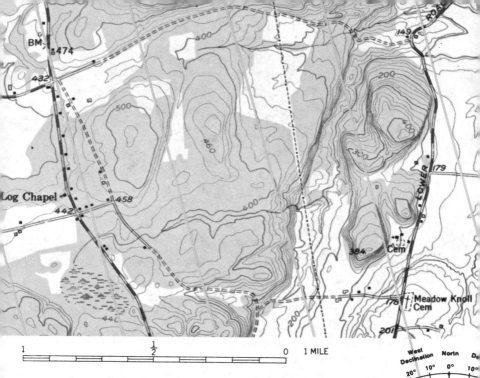

are going and when you expect to return. Thinking through your route will help you plan better adventures. Sharing your route with others will let them share your excitement and help insure your safety.

A map is drawn in the language of north. That means the top of the map points toward the North Pole. Compasses speak magnetic north because they point to the magnetic North Pole. The faint lines drawn across this map are extensions of the magnetic-north arrow in the margin. They allow your map to speak the language of magnetic north, the same as your compass.

1. The map has five different colors. What does each represent?

2. Use the contour lines to find the tops of hills. Which one is the highest?

3. In a straight line, how far is Log Chapel from Meadow Knoll Cemetery?

4. Use a piece of string to measure the distance by road from Log Chapel to Meadow Knoll Cemetery.

5. In which direction does the stream near Log Chapel flow?

6. How long will it take you to hike from the farmhouse at 149 to crossroads 432 if you walk 2 miles an hour? On what kind of road will you be walking?

Mapping

Drawing a map of an area is a great way to practice compass skills and to get a real feel for the terrain. You will need a compass, a pencil, and some notebook paper.

Start with a fairly small area such as a campsite. Make a list of all the features you want to include on your map. A campsite list might include a large rock, an oak tree, a tent, and the beginning of a trail.

Turn a sheet of paper sideways so the lines run up and down (north and south). In the center of the paper, draw a small symbol for the feature that will be in the middle of your map. That's point 1.

Stand at point 1 and take a compass bearing on another landmark (point 2), as explained on page 195. Lay the compass on the paper with one edge of the baseplate touching point 1. Turn the whole compass until the meridian lines in the compass housing are parallel with the north-south lines of the

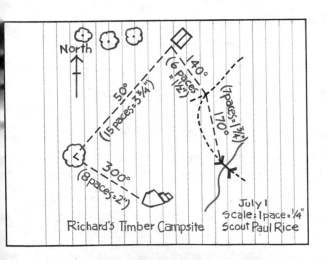

Above: Use your compass to take the bearings you need for drawing a map. **Left:** Finished map sketch should contain north arrow, scale, name of area, details of landscape features, name of mapmaker, and date. Color the map if you wish.

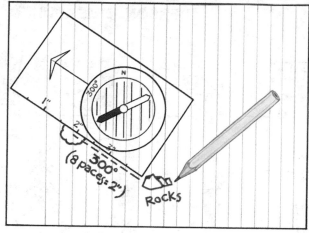

This is the way you start ▶
a map. It shows the
first bearing line in the
map at left.

paper. The *N* on the compass housing should point toward the top of the sheet. Draw a line along the edge of the baseplate.

Now count the number of steps it takes you to walk from point 1 to point 2. Use the scale on the compass baseplate to mark that distance on the line you've drawn. A quarter of an inch equals one pace — that's a good scale for a small map. If you took seven paces, measure 1¾ inch along the line from point 1 and draw a symbol there for point 2.

Stand at point 2 and take a compass bearing on point 3. Again use the meridian lines to orient your compass on the paper, and draw the new bearing line. Pace the distance, measure it on your map, and draw the point 3 symbol. Do the same for all the other landmarks, filling in your map as you go.

As on any good map, the margin of your creation should contain a north-pointing arrow, the map scale (in this example: 1 pace = ¼ inch), the name of the area, and the date you did the drawing. When you are done, you will have an accurate map drawn to scale.

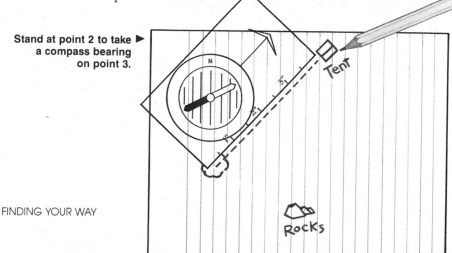

Stand at point 2 to take ▶
a compass bearing
on point 3.

FINDING YOUR WAY

PERSONAL MEASUREMENTS

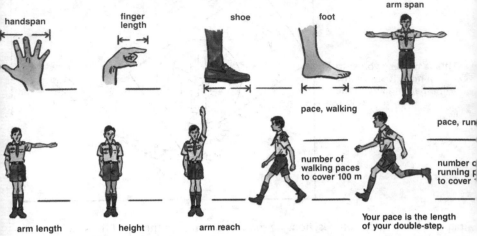

handspan   finger length   shoe   foot   arm span

pace, walking

number of walking paces to cover 100 m

pace, run

number of running paces to cover

arm length   height   arm reach

Your pace is the length of your double-step.

MEASURING IN METRICS

In the United States, we have traditionally measured distances with a system of inches, feet, yards, and miles. Our volume measures include ounces, pints, quarts, and gallons.

Most other nations rely on the *metric system* of measuring distance and volume. Because it is simple to use and very accurate, many people in the U.S. are learning the metric system, too. You may already use it in school, especially in your science classes. Some topographic maps give elevations in meters as well as in feet. Have you ever run a 100-meter dash? That's a metric measurement, too.

Practice using the metric system whenever you can. A good way to start is with your personal measurements.

Personal Measurements

Ever wanted to measure something but thought you couldn't because you didn't have a ruler? In fact, you carry a measuring tool with you all the time — yourself. The most useful measurements are shown above. You will need a tape measure to figure them out the first time. In the spaces, record the inches and feet as well as the metric measurements. You can use them to determine how far you hike, the true size of the fish you caught for dinner, and anything else you want to measure.

As you grow, your size will change. Update your personal measurements chart every 6 months.

[Ruler markings: cm 1 2 3 4 5 6 7 8 9 10]

METRIC SCALE

This scale is 10 centimeters long. It would take 10 of these scales to make 1 meter. The spaces between the numbers are millimeters.

LENGTH IN METERS

1 meter = 10 decimeters (*Deci* means 10 parts of a unit.)
  A meter is a little longer than a yard (1.1 yd.).
1 meter = 100 centimeters (*Centi* means 100 parts of a unit.)
  A dollar bill is 6.5 centimeters wide.
1 meter = 1,000 millimeters (*Milli* means 1,000 parts of a unit.)
  A dime is about 1 millimeter thick.
1 kilometer = 1,000 meters (*Kilo* means 1,000 units.)
  A kilometer is a little farther than a half mile (0.6 mi.).

WEIGHT IN GRAMS

1 gram = 1/1,000 kilogram
  A gram is a little more than the weight of a paper clip.
1 kilogram = 1,000 grams
  A kilogram is a little more than 2 pounds (2.2 lb.).

CAPACITY IN LITERS

1 liter = 1 cubic decimeter of liquid or gas
  A liter is a little larger than a quart (1.06 qt.).
1 milliliter = 1 cubic centimeter of gas or liquid
  A milliliter amounts to 18 drops.
1 kiloliter = 1,000 cubic decimeters of gas of liquid
  A kiloliter is about 265 gallons.

A cubic centimeter like this will hold 1 milliliter.
If it were filled with water, it would weight 1 gram.

TEMPERATURES

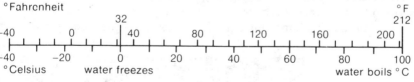

°Fahrenheit ... 32 ... °F 212
-40 ... 0 ... 40 ... 80 ... 120 ... 160 ... 200
-40 ... -20 ... 0 ... 20 ... 40 ... 60 ... 80 ... 100
°Celsius ... water freezes ... water boils °C

1 calorie is the ENERGY needed to raise the temperature of 1 gram of water by 1 degree Celsius.

ABBREVIATIONS

cl	centiliter	g	gram	km	kilometer	mg	milligram
cm	centimeter	kg	kilogram	l	liter	ml	milliliter
dm	decimeter	kl	kiloliter	m	meter	mm	millimeter

[Vertical ruler on right margin: cm 1 2 3 4 5 6 7 8 9 10 11 12 13 14 15 16 17 18 19 20]

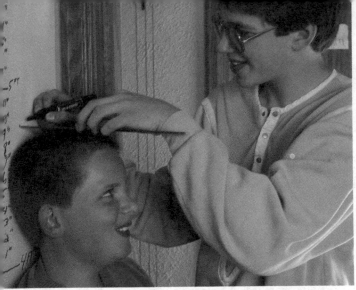

Use a yardstick to make a ruled measure on a piece of
paper. To keep a record of your growth, attach the ruled
measure in an out-of-the-way place and have someone
mark your height every few months.

MEASURING TIME

How long a period of time is 3 seconds? About as long as it takes to say,
"One thousand one, one thousand two, one thousand three." When you don't
have a watch, counting seconds by thousandths is a good way to measure short
amounts of time.

Here's another method. Sitting quietly, find the pulse in your wrist or neck
and count the number of beats you feel in 60 seconds. Remember that number, and you can always measure a minute by counting your resting pulse.

MEASURING HEIGHTS

Pencil method. Have a friend whose height you know stand beside a tree, or tie a ribbon around the tree at your own height. Step back and hold a pencil or a stick at arm's length in front of you. With one eye closed, sight over the stick so that the top of it appears to touch the ribbon or your friend's head. Place your thumbnail on the stick where it seems to touch the base of the tree. Now move the stick up to see how many times this measurement goes into the height of the tree. Multiply that number by the height of your friend or the ribbon, and you will know the height of the tree. You can also use this method to measure buildings, waterfalls, and walls.

Tree-felling method. Back away from a flagpole or tree that you want to measure. Hold a stick upright at arm's length. Sight over the stick so that its tip appears to touch the top of the pole and your thumb is at its base. Swing the stick 90 degrees to a horizontal position as if the flagpole were falling. Keep your thumb at the base of the pole, and notice where the tip of the stick seems to touch the ground. Pace the distance from that point to the base of the flagpole to get its height.

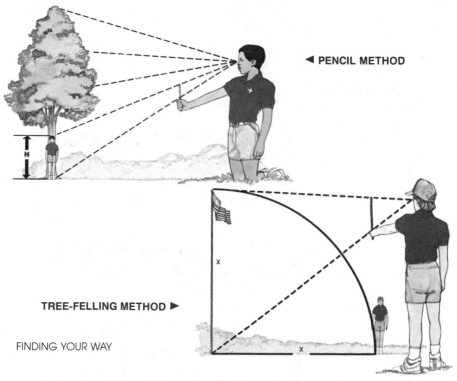

◀ PENCIL METHOD

TREE-FELLING METHOD ▶

MEASURING WIDTHS

Napoleon method. Stand on one shore of a stream. Bow your head, chin against your chest. Hold your hand to your forehead in a salute. Move your hand down until the front edge of it seems to touch the opposite shore. Without changing the position of your hand, make a quarter turn. Notice the point at which the edge of your hand seems to touch the near shore. Pace off the distance to that point, and you will know the width of the river. Napoleon might have used the brim of his hat instead of his hand. If you are wearing a cap with a visor, so can you.

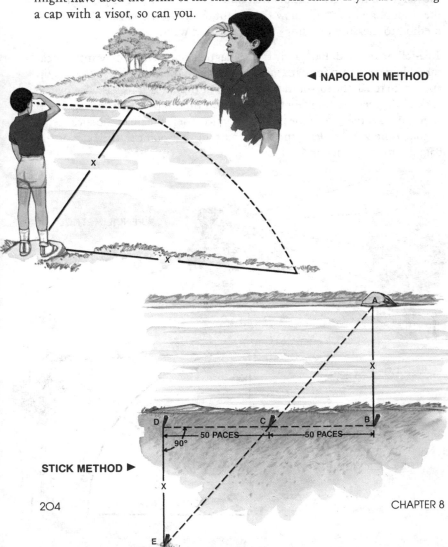

◄ **NAPOLEON METHOD**

STICK METHOD ►

Stick method. Locate a rock on the other side of the river (A). Place a stick by your side, opposite the rock (B). Walk along the shore at right angles to AB. Take any number of paces (50, for example), and place another stick there (C). Continue walking along the shore in the same direction for as many paces as before (in this case, 50 more). Put a stick there (D). Now walk away from the river at right angles to BD. When you can sight a straight line over stick C to the rock on the far side, stop and mark your spot (E). Measure DE to get the width of the river.

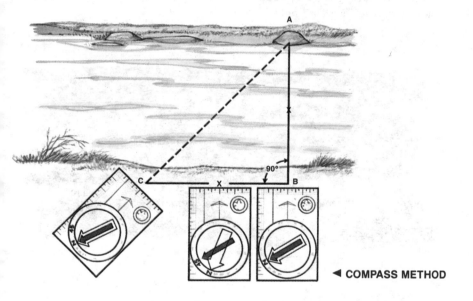

◄ COMPASS METHOD

Compass method. Locate a rock on the far side of a river (A). Stand on your side of the river, exactly opposite the rock (B). Take a bearing by pointing the direction-of-travel arrow of your compass at the rock and turning the compass housing until the needle lies over the orienting arrow. Read the degrees (in this case, 120). Add 45 degrees (120° + 45° = 165°). Set your compass at the new reading (in this case, 165). Walk along the shore, pointing the direction-of-travel arrow toward the rock. When the compass is again oriented, stop and mark your spot (C). Distance BC is the same as the width of the river.

By the Stars **1**

With the stars to guide them, ancient sailors crossed the seas, and travelers made their way through distant lands. Using the stars to find directions is the oldest method we know.

North star method. Find the North Star (see page 354). Because it is located directly over the earth's North Pole, the North Star appears to be stationary in the sky. For night travel, you need only look to it from time to time and adjust your route accordingly.

For a more lasting record, push a 2-foot-long stick into the ground. Hold a shorter stick in such a way that when you sight over the tips of both sticks, you see the North Star. A line scratched between the sticks is a true north-south line.

Constellation method. As you become familiar with the shapes of constellations of stars, pay attention to their locations. For example, the constellation Scorpius fills the southern sky in the summer. Orion rises in the southeast on winter evenings. Shaped like a horseshoe, the Northern Crown opens toward the north. Both the Big Dipper and Cassiopeia circle the northern sky.

By the Sun

For general orientation, remember that the sun rises in the east and sets in the west. (Never look directly at the sun.) For more exact direction finding, try one of the following methods:

Watch method. Hold your watch flat. Place a short twig upright against the edge of the watch at the point of the hour hand. (This method will not work with a digital watch.) Turn the watch until the shadow of the twig falls exactly along the hour hand — that is, until the hour hand points toward the sun. A line from the center of the watch, dividing in half the angle between the hour hand and the numeral 12, will point south. (Note: This method requires standard time. If your watch is on daylight savings time, turn it back 1 hour.)

◀
**WATCH
METHOD**

207

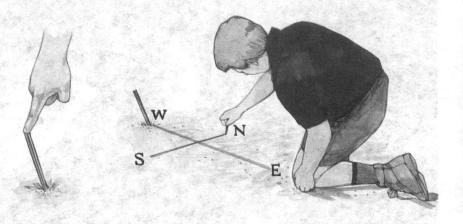

Shadow-stick method. Push a short, straight stick into the ground. Angle it toward the sun so that the stick makes no shadow. Wait until it casts a shadow at least 6 inches long. The shadow will be pointing east from the stick. A line at right angles across the shadow will be north-south.

Equal-length-shadow method. In the morning, push a straight 3-foot-long staff upright into the ground. Tie a string around the bottom of the staff with a bowline. Extend the string to the end of the staff's shadow. Tie a peg to the string at that point, and use it to scratch a smooth circle on the ground around the staff. Push the peg into the ground at the point where the tip of the staff's shadow hits the circle.

In the afternoon, place another peg where the tip of the staff's shadow again touches the circle. A straight line scratched between the pegs is a west-east line, with west at the morning peg. A line at right angles to that one is north-south.

▼

By the Moon

The moon comes up in the east and goes down in the west, just like the sun. The *shadow-stick method* described for use with the sun will work just as well with the moon on nights when it is bright enough to cast a shadow.
◀

LOST!

Someone once asked Daniel Boone, "Were you ever lost?" Dan thought it over for awhile, then replied, "No, I was never lost. But once I was a mite bewildered for five days." Dan had the right idea. No one is ever really lost if he knows how to find his way.

How Not to Get Lost

The best way not to get lost is to know at all times where you are. Before you leave home, plan your route and mark it on a map. Study the map to become familiar with the countryside. Where are the roads, lakes, and streams? Where is your campsite? What landmarks should you be able to see as you hike?

Be very alert while you are hiking. Notice the direction the trail goes. Look for hills, cliffs, streams, lakes, buildings, towers, and other landscape features. Find those landmarks on your map and use that information to pinpoint your location along the route.

If you don't have a map, jot down some notes on a piece of paper or sketch a map showing the major features of the land. Give special attention to the intersections of trails.

Stay with your patrol. If no one is sure of your location, you can put your heads together and probably figure out where you are. Should you become truly lost, there is strength in numbers.

Unless you are prepared for cross-country travel, stay on the trail. It's hard to become seriously confused when you have a path under your feet.

Finally, look over your shoulder often. You will see your route as it will appear upon your return.

Lost When No One is Looking for You

You may one day discover that despite your precautions, you are lost and alone. Perhaps you strayed from a trail and can't find it again. Maybe you've taken the wrong turn on a trail and now you aren't sure how to return to camp.

Stay calm. Sit down and have a sip of water and a bite of food. If you are chilly, pull on a warm shirt or sweater.

Quietly review how you got where you are. In your mind, trace your steps back to where you last knew where you were. Look for your boot marks in loose and muddy earth or in the snow. Scan the horizon for landmarks that may give clues about your location. Do you have a map? Orient it and see what you can learn from the symbols and contour lines.

If you still have no idea where you are or where you want to go, *stay put*. When your absence is noticed, people will come looking for you.

However, if you are fairly sure of a route that will take you to a known location, you can move cautiously. If you have a compass, set a bearing in the direction of your destination and follow it. Otherwise, line up two landmarks in the direction you want to go — two trees, rocks, bushes, etc. Sight along them to a third landmark in the distance. Walk to the middle landmark. Sight along it and the third feature to another landmark farther ahead. Move from one landmark to another, always keeping at least two features in a straight line in front of you.

Mark your route well with broken branches or strips of cloth in case you have to find your way back. Eventually you should come to a familiar spot or see a trail or a stream that will lead you to camp.

Strayed from Your Patrol

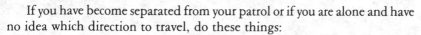

If you have become separated from your patrol or if you are alone and have no idea which direction to travel, do these things:

☆ Stay in one place and let *them* find *you*. A search will begin as soon as someone notices you are missing.

☆ Let searchers know where you are. The universal distress call is some signal repeated three times at frequent intervals. Three shouts, for instance, or three blasts on a whistle. A smoky fire in the daytime and a bright fire at night may also attract attention. For smoke, toss grass or green leaves on the flames. Is there an open field nearby? Spread your rain gear and bright-colored equipment on the ground to catch the eye of a rescue pilot. (For more on distress signals, see page 445.)

☆ Make yourself comfortable. Pitch a tent if you have one, or find shelter for the night against a rock or under the cover of trees. Use everything in your pack to stay warm and dry. A campfire can offer warmth and lift your spirits. Before dark, collect enough wood to last through the night.

☆ Don't worry. You can go for 3 days without water and 3 weeks without food. Lots of people will be looking for you. Whatever you do, stay calm and stay put. You will be found.

"The worst thing you can do is to get frightened. The truly dangerous enemy is not the cold or the hunger, so much as the fear. It robs the wanderer of his judgment and of his limb power; it is fear that turns the passing experience into a final tragedy . . . . Keep cool and all will be well . . . . Use what you have, where you are, right now."

Ernest Thompson Seton, 1906

CHAPTER 9

BACKPACKING

THE 1925 *Boy Scout Handbook* noted that "Scouts as a rule do not go into the big woods." How times have changed! Today, Scouts like you are roaming deep into the forests, hills, mountains, deserts, and plains, carrying food, clothing, and gear for treks lasting days or even weeks.

As miles of rugged trail roll beneath your boots, you leave behind the rush of the cities and pressures of school. Backpacking helps you break down the walls between yourself and the outdoors. It brings you together with good friends in your patrol or crew. By using your best Scouting skills, you can live simply and well.

John Muir, a famous American naturalist, urged people to "go to the mountains and get their good tidings." Nature has many lessons to teach. As you seek them out, you will also find that backpacking refreshes you, fills you with energy, and makes you strong in body and spirit. Travel lightly and get the good tidings of the backcountry. There is simply no finer way to go.

HOW MANY?

Scouts are among the more than 30 million Americans who enjoy backpacking and hiking. That's a lot of people eager to visit open country. We go to find solitude, inspiration, and excitement. Rangers help us do that by limiting the size of groups going into many backcountry and wilderness areas. For most treks, they allow no more than eight to ten persons to travel and camp together.

When your backpacking crew is the size of a Scout patrol, you will find it easy to live by the no-trace ethic. A troop going into the backcountry should split into patrols for the outing. You won't need big campsites, so you will have a wide choice of places to stay. A patrol hiking quietly will see much more wildlife than a big, noisy group. A small crew is less likely to disturb the treks of other hikers and campers.

On the other hand, the smallest safe size for a backpacking crew is three Scouts and two adult leaders. Should an accident occur far from a road, two people can give first aid and stay with the injured person. The other two can go for help if necessary.

If you want to be with groups larger than a patrol, plan your outings for developed campgrounds and Scout camps that can handle lots of people. There you can spread out your camp, work on all sorts of skills, play noisy games, and use as much gear as you want to carry. Save the backcountry for trips when you are willing to travel lightly and become a part of the environment. By practicing no-trace hiking and camping wherever you go, you can be sure you won't drown out nature's good tidings.

GET PREPARED FOR BACKPACKING

Getting prepared ahead of time is vital for the safety and success of a backpacking trip. There are no stores in the backcountry. The gear and food in your pack will have to serve you until you reach the end of the trail.

Carry the Scout Outdoor Essentials on every backpacking adventure. In addition, pay special attention to the following:

Footwear. Long miles of hiking and the weight of a pack put stress on your ankles and feet. Good hiking boots should give you plenty of support and protection. If the boots you wear on campouts and hikes fit well, they should be fine for backpacking, too. (For more on footwear, see page 162.)

Clothing. The "layering" system explained on page 164 lets you pull on extra clothing to stay warm, or remove some to cool off. Check the clothing lists for the season you will be hiking. Experience will help you decide what clothes and rain gear to take so that you can be comfortable but carry no more than you need.

Pack. The pack you use for overnight camping may be too small to hold enough gear, clothing, and food for a trek of several days or more. For those longer trips, a backpack is just right.

A backpack has *shoulder straps*, a *frame*, and a *hip belt* that allow you to shift the weight of the load from your shoulders to the strong muscles of your legs. Cinch the hip belt and adjust the straps until your pack rides easily on your back. Even though backpacks can hold a lot, keep the total weight of your load as light as you can—no more than one-fourth your body weight. For example, if you weigh 100 pounds, keep the pack weight under 25 pounds.

Backpacking Gear

Overnight camping gear and the Scout Outdoor Essentials form the heart of backpacking equipment. Carrying only what you need will help you travel lightly and live well in the backcountry.

Does your backpack ride hard on your hips and collarbone? For more padding, fold extra socks over the hip belt of your pack or tuck them under your shoulder straps.

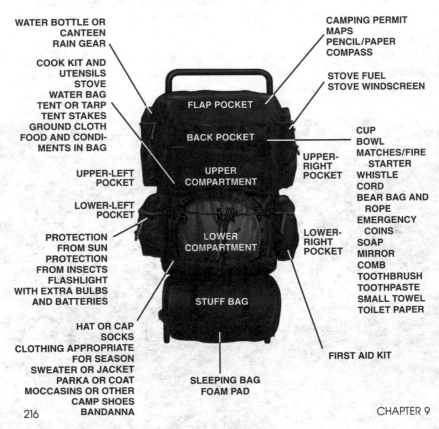

WATER BOTTLE OR
CANTEEN
RAIN GEAR

COOK KIT AND
UTENSILS
STOVE
WATER BAG
TENT OR TARP
TENT STAKES
GROUND CLOTH
FOOD AND CONDI-
MENTS IN BAG

UPPER-LEFT
POCKET

LOWER-LEFT
POCKET

PROTECTION
FROM SUN
PROTECTION
FROM INSECTS
FLASHLIGHT
WITH EXTRA BULBS
AND BATTERIES

HAT OR CAP
SOCKS
CLOTHING APPROPRIATE
FOR SEASON
SWEATER OR JACKET
PARKA OR COAT
MOCCASINS OR OTHER
CAMP SHOES
BANDANNA

FLAP POCKET

BACK POCKET

UPPER
COMPARTMENT

LOWER
COMPARTMENT

STUFF BAG

CAMPING PERMIT
MAPS
PENCIL/PAPER
COMPASS

STOVE FUEL
STOVE WINDSCREEN

CUP
BOWL
MATCHES/FIRE
STARTER
WHISTLE
CORD
BEAR BAG AND
ROPE
EMERGENCY
COINS
SOAP
MIRROR
COMB
TOOTHBRUSH
TOOTHPASTE
SMALL TOWEL
TOILET PAPER

UPPER-
RIGHT
POCKET

LOWER-
RIGHT
POCKET

FIRST AID KIT

SLEEPING BAG
FOAM PAD

PERSONAL GEAR

Scouting Outdoor Essentials

_____ Pocketknife

_____ First aid kit

_____ Extra clothing

_____ Rain gear

_____ Canteen or water bottle

_____ Flashlight

_____ Trail food

_____ Matches and fire starters

_____ Sun protection

_____ Map and compass

_____ Eating kit:

_____ Spoon

_____ Bowl

_____ Cup

_____ Cleanup kit:

_____ Soap

_____ Toothbrush

_____ Toothpaste

_____ Comb

_____ Washcloth

_____ Small towel

Additional Gear

_____ Map of the area

_____ Compass

_____ Clothing for the season

_____ Pack

_____ Sleeping bag **or** 2 or 3 blankets

_____ Foam sleeping pad **or** air mattress

_____ Ground cloth

Personal Extras (Optional)

_____ Watch

_____ Camera and film

_____ Notebook

_____ Pencil or pen

_____ Sunglasses

_____ Small musical instrument

_____ Swimsuit

_____ Insect repellent

_____ Prayer book or Bible

Group Backpacking Gear

_____ Tents with poles, stakes, and lines

_____ Nylon cord—50 feet

_____ Backpacking stoves and fuel

_____ Camp saw (where firewood cutting is allowed)

_____ Camp shovel

_____ Group cooking kit:

    _____ Pots and pans

    _____ Hot-pot tongs

    _____ Large spoon

    _____ Water container—2½-gallon, collapsible

    _____ Plastic sheets (2), 4 feet by 4 feet

    _____ Matches in waterproof container

    _____ Emergency fire starters

_____ Group cleanup kit:

    _____ Biodegradable soap

    _____ Sanitizing rinse agent

    _____ Scouring pads

    _____ Trash can liners

    _____ Toilet paper in plastic bag

_____ Repair kit:

    _____ Thread

    _____ Needles

    _____ Safety pins

Group Extras (Optional)

_____ Dining fly

_____ Grill

_____ Pot rods

_____ Spatula

_____ Ladle

_____ Ax

_____ Plastic wash basin

_____ Patrol flag

_____ Small U.S. flag

HIT THE TRAIL!

Hiking

The guidelines you use on any Scout hike will serve you well during a backpacking trip. Begin by studying a map and charting your route. Find out if you need camping permits. Leave a copy of your trip plan with your family.

Will you be following hiking trails? If so, stay on them to reduce impact on vegetation. If you are going cross-country, try to travel on dry, hard ground. Wet earth makes hiking much harder, and your boots can tear plants out of wet soil.

Stay together as you hike, and let the slower members of your group set the pace. You will appreciate being with each other as you enjoy the countryside.

Set reasonable distances for each day's hike so that you can see everything and not feel rushed. It's a good idea to reach each camp by mid-afternoon. You will have plenty of daylight for setting up tents, cooking your evening meal, and exploring the area around camp.

Take advantage of the fresh, cool hours of the morning. Get up, get dressed, and have breakfast. After you've broken camp and loaded your pack, take a last good look around. Any bits of litter? Any pieces of equipment? Does the area look better than how you found it? Then swing your pack to your shoulders, check your map, and hit the adventure trail again.

Resting

Give yourself time to rest while you are on the trail. For a short break, lean over with your hands on your knees and let the weight of your pack shift for

a moment from your shoulders to your back. Or slip off your pack and take it easy for a good 5 minutes or more. If you lean your pack against a tree, you can use it as a backrest.

At lunch you may want to pull off your boots and wiggle your toes. Maybe you can plunge your bare feet into a cold stream. Pull on clean, dry socks for the afternoon hike and your feet will feel like new. Damp socks tied to the outside of your pack will dry as you hike.

During long treks, you may want to plan a *layover day* — that is, a day without moving camp. Perhaps you can locate your layover camp near a lake for a day of fishing and swimming, or you may find a nearby mountain to climb. The main reason for going backpacking is to enjoy yourself. There is no need to be moving down the trail every day.

Cooking

Open fires are not allowed in many backcountry areas. This will not be a problem if you have a backpacking stove.

Since you will be carrying all of your food, too, rely on simple, hearty meals that are full of flavor. Try one-pot stews for supper, and instant puddings and custards for dessert. Hot or cold cereals, cocoa, drink mixes, and dried fruit will get you started in the morning. Cheese, crackers, peanut butter and jelly, sardines, and tuna make fine lunches. On the trail, a handful of nuts and raisins or some dried fruit will keep you going.

NO-TRACE BACKPACKING

America's backcountry is a true national treasure. Backpacking gives you an exciting way to visit it, learn from it, and find many terrific adventures. However, for unspoiled country to remain that way, you must do your part. Go backpacking whenever you can, but leave no trace. Take time to clean up campsites and trails left dirty by people less thoughtful than you.

Many Scout troops are working with agencies and other groups who care for the backcountry. You may be able to use your camping, hiking, and woods tools knowledge to help with worthwhile conservation projects. Helping to repair a damaged campsite or pathway can give you a real feeling of doing your part for the land.

CHAPTER 10

HIT THE PEDALS!

S COUTING adventures don't only happen when you are hiking with a pack on your back. If you have a bicycle, great times with your patrol are as close as the sunny back streets and empty roads near home.

You may already ride your bike to school, to the store, and to Scout meetings. Instead of just using it for transportation, plan a 1-day patrol bike-hike that lets you ride to an interesting destination. A few hours of steady pedaling may take you to a park, a museum, or the meeting place of another troop. You'll feel the strong effort of your legs and lungs as you power the pedals. Along the way, enjoy the freedom of the open road.

Once you have a few short treks behind you, stretch those day trips into bicycle campouts. Strap your overnight gear to your bike frame and you're ready to ride just about anywhere. As your skill increases, so can the length of your journeys. Someday you might even want to pedal 3,000 miles across the United States from the waters of the Pacific to the Atlantic shore. That's the sort of adventure that takes a lot of experience and planning. But if you like the idea of great adventures, you can start right now by getting out on bike-hikes with your patrol.

RIDING SAFETY

Safety on the road begins with a bicycle that's in good condition. Learn to adjust your bike's brakes, lubricate the bearings, and keep the chain clean. Carry a patch kit and small tire pump to fix flats. With an adjustable crescent wrench, pliers, and a screwdriver, you can make almost any roadside repairs.

Keep your bike in good working condition.

Whether you're riding your bicycle around the block or across the country, *always* wear a helmet. A hard plastic helmet made especially for cyclists will protect your head from serious injury. Your helmet should have a label from either the Snell Memorial Foundation or ANSI (American National Standards Institute), certifying that it is safe for cyclists. Put it on whenever you climb aboard your bike, and keep the chin strap snug.

Memorize the following road rules for safe bicycling:

☆ Ride in single file on the right side of the road with the flow of traffic. Stay close to the right edge of the roadway.

☆ Be visible! Reflectors and a bright flag on a wand make your bicycle show up. Light-colored clothing and a highway worker's orange vest caution drivers to give you room.

☆ Obey all traffic rules. Bicyclists must follow the same traffic regulations as the drivers of cars and trucks. Come to a full halt at stop signs and red lights. Make turns from the correct lanes. Look over your shoulder before making any turn.

☆ Use hand signals every time you make a left turn or a right turn, or come to a stop.

★ Pedestrians always have the right-of-way. If you must go on sidewalks, dismount and walk your bicycle. On bike trails shared with walkers, slow down as you come up behind them and let them know you are going by. Ring a bicycle bell or call out, "Passing on your left!" so they will not be startled.

★ Stay alert. Motorists may not expect to see bicycles on the road. Watch out for doors of parked cars opening into your path.

★ Look before you ride out of a driveway or alley into a street. Come to a full stop and look both ways for traffic. Go when it is clear.

BICYCLE TREKS

On long rides, toting your gear in a backpack can be tiring. The weight of a loaded pack may cause you to lose your balance. Its size can block your vision of traffic coming up behind you.

On a day trip, a *handlebar bag* will hold your patch kit, tools, and the Scout Outdoor Essentials. For overnight treks, mount a couple of *panniers*— bicycle saddlebags—on a carrier over the rear wheel. Stow your camping gear in them and lash your sleeping bag on top.

You will need the same equipment for long bicycle journeys as for any campout. However, if you plan routes that take you past grocery stores, you can buy each day's food along the way.

LOW-IMPACT RIDING

With knobby tires, strong frames, and low gears, some bicycles are built for rugged riding. Many trails are open to bicyclists. Other paths, however, are reserved for hikers, horseback riders, wheelchairs, or other users. Pedal your bicycle only on those trails where bikes are permitted.

Wherever you go, stay on roads or trails. Riding a bicycle cross-country is a sure way to start erosion. The tires of bicycles beat down vegetation. They loosen the soil, which allows it to wash away in the next rain.

The bicycle trails and roads of America are as much a part of the great outdoors as any campground or wilderness area. Properly dispose of trash during bike-hikes. Enjoy the land through which you ride, and leave no trace of your visit.

▲
Bags and panniers

227

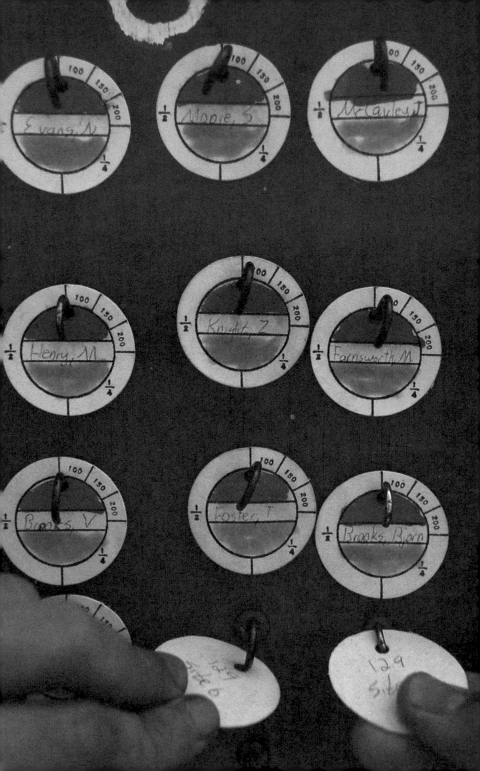

LET'S GO SWIMMING!

"**C**OME on in, the water's fine!" That's a cry heard at Scout camps and pools everywhere. On a hot summer day there's nothing better than swimming, splashing, and having fun in the water.

Swimming is also an important outdoor skill. Learn how to swim, and you will be able to take care of yourself if you ever fall out of a boat or slip into a stream. With training in lifesaving, you can come to the aid of a drowning person.

There is a right way to swim. Take the time to learn the basics, and then always practice safe methods. Begin by becoming acquainted with the rules of the Safe Swim Defense.

SAFE SWIM DEFENSE T 2

1. An adult is in charge during every swim. It is strongly recommended that he or she hold current certification in Scouting's Safe Swim Defense plan.

2. Each swimmer must provide a current and complete health history from his parent, guardian, or medical doctor.

3. The swimming place must be clear of hazards. Areas are marked: no more than 3½ feet (1 meter) deep for nonswimmers, deeper for beginners, over the head for swimmers (not over 12 feet).

4. Strong swimmers take turns as lifeguards. Two stand on shore with a lifeline, ready to help.

Left, the Safe Swim Defense plan includes a lookout who can see and hear all areas and, *above,* the buddy system.

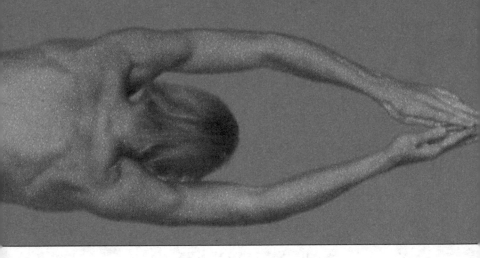

5. A lookout stands where he can see and hear all areas. He directs any help needed.

6. Scouts swim in ability groups in areas matching their skill level. A *non-swimmer* is just learning. A *beginner* can jump into the water and swim 50 feet (15 meters). A swimmer can swim 300 feet (100 meters) and float.

7. Everyone swims with a buddy who is of equal swimming ability. Buddies check in together. They stay near one another during the swim. They check out together.

8. Maintain good discipline in the swimming area. Everyone must understand and follow the 8 rules of the Safe Swim Defense.

CHAPTER 11

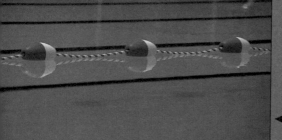

◀ A safe swimming area is marked for nonswimmers, beginners, and swimmers.

Learn how to swim by taking lessons from trained instructors. They can teach you the skills you need to have fun safely in the water.

LEARN TO SWIM

2 1

The best way to learn swimming is to take a course from trained instructors. Scout camps offer swimming classes. So do organizations like the American Red Cross and YMCA. Ask about lessons at local pools. Your Scoutmaster can help you find the swimming lessons you need. If you have a good swimmer or a lifeguard to watch you, you can try out some basic swimming methods yourself.

Did you know that you can float? Here's how you can prove it. With a good swimmer standing nearby, wade into water that is waist-deep. Hold your breath, bend down, and curl up in a ball. Clasp your arms around your shins. You will bob to the surface and float like a jellyfish.

Next, glide across the top of the water. Turn so you are facing the shore and take another deep breath. Push off with your feet and plunge forward with your arms stretched in front of you. Stand for a moment to get another breath, then push off and glide again.

Finally, practice the way a swimmer breathes. Stand in waist-deep water again. Take a breath through your mouth and put your face in the water. Slowly exhale through your nose. Repeat.

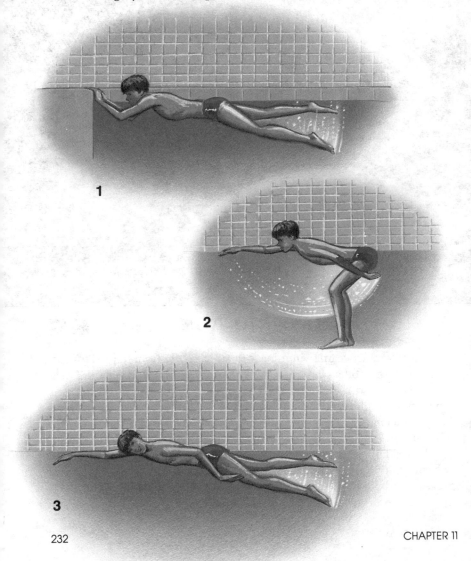

1

2

3

Crawl

The *crawl* is a swimming stroke that moves you quickly through the water. It's best for short distances, but tiring to use very long. The crawl has three parts: the leg kick, the arm stroke, and breathing.

Work on the *leg kick* by holding onto the edge of a pool or by resting your hands on the bottom in shallow water. Move your legs from the hips as you kick them up and down. Keep them straight but not too stiff. Then try gliding across the water using the leg kick to push you along.

Stand in waist-deep water to practice the *arm stroke*. Bend forward so that the top of your body is in a swimming position. Stretch your right arm straight ahead. Swing that arm down to your hip, then raise the elbow and stretch your arm forward again. Do the same with your left arm, then with both arms alternately.

Push off into a glide. Use the leg kick and arm stroke at the same time to move you through the water. When you need air, turn your head to the side and breathe through your mouth.

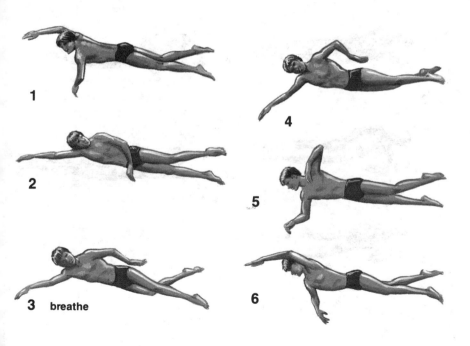

1

2

3 **breathe**

4

5

6

After you have learned the crawl stroke, master several others. The side-stroke, breaststroke, and backstroke crawl are effective strokes that will give you confidence in the water. Each of these strokes is more fully described in the *Swimming* merit badge pamphlet.

Sidestroke. A strong scissors kick is the power of the sidestroke. Your face is always above the water, so breathing is easy. Begin the sidestroke by pushing off and gliding on your side. Draw your knees toward your chest, then spread your legs and snap them together as if you were closing a pair of scissors. At the same time, thrust one arm forward and sweep the other down. Keep your hands cupped.

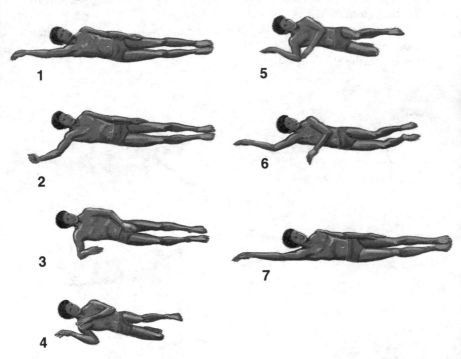

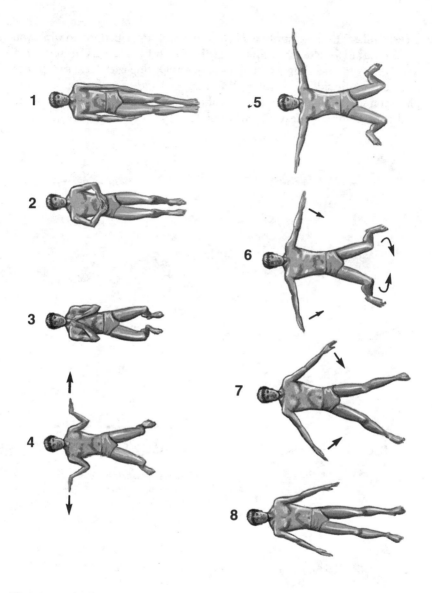

Elementary backstroke. The elementary backstroke conserves your energy during long swims. Use an inverted whip kick with your legs, pulling them up, apart, and together. With each kick, extend your arms and pull them down to your sides as though they were oars. Glide after each stroke.

Breaststroke. The breaststroke is a little like a backstroke performed while you are on your belly. Use the whip kick again. Extend your arms out in front of you as you did for a simple glide on the water. During each kick, sweep your arms out to the side. That will pull you forward and also lift your face from the water so you can breathe and look ahead. Extend your arms forward again and glide before the next kick and pull.

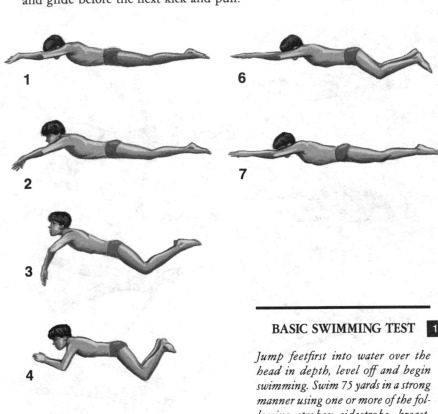

BASIC SWIMMING TEST 1

Jump feetfirst into water over the head in depth, level off and begin swimming. Swim 75 yards in a strong manner using one or more of the following strokes: sidestroke, breaststroke, trudgen, or crawl; then swim 25 yards using an easy resting backstroke. The 100 yards must be swum continuously and include at least one sharp turn. After completing the swim, rest by floating. This qualification test should be renewed annually.

WATER RESCUES

Six thousand Americans drown every year. You can take care of yourself in the water if you have learned how to swim. To help someone else who is in danger of drowning, you must also learn lifesaving techniques *before* you need them. Practice water rescues at Scout camp or take a course at a local pool. Many Scouts develop vital rescue skills by earning the Lifesaving merit badge.

Even with proper training, *never* attempt a water rescue by swimming if you can do it some other way. The safest methods are to *reach, throw*, or *go with support*.

☆ *Reach.* Most water accidents happen close to shore. Try to reach the victim with your hand or foot, a pole, branch, canoe paddle, towel, deck chair, or anything else close by. ▶

☆ *Throw.* Is there a ring buoy on shore? An air mattress, life jacket, or beach ball? Throw it to the victim. Or cast out a coil of rope, being sure you hang on to one end.
▼

☆ *Go with support.* When a victim can't be rescued by reaching or throwing, then go with support. Row out in a boat or paddle a canoe, a surfboard, or a sailboard. ▼ •

LET'S GO SWIMMING!

☆ *If everything else fails.* Under extreme circumstances, you may have to swim to the aid of a drowning person.

— *Never attempt a swimming rescue unless you are a strong swimmer!* A rescue effort is very tiring. It can put you at risk of drowning.

— *Go only if you have practiced lifesaving methods!* A person struggling in the water is fighting for his life. In his fear and panic, he may try to grab you and hang on. Unless you know what to do, he may pull you under.

When there is no other way to assist someone who is drowning, quickly strip down to your undershorts, keeping an eye on the victim the entire time. Take the collar of your shirt in your teeth and enter the water feetfirst. Use the breaststroke to swim toward the victim, but stay beyond his reach. Grasp the shirt in one hand and flip an end of it into the victim's hands. When he grabs it, tow him to safety.

Be very careful. If the victim panics and threatens your safety, back off. Wait until he becomes calm, even if that means he loses consciousness. Then pull him ashore.

SURVIVAL FLOATING

Sailors are trained to use survival floating to stay safe for many minutes or even hours awaiting rescue. Take a breath and relax completely, floating upright near the surface of the water. When you need air, push down with your hands and make one scissors kick with your legs to lift your mouth and nose. Then relax and float again.

CHAPTER 11

HAVE FUN SWIMMING

Playing in the water improves all your swimming and rescue skills. Once you have learned to swim, try some of the following:

Floating. Take a deep breath, arch your spine, and lay back on the water. Your feet may dangle, but your face should stay above the surface so that you can breathe.

Snorkeling. A mask, snorkel, and flippers will improve your underwater vision and swimming speed. In a pond or lake, you can explore an aquatic world full of wildlife, vegetation, and wonderful surprises. ▼

Swimmer rescues. Have a buddy ▶ pretend to be a struggling swimmer. Bring him to shore with a *chin tow* or a *cross-chest carry.* Propel the two of you with your free arm and the scissors kick. To do the *hair-pull rescue,* grasp your partner's hair with one hand and tow him with a sidestroke.

Tired-swimmer rescue. Try the *back-rest push* by having your partner float on his back with his hands on your shoulders. Push him ashore with the breaststroke.

Switch roles and let your partner practice the same rescues with you.

CHAPTER 12

CANOEING AND ROWING

CANOEING

"Our paddles keen and bright, flashing like silver!
Swift as the wild goose flight, dip, dip, and swing."

T HAT'S a Scout song you can sing when you canoe the wilderness lakes
of the Great North Woods. With smooth, powerful strokes of your paddle, you'll send your canoe flying across the water. Pull ashore late in the day
and make camp. Grill slabs of freshly caught fish over the coals of a campfire.
As night falls, watch for moose and beaver, and listen for the cry of a loon.

On a small pond near your home, on a lake at Scout camp, or slicing
through the vast wilderness of the Boundary Waters, a canoe will give you
hours of outdoor pleasure. It can float quietly across a city park lake, or crash
through whitewater rapids of a wild and scenic river.

The canoe is a direct link to America's past. For centuries, native Americans
built and paddled wooden dugouts, kayaks, and birchbark canoes. Today's
canoes are built of wood, aluminum, or sturdy man-made materials, but the
basic design has changed little. When you go canoeing, you are paddling a
part of outdoor history.

Follow the guidelines of the BSA Safety Afloat plan for all canoeing and
rafting trips. Become a good swimmer *before* you try canoeing. Always wear a
personal flotation device (PFD) while you are on the water. If you ever do tip
over, hang onto the side of a canoe. The craft will stay afloat even when it is full
of water. Flop back inside and you can splash your way to shore.

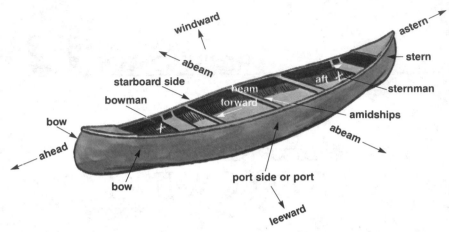

windward

astern

abeam

stern

starboard side

aft

beam

sternman

bowman

forward

bow

amidships

abeam

ahead

port side or port

bow

leeward

The *forward stroke* pushes a canoe ahead. It is used by the paddler in the bow of a canoe. Use the J-stroke when you are in the stern. Start it just as you would a forward stroke, but for a moment at the end of the stroke use the paddle blade as a rudder to hold the canoe on course.

There are other strokes, too, that you'll learn as you go. They are all described in the *Canoeing* merit badge pamphlet. Master them, and you will begin to think of the canoe as an important part of your backcountry travels. One day soon you may be launching your canoe on a wilderness lake and setting out for one of Scouting's best adventures.

Mastering certain skills will make your adventures on water safe and fun. All boaters must be with buddies. Three may go in one canoe, and up to four in a single rowboat.

A Scout who has not been classified as a "swimmer" may ride as a passenger in a rowboat with an adult swimmer, or in a canoe with an adult certified as a lifeguard or a lifesaver by a recognized agency. In all other cases, a person must have passed the basic swimming test (see page 236) before participating in activities afloat. Fulfilling the requirements of the basic handling tests will give you the minimum skills you must have to manage a rowboat or canoe.

ROWING

For fun on the water, rowing is a terrific way to go. A rowboat will carry you across lakes and streams, and let you poke along shorelines. If you like to fish, you can row to where the lunkers lie. Rowboat races are exciting, and so is drifting quietly, watching the water and the land.

Rowing is also a fine sport for strengthening your arms, back, chest, and heart. In an emergency, rowing gives you a way to rescue a struggling swimmer.

Summer camp is a good place to practice rowing. Even if you are an expert swimmer, you will learn that everyone in a boat wears a PFD at all times. You'll discover the right way to enter and leave a boat, and how to use the oars for power and steering. Before long, you'll be the captain of your boat, rowing it exactly where you want to go.

◄ **When you enter a boat, step into the middle of it.**

► **For good rowing, "feather" your oars by turning the oar blades flat when out of the water so that the wind doesn't catch them.**

To row a straight course, keep a landmark over center of stern.

BASIC CANOE HANDLING TEST

1. As a stern paddler in tandem with a partner, demonstrate your ability to launch a canoe properly, paddle a straight course for 100 yards, turn, come back, land, and store the canoe.

2. With a buddy, jump out of the canoe, hold onto it, then climb back in it without swamping the craft.

3. With a buddy, get into a swamped canoe and paddle it to shore.

BASIC ROWBOAT HANDLING TEST

1. Demonstrate your ability to launch a rowboat, row in a straight line for 100 yards, turn, come back, land, and properly moor the boat.

2. Participate in a swamped-boat safety demonstration, including a demonstration of the use and care of personal flotation devices (PFDs).

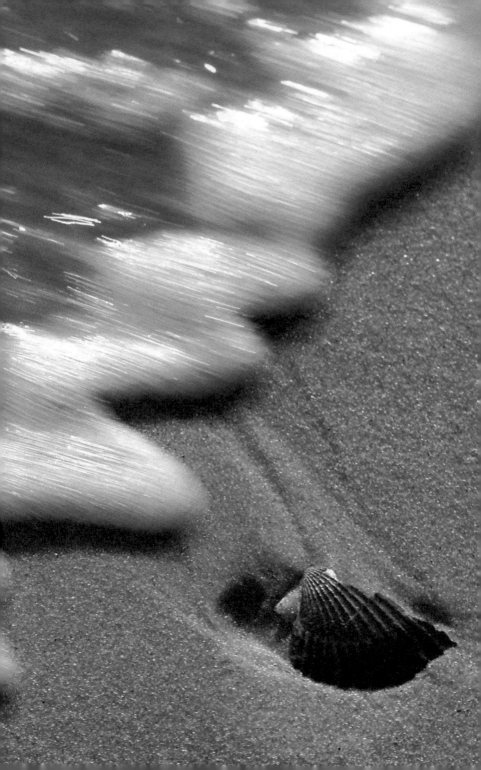

UNDERSTANDING NATURE

ONE morning a Scout patrol sat on the lawn near their troop meeting hall. They were waiting for everyone to arrive so they could bicycle to a state park for a nature hike. They wanted to see lots of wildlife.

As they waited, the patrol leader noticed a movement under the bush beside him. He looked closer and spotted a small leaf moving among the blades of grass like a shark fin above water. Then he saw that an ant was carrying the leaf. The ant was one of hundreds hurrying single file through the grass.

"Hey, look at this!" he said as the others gathered around. "Let's follow them!"

The Scouts got down on their hands and knees. They watched as the ants scrambled over dead blades of grass, around pebbles, and under twigs. Many ants were carrying leaves. The jaws of others were clamped around white bundles the Scouts thought might be ant eggs.

"It seems as if they have their own trail in the grass, and they all know where to go," said the patrol leader.

The line of ants led to an anthill under a bush. Near it the Scouts saw a little spider web spun between a twig and a blade of grass. At first they couldn't see the spider. They looked more closely, and finally located the spider hiding in the grass right next to the web.

"Do you think that spider is after the ants?" one of the Scouts asked. "It's not very big."

They kept watching. The minutes ticked away. One ant wandered very near the web, but didn't touch it. The Scouts waited. Then a small moth fluttered into the web. It tried to pull loose, but its wings were stuck. As it struggled, the moth became more tangled in the web.

Then the spider rushed from its hiding place and pounced on the moth. It turned the moth over and over, wrapping it in sticky thread. Then the spider pulled its motionless prey out of sight beneath the twig. The small patch of lawn was once again still, except for the line of ants carrying their leaves and eggs.

"That was cool! That moth never a had chance!" said one of the Scouts.

"It's like those films you see of lions hunting zebras," said another. "That spider really knew what it was doing."

As they talked, a clump of twigs in the branches of the bush caught their attention. "Look at this!" one Scout whispered. "It's a little bird nest! I didn't know that was here."

The patrol leader warned the Scouts not to touch it. "The birds may still be using it. You don't want to scare them away by leaving your scent on their nest."

The Scouts inspected the bush for other nests. They didn't find any more, but they did discover a shiny green cocoon hanging beneath a leaf.

"I didn't know there could be so much to see around one bush," a Scout said. "I like this. Let's make a list of everything we can find."

The patrol leader ran inside to get a pencil and some paper. He also brought a magnifying glass and a camp shovel from the troop equipment room. For the rest of the morning, the Scouts crawled slowly around the bush, writing down what they saw. The list included beetles, butterflies, worms, a mouse, and the birds from the nest. They examined many plants, too. Some had flowers in bloom. A moist, white fungus was growing on a stick of rotting wood. A vine with tiny thorns on its stem had twisted itself around the trunk of the bush.

The Scouts used the camp shovel to loosen and turn a square of soil. There were roots, worms, a centipede, and lots of tiny animals they didn't recognize. Under the magnifying glass, everything looked big, different, and exciting. They wrote down descriptions of everything they couldn't name. The list became very long.

You may have guessed that the Scouts didn't reach the state park that morning. They had found plenty of wildlife to observe without traveling anywhere. They simply opened their eyes and looked at what had always been right in front of them.

ECOLOGY

A hawk soars on still wings high above a mountain wilderness. The trees near your home sway in the wind. Ocean tides ebb and flow. Geese, whales, and Monarch butterflies journey thousands of miles a year in complex migrations. A worm turning silently in the cool earth goes no more than a few feet in its entire lifetime.

The natural world is beautiful and strange. It is spectacular beyond your wildest imagination. Some of it is gigantic — towering redwood forests, avalanches thundering down enormous mountains, broad rivers flowing for hundreds of miles. Nature is tiny, too — the eye of an insect, the nucleus of a cell, the secrets of an atom. At times, nature makes itself known with explosive power. Think of the eruption of a volcano, the jolt of an earthquake, or the howling winds of a blizzard. Nature also moves so slowly that we notice no change in an entire lifetime. Continents drift away from each other, a few inches every thousand years. Climates change a degree or two each century. Water flows over the land and becomes an ocean. An ocean retreats and leaves behind dry land.

The more we learn about nature, the more we realize that there is much we don't know. The relationships among plants, animals, and their surroundings are so intricate we can unravel only the most obvious mysteries.

On the other hand, we do know a great deal about nature. You can understand much of it, too, if you are willing to open your eyes and your mind. Learn about animals and plants. Investigate weather, climate, geology, and the effects of people both ancient and modern. Find clues that help you see the inner workings of the natural world.

UNDERSTANDING NATURE   249

Ecology is the word that describes this way of looking at nature. It comes from the old Greek word *oikos,* meaning "house," and *ology,* meaning "to study." Ecology is simply the study of your own house.

It may seem odd to think of your house as being more than just the building in which you live. Ecology helps us see that our home includes the area surrounding that building and all the land beyond it. In fact, the entire world is our home. We are affected by changes in nature happening everywhere on the globe.

Likewise, what we do has effects on nature that may reach far beyond our houses and our towns. The way we treat the environment today will leave its mark for hundreds of years to come.

We have a very great responsibility to take care of this earth-house of ours. We must keep it clean and repair it where it is damaged. It is the only home we have. We must cherish it and do it no harm.

CHAPTER 13

PEELING BACK THE LAYERS

Gaining knowledge is the first step toward making wise decisions about nature. You need to understand problems if you expect to solve them. You don't have to be a scientist or a scholar to study nature. Remember those Scouts on the lawn? They had the right idea. They were on their hands and knees, learning by observing. Their experience was like peeling back the layers of an onion. At first they saw the big things—a bush, a tree, a lawn, a stream. They noticed the bright colors of flowers, the big plants, and the birds, a squirrel, and a rabbit.

As they looked harder, they peeled back that layer and began to see smaller animals, too—insects, moles, mice, snakes, lizards. They discovered the *understory*—the grasses, weeds, and shrubs, living beneath larger bushes and trees. They peeled back the top of the earth and looked underneath at the root systems and the burrowing animals in the soil. Up to half of the living mass in an area can be underground.

If those Scouts looked the other way at larger ecological layers, they would see some of the ways individual plants and animals depend upon each other. One of the most important of those relationships is the *food chain*.

A Front Lawn Food Chain

Every living thing must have nourishment; food is converted into energy and into building blocks for growth. Those animals and plants that the Scouts found rely on each other to provide sources of food. They saw ants carrying

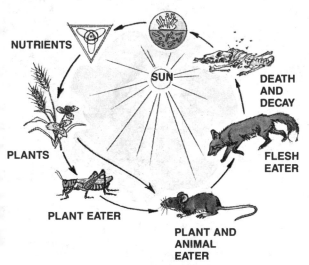

NUTRIENTS

SUN

PLANTS

PLANT EATER

DEATH AND DECAY

FLESH EATER

PLANT AND ANIMAL EATER

FOOD CHAIN. Plants get energy from the sun. Animals get energy from food. The mouse eats a root and gets energy from it. The fox gets energy from eating the mouse. Body waste from both gets into the soil as nutrients—food for plants. When animals die they also return to the soil.

leaves into their anthill for use as food. They also saw a spider trap a moth. Later, a field mouse might catch and eat the spider. A hawk drifting high overhead may see the mouse wander out from beneath the bush. With the wind rushing through its feathers, the hawk will dive on the mouse and grab it in its strong talons. It may eat the flesh or carry it to a nest for its young. When the hawk dies, its body falls to earth where ants, beetles, and other small creatures can feed on it. The hawk's remains will decay and be absorbed into the soil, enriching the roots of plants.

Those plants and animals living on that lawn make up a *food chain*. The plants grow because of energy from the sun and nutrients in the soil. Small animals eat the plants. Larger animals feed on them, and still larger ones on those. Upon their deaths, their bodies decompose and return to the soil. Plants absorb the fresh nutrients, and the chain is complete. Nothing is wasted in nature and nothing goes away. Energy simply changes form.

The food chain is a *cycle*. That's a process that continues in a circle with no start or end. Two other important natural cycles are the oxygen-carbon cycle and the water cycle.

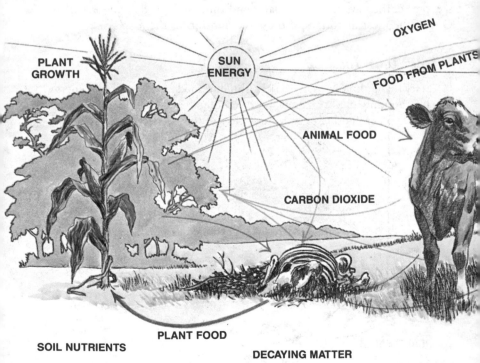

OXYGEN

PLANT GROWTH

SUN ENERGY

FOOD FROM PLANTS

ANIMAL FOOD

CARBON DIOXIDE

PLANT FOOD

SOIL NUTRIENTS

DECAYING MATTER

CHAPTER 13

Oxygen-Carbon Cycle

You and all other animals must breathe in order to stay alive. Your lungs absorb oxygen and use it to provide energy for your body through a process similar to burning. You exhale carbon dioxide. Carbon dioxide is also produced when dead plants and animals decay and when fuels are burned.

Plants must absorb carbon dioxide in order to stay alive. They don't have lungs, but plants do have a green substance in their leaf cells called *chlorophyll*. Powered by sunlight, chlorophyll allows plants to combine carbon from the air with water to produce the simple sugars that plants use for food. The process is called *photosynthesis* — making something with the aid of light. One product of photosynthesis is oxygen.

Animals use oxygen and exhale carbon dioxide. Plants use carbon dioxide and give off oxygen. Like the cycle of the food chain, the oxygen-carbon cycle makes life possible.

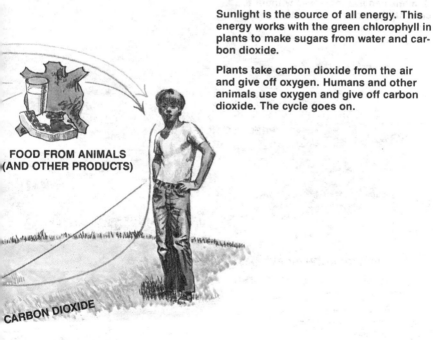

Sunlight is the source of all energy. This energy works with the green chlorophyll in plants to make sugars from water and carbon dioxide.

Plants take carbon dioxide from the air and give off oxygen. Humans and other animals use oxygen and give off carbon dioxide. The cycle goes on.

FOOD FROM ANIMALS (AND OTHER PRODUCTS)

CARBON DIOXIDE

Water Cycle

All living things must have water. It allows foods and gases to pass through the cells of plants and the tissues of animals. Water circulates through the environment in a cycle that, like the carbon-oxygen cycle, relies on the sun for power.

Heat from the sun evaporates water from oceans, lakes, and streams. The vapors form clouds that can be blown many miles by the wind. When the air cools or becomes loaded with moisture, the vapor falls as rain, snow, sleet, or hail.

Much of the water soaks into the soil where it can be used by plants. Some finds its way deeper into the earth and becomes part of the groundwater supply in the form of springs or wells. Eventually that water also returns to lakes and oceans where it can once again evaporate and continue its way through the cycle.

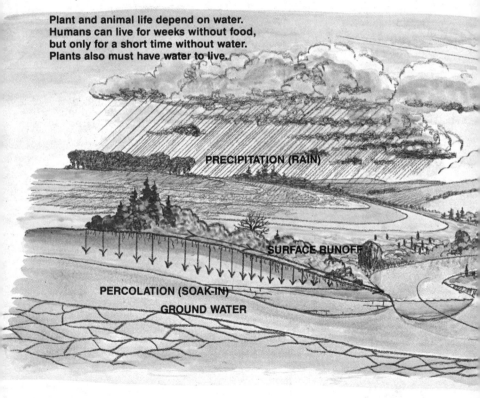

Plant and animal life depend on water.
Humans can live for weeks without food,
but only for a short time without water.
Plants also must have water to live.

PRECIPITATION (RAIN)

SURFACE RUNOFF

PERCOLATION (SOAK-IN)
GROUND WATER

Succession

Nature is forever changing. The changes may happen so slowly that we don't notice them, but change is essential if living things are to thrive.

If you could watch a pond near a forest for many decades, you would see a gradual, remarkable change. Soil washing from the hillsides into the water slowly collects along the edges of the pond. Grass seeds carried by the wind take root in that new mud and grow. As the small grasses die, they mat down and decay, creating a nutrient-rich bed for larger rushes and cattails. Frogs and little fish find safety among the roots and stalks. Insects lay their eggs on the leaves.

Those plants and animals will also die and fall into the mud. Their decay builds more of the fertile soil, slowly raising and drying the edge of the pond. Bushes and small trees move in. They, too, will fall and form more earth.

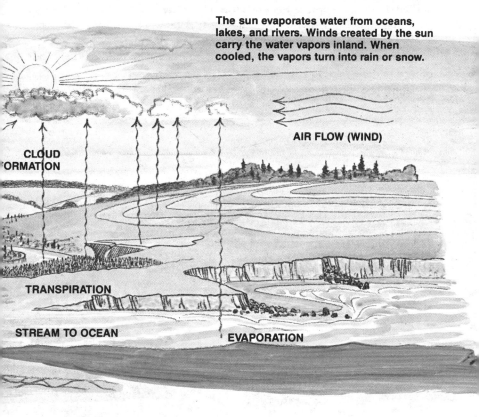

The sun evaporates water from oceans, lakes, and rivers. Winds created by the sun carry the water vapors inland. When cooled, the vapors turn into rain or snow.

AIR FLOW (WIND)

CLOUD FORMATION

TRANSPIRATION

STREAM TO OCEAN

EVAPORATION

Large trees may finally grow into a stand called a climax forest. The pond will have completely disappeared. The *succession* of stages from pond to mature forest can take hundreds or even thousands of years. Further changes will go on forever.

Diversity

A forest that has developed through the long process of succession has many kinds of plants and animals within it. From the bacteria in the muck at the bottom of the pond to the eagles, bears, and other predators feeding on the largest food sources, the food chain is very rich in its variety.

This variety of species is known as *diversity*. It is one of the ways nature regulates change. If a certain kind of plant or one type of animal should die out, other species can quickly take its place. For instance, an insect may infest and kill most of the spruce trees of a forest, but the forest will not disappear. Instead, aspens, firs, and pines will fill in the holes where the trees had been. The dead trees will decay and become nutrients for other species.

However, if there were only spruce trees in that forest and no other kinds of trees, the area would have lacked diversity. Any threat to the spruce would endanger the entire forest. Other trees would not be around to fill the void. The forest would be gone.

Diversity acts as a buffer against drastic change. It allows an area to adjust gradually to new conditions.

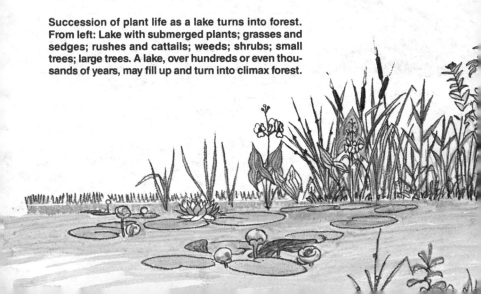

Succession of plant life as a lake turns into forest. From left: Lake with submerged plants; grasses and sedges; rushes and cattails; weeds; shrubs; small trees; large trees. A lake, over hundreds or even thousands of years, may fill up and turn into climax forest.

Fire/Disease/Death

Sometimes natural changes occur very quickly. A forest fire, a volcanic eruption, an earthquake, or a hurricane can dramatically alter an area. Because they are so spectacular, we may think of these changes as disasters. But like more gradual change, the swift actions of fire, disease, and death are natural stages of the succession process.

A forest fire caused by lightning may destroy thousands of acres of timber. To people who liked the forest the way it was, that may seem like a great waste. However, the flames that charred the trees also consumed much of the brush choking the understory of the forest. The fire burned great amounts of dead wood lying on the ground. Full of nutrients, ashes from the blaze mix into the soil and provide a fertile bed for new grasses. The cones of some pine trees open only after they have felt the heat of a fire, and soon new trees will sprout from the blackened remains of the old. Animals can move more easily through the open land, grazing on the grasses. The climax forest has been swept away, leaving the land open for the process of succession to continue.

A clearcut forest

Man-Made Succession

Aside from the spectacular effects of fires, storms, and volcanic activity, natural succession is a very slow process. When humans become involved, however, changes in the environment may happen quickly. We cut down trees for lumber, pave open land for highways and parking lots, and plow fields for planting crops.

Because we are capable of making vast changes in our environment, we often try to alter the earth to suit our needs, rather than adapting our needs to existing conditions.

Man-made change is not necessarily bad. However, we must remain aware of the impact our decisions have. We need to make wise decisions about land use. Our actions have consequences. If a forest of 800-year-old trees is cut down, there is no chance of having another forest like that in that place for 8 centuries. Any profit made from cutting those trees is insignificant compared to the loss of that climax forest.

We can't make decisions like that unless we know what we are dealing with. Understanding nature is an important first step.

POPULATED AREAS OF THE U.S.A.

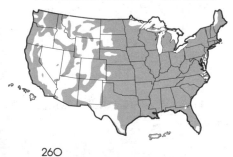

MAMMALS
1 Chipmunk
2 Cottontail rabbit
3 Raccoon
4 Gray squirrel

BIRDS
5 Blue jay
6 Common flicker
7 Mourning dove
8 American robin
9 Downy woodpecker

REPTILE
10 Box turtle

AMPHIBIANS
11 Bullfrog
12 American toad

ANNELID
13 Earthworm

INSECTS
14 Dragonfly
15 Monarch butterfly

ECOSYSTEMS

A *population* is a group of the same animal or plant species living together. A *community* is all the populations of plants and animals in an area. An *ecosystem* is made up of those communities and the physical surroundings — the land, weather, water, sunlight, and everything else that affects them.

No two ecosystems are alike. However, many share general similarities based on their locations, elevations, and other factors. Those similarities help us to compare one area with another and to make sense out of what we are seeing.

Lawns and Gardens

Many people work hard to have neat lawns around their homes or in nearby parks. Some yards look like smooth green carpets broken only by shade trees, shrubs, and flower beds. To keep your family's lawn in shape, you may help mow the grass, dig up weeds, run water sprinklers, and spread fertilizer. Each of these actions is necessary to maintain the appearance of the lawn. Each also alters the habitat in which many plants and animals struggle to live.

Living things must be able to adapt to their environment or they will not survive. For instance, grass that is kept short leaves larger animals nowhere to hide, and so the animals that live on lawns are

TREES AND SHRUBS	PLANTS
16 Scotch pine	27 Cattail
17 Cedar	28 Pond lily
18 Hemlock	
19 Blue spruce	
20 Dogwood	
21 Gray birch	
22 Lilac	
23 Sycamore	
24 White oak	
25 Blueberry	
26 Blackberry	

MAIN BIG-CITY AREAS OF THE U.S.A.

MAMMALS
1 Gray squirrel
2 Red squirrel

BIRDS
3 House finch
4 Chimney swift
5 House sparrow
6 Herring gull
7 Common nighthawk
8 European starling
9 Blue jay
10 American robin
11 Pigeon

INSECTS
12 Clothes moth
13 Mosquito

TREES
14 Ailanthus
15 Silver maple
16 Locust
17 Sycamore
18 Mulberry
19 Cedar

CHAPTER 13

small—squirrels, rabbits, songbirds, and garter snakes. Peer into the grass and you will see beetles, earthworms, ants, spiders, and plenty of other animals. Look for more small animals on the bark of trees and the leaves of bushes and flowers.

But there are changes occurring in lawns and in all ecosystems that have nothing to do with the efforts of humans. Ignore a lawn for a year and it will become covered with tall weeds and brush that grew from seeds carried by birds and the wind. Leave that lawn alone for a hundred years and it may become a towering forest or a prairie that is home to many kinds of plants and animals.

The slow, constant process of succession is at work everywhere on the face of the earth. To see it—and to see how man can alter the environment—you need go no farther than your own yard.

Towns and Cities

Office buildings, shopping centers, and city streets may not seem very inviting habitats for animals and plants, but open your eyes and you will find life everywhere. Grasses push up through cracks in the sidewalk and along the edges of buildings. Pigeons and sparrows make their nests on rooftops and ledges, and prowl the pavement in search of food. Lawns, parks, streets lined with trees, and even window boxes full of flowers add diversity to the mix of plants and animals.

You will also see lots of people in our towns and cities—thousands and perhaps even millions of us. In fact, an urban area is an ecosystem dominated by humans. Like all animals,

PLANTS
20 Grass
21 Red-tipped photenia
22 Burford holly

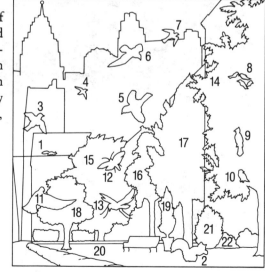

MAIN PRAIRIE AREAS OF THE U.S.A.

264

FIELDS

MAMMALS
1 Red fox
2 Cottontail
3 Striped skunk
4 Meadow vole

BIRDS
5 Red-tailed hawk
6 Barn swallow
7 Ring-necked pheasant
8 Common bobwhite
9 American crow
10 Eastern bluebird
11 Meadowlark
12 Lark sparrow

REPTILES AND AMPHIBIANS
13 Leopard frog
14 Garter snake

TREES AND SHRUBS
15 Cottonwood
16 Walnut
17 Pin cherry
18 Sumac
19 Apple
20 Multiflora rose
21 Blackberry

PLANTS
22 Wheat
23 Corn
24 Lichen
25 Pasture (grasses)

we must eat, and so we have developed ways of gathering our food from distant farms, oceans, and rivers and then moving it to our neighborhood grocery stores. Without fresh water piped in from wells and reservoirs, our cities would shut down.

What we do in our cities and towns has an impact on ecosystems many miles away. There are holes in the ground where iron and stone were dug up to make our buildings. Dams have changed wild rivers into still lakes that provide some of our electrical power. Trees are cut down so we can have newspapers and cardboard boxes. Exhaust from our factories and cars falls as acid rain on distant woodlands and waters. The tons of trash we do not recycle must be buried in landfills or dumped in the ocean.

Towns and cities are remarkable human inventions. Much that happens in them is wonderful. But all of us must realize that what we do in an urban area can affect ecosystems far away. That understanding will help us make wise decisions about using resources and caring for the earth both within and beyond our city limits.

Fields and Prairies

You won't be far out of town before you see farms, fields, or prairie. In the East, many of these open areas were once great forests. Colonists felled the trees for lumber and sowed crops in the new fields.

Pioneers moving farther west found a vast prairie covering the center of the continent. Long-stemmed grasses moved like waves in the wind. Herds of bison darkened the plains, their hooves thundering against the earth.

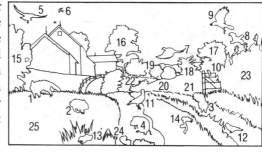

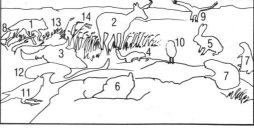

PRAIRIES

MAMMALS
1 Coyote
2 Pronghorn antelope
3 Bison skull
4 13-lined ground squirrel
5 Jackrabbit
6 Badger
7 Prarie dog

BIRDS
8 Lark bunting
9 Prairie falcon
10 Burrowing owl
11 Horned lark

REPTILES
12 Prarie rattlesnake

PLANTS
13 Sagebrush
14 Grama-grass

265

MAIN STREAMS AND LAKES OF THE U.S.A.

MAMMALS
1 Beaver
2 Raccoon

BIRDS
3 Tree swallow
4 Osprey
5 Belted kingfisher
6 Canada goose
7 Common loon

REPTILES
8 Ribbon snake
9 Painted turtle

AMPHIBIANS
10 Spotted newt
11 Bullfrog

FISH
12 Trout
13 Pickerel
14 Crappie
15 Black bullhead
16 Yellow perch
17 Pumpkinseed
18 Largemouth bass

CHAPTER 13

Early settlers, "sod busters," used their plows to break open the dense top-soil of the prairie. They planted corn, soybeans, hay, and other crops. They fenced their land and brought in cattle, sheep, and hogs. Today the farms and ranches of the Great Plains produce food for the nation and the world.

The original prairie ecosystem has all but disappeared. Still, there is much for you to see. Deer and foxes find shelter in stands of timber along creeks. Hawks ride the rising air, their sharp eyes scanning the thick grasses along fence rows where pheasants, rabbits, and mice make their homes. Coyotes and antelope range the open spaces of the western prairie.

As producers of food, prairies and fields are vital to the well-being of the nation. The plains represent an ecosystem that has undergone dramatic changes in a relatively short time.

Lakes and Streams

America's lakes and streams act as arteries carrying life-giving water through the land. Where water flows, vegetation and wildlife usually abound.

The beds of many large lakes in the northern states were scooped out by glaciers millions of years ago. Rivers carrying water from rain, snowmelt, and springs have cut their own channels across the landscape. The Grand Canyon, over a mile deep, is still being carved by the Colorado River.

In dry regions of the western United States, the importance of water is especially clear. Banks along streams often develop into strips of lush life surrounded by almost barren countryside. Biologists refer to them as *riparian areas*.

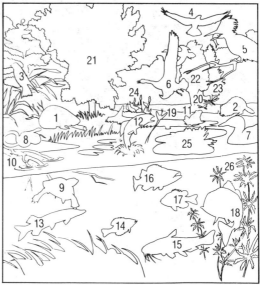

INSECTS
19 Mayfly
20 Dragonfly

TREES AND SHRUBS
21 Cottonwood
22 Alder
23 Tamarack

PLANTS
24 Pickerelweed
25 Pond lilies
26 Hornwort

MAIN WETLAND AREAS OF THE U.S.A.

268

MAMMALS
1 Muskrat
2 Mink

BIRDS
3 Mallard
4 Northern harrier
5 Great blue heron
6 Red-winged blackbird
7 Black-crowned night heron
8 American coot
9 Bank swallow
10 Sora
11 American bittern
12 Pied-billed grebe
13 Common pintail
14 Green heron
15 King rail

REPTILES
16 Water snake
17 Cottonmouth
18 Snapping turtle
19 Painted turtle

AMPHIBIANS
20 Leopard frog
21 Bullfrog
22 Spring peeper

INSECTS
23 Damselfly
24 Dragonfly

Like all ecosystems, streams and lakes are very complex. Much of an area's living matter is underground in the form of roots, burrowing animals, and the eggs and larvae of insects. Small crustaceans and mites live in the mud beneath the water, too, feeding on insects and decomposed plants.

Light and dark reveal more complexity. Many animals that are active during the day seek shelter as the sun goes down. In the cool of the night, animals from miles away use the darkness to protect them as they come close to the water to drink and to hunt.

Each season by a stream gives you a different view of nature, too. Spring snowmelt may send water thundering down a streambed. Snails and flat beetles are shaped so the water flows over them rather than washing them downstream. Some fish use their sucker mouths to hold fast to boulders. Insects hatching in quiet pools provide food for fish, frogs, and birds.

Summer heat and drought may lower the levels of streams and lakes. Autumn leaves falling in the water sink to the bottom and decay, creating a food source for the next year's smallest creatures. Winter weather locks bodies of water in ice and snow. Many animals hibernate until spring while others remain active, using trees and brush for shelter. They are reminders that even in the cold silence of January, the intricate cycles of an ecosystem continue.

Wetlands

Wetlands form when a stream slows and floods flat land, or when a lake gradually fills with vegetation. The shorelines of rivers like the lower Mississippi can hold enough water to be considered wetlands, too.

TREES AND SHRUBS
25 Red maple
26 Poison sumac
27 Pussy willow
28 Black willow

PLANTS
29 Cattails
30 Arrowhead

31 Reeds
32 Spatterdock
33 Sedges
34 Rushes
35 Wild rice
36 Wild celery
37 Sundew
38 Pitcher plant

MAIN DESERT AREAS OF THE U.S.A.

MAMMALS
1 Peccary
2 Spotted skunk
3 Kit fox
4 Yuma antelope squirrel
5 Black-tailed jackrabbit
6 Kangaroo rat

BIRDS
7 Gila woodpecker
8 Red-tailed hawk
9 Turkey vulture
10 White-winged dove
11 Elf owl
12 Road-runner

13 Gambel's quail
14 Cactus wren

REPTILES
15 Diamondback rattlesnake
16 Desert tortoise
17 Collared lizard
18 Gila monster
19 Sidewinder
20 Zebra-tailed lizard
21 Garter snake
22 Horned toad

Wetlands like those in the southeastern United States are called *swamps* because they support trees. The *marshes* of the upper Midwest are predominantly grass-covered.

A wetland is an in-between stage in the natural succession of an area. It is no longer a body of water, but it's not yet solid land, either. That makes it an ideal home for all sorts of plants and wild animals. When it comes to numbers of animals and plants, wetlands are among the bountiful regions in America.

The water and mud of the wetlands are home to insects and other tiny animals that feed on plants. Turtles, salamanders, and frogs feast on those smaller creatures, and so do many fish and dozens of kinds of birds. Raccoons, otters, muskrats, and other swimming mammals find shelter and plenty to eat in the heavy vegetation. Immense flocks of ducks and geese use wetlands as rest stops and nesting areas.

Wetlands also serve as huge filters purifying the water that flows through them, and they limit the damage caused by floods. Yet for all the natural values of wetlands, they are rapidly disappearing. Many thousands of acres of marsh and swamp are drained each year to make dry land for fields and buildings. Once the water goes, so do the plants, the wildlife, and the diversity of an entire ecosystem. We have the power to alter our environment, but we must remain aware that using that power may have a high price.

If there are wetlands near your home, visit them. Your feet may get wet and you may need a rowboat or a canoe, but go. You won't be disappointed.

Deserts

Four magnificent deserts cover much of the western United States. The deserts of the Great Basin and northern New Mexico are "cold"— they sometimes

DESERT CREATURES
23 Centipede
24 Tarantula
25 Scorpion

TREES AND PLANTS
26 Saguaro cactus
27 Palo verde
28 Cholla cactus
29 Yucca
30 Barrel cactus
31 Ocotillo
32 Creosote bush
33 Mesquite
34 Staghorn cholla cactus
35 Prickly pear cactus
36 Beaver tail cactus

MAIN SEASHORE AREAS OF THE U.S.A.

MAMMALS
1 Porpoise
2 Deer mouse

BIRDS
3 Herring gull
4 Bald eagle
5 Common tern
6 Sandpiper

FISH
7 Skate egg case
8 Common mackerel
9 Bluefish
10 Porgy
11 Sand shark
12 Flounder

SEA CREATURES
13 Horseshoe crab
14 Left-handed whelk
15 Razor clam
16 Common starfish
17 Sand shrimp
18 Ghost crab
19 Scallop shell
20 Moon shell
21 Sand dollar
22 Fiddler crab
23 Hermit crab
24 Portuguese man-of-war

experience freezing weather. Farther south, the Sonoran and Chihuahua deserts are "warm."

Some regions of the deserts are the flat, sandy remains of ancient sea beds. Other areas are mountainous or cut by deep canyons. Wind and water have shaped towering sandstone fins and pillars of stark beauty.

All deserts are dry most of the year, forcing plants and animals to find special ways to survive. Some plants produce seeds that can lie in the soil for months or even years. When rain does moisten them, they sprout and burst into bloom. In as little as 6 weeks, they produce a new crop of seeds that will lie waiting for the next rain.

Cacti are succulent desert plants that rapidly absorb rainwater and store it in fleshy leaves, stems, and roots. Tough, waxy skins prevent water from escaping by evaporation. A cactus can draw on its stored water through months of dry weather.

Some desert animals endure drought by lying in burrows or burying themselves in the soil until clouds bring rain. Others obtain water from diets of insects, other animals, and juicy plants.

Desert treks may be among your most exciting Scout adventures. From the lives of tiny plants and animals to the grandeur of vast geological formations, you will find the desert a magical part of the outdoors.

Seashores

A seashore is a boundary between two environments—the land and the sea. The vegetation and wildlife of seashores are greatly affected by temperatures, tide, wind, and the

SEA CREATURES (continued)	PLANTS
25 Soft-shell clam	36 Rockweed
26 Mole crab	37 Kelp
27 Sea anemone	38 Sea lettuce
28 Limpets	39 Blue-green algae
29 Common mussels	
30 Sea urchin	
31 Oyster drill	
32 Oyster	
33 Rock barnacle	
34 Blue crab	
35 Periwinkle	

MAIN BROADLEAF AREAS OF THE U.S.A.

274

MAMMALS
1 Gray squirrel
2 White-tailed deer
3 Raccoon
4 Long-tailed weasel
5 Eastern chipmunk
6 White-footed mouse
7 Shrew

BIRDS
8 Red-eyed vireo
9 Blue jay
10 Common screech owl
11 Cooper's hawk
12 Scarlet tanager

13 Black-capped chickadee
14 Hairy woodpecker
15 Wood thrush
16 Ruffed grouse
17 Ovenbird

REPTILES
18 King snake
19 Box turtle
20 Ringneck snake

salty spray. Along a rocky coast you might walk through groves of storm-twisted pines. On sandy shores you might reach the water's edge through dunes held in place by beach grass.

The signs of life are everywhere. Damp sand holds tracks of crabs and of long-legged birds in search of food. Gulls and terns glide on long, pointed wings, watching the water and land for a meal. Seashells scattered along the beach once sheltered mussels, oysters, and other crustaceans. Hermit crabs crawl into empty shells and use them as their own homes.

Rising tides wash ashore jellyfish, seaweed, starfish, sand dollars, and other ocean dwellers. Waves also clean shorelines, carrying nutrients into the sea where aquatic animals and vegetation can use them.

Trapped behind sandbars and in depressions in rocks, seawater may form tidal pools. Snails, crabs, periwinkles, rockweed, and barnacles in each pool develop a small ecosystem of their own.

Visit seashores often and you will see many changes throughout the seasons. But even if you go only once, you'll find the shoreline is a magnificent, complex environment full of natural mysteries and surprises.

Forests

Broadleaf forests dominate the eastern United States, while conifer forests cover much of the West. Those great stands of trees shield the earth from the full force of wind, rain, and sunlight. They slow erosion, act as watersheds, and provide havens for animals. Photosynthesis, the process by which trees produce food, freshens the air.

AMPHIBIANS
21 Wood frog
22 Red eft

TREES AND SHRUBS
23 Sassafras
24 Gray birch
25 White ash
26 Dogwood
27 White pine
28 White oak
29 Spicebush
30 American beech
31 Viburnum
32 Shagbark hickory
33 Sugar maple
34 Rhododendron

PLANTS
35 Ferns

MAIN EVERGREEN WOODLAND AREAS OF THE U.S.A.

MAMMALS
1 Abert squirrel
2 Elk
3 Mule deer
4 Bobcat
5 Red squirrel
6 Fisher
7 Porcupine
8 Black bear
  (brown phase)

BIRDS
9 Northern goshawk
10 Golden eagle
11 Great horned owl
12 Steller's jay
13 Western tanager
14 Clark's nutcracker
15 Oregon junco

From the highest branches to the deepest roots, a forest forms a belt of life several hundred feet thick. That belt contains hundreds of species of plants and animals. If drought, disease, or disaster wipe out most of one kind of plant or animal, others that are similar to it will soon take its place. As a result, changes in a forest tend to be gradual, and that creates stability throughout the environment.

Forests are important sources of raw materials. Lumber for houses, pulp for paper, and many other products come from the harvest of trees. Managed wisely, many forests produce timber as a renewable resource that can be harvested with minimal environmental damage. On the other hand, thoughtless cutting of entire forests has left some areas without shelter for wildlife or erosion control for the land.

Recreation is another vital use of forests. As more people live in cities, the need to escape to an unspoiled environment becomes increasingly important. Hiking trails, campgrounds, and open country are natural resources every bit as important as raw materials that can be harvested.

Much of America's forested land is in national and state forests and parks and other public holdings. As an American citizen, you share ownership of that land. Practicing low-impact and no-trace methods of camping and hiking allows you to use forests responsibly. Through elected representatives and agency officials, you can help decide how public lands will be used. Learn all you can about nature, spend time outdoors, and be prepared to act in the best interests of your environment.

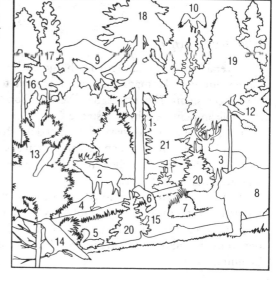

TREES
16 Lodgepole pine
17 Ponderosa pine
18 Douglas-fir
19 Quaking aspen
20 Englemann spruce
21 White fir

Wilderness Areas

Several hundred years ago, nearly the entire North American continent was a wilderness. Humans had done very little to affect the natural balance of vast ecosystems. The remarkable diversity of plants and animals helped keep the environment healthy and stable.

Over the centuries, we have transformed much of that wilderness into cities and fields. The numbers of animal and plant species has dwindled. The true wilderness that once stretched from the Atlantic to the Pacific has shrunk to a limited number of areas.

In 1977, Congress established the National Wilderness Preservation System to protect some of the remaining unspoiled wilderness. To be considered wilderness, an area had to be at least 5,000 acres in size. No public roads could penetrate it, and it could have no significant ecological disturbances caused by human activity.

The intent of Congress was that people would be able to see and enjoy land as wild and unchanged as though no humans had ever visited it. To that end, motorized machinery, resource harvesting (except some hunting and fishing), and developments are prohibited. Activities that are allowed in wilderness areas include primitive camping, hiking, horseback riding, mountaineering, snowshoeing, and cross-country skiing.

When you visit a wilderness area, you are entering a land that is still in its most natural condition. Go to the wilderness only when you are ready to open yourself to the magnificence of unspoiled territory. Practice no-trace methods of camping and hiking so that you can help preserve the wilderness for the enjoyment of generations to come.

OBSERVING NATURE

N ATIVE Americans have a long heritage of being good observers of nature. Over the centuries, their lives have often depended upon their skills in tracking animals, reading the weather, and finding their way through forests and plains. From early childhood, they learned the ways of the environment in which they lived. Their eyes became accustomed to seeing the shapes of animals hiding in the wild. They noticed prints left by animals — a bent blade of grass, an overturned stone, a scuff of soil. Their ears picked up faint, far-off sounds, and they could sometimes smell concealed prey.

They could also make sense out of the information they gathered. Sounds, aromas, and sights meant as much to them as telephones, radios, and televisions mean to us. By observing nature, they knew what was going on around them, where they could find food, and when they should seek shelter.

Today, most of us can travel through our hometowns without much thought. We know where to find food, how to stay safe, and when to take cover from storms. Our senses are highly developed toward life in cities and towns.

In the previous chapter, you discovered that nature is all around us. But to actually *see* it and make sense of it, you may need to learn new skills. In a way, it's like learning a foreign language — the language of the woods, the prairies, the forests, and the peaks. It's a new way of using all of your senses.

Looking. Hawks can see small movement from great heights. Owls see well enough in the dark to fly among the branches of trees. Human eyes are not as sharp as those of hawks and owls, but ours are very good compared to the eyes of many animals. With binoculars and magnifying glasses we can make them even better.

However, most of us aren't very good at using our eyes to see nature. To do that, you have to slow down and give your eyes time to notice things. Let them roam over familiar outdoor areas. Instead of seeing an entire lawn, look at individual plants. Rather than glancing at a forest, study one tree. Watch the motion of the clouds. Be alert to movement in the brush.

Most of us rely on our eyesight for information about what's going on around us. But you do have other senses, and you can use them to observe nature, too. Sometime when you are outdoors, blindfold yourself with a bandanna. Sit quietly against a tree for a half hour or more. At first you may have an uneasy feeling of being lost, but slowly your brain will begin to rely on your other senses. First among those is hearing.

Listening. The outdoors is awash with sounds. The buzz of cicadas and the croak of bullfrogs are mating calls. Birds use their songs to mark off their territory. The whistle of a marmot and sharp cry of a squirrel are warnings of danger. There are sounds humans can't hear, like the sonic echoes of bats in flight. Sometimes it's the absence of sound that is important. When birds suddenly stop singing, it may be because a cat is prowling nearby.

Sound is so important that many animals have developed very keen hearing. The ears of a deer are shaped like big scoops that the animal can easily turn to pick up faraway sounds. You can increase your own hearing by cupping your hands behind your ears. Turning your head from side to side may help you pinpoint the location of a sound.

Smelling. You may have heard stories about bloodhounds that found lost persons by following their scent. Tracking dogs can sniff a piece of a person's clothing and then follow the scent of his footsteps for long distances.

The noses of many animals are very sensitive. Unlike most eyes, noses work just as well in the dark as at high noon. Ants lay down scent trails to find their way back to their nests. Wolves sniff the wind for signs of prey. Deer are startled by the smells of predators nearing them. Mountain lions mark their domain with the scent of their urine. Many animals are attracted to their mates by their odor.

Humans are aware of the natural aromas of flowers, trees, earth, and moss. Stagnant water smells different from a fresh stream. The stench of an animal carcass can lead you to its location. In general, though, our ability to smell is limited because we seldom rely on it.

Foxes improve their sense of smell by licking their noses. You can increase your own sensitivity to aromas by moistening your upper lip with a little water. Then pay attention to outdoor smells. They are valuable clues as to what's going on around you.

Touch. A snake flicking out its tongue is picking up vibrations in the air. Brook trout have nerves running down their bodies to alert them to changes in the water. With whiskers or feelers, some animals rely on touch more than any of the other senses. Even those with keen eyesight or finely tuned noses are aware of the feel of the world around them.

While you can't sense the faint vibrations felt by snakes and fish, you can use touch to better understand nature. Feel the texture of leaves; some are rough, others smooth. Weigh stones in your hand. Wade in ponds. Crawl through tall grass. Roll in the snow. Touch plants and animals, and let them touch you. Run through the woods like a deer. Slither along the ground like a snake. Swim along the bottom of a lake like a fish. Imagine what it would be like to live as different animals and plants.

OBSERVING NATURE

SEEING ANIMALS

Drop a pebble into a pool of water and watch how the ripples run out in circles, one outside the next. A skilled observer's line of sight is similar to those rings of ripples. First, scan the area a few feet to the front and sides of you. Sweep your eyes along, taking in the whole scene rather than focusing on just a few highlights.

Then sweep your eyes to take in the next line of "ripples"—an arc about 20 feet away. Look out a little farther and make a third sweep. With practice, you can scan a wide area very quickly. Animals, interesting plants, tracks, and other signs of wildlife will seem to pop out of the background. You'll also have a sense of the area as a whole, rather than seeing just one or two things within it. Sweeping with your eyes helps you look beyond the obvious and see those plants and animals that may be trying to escape your gaze.

TRACKING

Following the tracks of an animal can teach you much about what it eats, where it sleeps, and its daily habits. Your tracking skill may lead you right to the animal itself.

Tracking is not limited to following mammals. Insects leave tracks, too. So do reptiles. You can spend an hour of careful tracking and not move more than a few feet. In fact, if you can track a beetle through the jungles of a grassy lawn, you probably have the skill to track larger animals across any terrain.

Tracking is a skill that you can learn only by doing a lot of it. You can learn in your own yard, vacant lots, fields, and forests. The following guidelines will help you get started:

☆ You must find some tracks before you can follow them. Winter snows hold a surprising number of tracks. During other seasons, try the soft soil near ponds and streams. In dry country, scan the dust for prints and look for pebbles and rocks that have been disturbed.

☆ Study a single track. Get down on your hands and knees to study the shape of the track you wish to follow. Fix its details in your mind. You might even measure it and make a sketch of it. That will help you find it later, even when other tracks are mixed in with it.

☆ Track early or late. Tracking is easiest early in the morning and late in the day, when shadows cast in the prints make them more obvious.

☆ Look for more than just the prints. As you follow a trail of tracks, keep your eyes peeled for other evidence of the animal. Bent grass, broken twigs, and displaced pebbles help you see the animal's path. Watch for places where the animal has scratched or rubbed against trees or rocks.

Droppings, or *scat,* give evidence of an animal's diet. Break scat apart with a stick. Hulls of seeds, skins of berries, and bits of leaves suggest the animal is a vegetarian. Small bones, fur, and feathers appear in the scat of meat eaters.

Scat tends to dry from the outside in. If it is completely dry, you know the animal passed by some time ago. Moist scat was left more recently. The animal may be near.

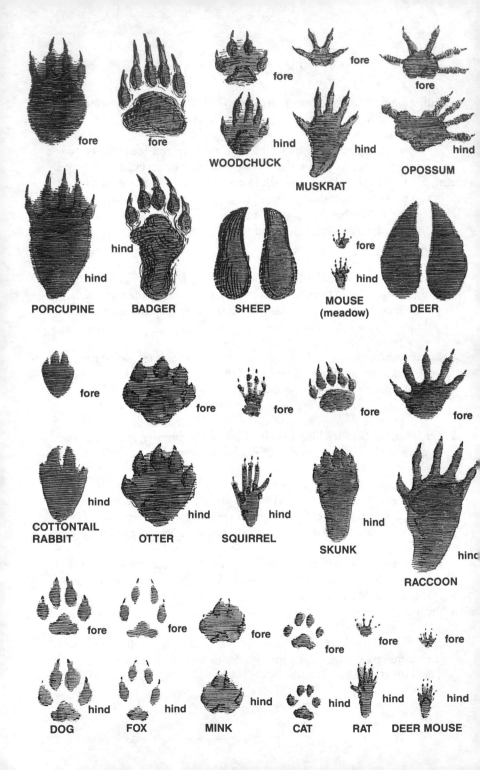

fore

fore

WOODCHUCK
fore
hind

fore
MUSKRAT
hind

OPOSSUM
fore
hind

PORCUPINE
hind

BADGER
hind

SHEEP

MOUSE
(meadow)
fore
hind

DEER

COTTONTAIL
RABBIT
fore
hind

OTTER
fore
hind

SQUIRREL
fore
hind

SKUNK
fore
hind

RACCOON
fore
hind

DOG
fore
hind

FOX
fore
hind

MINK
fore
hind

CAT
fore
hind

RAT
fore
hind

DEER MOUSE
fore
hind

☆ Imagine yourself in the place of the animal. If you lose the trail, ask yourself where you would go if you were the animal. Look in that direction. Mark the last track with a stick, then explore all around it until you find the trail again.

☆ Notice important landmarks as you proceed. Don't become so interested in following a trail that you get lost. Be alert to your surroundings. Notice and remember landmarks that will guide you back to your starting point.

☆ Don't disturb human artifacts. Over the centuries, humans have left traces of their passing. You may be fortunate enough to discover an arrowhead, broken pottery, or other artifacts of earlier cultures.

If so, let them lie where you find them. Note the location very well and draw a map so you can find the spot again. Then alert local authorities. They will know if archaeologists should examine the site. The position in which artifacts are found can tell scientists a great deal about the people who made and used them. That's why it is important not to disturb them.

Collecting Tracks

Perhaps you've heard the old saying about low-impact hiking: "Take only photographs, leave only footprints." By making plaster casts, you can bring home some footprints, too.

When you find a track you want to preserve, mix up some plaster of paris. (You can get the plaster at a drugstore. The label will have mixing instructions.) Turn a cardboard strip into a collar by notching the ends together. Place the collar around the track and pour in the mix. Let it harden — 10 to 15 minutes in warm weather. Remove it and brush off the dirt. On the back of the cast, write the date and the location where you found the track.

You can also cast plaster molds of tracks in the snow. In addition to plaster of paris, you'll need a mist bottle such as those used with window cleaner. Spray the track with a fine mist of water and wait a few moments while it freezes. Mix the plaster using cold water (warm plaster will melt the print). Put a collar around the track and pour in plaster. Allow it time to harden.

By themselves, casts of prints are fine souvenirs of your adventures. You can also press them into damp sand to recreate the original prints — a valuable study aid for improving the tracking skills of everyone in your patrol.

STALKING ANIMALS

When you have animals in sight, stalking them lets you get closer. It allows you to observe their habits, watch where they go, and see what they do.

Stalking is also a fine mental exercise. To do it well, you must be very patient. You need to control your body so that you move smoothly and quietly. All your senses will be heightened as you concentrate on moving near a wild animal. Whenever you are stalking, think of yourself as a shadow. Become so much a part of your surroundings that you seem to disappear.

Stalking by waiting. The easiest way to get close to wild animals is to let them come to you. Many animals are quite regular in their habits. Sit near well-worn animal tracks, and there is a good chance you'll see them coming by. Hide in the brush, bury yourself in leaves, or float among the water lilies in a pond. Climb into a tree and wait to see what animals pass below you. Crouch behind a wall of snow.

Many animals are active at night. Under a full moon, you are likely to see wildlife activity if you hide quietly at the edge of a meadow or near a lake or pond. As with all stalking, patience is absolutely essential.

Stalk against the wind. Many animals can smell you from long distances, especially if your scent is carried toward them by the wind. Try to keep downwind (with the wind blowing toward you) as you stalk toward an animal. If you come upon an animal from the upwind side, you may be able to make a wide half circle around it until the wind is in your face.

CHAPTER 14

Move slowly and carefully. Animals will be startled if you make jerky motions or walk noisily through leaves and twigs. Move with care. When an animal looks in your direction, freeze. Don't move a muscle until it turns its attention elsewhere.

Make use of anything that will hide you. Hide behind trees, stumps, and rocks. Stay near the ground and watch from around the sides of your cover, not over the top. Your shape shows up sharply against the sky, so keep low as you cross ridges.

Fun with Tracking and Stalking

You can practice tracking and stalking just about anywhere. At home, try sneaking up on the family dog, the cat, and your brothers and sisters. In camp, sit very quietly near a trail and see how many Scouts pass by without noticing you.

Would you like to play some tracking and stalking games with your patrol? Here are several that have been popular with Scouts for many years:

Cross-Country Runner. The Scout who is the runner has a 1-minute head start. Every few steps he drops a few kernels of corn. The others in the patrol follow the kernel trail and try to catch up with the runner before he reaches a finish line about a mile away.

Sleeping Pirate. A blindfolded "pirate" sits on a log with his "treasure" (a bandanna) at his feet. The other Scouts form a large circle around him, each Scout about a hundred feet away. They try to stalk up to the pirate, take the treasure, and get away without being heard. If the pirate hears someone, he claps his hands and points. That Scout is out of the game. Whoever successfully takes the treasure becomes the next pirate.

Deer Stalking. The "deer" (a Scout) stands in a forest or field. The other patrol members walk away from him several hundred feet in different directions. On a signal, they begin stalking toward the deer, using whatever cover is available. If the deer sees a Scout, he points and yells to him to stand. The Scout who comes the closest without being noticed is the next deer.

Wary Wolf. One Scout is the "wary wolf." The others stand in a line 200 feet from him. Whenever the wolf turns his back, they stalk toward him. Whenever he turns toward them, everyone freezes. Any Scout making the slightest movement must go back to the starting line and begin again. The first Scout to touch the wolf takes his place for the next game.

Of course, the best fun of all for a tracker and stalker is following and observing wild animals in their own surroundings. You'll have plenty of chances to do that on patrol and troop hikes and campouts.

NORTH AMERICAN ANIMALS

Mammals

What do a field mouse and a grizzly bear have in common? For one thing, they are both *mammals*. That's a word used to describe animals that have mammary glands for feeding their young. All mammals, including humans, also have backbones. Their bodies are usually covered with fur or hair. Mammals are warm-blooded, which means they maintain the same body temperature in both cold and hot weather.

You're sure to see many mammals on your Scout adventures. Take time to watch them closely. Try to figure out what they are eating, how they find shelter, and the ways they defend themselves. That little field mouse, for instance, scurries among the grasses in search of insects and seeds. When startled, it relies on speed to carry it to a safe hiding place.

Rabbits also use bursts of speed to escape predators. Powered by muscular hind legs, they scamper away from danger in a zigzag course that larger animals cannot easily follow. Rabbits and mice use their smaller front legs to hold the grasses on which they feed.

Perhaps you have seen squirrels near your campsite. Their long tails give them balance as they run along branches. Sharp claws allow them to grip the bark of trees. Like chipmunks, they fill their cheeks with nuts and grains. Sometimes they store food in holes in trees or in the ground, returning to eat it when food sources are scarce.

mole

chipmunk

flying squirrel

squirrel

rabbit

shrew

meadow
mouse

white-footed
field mouse

The opossum does not have the speed of a rabbit. Instead of fleeing, it goes limp when threatened and lies very still until danger has passed. The opossum is a close relative of the kangaroos of Australia. Both are *marsupials,* or pouched mammals. A mother opossum carries her newborn babies in a pouch formed by a fold of skin on her abdomen.

Although slow, the porcupine has little to fear. When crowded too closely, it uses a quick slap of its tail to drive sharp quills into the flesh of an attacker. In the North Country, you may have a porcupine waddle into your camp eager to chew on boots or pack straps that are salty with sweat.

Skunks can spray an attacker with a chemical that stings the eyes and leaves a foul, long-lasting odor. Close relatives of weasels, skunks feed on insects, reptiles, eggs, and small rodents.

As you hike along a stream, you may notice the stumps of trees cut by beavers. They eat the bark of smaller branches and use the wood for improving their dams. The pond formed behind a dam gives beavers quiet water in which

opossum

skunk

beaver

porcupine

woodchuck

CHAPTER 14

mink

muskrat

weasel

otter

raccoon

to swim and feed. Look in the pond for a large, dome-shaped lodge that is the beavers' home. If a beaver becomes startled, it will warn the others by whacking its tail on the water.

Beaver dams sometimes play a role in the natural succession of an area. Slowed by the dam, a stream may drop its silt. Eventually the beaver pond fills and becomes dry land where grasses and trees can take root.

Ponds are also home to muskrats, but you may see little more of one than its nose parting the surface of the water. Muskrats build lodges out of sticks just as beavers do. The entrances are beneath the water so that the animals can slip in and out unseen. Muskrats feed on tender stems of aquatic plants.

Otters dig burrows in the banks of lakes and streams. Strong, sleek swimmers, they prey on fish. You may come upon an "otter slide" where otters have been tobogganing on their bellies down stream banks into the water. Otters were once found throughout much of America. However, they were hunted so much for their fine fur that they are now rarely seen.

In the damp soil along a stream, you might find tracks that look like small hands with five long fingers. Those are the marks of a raccoon. A night traveler, it comes to the water for frogs and crayfish. Raccoons are expert climbers that often live in hollow trees.

In more remote forests you may come upon the tracks of a black bear. Bears eat a wide range of food including berries, grubs, fish, and other small animals. Wild bears are usually shy. They try to avoid people. However, a bear that gets easy meals from campsites and garbage cans may lose its fear of humans. If it endangers campers, the bear may have to be destroyed. Help prevent that from happening by keeping your campsites very clean. At night, hang your food from a high branch of a tree.

Grizzly bears grow to be much bigger than black bears. Each of these bears must have a large territory in which to roam and feed. Grizzlies once ranged throughout the western states, but their population has been severely reduced by hunters and by the rapid development of farms and cities. Most grizzly bears are now found in Yellowstone and Glacier national parks, and in Canada and Alaska.

grizzly

black bear

gray fox

red fox

CHAPTER 14

coyote

wolf

mountain lion

lynx

bobcat

The wolf also has been driven almost to extinction in much of the nation. Humans have long misunderstood and feared wolves, and have killed them with guns, traps, and poison. In fact, wolves were a key link in many food chains. Feeding on old and sickened deer, elk, and caribou, wolves helped keep the size of those herds under control. Today some land managers who recognize the importance of wolves are working to return them to some of our national parks.

Bobcats and mountain lions have also suffered from the actions of man. Each must have plenty of open space in which to thrive. Each is a tempting target for hunters. Their decreasing number is a loss for all of us and a grim reminder that what we do to animals may lead to the destruction of entire species.

mule deer

white-tailed
deer

black-tailed
deer

elk

moose

caribou

CHAPTER 14

You can see deer in almost every part of North America. As their names suggest, white-tailed deer and black-tailed deer can be identified by the distinctive coloration of their tails. The mule deer, a native of the foothills of the Rocky Mountains, has a white tail tipped with black.

Moose are the largest members of the deer family. Moose range through the northern forests of the United States and far into Canada. Like all deer, a moose is a *ruminant* — an animal with four stomachs for digesting grasses, leaves, and twigs.

Wapiti is the Indian name for the North American elk, another large deer. Great herds of elk live in Yellowstone National Park and other parts of the western states. Male elk grow antlers each year. They use them as weapons to fight off rival males. After mating season in the autumn, they shed their antlers. The same holds true for other deer, too.

Although deer can kick with their sharp hooves, most flee their enemies rather than trying to fight. In the deer family, the pronghorn antelope is one of the fastest animals of North America, sometimes reaching speeds of more than 40 miles an hour.

Mountain goats are close relatives of deer. They are surefooted enough to scale steep mountain cliffs where they have little to fear. Their shaggy white coats keep them warm and help them blend into snowy backgrounds. In warm weather, bighorn sheep also move into the high country to graze on summer grasses.

pronghorn

mountain
goat

bighorn

Birds

Observing birds is an exciting, satisfying part of outdoor adventures. Scan the trees as you hike, and take time to watch the birds that are part of your surroundings. Binoculars will help you make out small details. Use a bird identification book to learn the names of the birds you see and to read about their habits. Your patrol may even keep a notebook of all the birds you see on your outings.

Some Scouts can attract birds by whistling. With a duck or goose call like those used by hunters, you may bring waterfowl close. Another old stalking trick is to make a smacking sound by kissing the back of your hand. Birds that recognize that as a distress call may be drawn toward it.

As you observe birds, the six S's give you a quick way to gather clues that will lead to a bird's identification. Even if you aren't interested in finding out its name, the S's can solve some of the mysteries about a bird.

☆ *Size.* A hummingbird is just a few inches long and weighs only ounces. A turkey vulture weighs several pounds and has a wing span of 3 feet or more. When you see a bird, compare its size with those of birds you know. Is the new one larger than a house sparrow? About the same size as a robin? Smaller than a crow? Can you think of ways the size of a bird may affect its methods of gathering food, making its nests, and avoiding predators?

scarlet tanager

yellow warbler

American goldfinch

indigo bunting

blue jay

red-headed woodpecker

brown-headed cowbird

CHAPTER 14

red-winged
blackbird

prairie
warbler

northern
cardinal

Baltimore
oriole

American
robin

rufous-sided
towhee
(or chewink)

common
grackle

brown
thrasher

wood
thrush

☆ *Shape.* A bird's shape helps it thrive in a particular environment. For instance, the powerful talons of eagles and owls allow them to snag their prey and lift it into the sky. The long, skinny legs of the heron enable it to wade out into water where it can feed on small fish.

☆ *Shadings.* Bright feathers help many birds attract mates. For others, drab colors act as camouflage so that the birds can blend into their backgrounds. The ptarmigan is a good example. Its brown feathers hide it during summers in mountain forests. When winter comes, the ptarmigan's feathers become as white as the snow.

☆ *Song.* Birds use their songs to warn of danger, mark their territories, and find mates. Sometimes they sing for the sheer joy of making noise. When you know the songs of birds, you can identify them even without seeing them. A good way to learn bird songs is to hike with bird watchers who already know a few. They can teach you how the songs of each species differ from all others.

belted kingfisher

killdeer

common snipe

wood duck

blue-winged teal

mallard

American coot

☆ *Sweep.* Sweep refers to the movement a bird makes. Some hop across the ground or scurry along in a fast waddle. Others flit from tree to tree. Soaring birds catch updrafts of wind and hover for many minutes without flapping their wings. Some water birds dive into cold mountain streams. Close observation of the sweep of a bird may lead to the most interesting part of bird watching—seeing how each has adapted to its environment.

☆ *Surroundings.* From the Arctic to the equator, birds seem to be everywhere. Like all animals, a bird must learn to live in its habitat or it will die. It must find food, escape predators, mate, and raise its young. The first five S's (size, shape, shadings, song, and sweep) are ways that birds have adapted to S number six, their surroundings.

You can improve birds' surroundings by putting up birdhouses near your home. Bird feeders containing seed and suet are especially important in northern states when winter snows have covered the usual sources of food. The *Bird Study* merit badge pamphlet has building plans for birdhouses and feeding stations.

osprey

northern harrier

Cooper's hawk

peregrine falcon

red-tailed hawk

turkey vulture

swallow-tailed kite

common nighthawk

common tern

chimney swift

barn swallow

herring gull

Reptiles

Unlike mammals, reptiles are cold-blooded. Since they cannot generate heat to keep warm, their bodies are the same temperature as their surroundings. Many reptiles survive the winter by hibernating until warm spring weather revives them.

Reptiles have important roles in food chains as both predators and prey. Small reptiles make meals of snails, worms, insects, and grubs. Larger ones may also feast on rats, mice, and other rodents. In turn, reptiles are a part of the diets of many mammals, fish, and birds.

Reptiles and humans have had a stormy history. People have often looked more kindly upon furry or feathered animals than they have upon cold-blooded beasts with scales and fierce-looking faces. Where humans are concerned, though, reptiles are very beneficial. They help control populations of rodents and insects that could otherwise devastate farm crops.

Snakes

Snakes are very shy animals. They will do all they can to get out of your way. As you watch a snake slither along the ground, you may wonder how an animal without legs can move so well. The secret is in the way a snake makes S-shaped bends with its body. The snake goes forward by pushing those bends against twigs, pebbles, and bits of grit on the ground.

Several kinds of American snakes have hollow fangs through which they can inject venom into a victim or attacker. The rattlesnake may be the best-known of these reptiles. Its tail is equipped with dry, horny rattles that sound a warning whenever the snake is alarmed. Rattlesnakes are found in the continental United States, Mexico, and some parts of Canada.

The copperhead snake lives in woodlands and rocky outcroppings of the eastern half of the country. It has no rattles to announce its presence, but you can recognize it by its copper-brown color with an hourglass pattern of darker shade.

The cottonmouth, or water moccasin, lives in streams and marshes of southern states. A chunky, muddy-brown

rattlesnake

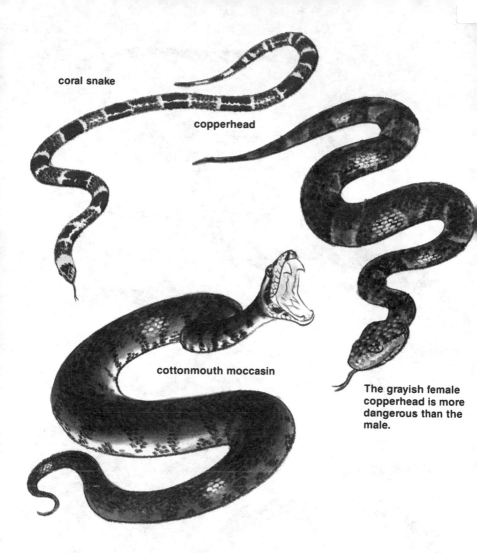

coral snake

copperhead

cottonmouth moccasin

The grayish female copperhead is more dangerous than the male.

snake, it may rest in low tree branches overhanging the water. Its name comes from the cotton-white color of the inside of its mouth.

Rattlesnakes, copperheads, and cottonmouths are all *pit vipers*. In addition to their long, thin fangs, they all have a distinctive pit beneath each eye.

The only poisonous American snake that is not a pit viper is the coral snake. It ranges from North Carolina south to Florida, and west into Texas. Small and slender, the coral snake has bands of bright yellow scales separating broader bands of black and red. Because it hunts at night, it is seldom seen.

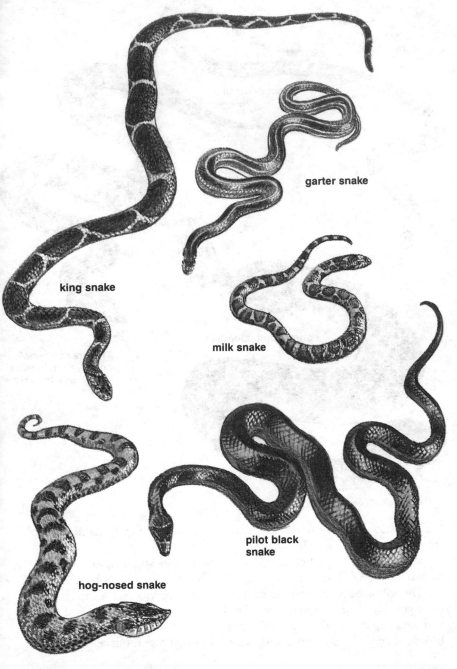

garter snake

king snake

milk snake

pilot black
snake

hog-nosed snake

Many nonpoisonous snakes have names that seem to fit their appearance. The worm snake is about the same size, shape, and color as an earthworm. The ring-necked snake is steel-gray with a yellow-to-orange ring around its neck.

Snakes such as the brown snake, red-bellied snake, and green snake take their names from their colors. Like all snakes, their jaws are hinged so that they can swallow prey larger than their heads.

The hog-nosed snake, or *puff adder,* is named both for the shape of its head and for its habit of puffing itself up when frightened. The common water snake takes its name from the ease with which it swims. It feeds on small fish and frogs.

Among the largest American snakes, the king snake eats rats, mice, and other snakes. The common king snake is black with white or yellow bands. The bright red, yellow, and black bands of the scarlet king snake make it look much like the poisonous coral snake.

The black racer of the eastern states has a smooth, black back. The brownish coach whip of the South and the striped whip snakes of the West are close relatives of the racer.

Bull snakes are the largest American nonpoisonous snakes. They are grayish brown with large patches on their backs. An eastern variety is often referred to as the pine snake while a western form is called the gopher snake.

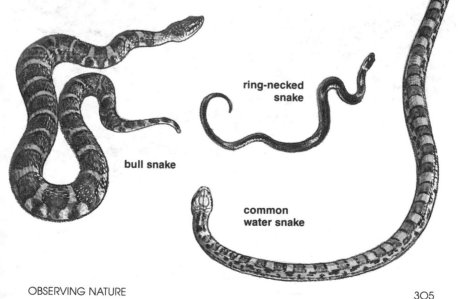

bull snake

ring-necked snake

common water snake

Lizards

Lizards are much like snakes. Among the most important differences are that lizards have legs, their eyelids move, and they have small ear openings on their heads.

Many lizards make their homes in arid regions. Perhaps the best known is the horned lizard. Its thick, rough skin protects it from its enemies and helps it conserve vital moisture. Collared lizards and swifts are also desert dwellers. Their speed and their long, slender tails set them apart from the fat, sluggish Gila monster. It is covered with black and pink warts that look like beadwork. The Gila monster is America's only poisonous lizard.

gila monster

horned toad

collared lizard

swift

snapping turtle

spotted turtle

wood turtle

painted turtle

box turtle

diamondback
terrapin

musk turtle

gopher tortoise

Turtles

The shells of turtles make them easy to recognize. Made of hard scales attached to a cagelike skeleton, the shell encloses a turtle's vital organs and provides some protection for its head, legs, and tail.

Some turtles spend most of their lives on dry land. Others dwell in ponds, streams, and marshes. A few thrive in the open sea.

Turtles have no teeth, but the edges of their jaws are tough enough for them to feed on insects, snails, and other small aquatic animals. The snapping turtle settles to the bottom of a pond and lies still with its mouth open. A wormlike appendage on the floor of its mouth lures fish close enough for the turtle to catch them.

Amphibians

The name *amphibian* comes from two old Greek words—*amphi* meaning "both," and *bios* meaning "life." Amphibians lay their eggs in water, and most of them begin life swimming as tadpoles. As they mature, they develop legs and begin spending some of their time on land. Frogs and toads lose their tails by the time they become adults, while salamanders keep theirs.

Frogs and Toads

Frogs and toads have similar body shapes, but frogs have moist, smooth skin. The skin of toads is dry and warty.

Frogs and toads propel themselves over the land with their powerful hind legs. Those same legs make them strong swimmers.

The croaking you hear near a pond may be a bullfrog, the largest American frog. Like many kinds of frogs, it catches insects with a flick of its tongue.

Spring peepers and tree frogs have sticky pads on their toes that enable them to hang onto branches and leaves. Some of them lay their eggs in tiny pockets of water in tree knots, and the tadpoles mature high above the ground.

bullfrog

American toad

spring peeper

leopard frog

mud puppy

newt

The shorter legs and heavier bodies of toads make them less mobile than frogs. As a defense, some toads can secrete a poison that irritates the eyes and mouths of predators.

Salamanders 2

Like frogs and toads, adult salamanders live both in and out of water. Even though they may be similar in appearance to lizards, they aren't. Lizards have scales while salamanders have smooth, moist skin.

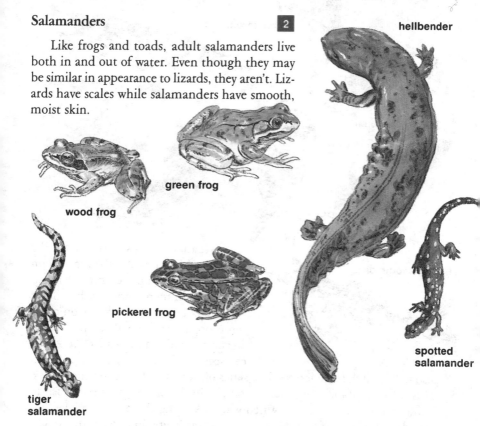

hellbender

green frog

wood frog

pickerel frog

spotted salamander

tiger salamander

Fish 2

Fish are ancient animals. Fossils show us that fish were thriving in the oceans of the Earth millions of years before beasts with backbones walked on dry land. They have endured for so many eons because they are well-suited to their environment.

Over 30,000 kinds of fish are alive today. You can find them in almost every body of water except for salty, alkaline waters like the Great Salt Lake, and water that has become badly polluted.

FRESHWATER FISH

rock bass

bluegill sunfish

brook trout

muskellunge

yellow perch

walleyed pike

catfish

largemouth bass

Instead of lungs, fish have gills through which they absorb oxygen from the water. Oxygen passes into the blood through thin membranes in the gills.

Like land animals, fish rely on many sense organs to help them find food, escape predators, and locate mates. Most can see, smell, hear, taste, and feel. Fish also have a sixth sense located in a series of nerves and pores on their sides. This *lateral line* picks up small vibrations in the water and alerts a fish to changes in its surroundings. When you walk along the bank of a lake, fish may dart away even if they can't see you. Their lateral lines sense the weight of your footsteps upon the ground.

Every fish has an air-filled internal organ called a *swim bladder*, which gives the animal buoyancy. Fins help the fish stay upright, propel it forward, let it turn, and act as brakes when it must stop. The long, sleek shape of many fish helps them swim fast enough to catch their prey and to escape becoming dinner themselves.

Coloration also protects fish. Most are dark on top so that predators looking down into the water have difficulty seeing them. Light, shiny undersides blend with the sky when seen from below. Perch, bluegills, and other fish that

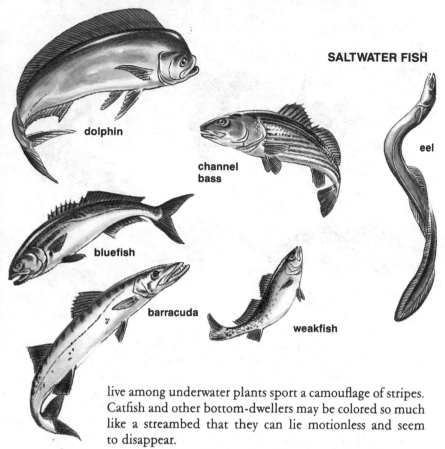

dolphin

channel
bass

eel

bluefish

barracuda

weakfish

live among underwater plants sport a camouflage of stripes. Catfish and other bottom-dwellers may be colored so much like a streambed that they can lie motionless and seem to disappear.

Catfish have mouths designed for suction. They vacuum food from the bottoms of rivers and lakes, feeling their way through murky waters with the long "whiskers" on their faces. Since their diet includes dead and decaying matter, they help keep the water clean.

Thin, sharp teeth that can tear flesh let fish like the muskellunge, pike, and barracuda feed on other fish. Trout, crappie, and other fish that feed on insects and their eggs make do with less fearsome teeth. Sardines are among the little fish that feed on plankton. They don't need teeth at all.

A mass of tiny plant and animal organisms drifting in the water is called plankton. Plant plankton combines sunlight with minerals and gases to make food. Plankton serves as food for small fish and also for some whales, the largest animals on Earth. The relationship between plankton and aquatic animals is one part of a vast aquatic food chain that also includes insects, amphibians, birds, and many other kinds of vegetation.

SALTWATER FISH

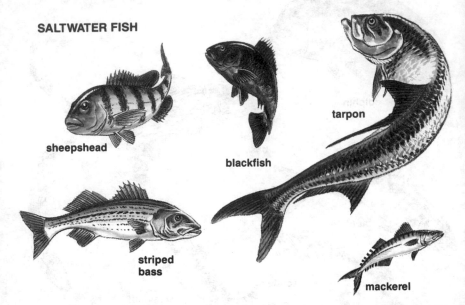

sheepshead

blackfish

tarpon

striped
bass

mackerel

Even though they spend their lives in seawater, whales are mammals, not fish. Whales are warm-blooded. They breathe through lungs rather than gills, coming to the ocean's surface to inhale fresh air. Instead of laying eggs like fish do, whales bear their young alive and nurse them with milk. *Baleen* whales live mainly on plankton; they strain seawater through their mouths, trapping the plankton in bristled screens called *baleen* or *whalebone*. *Toothed* whales swallow their food whole; they use their teeth for capturing, not chewing, their prey.

Different species of fish distribute their eggs in many different ways. Some simply scatter them in open water. Others make nests of gravel or mud. A few species gather their eggs in their mouths to protect them from predators.

Salmon eggs hatch in fresh water and the young salmon swim to the sea where they mature for several years. Drawn by powerful instincts, adult salmon fight their way back upstream to lay and fertilize their eggs in the same shallow waters where they themselves began life. Only a few adults complete the journey, and even they die once the eggs are deposited among the gravel on the streambed. Fingerling salmon hatching from those eggs swim off to start the migratory cycle for the next generation.

Fish are important to humans as a source of food. Many species of fish help control mosquitoes and other insects that are harmful to man, by eating both insect eggs in the water and adult insects hovering just above the surface.

CHAPTER 14

Insects

When it comes to sheer numbers, insects rule the world. Five out of six animals are insects. They thrive almost everywhere on land except for the ice of the North and South poles. Every insect is a tiny wonder, full of mysteries for you to discover. Each one is doing all it can to survive. Some insects fly, some swim, and some scurry across the ground. Different species eat everything from leaves and flower nectar to blood, dead animals, and each other. Some display brilliant hues, while others are drab in color and shaped like dried leaves or twigs.

With so much spectacular variety, you may wonder if these creatures have anything in common. In fact, they do. Every one of them has six legs and a body with three sections—head, abdomen, and thorax. That's what makes them insects. (Spiders are sometimes confused with insects, but look closely. They are *arachnids*—animals with eight legs and just two body parts.)

Butterflies and Moths

You probably have seen butterflies and moths flitting over fields and among trees. Many of them sip nectar from flowers and carry pollen on their legs from one blossom to another.

Both butterflies and moths have four broad wings covered with scales so tiny that they may look like fine dust. At rest, butterflies tend to hold their wings

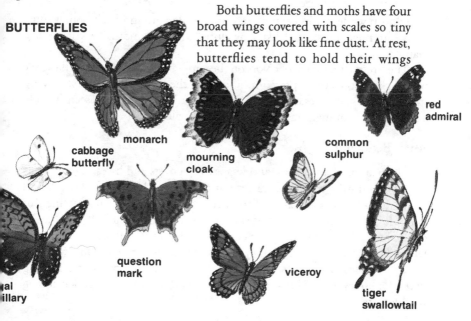

BUTTERFLIES

monarch

cabbage butterfly

mourning cloak

red admiral

common sulphur

question mark

viceroy

tiger swallowtail

al illary

MOTHS

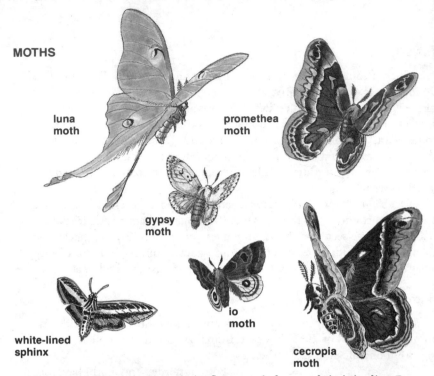

luna
moth

promethea
moth

gypsy
moth

io
moth

white-lined
sphinx

cecropia
moth

straight up while moths keep theirs flat or curled around their bodies. Butterfly antennae are shaped like tiny clubs. Those of moths look more like
feathers.

The irregular patterns of colors on the wings of moths and butterflies may
play tricks on the eyes of predators and make the insects harder to see. Wing
spots that look like eyes may cause birds to think one of these insects is really
a much larger animal, one they should leave alone.

Ants, Bees, and Wasps

Many kinds of ants, bees, and wasps live in nests and hives. As members
of a community, each insect carries out duties that help feed, defend, and
maintain its home. The habits of these communal insects are fascinating. For
example, some ants look after tiny sucking insects called aphids. When stroked
on the back, the aphids make a sweet liquid which the ants feed to their own
larvae. Other ants are farmers, preparing soil and raising small fungi for food.

Some wasps feed on insects that are destructive to crops. Bees collecting
nectar for honey help pollinate fields and orchards by scattering pollen among
the blossoms.

Bees and wasps also carry stingers with which they can inject a painful poison. Some ants can do that with their jaws. A great many more people are injured each year by insect stings than by snakebites. Take a moment before your next Scout outing to review the first aid treatment for insect stings and bites (see page 423).

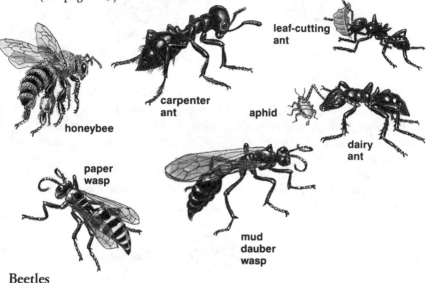

leaf-cutting
ant

carpenter
ant

aphid

honeybee

dairy
ant

paper
wasp

mud
dauber
wasp

Beetles

When asked what he thought of God, a famous scientist replied, "He certainly likes beetles." In fact, 40 percent of all insects are beetles. They range in size from the ¼-inch-long snout beetle to the stag beetle which, with its great pincers, can be several inches long.

Every beetle has two pairs of wings. The back pair is used for flying. The front pair joins to make a hard shell that protects the abdomen. The line between the two halves of the shell runs straight down the beetle's back.

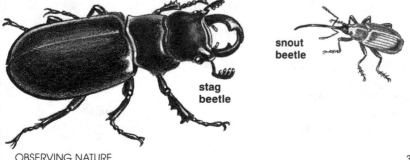

snout
beetle

stag
beetle

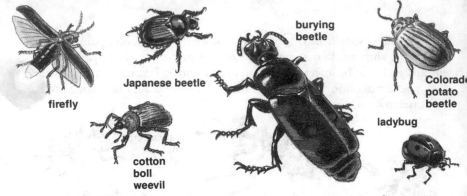

firefly

Japanese beetle

burying beetle

cotton boll weevil

Colorado potato beetle

ladybug

The ladybug is a beetle that eats many times its own weight of insects that are harmful to vegetables. Gardeners sometimes scatter ladybugs among the rows rather than spraying their plants with pesticides. Many other beetles are scavengers that devour dead plants and animals. Without them, some food chains would collapse.

One of the most remarkable beetles is the firefly. A chemical reaction in an organ near its tail creates a glowing light. Fireflies flash their lights as signals in their mating rituals.

mosquito

housefly

Flies and Mosquitoes

Each of these insects has just two wings. The long proboscis of the mosquito allows it to pierce the skin of a mammal and draw out blood. The mouth parts of a fly are more like a sponge made for lapping up liquids.

Mosquitoes lay their eggs in still water. Flies may leave their eggs in dead and decaying matter. While important to some ecosystems, flies and mosquitoes may also carry diseases that affect humans.

Grasshoppers and Their Relatives

These are the musicians of the insect world. Grasshoppers click and whir when they fly, and sometimes make a raspy sound by stroking their wing covers with their hind legs. Male katydids rub their front wings together to produce a rhythmic buzzing. Cicadas do the same by vibrating a membrane, the *timbal,* in their abdomens.

The dry shells of cicadas that Scouts often find on tree trunks are evidence of a very interesting life cycle. Cicada nymphs hatch from eggs laid in trees.

The young insects burrow into the ground and suck sap from roots. They may stay buried for up to 17 years. When they do come out they crawl up a tree, shed their old shells, and emerge as full-grown adults ready to lay eggs and keep the cycle going.

Bugs

Many people call all insects "bugs." But true bugs form a definite group. Like a beetle, each bug has four wings, and the front ones form a protective shell over the rear flight wings. However, where a beetle's shell halves form a straight line down its back, those of a bug fold into an X shape.

All true bugs have mouth parts made for sucking. Many suck sap out of plants and trees. Others get nourishment from berries and grains.

An interesting member of this group is the spittle bug which hides in frothy spittle it hangs on weed stalks. The water strider is a bug that hurries along the surface of the water. So are two other bugs, the back swimmer and water boatman.

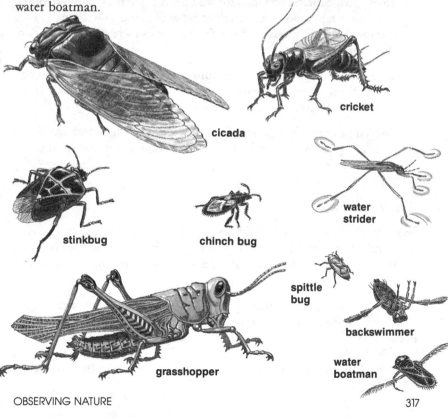

cricket

cicada

stinkbug

chinch bug

water strider

spittle bug

backswimmer

grasshopper

water boatman

OUR AMERICAN TREES

The largest and oldest living things on earth are trees. Over a thousand kinds grow in the United States, and thousands more flourish in other parts of the world. Trees play a very important role in the health of the environment and in the lives of people. The following are a few of the benefits we enjoy from trees:

☆ Trees pump oxygen into the air. The great forests of the world are essential for purifying the air and maintaining the right balance of oxygen in the atmosphere.

☆ Leaves on branches and on the ground slow falling rain so that it can seep into the earth. Roots keep dirt from washing away. Fallen leaves decay in the soil and enrich it.

☆ Trees provide shelter and food for wildlife. A forest is a complicated web of relationships among hundreds of types of plants and animals. That diversity helps all species survive. Strong forests increase the stability of the environment.

☆ Trees provide shelter and food for humans, too. Lumber goes into homes. Fruits, berries, nuts, and oils feed us. Other products of trees include paper, rubber, spices, and medicines.

☆ Shaded yards and city parks offer us places close to home where we can relax and play. Hiking and camping let us explore vast forests and wilderness areas.

Parts of a Tree

Roots. Much of a tree is out of sight beneath the ground. Growing very quickly, thousands of tiny root hairs push through the earth, absorbing moisture and sending it up into the tree. A root system is also the anchor holding a tree upright even in storms and high winds.

Trunk. The *bark* on a tree trunk gives the plant a tough outer armor. *Sapwood* underneath the bark transports moisture from the roots up to the leaves. Between the sapwood and bark is a thin layer of tissue called the *cambium* layer. It channels food produced by the leaves down into the tree trunk and the roots. In the center of the trunk is hardened sapwood called *heartwood*

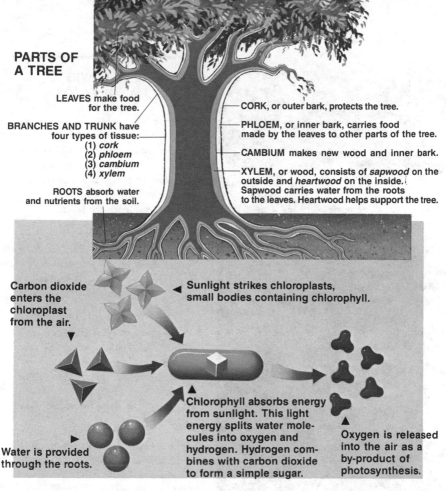

PARTS OF A TREE

LEAVES make food for the tree.

BRANCHES AND TRUNK have four types of tissue:
(1) *cork*
(2) *phloem*
(3) *cambium*
(4) *xylem*

ROOTS absorb water and nutrients from the soil.

CORK, or outer bark, protects the tree.

PHLOEM, or inner bark, carries food made by the leaves to other parts of the tree.

CAMBIUM makes new wood and inner bark.

XYLEM, or wood, consists of *sapwood* on the outside and *heartwood* on the inside. Sapwood carries water from the roots to the leaves. Heartwood helps support the tree.

Carbon dioxide enters the chloroplast from the air.

Sunlight strikes chloroplasts, small bodies containing chlorophyll.

Chlorophyll absorbs energy from sunlight. This light energy splits water molecules into oxygen and hydrogen. Hydrogen combines with carbon dioxide to form a simple sugar.

Water is provided through the roots.

Oxygen is released into the air as a by-product of photosynthesis.

that gives the tree strength. Each year the cambium builds a new layer of sapwood around the trunk. Count the rings formed by the layers and you'll know how many years a tree was alive.

Leaves. The green chlorophyll in the leaves draws power from sunlight and converts carbon dioxide in the air into nutrients for the tree. Called *photosynthesis,* this process returns oxygen to the atmosphere. It is an important way for the air to be cleaned and refreshed with oxygen.

The two large groups of American trees are *conifer* trees and *broadleaf* trees. Conifers, also known as *evergreens,* have needlelike or scalelike leaves that usually stay on the trees for several years. Broadleaf trees have flat leaves that generally fall off in the autumn.

Conifers

1

In addition to having needle-shaped leaves, all conifers bear cones containing seeds and pollen. The seeds have no protective cover except for the cones. Once freed from its cone, a seed must quickly reach soil in which to grow or it will die.

Douglas fir **ponderosa pine** **western hemlock**

balsam fir **eastern white pine** **white spruce**

The man at the base of each tree shows relative height of a mature tree. Most evergreen trees have the Christmas-tree look of an inverted cone.

The trunks of most conifers extend straight to the tops of the trees. Tapering branches give these evergreens the pyramid shape of a Christmas tree. Woodworkers refer to conifers as *softwoods* because lumber from them is easy to cut and shape. Experienced campers know that firewood from conifers burns quickly with hot, smoky flames.

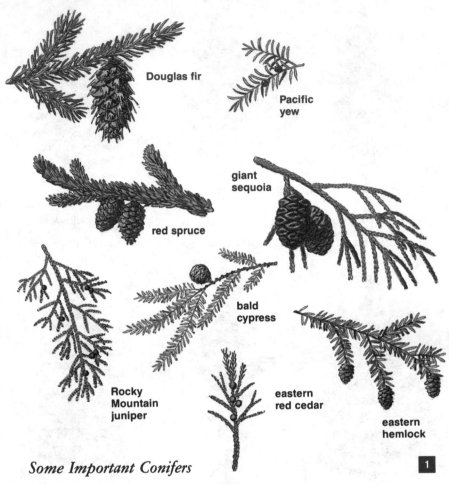

Douglas fir

Pacific yew

giant sequoia

red spruce

bald cypress

Rocky Mountain juniper

eastern red cedar

eastern hemlock

Some Important Conifers

1

Pines. The needlelike leaves of pines almost always grow in clusters of two to five leaves each. The bark of a pine tree is usually thin. The straight trunks of mature pine trees often have no branches near the ground. Higher up, branches may form the shape of a cone.

Carpenters like to use the straight-grained wood of the white pine. It has a smooth, tight bark and five needles in each leaf cluster. Found especially in the Northeast, the white pine is the tree on the state flag of Maine.

Other pine trees common in the eastern states include the pitch pine with three needles per cluster and the jack and red pines with two needles per cluster. In the Southeast, the longleaf and loblolly pines have three needles to a cluster, while slash and shortleaf pines display two.

The largest pines grow in the mountains of the West. Sugar pines can reach a height of 200 feet. Look for five needles in each of its leaf clusters. The cones of sugar pines can be 18 inches long and quite heavy.

Jeffrey pines have groups of three long needles. Get close to the bark of a Jeffrey pine and you may smell a pleasant vanilla-like aroma. Ponderosa and knobcone are other western pines with three-needle clusters. Lodgepole pines, named for their straight, clean trunks, have clusters of two needles each.

Spruces. The needles of spruce trees are four-sided in shape. They grow singly all around a branch. The Engelmann spruce of the North and Northeast has soft needles with a blue-green hue. The blue spruce of the same regions has needles that are stiff. The tallest American spruce is the Sitka spruce of the Pacific Northwest.

Firs. Fir needles are flat. They appear to be arranged in orderly rows along the sides of branches. The flat needles are dark green on top while the undersides show two white lines. Fir cones grow upright on the upper branches of the trees. The balsam fir of the East and the white fir of the West are stately, fragrant representatives of these evergreens.

redwood

tamarack

balsam fir

eastern
white pine

Larches or tamaracks. The soft needles of the larch grow in tufts out of old-growth bumps on the branches. Unlike those of most other pines, larch leaves fall off in the winter. The tree is very tall and slender, and the cones are quite small.

Hemlocks. Hemlocks are large evergreens identified by short, flat needles with dark green tops and silvery undersides. The small cones hang from branches that droop in the shape of a graceful pyramid.

Douglas firs. A close relative of the hemlock is the Douglas fir, a giant tree of the West. Also known as the Douglas spruce, red fir, and Oregon pine, it is actually not a spruce, fir, or pine, but is something of a botanical mystery. Its flat, needlelike leaves spiral around the branches, giving them the appearance of bottle brushes or squirrels' tails.

Sequoias and redwoods. The largest trees in the world are the redwoods and giant sequoias of California. Some redwoods are over 300 feet tall—higher than the length of a football field. Sequoias can grow to a thickness of 25 feet. Some of these trees are more than 4,000 years old.

Cedars, junipers, and cypresses. The leaves of cedars are tiny, bright-green scales arranged like small shingles on flattened twigs. Landscapers use cedars to increase the beauty of lawns and parks.

Western red cedar is, in fact, a juniper. Junipers have two kinds of leaves. Some are scaly and flat like a cedar, while others are awllike and prickly. Juniper cones look like blueberries.

The bald cypress of the South "goes bald" by dropping its needles each winter. Some kinds of cypress grow in swamps where they send up cone-shaped stumps called *knees*.

Broadleaf Trees

1

While most of these trees have wide, flat leaves, a more important characteristic is that their seeds are enclosed in a nut, fruit, or other seed case. Unlike conifers, their seeds do not grow in cones. Many broadleaf trees have trunks that branch out and give the trees round, airy shapes. The lumber from most broadleaf trees is called *hardwood*. It is used to build furniture and other structures where great strength is required. Hardwood campfires burn down slowly into long-lasting beds of coals.

Another term for broadleaf trees is *deciduous*—from the Latin word *decidere*, meaning "to fall off." Most deciduous trees lose their leaves in the winter.

tulip tree   American elm   shagbark hickory

oak   sweet gum   maple

The man at the base of each tree shows the relative height of a mature tree. Deciduous trees flourish in the temperate climate of the Northeast.

Some Important Broadleaf Trees

Willows and poplars. The pussy willow takes its name from its furry flower clusters. You may think they look like tiny kittens clinging to the willow's long, straight branches. The sandbar willow is often one of the first plants to grow on new ground formed by shifting river currents.

Poplars, or aspens, thrive on sunlight. They sprout on mountain slopes burned by fire, providing shade for the seedlings of pines, firs, and other trees. As those trees mature, they tower above the aspens and eventually crowd them out of the forest.

Nut trees. Walnuts and hickories have a number of leaflets making up each of their leaves. Every hickory leaf has three to nine leaflets, while a leaf of the walnut tree may have more than a dozen. Walnuts and hickory nuts are the

black willow

glaucous willow

large-tooth aspen

canoe birch

gray birch

yellow birch

quaking aspen

weeping willow

sandbar willow

mockernut

American hornbeam

black walnut

butternut

American beech

cottonwood

pignut hickory

alder

shagbark hickory

chestnut

seeds of their trees. Both are good to eat. So are the nuts of the pecan tree. Mockernut, bitternut, and pignut have small, bitter kernels.

Birches. This family of broadleaf trees includes birches, hornbeams, and alders. The trees are most commonly found in the East and Northeast. Their oval leaves have jagged edges and shiny surfaces.

honey locust

persimmon

tupelo

buckeye

flowering dogwood

western catalpa

black locust

basswood

white ash

wild crabapple

tulip

sycamore

pawpaw

sweet gum

wild black cherry

silver maple

slippery elm

sassafras

red mulberry

mountain ash

red maple

American elm

burr oak

scarlet oak

redbud

sugar maple

white oak

chestnut oak

hingle oak

red oak

pin oak

black oak

staghorn sumac

Native Americans peeled sheets of white bark from the paper birch and used it to build their canoes. The bark of yellow birch peels away from the trunk in curls. Gray and black birches have much tighter bark.

The wood of the smooth-barked American hornbeam is so tough that the tree is sometimes called *ironwood*. The trunk resembles the muscular arm of a man.

Alders grow in moist ground throughout the country. They have broad leaves, stalked buds, and small, conelike fruits.

Beeches and chestnuts. You can identify a beech tree by its smooth, pale gray bark. Like those of the birches, each beech leaf has a strong midvein and parallel side veins. Its burrlike fruit contains two triangular nuts.

The chestnut was once a tree common to eastern forests. A fungus called chestnut blight has killed a great number of the trees, so you may have to look hard to find one.

Oaks. Wood from America's oak trees has long been prized by builders. Oak timbers are slow to rot, even if they are wet. The ship *Old Ironsides* was made from oak. Hand-hewn oak beams were used in many colonial homes.

The acorn is the fruit of an oak. Look for acorns on the ground under these trees. Though edible, acorns of American oaks have a bitter taste. Most oaks have notched leaves. The lobes on the leaves of some oaks are rounded. Lobes of other species come to sharp points. An exception is the live oak. Its leaves have smooth edges and no lobes at all, but its acorns still let you know it is an oak.

Elms. The elm is another tree prized for its grace and beauty. Once planted as a shade tree in American cities, many elms have been killed by a fungus called Dutch elm disease.

American elms and slippery elms have leaves that are egg-shaped and lopsided with saw-toothed edges. Leaves of American elms are shiny and smooth. Despite the name, those of the slippery elm have dull, rough surfaces.

Magnolias. Magnolia trees are found in the southeastern United States. Their large, distinctive leaves are shiny dark green on top and pale underneath. One magnolia, the cucumber tree, bears a mass of many small *pods* that resembles a cucumber.

Another member of the magnolia family is the tulip tree, named for the tuliplike appearance of its flowers. A very tall tree, it is found in Southern states where the winters are mild.

Papaws and sassafras. The common papaw belongs to the custard apple family. It is found in timbers of the East and Midwest. The fruit of the papaw looks and tastes like a chubby, overripe banana.

Tea made from the root bark of the sassafras tree is an old household remedy for colds. On the same tree you can find leaves of many shapes — some

LEAF CASTS

If you have some plaster of paris, you can make a three-dimensional print of a leaf. Start by smearing the underside of the leaf with petroleum jelly. Do the same to the top of a lid of a cottage cheese container. Place the ungreased side of the leaf on the lid. Pour enough plaster over the leaf to fill the lid to its lip. After the plaster has hardened, gently remove it from the lid and peel away the leaf.

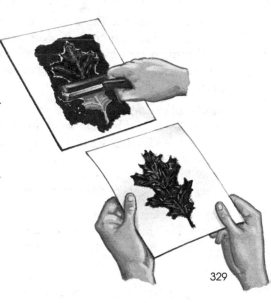

INK PRINTS

Use a rubber roller to spread a dab of printer's ink on a glass plate. Place a leaf on the glass with the veined side against the ink. Run the roller over the leaf several times. Lay the leaf, inked side down, on a clean sheet of paper. Cover with a piece of newspaper and run the roller over it to make a print.

TREE FRUITS

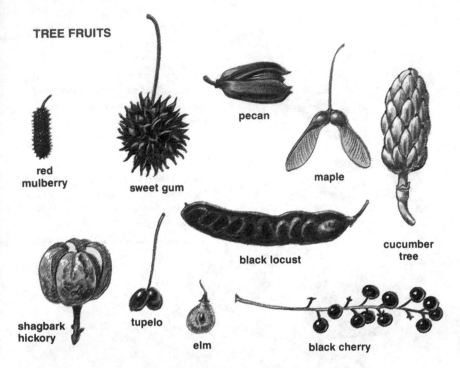

red mulberry

sweet gum

pecan

maple

cucumber tree

black locust

shagbark hickory

tupelo

elm

black cherry

oval, some like three-fingered mittens, some that may remind you of the trefoil of the Scout badge.

Gums and sycamores. The sweet gum tree has star-shaped leaves that turn a brilliant red in autumn. Its fruits look like spiny balls.

The fruit of the sycamore has a similar shape but has no spines. The bark of a sycamore gives the trunk a distinctive patchwork of large blotches of white, green, and yellow.

Plums and cherries. A dozen varieties of wild plum trees grow in the eastern United States. Watch in the woods for small trees with shiny oval leaves and purple or reddish fruits. The hard pit inside each fruit contains the seed of a new tree.

Wild bird cherry or pin cherry are small trees with tiny red fruits in clusters of two or three. Other wild cherries have fruits arranged in bunches like grapes.

Maples. The leaves of maples are arranged in pairs opposite each other on the branch. Their main veins come out like fingers from the base of the leaf. Fruits of maple trees are called *keys* because of the "wing" attached to each one.

Buckeyes. Inside a tough, spiny burr is the fruit of the buckeye. Its size and shiny brown surface make it look something like the eye of a deer, and thus its name. Leaves of buckeyes have five long leaflets. Ohio takes its nickname, the Buckeye State, from this tree.

Ashes. Baseball bats and ax handles are often made from the hard, smooth wood of the ash tree. Each ash leaf is made up of many leaflets that grow in pairs on either side of the leaf stalk. The leaves are in pairs, too, and so are the branches of the tree.

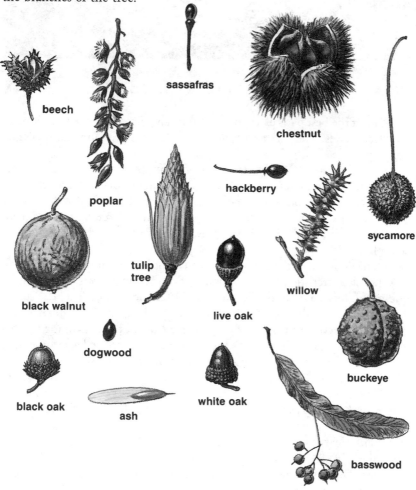

beech

sassafras

chestnut

poplar

hackberry

tulip tree

sycamore

black walnut

willow

live oak

dogwood

buckeye

black oak

ash

white oak

basswood

FLOWERS OF THE YEAR 1

One of the best parts of a spring hike is seeing flowers poking up through the dead leaves. They are a sure sign that winter is over and summer is on the way.

Flowers are the reproductive parts of many plants. The petals are the flower parts we often notice first. Their shapes and bright colors attract insects and other animals that spread pollen among the plants. The stamen is the male part of the flower that produces pollen. The female part of the plant that receives the pollen is called the pistil. It's often shaped like a stalk with a knob on top.

Many flowers take their common names from their appearances, aromas, or other characteristics. Under a hooded leaf, the tiny flowers of the jack-in-the-pulpit look something like a little minister about to preach. The turtle-head, a plant that likes wet places, has flowers that look much like small turtles.

Have you ever seen flowers that look like pairs of pants hanging upside-down? Those may be dutchman's breeches. Have you noticed colorful flowers in the shape of shoes? Those could be pink moccasin flowers.

Examine the long, yellow blossoms of the goldenrod and the dark centers of black-eyed susans. Their colors are an important part of those flowers' names. A bright splash of color also helps identify the butterfly weed when it blooms in midsummer.

A large leaf wrapping itself around skunk cabbage flowers protects them from the cold. Take a sniff and you'll quickly understand where the plant gets its name. The wake-robin also has a foul aroma. It blooms in the spring about the time robins return.

Spring Marches North

The time of the year that flowers appear in your part of the nation depends on where you are located. In early March in Georgia, for instance, you will see spring flowers that people in New York will not see until late in April. At high elevations in the mountains, spring may not arrive until June or even early July, and the growing

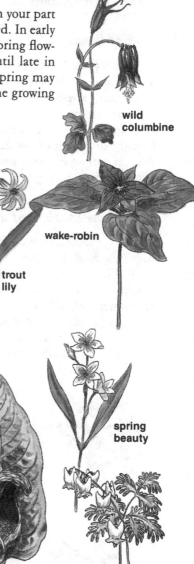

wild columbine

FLOWERS OF SPRING

hepatica

wake-robin

trout lily

jack-in-the-pulpit

bloodroot

spring beauty

pink moccasin flower

rue anemone

skunk cabbage

dutchman's breeches

season may last only a few weeks. In desert regions, plants must wait for rainstorms to moisten them before they put out their flowers.

Uses of Plants 1

When you are fishing or canoeing, you may see the leaves of yellow pond lilies floating on the water. Long roots anchor each plant to the lake bed. Native Americans harvested those roots for food.

In fact, many plants are useful to humans. The woolly leaves of common mullein have been used for lamp wicks and the insoles of shoes. Yarrow was brought to America from Europe because it could be used as a medicine. Boneset earned its name when people thought it helped with the setting of broken bones.

North and South, East and West 1

Most of these flowers are found throughout our country, but some sections have flowers of their own.

It is in the Northeast where you may find the fringed gentian, Virginia cowslip, day lily, Oswego tea, and showy aster. On the West Coast grow the golden-yellow California poppy, shooting stars, blue and scarlet wonder, and the snow flower. In the dry parts of the Southwest you will come upon cactus in bright colors. In the South there are coral plant, orange milkwort, purple gerardia, and meadow beauty.

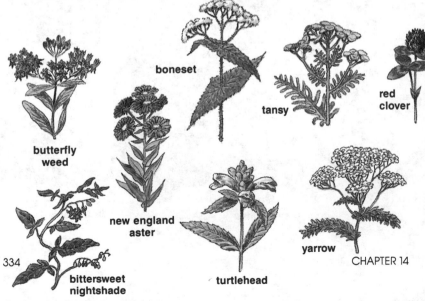

boneset

tansy

red clover

butterfly weed

new england aster

yarrow

bittersweet nightshade

turtlehead

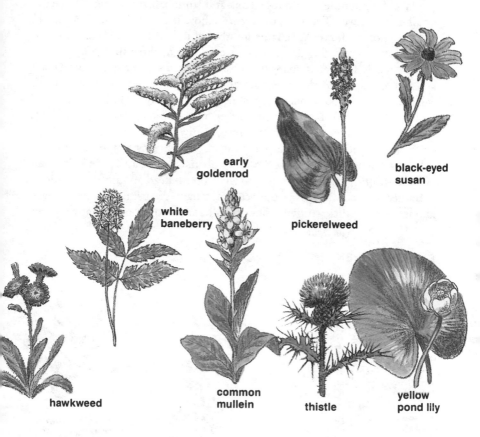

early
goldenrod

black-eyed
susan

white
baneberry

pickerelweed

hawkweed

common
mullein

thistle

yellow
pond lily

Families of Flowers   1

The flowers shown on these pages are just a few of thousands of varieties that bloom in America. There are so many that you may think it is impossible to tell them apart.

However, botanists — naturalists interested in flowers — have tackled this problem by writing *plant keys,* which are books that group flowers into families based on similarities they share. You can find plant keys at your library or local bookstores. They will help you figure out what a flower is, as well as help you learn about other flowers in the same family.

Studying a Flower

Take, for example, a wild rose. Look at it from below and you will see five small, green leaves. Those are the *sepals*. Above them are five pink *petals*. In the center of the flower are a large number of pollen-bearing pins—the *stamens*. They form a ring around a cluster of green, threadlike *pistils*.

Five sepals, five petals, many stamens, many pistils—search through a plant key and you will find that these are all features of the rose family. The key will also tell you about other members of the rose family, including wild strawberry, meadowsweet, raspberry, cinquefoil, and agrimony. Apple, pear, plum, and cherry are trees that are in the rose family, too.

From dandelions pushing up through cracks in a city street to lupine covering a high mountain meadow, flowering plants are a beautiful and vital part of our environment. Take the time to enjoy them. Read about them in books. Whether you know flowers by their common names or use a plant key to learn about their families, studying flowers will enrich your outdoor adventures.

PLANT FAMILIES

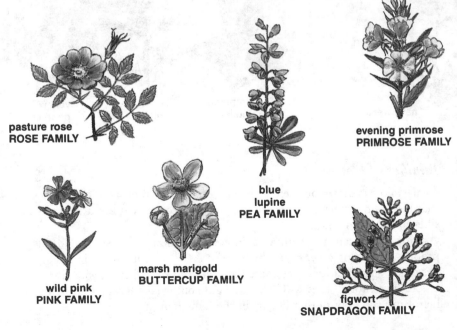

pasture rose
ROSE FAMILY

evening primrose
PRIMROSE FAMILY

wild pink
PINK FAMILY

marsh marigold
BUTTERCUP FAMILY

blue
lupine
PEA FAMILY

figwort
SNAPDRAGON FAMILY

ROSE

MUSTARD

LILY

DAISY

PLANT FAMILIES

Each plant family has its own characteristics. In a flower belonging to the rose family, the parts are divisible by 5, in the mustard family by 4, in the lily family by 3. What looks like a single flower of the composite (daisy) family may actually be hundreds of flowers, some of them tube-shaped, some of them tongue-shaped.

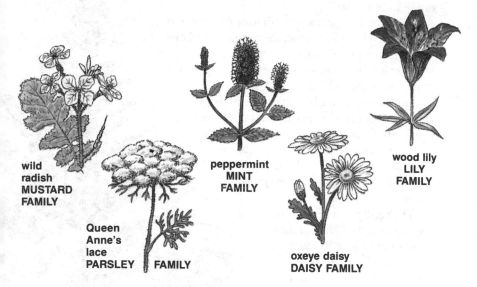

wild radish
MUSTARD FAMILY

Queen Anne's lace
PARSLEY FAMILY

peppermint
MINT FAMILY

oxeye daisy
DAISY FAMILY

wood lily
LILY FAMILY

Not All Plants Are Flowers

1

The flowers, of course, are all plants, but not all plants are flowers. You will come upon many flowerless plants on your hikes, and it is good to know a bit about them.

Plants are arranged into two large groups: those that produce seeds and those that don't.

On the list of plants without seeds are the algae. Some of them are tiny—the blue-green scum on a quiet lake. Others grow to great sizes—the green, brown, and red algae, or seaweeds, of our coasts. One of them, the big brown kelp, may grow to be 150 feet long.

To see the bacteria you need a microscope. But in spite of their tiny size they have a great effect on our lives. Some of them are harmless. Some are useful. Others cause infection and diseases. Strep throat is an infection caused by bacteria. The diseases of cholera, pneumonia, tuberculosis, and some venereal diseases also are caused by bacteria.

The fungi are seedless plants of wide variety: Green mold grows on bread. Mildew makes black spots on tents packed down while still damp. Blights and rust kill chestnuts and pine trees. Yeast raises bread. Mushrooms grow in woods and fields. Some of the mushrooms make good eating. Others are poisonous. Only an expert can tell them apart.

The lichens appear as grayish scale patches on trees, rocks, and soil. These patches are not individual plants. Each lichen is two plants, alga and fungus. They grow together in an amazing partnership, depending upon each other for life.

Liverworts—flat, ribbonlike, green plants—and mosses of many shapes are among the seedless plants. So are the horsetails, the ferns, and the club mosses. Some of the ferns are so tiny that you hardly see them in the rock cracks where they grow. Others grow to tree size.

The seed producers are very important to us. Without them there would be no human life on earth. They nourish us, clothe us, and give us shelter. They range from grasses and trees to the vegetables of our gardens, and the flowers in florists' shops.

mushroom
(fungi)

fern

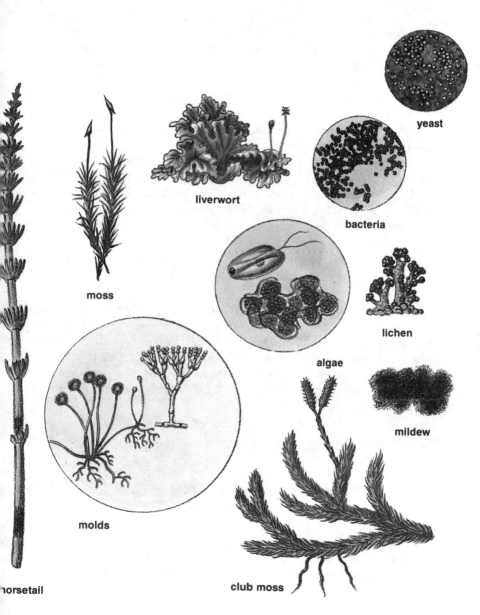

yeast

liverwort

bacteria

moss

lichen

algae

molds

mildew

horsetail

club moss

EDIBLE WILD PLANTS

Wild plants have been part of human diets for centuries. Early native Americans depended on roots, berries, and leaves for many of their meals. Explorers, hunters, and hikers have sometimes lived for long periods of time eating nothing but wild foods.

Preparing and eating wild plants can be an interesting part of your Scout outings. Bring foodstuffs from home, too, so you don't have to rely completely on natural food. It's often difficult to find enough nourishment in the wild to satisfy your hunger. On the other hand, a lost person can survive without any food at all for 3 weeks or more.

The best way to learn which wild plants are safe to eat is from Scout leaders who know plants well. They can point out which vegetation makes good salads, desserts, beverages, and cooked greens. They will also show you poisonous mushrooms and other plants that may be dangerous to eat.

Here are a few pointers to consider as you select edible plants:

☆ The plant must be **eatable.** You should be able to chew it easily, either in its raw state or after cooking has made it tender.

☆ It should be **wholesome.** The plants pictured on these pages are good for you. But there are many plants that are not wholesome, and a few that are poisonous. Before picking plants on your own, learn from someone who knows which wild plants are safe to eat. Learn them well enough to identify them positively even when they are not in flower. Don't pick plants along roadsides where they may be contaminated by motor oil or automobile exhaust.

☆ It should be **nutritional.** Many wild plants are rich in vitamins and minerals.

☆ It should be **palatable.** That means it should taste good. If you don't like it, you won't want to eat very much of it.

☆ It should be **appropriate.** Harvest wild plants only where they are abundant. Notice whether they are helping to prevent erosion. If gathering plants might harm the environment, then enjoy looking at them but leave them alone.

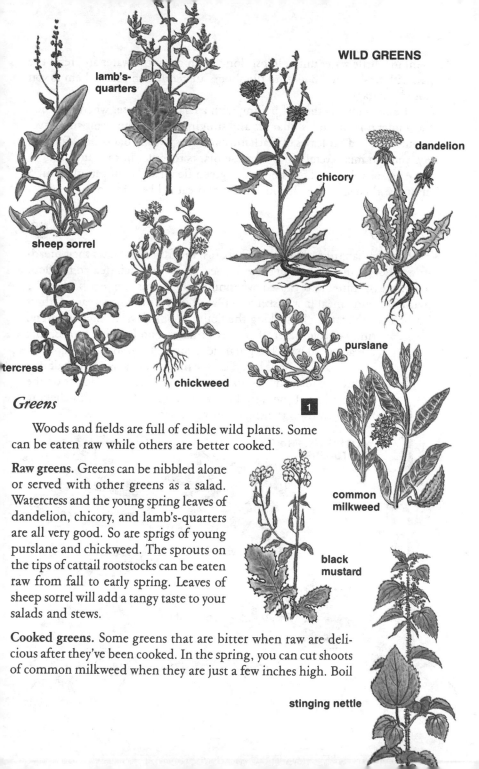

lamb's-quarters

dandelion

chicory

sheep sorrel

purslane

tercress

chickweed

1

common milkweed

black mustard

stinging nettle

Greens

Woods and fields are full of edible wild plants. Some can be eaten raw while others are better cooked.

Raw greens. Greens can be nibbled alone or served with other greens as a salad. Watercress and the young spring leaves of dandelion, chicory, and lamb's-quarters are all very good. So are sprigs of young purslane and chickweed. The sprouts on the tips of cattail rootstocks can be eaten raw from fall to early spring. Leaves of sheep sorrel will add a tangy taste to your salads and stews.

Cooked greens. Some greens that are bitter when raw are delicious after they've been cooked. In the spring, you can cut shoots of common milkweed when they are just a few inches high. Boil them in a little water until almost done, then drain the water and refill the pan with fresh water. Boil until the shoots are tender, and serve them as you would asparagus.

Use the same method of boiling with a change of water when you cook the tender tops of lamb's-quarters and stinging nettles, the stems and leaves of purslane, and the leaves of black mustard, chicory, and dandelion. For variety, you can mix several kinds of these plants together in the same pot.

As a special treat, boil the young, green flower spikes of cattail about 5 minutes, then spread each with butter and eat it like corn on the cob.

Breadstuffs 1

Many Indian tribes depended on acorns, the fruit of oaks, for their breadstuff. They ground the raw or dried kernels into flour, then treated the flour to remove the bitter taste caused by tannin in the acorns. Some tribes put the coarsely ground meal in a basket and placed it in a running stream. Others leached out the tannin by soaking the flour in boiling water, then in several rinses of cold water. If you try grinding and leaching acorns, mix the acorn flour with regular flour for better-tasting bread.

A more delicious bread can be made from a half-and-half mix of cattail pollen and regular wheat flour. The pollen forms on the flower spikes of the cattail in early summer. Collect it by shaking the pollen from the spikes into a paper bag.

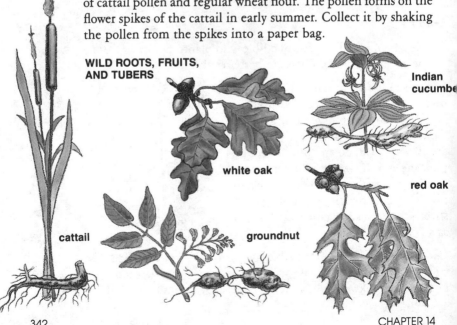

WILD ROOTS, FRUITS, AND TUBERS

Indian cucumbe

white oak

red oak

cattail

groundnut

Roots and Tubers 1

There is plenty of nourishment in the roots or tubers of arrowhead, cattail, prairie turnip, groundnut, hog peanut, Jerusalem artichoke, day lily, and the first-year roots of common burdock, dug in the fall.

These roots and tubers can be peeled and eaten raw, but they are better boiled or roasted in the coals of a campfire. For roasting, wrap the roots in several layers of large leaves that have been dipped in water. The wet leaves will steam the roots as they roast.

The crisp roots of the Indian cucumber can be eaten "as is." They have a pleasant cucumber flavor. As with all wild edibles, harvest only what you need.

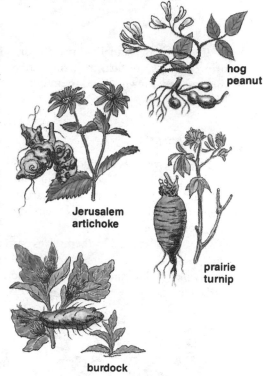

hog peanut

Jerusalem artichoke

prairie turnip

burdock

arrowhead

day lily

Beverages 1

The red fruit clusters of staghorn sumac make a refreshing cool drink. Put them in a pot and cover with cold water. Let them stand for an hour, then strain the liquid through a bandanna. Sweeten to taste.

For a pleasant-tasting tea, pour boiling water over the leaves of spearmint, peppermint, or wild bergamot, over the flowers of elderberry or basswood, or over the twigs of spicebush. Try the same method to make tea from the dried leaves of wild strawberry, black birch, wintergreen, or fireweed.

343

The roots of dandelion and chicory are sometimes used as coffee sub-stitutes. Dry them first, then chop them up and roast them in a pan until they are dark brown. Grind them between stones, and steep the grounds in hot water.

Wild Desserts

1

Wild berries, fruits, and nuts are delicious outdoor treats. Wild straw-berry, red raspberry, blackberry, huckleberry, and blueberry are tasty snacks you may find along the trail. You can also stir them into puddings and cob-blers for special desserts, or mix them into pancake batter for a breakfast you'll long remember.

Nuts are also good by themselves or in recipes. Try black walnuts, butter-nuts, pecans, hickory nuts, hazelnuts, chestnuts, and piñon nuts. The fruit of pawpaw and persimmon trees are good when fully ripe in late autumn or early winter.

staghorn sumac

elderberry

black birch

wild bergamot

basswood

fireweed

spicebush

spearmint

wintergreen

CHAPTER 14

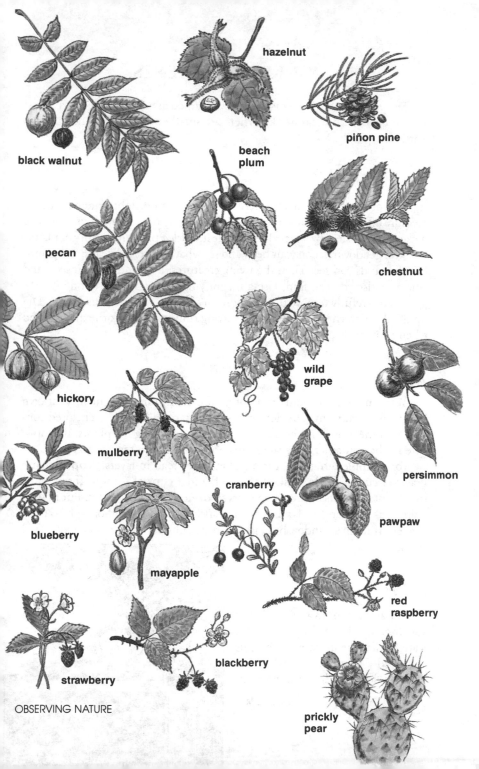

hazelnut

piñon pine

black walnut

beach plum

chestnut

pecan

wild grape

persimmon

hickory

mulberry

cranberry

blueberry

mayapple

pawpaw

red raspberry

strawberry

blackberry

OBSERVING NATURE

prickly pear

MINI-ENVIRONMENTS

The environments in which you have roamed as a Scout have been as vast as your eyes could measure. But there are small environments that are also worth your study.

Plot of Ground

One of these mini-environments is in the ground right under your feet. Measure off a square plot with sides 1 yard long: 1 square yard of ground. (Or make it a plot 2 feet by 5 feet: 10 square feet.) Pick a plot with plenty of plants.

Now get down flat on your belly and see what's there. Start with the plants. List the kinds you see. Then the living creatures: ants and other insects and whatever else you can find. Use a magnifying glass if you have one.

Then carefully remove the sod from an area two spadewidths square. Dig up the dirt and check it out for more living things. Put back the dirt and sod when you are through.

Terrarium

You can continue your study of a mini-environment right in your own home, in a terrarium. The definition of a terrarium is "a fully enclosed container for the indoor cultivation of plants." By enclosing the plants, the moisture in the container stays the same. You need do no regular watering.

For a simple terrarium, use a gallon jar. Spread in layers 1 cup of coarse gravel, 1 cup of finely crushed charcoal, and 3 cups of topsoil. Insert some small rooted plants or sow some grass seed. Add ¼ cup of water. Put in such animals as salamanders, land snails, and crickets. Screw the lid on tightly. Place the terrarium in a window but out of direct sunlight. Open as needed to feed the animals.

Aquarium

An aquarium, as the word tells you (*aqua* is Latin for water), is a watery mini-environment. For this you need a fishtank or bowl with a layer of clean sand on the bottom.

AQUARIUM ▶

Fill the tank with pond water. Anchor a couple of local aquatic plants in the sand. Then introduce a few water snails and a couple of minnows or other small fish.

If you can't get pond water, use tap water and let it stand a few days to lose its chlorine. And if you can't collect your own plants and fish, get them from a pet shop. Here you can also buy aquarium fish food. The main point in feeding is: Don't overfeed. Feed once a day and only enough to last the day.

WIND AND WEATHER

"Some are weather-wise, some are otherwise," Benjamin Franklin once said. Back in Franklin's time, farmers, sailors, and native Americans had to be wise about the weather. Their livelihoods and sometimes their safety depended upon their ability to predict the weather. They searched the land and sky for signs of changing conditions.

Today most of us get our weather information from radio and television. Scientists called *meteorologists* make weather predictions after studying photographs from satellites and reports from thousands of other meteorologists around the world.

You won't have radios or televisions on Scout campouts and hikes, but you can use your eyes to read the weather signs around you. You, too, can become "weather-wise."

Weather Signs

Through the ages, people have used sayings as a way of passing on their weather knowledge. The weather sayings below are very old. You will be surprised how often they foretell the weather.

Fair-Weather Signs

Expect pleasant weather when you see some of these signs:

☆ "Red sky at night, sailor's delight." The dust particles in the dry air of tomorrow's weather produce a glowing red sunset.

☆ "Swallows flying way up high means there's no rain in the sky." Swallows are birds that catch and eat flying insects. In the high air pressure that comes with fair weather, insects may be carried aloft by air currents.

☆ "If smoke goes high, no rain comes by." Campfire smoke rises straight up when there is no wind. Still air does not move moisture into an area.

☆ "When the dew is on the grass, rain will never come to pass." Dew forms when air moisture condenses on cool leaves and grass. That happens especially during the cool, clear night skies that come with good weather.

Stormy-Weather Signs

The following signs suggest bad weather is on the way:

☆ "Red sky at morning, sailor take warning." Dry, dusty air is moving away from you toward the east. Moist air may be coming in from the west.

☆ "Swallows flying near the ground means a storm will come around." The low air pressure that pulls in stormy weather causes insects to fly close to the ground on heavy, moist wings. Swallows follow.

☆ "If smoke hangs low, watch out for a blow." Low air pressure can prevent campfire smoke from rising very high.

☆ "When grass is dry at morning light, look for rain before the night." On a cloudy night, grass may not cool enough for dew to form.

☆ "Mackerel scales and mares' tails make lofty ships carry low sails." *Scales* and *tails* are cloud formations that warn of changing weather.

◄ CIRRUS or "FEATHER" clouds are the highest of formations, from about 5 to 6 miles.

CIRRO STRATUS or "TANGLED ► WEB." A high thin whitish cloud. Altitude about 5½ miles. Can produce halos.

◄ CIRRO CUMULUS or "MACK-EREL" clouds. Small flakes arranged in groups or lines. Height about 4 miles.

ALTO CUMULUS or "SHEEP." ► Rather large white masses or groups often spread into lines. Height varies from 3 to 4 miles.

◄ ALTO STRATUS. A thick gray "CURTAIN" like cloud. Shows a bright patch where sun or moon hides. Height about 3 miles.

349

◄ STRATO CUMULUS. "TWIST" shaped clouds of dark color. Not very thick showing blue sky in spots. Does not bring rain. Height about 1 mile.

NIMBUS. "UMBRELLA." "OVER ► ALL." Rain clouds. Thick and dark. Small ragged pieces floating at low level are known as "scud." Holes may be seen.

◄ CUMULUS "WOOL PACK." Huge masses of varying height. Some are brightly lit by the sun; others may be darker with glowing edges.

CUMULO-NIMBUS—"THUNDER" ► or "SHOWER." Like Cumulus but has "False Cirrus" at top and "Nimbus" underneath. These clouds come very low.

◄ STRATUS—"SPREAD-OUT SHEET." Horizontal sheet of lifted fog. Torn apart is known as "Fracto Stratus."

WEATHER RECORD

Date _____

	a.m.	p.m.
Temperature		
Relative humidity		
Wind direction		
Wind velocity		
Rainfall		
Sunshine		
Clouds		

YOUR WEATHER RECORD

Know your climate and you'll better understand your own environment. Weather records will help you learn. Use information from local newspapers, radio, or TV, if available. If not, set up a simple weather station. Take readings twice a day for those weather features listed on the chart. At the end of the month use the information to interpret your weather.

WEATHER AS A HOBBY. If you want to make weather one of your hobbies, get in touch with people interested in meteorology. Your science teacher may suggest names to you. Get a *Weather* merit badge pamphlet and meet the requirements.

WIND-SCALE NUMBERS
(Simplified Beaufort Scale)

When you see this:		Wind speed is:	
		MPH	**KM/H**
0 Calm. Smoke goes straight up. *No wind.*		0–1	0–1.6
1 Direction of wind shown by smoke drift, but not by wind vane. *Slight wind.*		1–3	1.6–5
2 Wind felt on face. Leaves rustle. Wind vane moves. *Light breeze.*		4–7	6–11
3 Leaves and small twigs move steadily. Small flag held straight out. *Gentle breeze.*		8–12	13–19
4 Dust and loose paper raised. Small branches move. *Moderate wind.*		13–18	21–29
5 Small trees sway. Waves form on lakes. *Fresh wind.*		19–24	30–38
6 Large branches move. Wires whistle. Umbrellas are hard to use. *Strong wind.*		25–31	40–50
7 Whole trees in motion. Hard to walk against wind. *High wind.*		32–38	52–60
8 Twigs break from trees. Very hard to walk against the wind. *Gale.*		39–46	62–72
9 Small damage to buildings. *Strong gale.*		47–54	74–87
10 Much damage to buildings. Trees uprooted. *Whole gale.*		55–63	88–101
11 Widespread damage from wind. *Violent storm.*		64–72	102–116
12 Violence and destruction from wind. *Hurricane.*		73 +	117 +

MPH—miles per hour   **KM/H—kilometers per hour**

WEATHER INSTRUMENTS

RAIN GAUGE. Use a No. 10 can or a coffee can. Whatever you use must have top, sides, and bottom the same diameter. Measure rainfall daily with a ruler. Empty the can after each measurement.

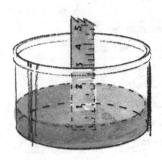

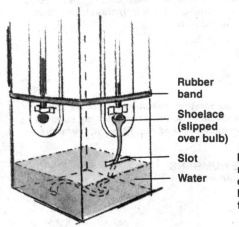

Rubber band

Shoelace (slipped over bulb)

Slot

Water

HUMIDITY. Use a milk carton and two thermometers. Measure humidity by noting the difference between the wet-bulb and dry-bulb thermometers. Use the chart below to find the percent of relative humidity.

TABLE OF RELATIVE HUMIDITY—MEASURING MOISTURE

Difference between wet-bulb and dry-bulb readings		Temperature of air, dry-bulb thermometer in Celsius (°C) and Fahrenheit (°F)							
°C	°F	−1°/30°	5°/40°	10°/50°	15°/60°	21°/70°	26°/80°	32°/90°	37°/100°
.5	1	90%	92%	93%	94%	95%	96%	96%	97%
1.1	2	79%	84%	87%	89%	90%	92%	92%	93%
1.6	3	68%	76%	80%	84%	86%	87%	88%	90%
2.2	4	58%	68%	74%	78%	81%	83%	85%	86%
3.3	6	38%	52%	61%	68%	72%	75%	78%	80%
4.4	8	18%	37%	49%	58%	64%	68%	71%	74%
5.5	10		22%	37%	48%	55%	61%	65%	68%
6.6	12		8%	26%	39%	48%	54%	59%	62%
7.7	14			16%	30%	40%	47%	53%	57%
8.8	16			5%	21%	33%	41%	47%	51%
9.9	18				13%	26%	35%	41%	47%
11.0	20				5%	19%	29%	36%	42%
12.1	22					12%	23%	32%	37%
13.2	24					6%	18%	26%	33%

STARS AND CONSTELLATIONS

One of the pleasures of camping is looking up at night into the heavens. Away from the lights of the city, you can see thousands of stars. At first, the night sky may seem to be a random scattering of brilliant points of light. Look more carefully, though, and you will notice that some stars are brighter than others. Night after night they appear in the sky at almost the same place. There is an order to their location. Learn about that order, and you will have a powerful skill for finding directions at night.

For thousands of years, people have grouped stars into pictures called *constellations*. The word comes from *con,* meaning "together," and *stella,* meaning "star." The custom may date back to times when Greek and Roman shepherds spent their nights under the open sky. They imagined that different groups of stars formed the shapes of their kings and queens, warriors, maidens, animals, and monsters. The names they gave the constellations are still with us today. You will find those same constellations in the sky over your camp. Read about them, and you can discover much about the history and legends of ancient people who, like you, gazed with wonder at the stars above.

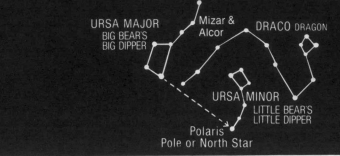

URSA MAJOR
BIG BEAR'S
BIG DIPPER

Mizar & Alcor

DRACO DRAGON

URSA MINOR
LITTLE BEAR'S
LITTLE DIPPER

Polaris
Pole or North Star

This is the way the North Star and the "pointers" appear on a star map.

Stars to the North

Ursa Major is the ancient name for a constellation called the Big Bear. Today it is also called the Big Dipper. You may have noticed it before—four bright stars in the shape of a bowl, and three stars making up a handle. Look closely and you may see that the middle star of the handle is really two stars. The Greeks called them Mizar and Alcor. Native Americans thought of the larger star as a horse, the smaller as a rider.

To find the North Star, train your eyes on the "pointer stars" of the Big Dipper—the two stars farthest from the handle. Extend an imaginary line through them. The North Star is on that line at a distance of about five times the distance between the two pointers. True north on the Earth lies at the horizon directly under the North Star.

Like the sun, most stars seem to move from east to west across the sky. That is because the Earth is revolving beneath them. Since it is directly over the Earth's North Pole, the North Star does not appear to move at all.

The North Star is also the last star in the handle of the Little Dipper, or Ursa Minor, the Little Bear. The Little Dipper appears to be pouring into the Big Dipper. Between the two dippers dangles a long line of faint stars—the tail of Draco the Dragon.

Remember the pointer stars of the Big Dipper? Follow that line beyond the North Star and you will come to five bright stars forming the shape of the letter **W**. That's the constellation Cassiopeia, also known as the Queen's Chair.

Find the North Star. Draw a line from it to the ground. A landmark here will be true north of you.

This is how the "pointers" help you find the North Star in the starry sky.

Summer Stars

Due to the Earth's yearly rotation around the sun, the location of each constellation is different in the summer from its location in the winter. Constellation maps like those on the following pages give the dates and hours when they best represent what you will see in the sky. If you can, select a viewing spot far from streetlights and the glow of the city. Choose a night when there is little or no moonlight to obscure the brilliance of the stars.

Just as you travel the backcountry by going from one landmark to the next, you can travel about the night sky by using the constellations you recognize as reference points leading you to star groups that are new to you.

Begin by finding the constellations that swing around the North Star: the Dippers and Cassiopeia. Draw an imaginary line through the pointers of the Big Dipper all the way to Cassiopeia.

Now draw a second line across the first, crossing at the North Star to form a huge "plus sign" in the sky. Follow the second line in one direction and you will come to a bright star near a tilted box made of four fainter stars. The bright one is Vega in the constellation called the Lyre. Trace the line the other way from the North Star to Capella, a bright star with three faint ones close by. They are part of a five-sided constellation known as the Charioteer.

Return to the pointer stars of the Big Dipper. This time, follow a line through them *away* from the North Star. It will lead you to the constellation Leo the Lion. Regulus is Leo's brightest star. Between the Lion and the

N

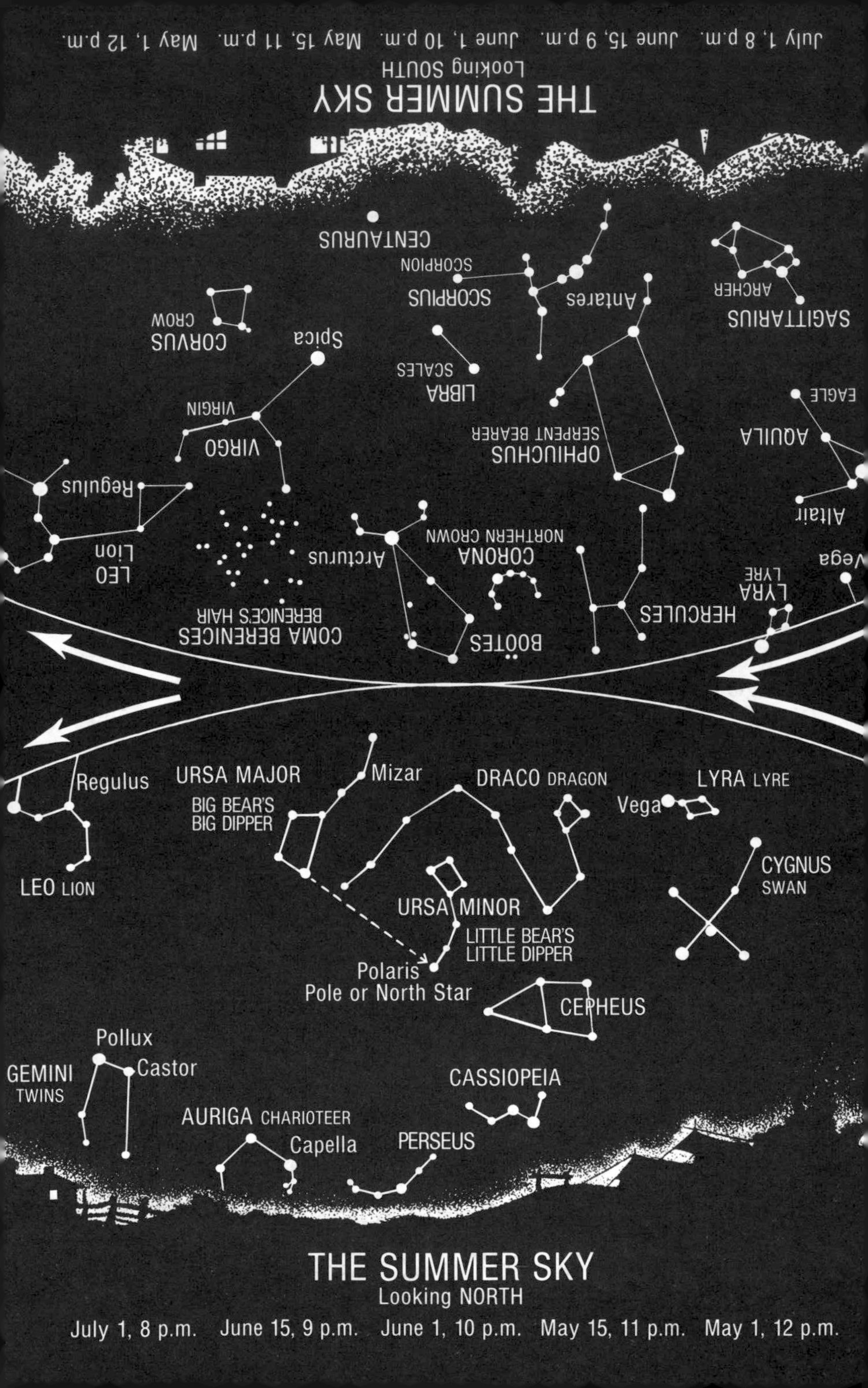

July 1, 8 p.m. June 15, 9 p.m. June 1, 10 p.m. May 15, 11 p.m. May 1, 12 p.m.
Looking SOUTH
THE SUMMER SKY
CENTAURUS
SCORPION
SCORPIUS
Antares
ARCHER
SAGITTARIUS
CROW
CORVUS
Spica
SCALES
LIBRA
VIRGIN
VIRGO
SERPENT BEARER
OPHIUCHUS
EAGLE
AQUILA
Regulus
Altair
NORTHERN CROWN
CORONA
Arcturus
Lion
LEO
Vega
LYRE
LYRA
HERCULES
BERENICE'S HAIR
COMA BERENICES
BOÖTES
Regulus
URSA MAJOR
BIG BEAR'S
BIG DIPPER
Mizar
DRACO DRAGON
LYRA LYRE
Vega
CYGNUS
SWAN
LEO LION
URSA MINOR
LITTLE BEAR'S
LITTLE DIPPER
Polaris
Pole or North Star
CEPHEUS
Pollux
GEMINI
TWINS
Castor
CASSIOPEIA
AURIGA CHARIOTEER
Capella
PERSEUS
THE SUMMER SKY
Looking NORTH
July 1, 8 p.m. June 15, 9 p.m. June 1, 10 p.m. May 15, 11 p.m. May 1, 12 p.m.

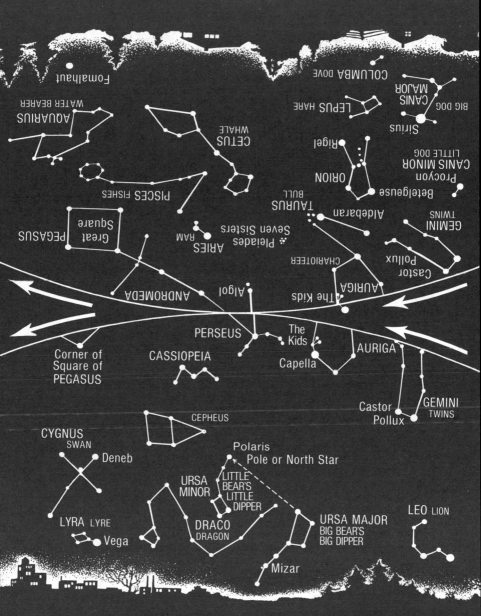

THE WINTER SKY
Looking NORTH

Charioteer are two bright stars called Castor and Pollux—the Twins. Between the Charioteer and Cassiopeia is the Perseus constellation. And finally, between Cassiopeia and the star Vega, five stars form a wide cross called Cygnus the Swan, or the Northern Cross.

Now, turn the book upside down.

For a look at the rest of the night sky, return once more to the Big Dipper. Follow the curved line of the handle to Arcturus; it is the brightest star in Boötes, the Herdsman, a constellation that looks like a big kite. Next to the Herdsman is a half circle of faint stars making up Corona, the Northern Crown. Nearby is Hercules, a group of stars shaped like a crooked letter H. Go a little farther in the same direction and you will find yourself back at Vega. Turn and look south. Filling much of the southern sky are the tail, shoulders, and claws of Scorpius, the Scorpion. The tail hangs down near the horizon. Its head points toward Spica, the bright star of the Y-shaped Virgin. Seeming to fly away in the other direction is Aquila, the Eagle. It resembles a great bird spreading its wings.

Winter Stars

On a winter night, find the Big Dipper. Trace a line from the pointers through the North Star and beyond the W of Cassiopeia to a string of three stars called Andromeda. The last of the three bright stars is a corner of the Great Square in the Pegasus constellation. The other end of Andromeda points toward Perseus.

Now, turn the book upside down.

An obvious winter constellation is Orion the Hunter. Two bright stars mark his shoulders. Three small ones form his head and two more his legs. Three stars are his belt. Three more represent the sword hanging from the belt. Above Orion's lower shoulder is the red star Aldebaran, the "eye," in the V-shaped head of Taurus the Bull. Farther up the sky are the Pleiades, or Seven Sisters—a tight cluster of faint stars. Six stars are visible to a person with average eyesight. Through a telescope, you will discover that the Pleiades are really several hundred stars. Return to Orion. Follow a line to the left through Orion's belt until you reach Sirius in Canis Major, the Big Dog. Sirius is the brightest star in the night sky.

CHAPTER 14

THE PLANETS

From earliest times, star watchers have noticed that five points of light did not behave like all the others. Rather than holding positions in constellations, these five moved about among the stars. The ancient Greeks called them *planetes,* meaning "wanderers."

Today we know that these wanderers are planets that, like the Earth, revolve around the sun. Those visible with the naked eye are Mercury, Venus, Mars, Jupiter, and Saturn. All look like bright stars except Mercury. The closest to the sun, it makes faint appearances near the western horizon just after sunset. The planets Uranus, Neptune, and Pluto can be seen only with the aid of a telescope.

In fact, a telescope or binoculars will reveal many wonders in the night sky. You may be able to see the rings of Saturn, the craters of our moon, and the great gas clouds called nebulas.

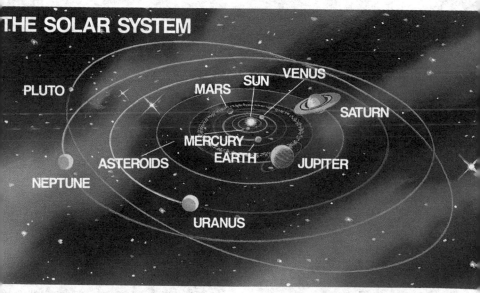

Many objects in the solar system travel around the sun—large and small planets, many with moons; meteorites; comets; and dust particles.

CHAPTER 15

CARING
FOR THE EARTH

I MAGINE being a crew member of a shiny, round space station cruising among the galaxies. On board are gardens full of plants, growing by the light of stars. Those plants purify the air you breathe and provide you with food. The space station's fine balance of air, water, vegetation, and starlight makes your survival possible.

But what if the crew gets lazy and forgets to take care of the gardens, or becomes greedy and harvests all the vegetation at once? What will happen if you dump raw sewage into the station's water tanks instead of mixing it with soil where it can nourish the plants? And what if exhaust from the rocket engines seeps into the air supply?

It's clear that you and the rest of the crew must protect the water, air, and gardens from abuse, and repair any damage that does occur. If you don't look after your environment, the space station may no longer be able to support life. You will have to abandon ship.

Now imagine a planet that, like the space station, is floating through the universe. The planet has gardens and also forests, prairies, deserts, and seas. Its water, air, and vegetation are part of a vast ecosystem that includes millions of species of animals and billions of human beings.

Of all the stars and planets in the cosmos, this may be the only one that supports life. Its inhabitants cannot travel to another planet to live. Their entire supply of air, water, and resources is aboard the planet right now. If they spoil what they have, there is nowhere they can get more.

Since their lives depend on it, you would think those people would do everything they could to protect their environment. Over the years, though, many of the planet's inhabitants have become careless, greedy, and wasteful. They have polluted their air and fouled their oceans, rivers, and lakes. Overuse and erosion have spoiled much of their land. The result is a growing environmental disaster.

There is hope for that planet. With hard work, the people can reverse much of the damage they have caused. But if they continue to mistreat their space home, they may turn it into a lifeless ball of stone drifting in the blackness of space.

What you have just read is not a science fiction story. That planet is Earth, and we are the people living on it. This is a place of great beauty, variety, and possibility. It is also a planet in serious trouble.

Today, there are five billion of us making the Earth our home. Each of us must have food, water, clothing, and room in which to live. The needs of so many people place tremendous demands upon the environment. We are in danger of damaging our planet so badly that we will limit the freedom with which we can live.

The signs of environmental abuse are all around us. You've seen litter in vacant lots, along roads, and in open fields. Many streams and lakes that should be clean and full of aquatic life are instead clouded with chemicals, refuse, and silt. The air we breathe is sometimes hazy with exhaust and smoke.

News reports tell us of other symptoms of harm to the ecology. The tons of garbage we dump every day are choking our landfills. Acid rain caused by our automobile and factory emissions is killing forests and polluting lakes. Sewage and industrial pollution are fouling rivers and parts of oceans. Throughout the world, inappropriate methods of farming, mining, logging, and manufacturing are eroding land, poisoning water, and threatening wildlife.

Of course, we must use some of the Earth's resources to make our lives possible, but we can do that in ways that are appropriate and safe. It's when we waste, pollute, or otherwise abuse the environment that the planet suffers. Learning how to act for the good of the land may require that we change how we think about our environment and ourselves.

Our language is full of phrases suggesting that we have long battled against nature rather than caring for it. "Taming the wilderness" and "defeating the elements" are slogans that describe the way we used to think about the environment. But there can be no victory in fighting against nature. It is time instead to work on the side of nature to heal the wounds that humans have caused.

A FRESH OLD IDEA

Peering through the trees, an Indian boy watched a deer crossing a meadow. Slowly he drew his bow and sent an arrow through the deer's heart. He and his family needed the meat for food and the hide for clothing.

The young hunter knelt beside the deer. He took some corn pollen from his pouch and gently placed it in the nostrils of the dying deer as a reminder of the natural cycle of life and death. Just as the corn had once nourished the deer, the deer would now sustain the boy's family. One day when their bodies were buried in the earth where they would become food for corn and other plants, the cycle would continue.

The boy belonged to a tribe that believed life is sacred and that everything has life. Animals, plants, soil, sky, water, and fire are full of the spirit of life — including deer and humans. Because they have life, all things have a right to exist. Knowing that, the tribe members lived *with* nature rather than struggling *against* it.

Unlike that boy, many of us today live in cities that limit our contact with the outdoors. Streetlights dim the night sky. Asphalt blankets the open ground. The vehicles that save us from walking also prevent us from feeling the shape and texture of the land beneath our feet. We are so entertained by the sights and sounds of television and radio that we pay little attention to the natural world around us. Insulated from the Earth, we may not be very aware of the importance of our environment.

Scouting brings you close to nature. On hikes, you feel the rise and fall of the land. On campouts, you can look up at the black dome of the sky and see more stars than you ever imagined. You may feel the force of a storm, and hear the long, distant roll of mountain thunder. As you learn how to observe, you will discover much about animals, plants, and the forces of nature.

The more time you spend in the outdoors, the better you will understand why Indian tribes believe everything in the environment is sacred. Perhaps you will find yourself agreeing with them. With understanding comes caring, and when you care about what happens to the environment, you will want to do all you can to protect it from harm. A good place to begin is on Scout outings.

THE LOW-IMPACT ETHIC

Scouts often enjoy campgrounds, trails, roads, swimming beaches, and other developed recreation areas. Whenever you leave those areas in better shape than you found them, you are practicing the *low-impact ethic.*

For example, a campground your patrol uses may have picnic tables, metal fire rings, and an outhouse. Whenever you break camp, you'll be sure to pick up litter and put it in a trash can. You might also shovel ashes from the fire ring into trash bags for proper disposal, and leave a stack of firewood for the next group of campers. If the outhouse is in poor shape, you may spend a few hours helping a park ranger make necessary repairs.

Your low-impact efforts can extend beyond your own campsites. Whenever you see a trashy fire ring, a littered tent site, soap suds floating on a lake, or litter on a trail, you know something is wrong. By cleaning up the mess, you'll mend the damage some thoughtless person has caused.

The low-impact ethic keeps land, water, and man-made facilities in the best possible condition. Use low-impact methods to protect outdoor recreation areas and the environment around them.

THE NO-TRACE ETHIC

Land and water that show few signs of human activity deserve the same low-impact attention you give to any area, plus an extra effort to remove all evidence that you or anyone else has ever been there. This *no-trace ethic* is especially important when you hike off the trails or cook and sleep where there are no developed campsites.

Your patrol may spend the night in a forest where it appears no one has camped before. By preparing meals over stoves instead of fires, pitching your tents where they will not crush vegetation, and carrying home your trash, you will leave no trace of your camp. You can take pride in knowing you have protected the environment.

Practicing low-impact and no-trace methods allows you to travel lightly on the land. This shows that you respect the Earth and that you are willing to make a real difference in the kind of world we have.

TAKE RESPONSIBILITY
FOR THE EARTH

A *land steward* is a person who looks after property that belongs to someone else. The steward keeps the streams clean, the forests strong, and the wildlife healthy. Stewards of farm lands use cultivation methods that do not harm the soil. Stewards strive to keep wastes out of rivers, lakes, and streams.

The Earth does not belong forever to any one of us. During our lifetimes we enjoy the land and the seas, and we use some of their resources. But then we will pass the planet on to the generations that live after us. People born a hundred years from now will use the same land, drink the same water, and breathe the same air as we do today. So will people a thousand years from now, and people many thousands of years after that.

Each of us is a steward of the Earth. We are caring for the planet on behalf of other people alive today. We are also watching over it for the animals and plants. We look after the land, the water, and the atmosphere so that we can give to future generations an environment that is healthy and clean.

Accepting responsibility for the environment is a sign of great maturity and wisdom. Here are some of the ways you can become a good steward of the Earth:

In the Outdoors

By using low-impact and no-trace methods whenever you are hiking and camping, you can

☆ Protect the areas you visit.

☆ Increase your awareness of the world around you.

☆ Encourage others to care for trails and campgrounds, too.

Many Scouts are also rolling up their sleeves and going to work for the land. Most troops are close to national parks and forests, state and city parks, or other recreation areas. With the help of rangers, Scout troops can make important conservation projects a part of their outdoor programs. Meaningful efforts include

☆ Repairing hiking trails

☆ Restoring eroded meadows

☆ Reseeding campsites damaged by overuse

☆ Building stream structures that improve fish habitat

☆ Setting up birdhouses and feeding stations

☆ Observing wildlife and keeping records of their habits and the areas in which they live

In Your Neighborhood

The environment of your neighborhood is just as important as any park, forest, or wilderness area. Low-impact methods work as well at home as on a Scout outing.

Disposal of trash is a good example. While camping, you would never think of dumping bags of trash into a stream. You wouldn't throw piles of litter under bushes and trees. From our homes, however, we dump 150 million tons of garbage every day. Much goes into landfills that are already overflowing. Some is thrown into the ocean.

Not only does that harm the land and the sea, it wastes valuable resources. Americans throw away enough aluminum each year to rebuild every commercial jet airplane in the country. We toss out enough paper to make a wall 12 feet high stretching from New York to Los Angeles. This means we must dig up more minerals, cut down more trees, and use more energy to make new cans, paper, boxes, and glass.

We can recycle our glass, metal, paper, and plastic instead of throwing it away. Land and water will stay cleaner, and we will need fewer raw resources.

Here are other ideas for improving the environment of your neighborhood:

☆ Cleaning up vacant lots

☆ Planting trees and shrubs

☆ Composting garbage

☆ Collecting cans, bottles, and paper from neighbors for recycling, and encouraging them to recycle

Each of these projects is a low-impact way of healing environmental damage. They also remind us that we don't have to look very far from home to find ways we can work for the good of the Earth.

LIVING A LOW-IMPACT LIFE

Perhaps you have seen a poster showing a heap of litter on the ground. The message on the poster says, "Johnny didn't think it would hurt to drop a piece of paper. Neither did Mary or Bill or Ted or Jane or Scott . . ." The point is that even our little actions have an impact on the environment. Small, individual abuses of land, water, and air can add up to serious injuries. On the other hand, everything we do that helps the environment will improve the quality of the entire planet. Your actions, both good and bad, make a real difference.

This chapter has traveled from space stations to the traditional beliefs of native Americans. It has discussed the whole planet and your own neighborhood. It has suggested appropriate ways to treat the environment wherever you are, and has encouraged you to practice wise stewardship of the land.

Living in harmony with the environment rather than abusing it or fighting against it is a special way of seeing your place in the world. You alone make the decision to respect the land. You alone decide if you will be part of the answer to environmental problems. By seeing the value of a healthy environment and working in harmony with it, you can make a priceless contribution to your home planet, the Earth.

GROWING FROM
BOY TO MAN

TROOP 46

D. Adair

During your years as a Scout, you are developing from a boy into a man. You are becoming stronger. You are gaining wisdom and experience. Every day, you are accepting more adult responsibilities in your family, community, and nation.

As you grow and learn, it helps to have the support of people you trust. Family members, teachers, and religious leaders may all provide valuable guidance. So can your Scout leaders and this section of the *Scout Handbook*.

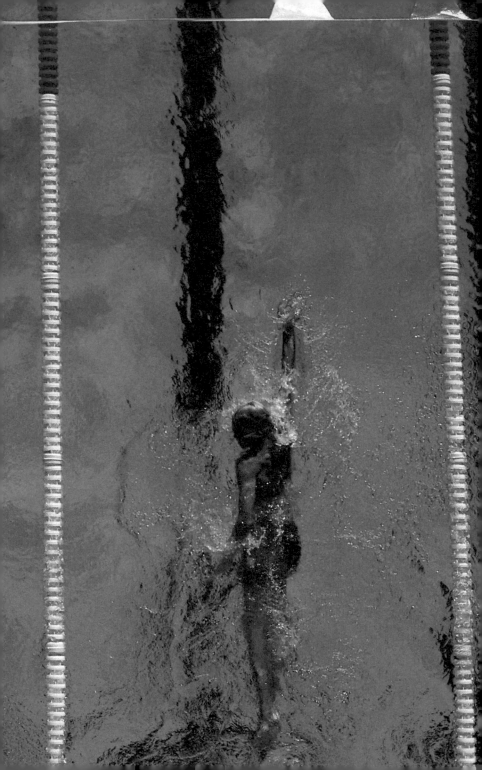

PHYSICALLY STRONG

S OME boys on a baseball team were poking fun at a Scout who had come to bat. He had a big nose, and they thought they could make him mad by teasing him about it. "Nothing I can do about that," he laughed. "You play the game of life in the uniform you were issued."

Perhaps your nose is small. Maybe it's wonderfully large like that Scout's. Your body may be long and lean, or thick and muscular. The color of your skin may be a rich brown, black, yellow, or white. Your hair might be straight, curled, or wavy. You might walk with a strong, steady stride, or get around in a wheelchair or on crutches. However your body looks, you can be proud of it. It's like no one else's in the world. It's a sign you are special.

While we can celebrate our differences, there is also much about our bodies that is the same. Each of us has more than 200 bones, more than 600 muscles, and miles of blood vessels. We each have organs, nerve cells, and thousands of other parts that make our bodies work like a finely tuned machines.

Follow wise health practices and you can build a body ready for action. You will always be in top shape for hiking, camping, and other adventures. Best of all, the health habits you develop now will stay with you for a lifetime.

GROWING INTO MANHOOD

During the years you are a Scout, you are going through one of the most important growing periods of your life. You are getting taller. Your voice is becoming deeper. You are gaining strength and speed.

See how quickly you are changing by filling in the Body Growth Chart on pages 397–398. Wait 3 months, then repeat the measurements. You may be very surprised at how quickly growth is taking place.

GOOD POSTURE

When you feel good about yourself, you stand proudly. You hold your head high, ready to face life directly. You sit with your shoulders easily back, your chest up, and your stomach in.

Backpackers walk tall in order to properly support the weight of their packs. Motorcycle police officers sit up straight so their backs won't tire during the long hours they ride. Good posture gives your internal organs room to work properly. It is also good for your spine and relieves strain on your neck and lower back.

Here's a simple trick for checking your posture: Stretch upward as if you are trying to touch the ceiling with the top of your head. Try it while sitting and while standing.

STRETCHING

Have you ever seen athletes stretching before a track meet or a big game? They slowly lean from one side to the other, bend down, and twist this way and that.

Before exercising, playing sports, or setting out on a hike or backpacking trip, take a few minutes to stretch. Stretching relaxes the tendons and ligaments. It warms up the muscles and gets them ready to work hard. It makes your body more flexible and less likely to be injured.

Try each of the following stretches with just enough effort to put a little strain on your muscles. Stretch smoothly without bouncing. At first you may feel stiff, but over time your range of motion will increase. Stretching after games and hikes will help keep your muscles and joints from becoming stiff and sore.

Thigh stretch. Place your left hand on a wall for support. Grab your right ankle with your right hand and gently pull your heel toward your buttocks. Hold for 30 seconds, then repeat with your left ankle.

THIGH STRETCH

STRADDLE STRETCH

HURDLER'S STRETCH

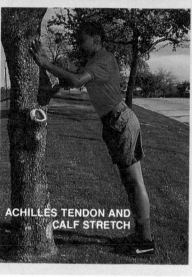

ACHILLES TENDON AND CALF STRETCH

Achilles tendon and calf stretch. Your calf muscles are in the back of your lower leg. The Achilles tendon attaches them to your heel. To stretch those muscles and tendons, stand about 3 feet from a wall. Place your palms flat against it. Keeping your heels on the floor and your back straight, lean closer to the wall and hold for 30 seconds.

Hurdler's stretch. Sit on the floor with your left leg straight ahead. Bend your right knee so that the sole of your right foot touches the left thigh, forming a triangle. Extend your hands along the straight leg and hold for 30 seconds. Repeat with the other leg.

Straddle stretch. Sit on the floor and spread your legs out flat. Lean forward as far as you can, sliding your hands on the floor. Hold the position for 30 seconds.

A STRONG BODY

Your body thrives on exercise. Like any good machine, it is made to be used. In fact, if you don't use it or if you do things that harm it, your body can become weak and useless.

Opportunities for daily exercise are everywhere. Walking, jogging, bicycling, mowing lawns, and working around the house are all good. So are the canoeing, backpacking, swimming, and climbing you do on Scout outings. In the Varsity program, you can learn and play team sports. Find out how to participate on school teams and in local leagues, too.

Exercise must be *regular*. Get in a routine of working out at least three times a week. Once you have started, you will come to enjoy it so much that you won't ever want to miss a chance to be active.

A STRONG HEART

The most important muscle in your body is your heart. Place your first two fingers on your wrist or along the side of your neck and feel your pulse. Each time your heart beats, it sends blood through your arteries and veins, carrying nourishment to every cell.

Your heart works very hard, pumping 2,000 gallons of blood each day. Regular exercise will strengthen your heart muscles. A diet low in fat helps keep your arteries clear. Don't smoke or use illegal drugs — they can weaken your heart, make you ill, and even lead to death.

GAINING STRENGTH

Here's how you can test yourself to see how well your exercises are strengthening your body:

☆ First, try each of the exercises on pages 393–395. Record your best results on the top line of the chart on page 396.

☆ Decide how much you want to improve in 30 days. Write your goals next to the word *Aim*.

☆ Work at each exercise three times a week or more. Push yourself to do your best.

☆ Test yourself again at the end of a month, and write the new results on the chart. You will see a difference. Keep at it until you reach the standard of excellence for your age in all five tests.

Relative Physical Fitness Values of Sports

You will enjoy many different sports over your lifetime. No matter what your size or ability, some sports will be just right for you.

PROPER NOURISHMENT

Your Food

Almost anything you eat and drink provides some nourishment, even a bag of potato chips and a bottle of pop. But if you try to get along on a steady diet of junk foods, you'll soon run into trouble. Why? Because they lack a lot of necessary nutrition.

The food you eat should do these three things:

☆ *Build up your body and keep it in good repair.* Protein and minerals are the body's building blocks. They are found in meat, fish, eggs, milk products, and in combinations of grains.

☆ *Give your internal organs — liver, spleen, intestines, and the others — what they must have to stay healthy.* Vitamins and minerals in vegetables and citrus fruits help do this, along with fiber and bulk in other foods.

☆ *Serve as a source of energy for what you want to do.* There is some fuel in everything you eat, especially breads, grains, fats, and oils.

A Balanced Diet

The four food groups listed below are the foundation of a balanced diet. They provide you with nutrition essential for good health.

Because of family background, religious beliefs, or medical limitations, many people choose not to eat certain foods. Vegetarians, for example, avoid meat. Combinations of grains give them diets as rich in protein as if they ate hamburgers and steaks.

Don't pass up chances to try different kinds of meals. Eating new dishes is a fun way to learn about other parts of the country and about foreign customs.

MILK GROUP

Milk, Cheese, Ice Cream, and Yogurt
One or more servings daily

PROTEIN GROUP

Meat, Fish, Poultry, Lentils, Beans, and Dried Peas
Two or more servings daily

BREAD-CEREAL-GRAINS GROUP

At every meal

VEGETABLE-FRUIT GROUP

Citrus Fruits and Tomatoes
At least one serving daily

Leafy Green and Yellow Vegetables
At least one serving daily

Other Vegetables and Fruits
Two or more servings daily

381

What About Caffeine and Sugar?

Coffee, tea, and many cola drinks contain *caffeine,* a mild drug that temporarily stirs up the nervous system and speeds the heart. None of these beverages has much food value. The caffeine in them may make you edgy and uncomfortable. Water, fruit juices, and milk are far better for you.

Sugar is an ingredient in many candies, cereals, and other foods. A can of soda may contain 6 teaspoons of sugar. Sugar is also a major part of pancake syrup, molasses, and honey. Sugary foods and sodas will give your body a quick surge of energy by lifting your blood sugar level. It wears off quickly, though. The letdown can leave you feeling tired and irritable. Try to limit the amount of sugar you eat. Fresh fruits and juices are nutritious substitues.

Drink Water

Did you know that 70 percent of your body is made up of water? Water helps your system digest food. It washes wastes through your intestines and kidneys. When you perspire, the evaporation of moisture from the surface of your skin cools you. Drink six to eight glasses of fresh water every day.

Getting Rid of Wastes

Eat the right foods, get enough exercise, drink plenty of water, and your body will take care of eliminating wastes. Grains and fresh vegetables provide *fiber* which keeps food moving smoothly through your system. Your digestive tract will develop its own rhythm for bowel movements.

CLEANLINESS

Your skin is your body's largest organ. Sweat glands in the skin help control body temperature. Nerve endings are sensitive to heat, cold, and touch. Your skin is also the armor protecting you from injury and disease.

Skin is very tough, but it needs regular care. Keep it clean. When you are in the sun, protect your skin from harmful rays by applying a sunscreen with a sun protection factor (SPF) rating of 15 or more. If your skin becomes dry or irritated, soothe it with lotion.

Bathing

Bathe regularly—once a day if you can. A shower or bath is best, or you can wash your whole body with a wet cloth. In camp and on the trail, carry water at least 200 feet from lakes, streams, and springs before you wash. That way, there is little chance of getting soap in open water where it may harm plants and animals. A hot shower always feels great after a campout, a long hike, or an afternoon of sports.

Your Hands

When you work and play hard, your hands will become dirty. Don't be ashamed of that. But when you are done, scrub your hands with soap and water, just as you do before handling food and after using the bathroom. Special hand soaps will cut through grease and grit. Clean under your nails, too, and keep them trimmed with clippers or nail scissors.

Before doing work that may cause dirt to collect under the nails, try scraping them over a piece of soap. The soap will keep out dirt and make cleanup easier. Or you may want to wear gloves to protect your hands from injury and grime. Leather or cotton gloves are fine for outside chores. Rubber gloves shield your hands from detergents and grease.

Your Feet

Your feet contain one-fourth of all the bones in your body. They give you balance. They absorb the impact of millions of footsteps. You land on them when you jump. They twist, turn, and spring back for more.

Wash your feet thoroughly whenever you bathe. Cut your nails straight across to prevent them from becoming ingrown. For hiking and hard play, wear properly fitted shoes or boots that support your feet and give you traction. Blisters, bunions, and aching feet are often caused by shoes that are too narrow or too short. On the trail and the playing field, treat "hot spots" before they become blisters. If a blister does form, stop and treat it (see page 422).

Hair

Wash your hair often enough to keep it clean. Exercise your scalp by massaging it with your fingertips.

Your Teeth

Your teeth can last a lifetime, but only if you keep them in good shape. Gentle brushing removes the sticky, colorless *plaque* that causes tooth decay and gum disease. Flossing loosens food particles and plaque from between your teeth. Brush and floss your teeth at least twice a day — right after meals is a good time to do

it. Eat a well-balanced diet, avoid sugary snacks, and have a dentist check and clean your teeth twice a year.

Your Eyes

Look in a mirror. Are your eyes clear, bright, and healthy? If they are bloodshot or if they hurt, you may be suffering from eyestrain. The cause can be wind or smoke, lack of sleep, watching too much television, reading under a poor light, or a need for glasses. Have your eyes examined by an eye specialist if you have any concerns. Good vision is so important that you will want to do all you can to care for your eyes.

Rest your eyes when you are studying by looking out a window now and then and focusing on distant objects. Wear sunglasses in bright light, especially on open water and snow. Goggles or a snorkel mask will keep swimming pool chemicals from irritating your eyes. Put on safety goggles whenever you use power tools.

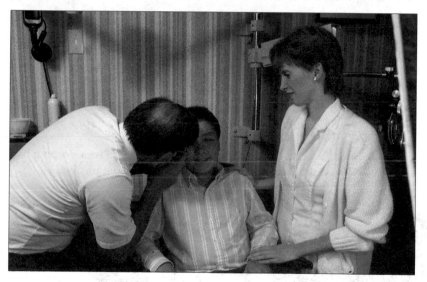

Your Ears

Clean the outside of each ear with a damp washcloth wrapped over the end of a finger. Let the inside of your ears take care of themselves. Never dig in your ears—that may infect them or even damage the eardrums.

Very loud noises, especially those that persist, can injure your ears. Wear ear protection around noisy machinery, engines, and on a firing range. Keep the volume of stereos and tape players at a reasonable level, especially if you are listening with headphones.

An earache, constant ringing, or fluid running out of an ear are all signs of trouble. See a doctor if you suffer from any of these symptoms.

FRESH AIR

The air you breathe provides the oxygen your body must have in order to live. Without a steady supply of air, you would die within a few minutes.

Breathe the cleanest air you can by staying away from exhaust fumes, smoke, and chemical vapors. Use paints, glues, and sprays outside, or in well-ventilated areas. Refuel and light camping stoves and lanterns outdoors, and never bring them inside a tent.

REST AND SLEEP

Sleep is your body's way of renewing its energy. Rest also gives your body a chance to replace old tissues and build new—in other words, to grow.

You are at an age when you are growing very quickly, and that requires plenty of sleep. How much is enough? A boy 11 to 14 years old needs 9 to 10 hours of sleep each night.

On campouts, you will be tired by nightfall. Crawl into your sleeping bag and you will probably fall asleep quickly and not awaken until dawn.

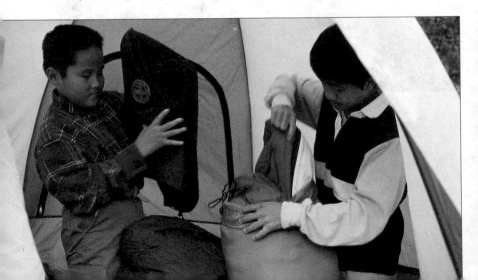

It can be a little different at home. With school activities, Scout meetings, homework, and reading for pleasure, there is much to do in the evening. Sometimes sleep may not seem very important.

But it's not how little you can get by on, it's how much rest you should have to be at your best. Do some planning so that you can get enough sleep and also finish everything else you want to do.

In the woods, you know how to make a good bed with your sleeping bag or blankets, ground cloth, and pad. Your bed at home should be just as comfortable. If the mattress sags, place a sheet of plywood under it. Open a window during the warm months to let fresh air into your room. Better yet, sleep outdoors whenever you can.

Go to bed at the same time every night and get up at the same time each morning. Your body will get used to the schedule. You'll fall asleep quickly and awaken refreshed.

STAYING HEALTHY

Protect Yourself Against Accidents

More young people die from accidents than from any other cause. Every year, thousands of others are injured, many of them seriously. That doesn't have to happen to you.

Here's what you can do:

Learn skills to make you safe. There are safe ways to do everything: swimming, bicycling, paddling a canoe, using an ax, playing sports. A good example is lifting. Instead of leaning over at your waist and grabbing a heavy object, bend your knees. Protect your back by keeping it straight and lifting with the strong muscles of your legs.

"Safety through skill" is a good slogan to follow. It means practicing the proper use of tools. Learn and follow the rules of the sports you enjoy. Hike and camp with care. Anytime you aren't sure how to do something safely, ask. Understand the dangers of an activity and know how to avoid them.

Common sense can keep you safe. It doesn't take much skill to cross a railroad track. But if a train is coming, common sense tells you to wait. It is common sense to use a sturdy stepladder instead of a wobbly chair when you have to reach high. It is good judgment to stay away from strange dogs that could bite you, and to sweep up broken glass before someone steps on it and is hurt.

Be on the lookout for situations that may become dangerous and do something to correct them. Is a campfire getting too large? Douse it. Is a sidewalk crowded? Keep your skateboard under your arm.

Protect yourself against disease. The best defense against illness is a healthy body. Good food, regular exercise, and plenty of sleep help you stay strong and well. You have also had a number of *immunizations* that guard you against diseases such as tetanus, polio, mumps, and measles.

Germs that cause sickness can be avoided in many ways.

☆ Wash cups and utensils used by others before you drink or eat from them.

☆ Use your own bath towel, washcloth, and handkerchief.

☆ Stay clear of persons who are coughing or sneezing.

☆ Keep flies away from yourself and your food.

☆ Wash your hands after using the bathroom and before handling food.

Protect Yourself Against Yourself   2

On a hike, you trust your map and compass to show you the way. When it comes to drugs, alcohol, and tobacco, you can trust that part of the Scout Oath in which you promise to keep yourself physically strong and mentally awake. You lose the power to guide your own life if you hurt your body or your mind. Just as you trust your compass, trust what you know is right.

Tobacco. You may have friends who think smoking makes them look grown up. Ads in magazines and newspapers pretend that smoking is very exciting. Many of those ads are aimed at young adults not much older than you.

Don't let advertisements fool you. Smoking shortens your breath and makes it hard for you to be good at sports. Smoke coats your lungs with sticky tars that can cause cancer, a disease that kills hundreds of thousands of people every year. Smoking can also lead to a sickness called emphysema which weakens the lungs so much that those who have it may not be able to blow out a candle. Chewing tobacco is also dangerous. Stuck behind the lip, it can cause gum disease and cancer of the mouth.

Tobacco contains a drug called *nicotine*. Nicotine raises blood pressure and increases the heart rate. A smoker's body gets in the habit of expecting those changes and becomes uncomfortable without nicotine. Once they have begun using tobacco, many people find it very hard to quit.

It's best never to start smoking in the first place. If you do smoke, stop now. Your lungs will slowly heal, and you can look forward to a much healthier, happier, and longer life.

Alcohol. Like tobacco ads, commercials for beer, wine, and liquor are all around us. But flashy ads don't change the fact that drinking is bad for you. Alcohol will cloud your mind and affect your good judgment. It can injure your body, especially your liver and brain.

Alcoholism — a dependence on liquor — destroys many people. The craving for alcohol saps their resources and their health, ruins families, and can lead to early death. If you want to make the most of your life, don't drink.

Although you may be too young to operate an automobile, be aware of the dangers of drinking and driving. Even a small amount of alcohol can make a person an unsafe driver. The results are often tragic. Thousands of teenagers die every year in crashes involving drivers who have been drinking.

Never ride in a car driven by someone who has been drinking. You can always find another way home, but you won't always live through a crash caused by a drunken driver.

Drugs. Drugs are chemicals that alter our bodies. When you are sick, drugs given by a doctor can help you get well. Unfortunately, some young people use drugs that don't come from a doctor. Marijuana, cocaine and crack, codeine, downers, LSD, and heroin have powerful effects on the mind as well as the body. They may produce temporary feelings of pleasure, energy, and peace. However, they can also cause nightmares, fear, and loss of reason. Users may lose interest in the rich life going on all around them. Because the amount of a drug that is swallowed, smoked, inhaled, or injected is not controlled by a doctor, a user never knows how much of a drug he is taking. An overdose may lead to serious illness or death.

Stand up for what is right and refuse drugs. Say no over and over again if you have to. Drugs are dangerous and can harm your body and your future. Show your friends there is a better way to live.

Many drugs are addictive. If you begin using a drug, you may soon find that you want more and more of the substance. You may lie, cheat, and steal to get it. Using drugs can become more important to you than your friends, your family, and even your own life.

Since illegal drugs, alcohol, and tobacco are so dangerous, why would anyone ever start using them? The following are some of the reasons users might give you, and ways you can respond to them:

☆ All my friends are doing it. Sometimes it seems as though everyone is doing something. To be like them, you may be tempted to try it, too. But if their actions are wrong, you don't have to follow the crowd. Show your friends there is a better way to live. Get more involved in school activities, sports, clubs, and Scouting. If you have to, find new friends who aren't developing dangerous habits.

WHAT TO DO ABOUT DRUGS

Baden-Powell, the founder of Scouting, almost added one more point to the Scout Law: "A Scout is not a fool."

Baden-Powell had faith in the ability of Scouts to judge what is healthy and right. Have faith in yourself and in your judgment. Don't let others pressure you into harming your body with drugs, alcohol, or tobacco. If you have been foolish, there is no law that says you have to stay that way.

☆ I want to get away from problems. On campouts, you learn that the outdoor life is not always easy. Perhaps you've been caught in a thunderstorm. Maybe another Scout fell and injured himself.

You didn't run away from those problems. Instead, you used your skills to make a safe camp or to give first aid. You faced the tough times squarely and made the best of them.

Demands at home and in school can seem very heavy. You may feel as though there's a lot of weight on your shoulders, or that parents and teachers expect too much of you. Instead of turning to drinking and drugs to escape problems, look for ways to solve them. Use your skills and sharp mind to find solutions. You don't have to do it all alone. Friends, parents, teachers, religious leaders, school counselors, and your Scoutmaster will all be able to help.

☆ I want to feel grown up. Because of the way they are often shown in movies and on TV, smoking, drinking, and drugs may seem like adult things to do. But hurting your body and your future is really very childish.

You can prove you are becoming an adult by accepting worthwhile responsibilities. Helping with household chores shows you are doing your part to make family life better for everyone. Earning Scout badges and holding troop offices are signs you are maturing. So is doing your best in class and in school activities. Those are the real ways to let the world know you are becoming a respected adult.

☆ There's nothing else to do. Some young people say they use drugs, alcohol, and tobacco because they are bored. What they are really saying is that they are too lazy to go out and take part in the real excitement of being alive.

If you look around, boredom should be the farthest thing from your mind. Athletics, libraries, Scouting, school projects, music, exercise, travel, helping others—the world is full of opportunities. Each of us gets just one shot at life. Make the most of every moment.

Finally, you can simply turn your back on anything that would harm you. Say no. That is a real sign of courage. Say it over and over again if you have to. Nobody can make you do something wrong if you don't want to do it. People will admire you for standing up for what is right. With a strong body and clear mind, you will be far ahead of those who choose instead to risk their friends, their families, and their lives on the dangers of drugs, tobacco, and alcohol.

PRESIDENTIAL
PHYSICAL FITNESS AWARD

These tests are a part of the nationwide fitness program for schools, clubs, and Scout troops. If you wish to earn the award certificate and emblem, write to the President's Council on Physical Fitness and Sports, 450 Fifth Street NW, Room 7103, Washington, DC 20001. Share this information with your Scoutmaster.

FITNESS TESTS

The following tests are required for the Tenderfoot rank. Use the chart on page 396 to mark your progress.

Situps

Lie on your back with legs bent. Have someone hold your ankles, or put your feet under a heavy object. Cross your arms with hands placed on opposite shoulders and elbows held close to the chest. Keeping this arm position, raise your trunk and touch elbows to thighs, then lower your back until your shoulder blades touch the floor. Count one situp each time you lie down.

Pullups

With the palms facing forward, grasp an overhead bar. Hang with arms and legs fully extended and feet off the ground. Pull yourself up with your amrs, without kicking your legs and without swinging, until you can place your chin on the bar. Now lower yourself. Count one pullup each time your chin is over the bar.

PHYSICALLY STRONG

Pushups T

Lie facedown on the floor with your legs together and your hands on the floor directly under your shoulders. Extend your arms so that your weight rests on your hands and toes. Keep your body straight. Lower your body until your chest or chin touches the floor.

Standing Long Jump T

Stand on a level surface with your feet comfortably apart. Flex your knees. Swing your arms back and forth. Then jump, swinging your arms forcefully forward and up. Measure the distance from the takeoff line to the spot where your heel or any part of your body touched the ground.

500-Yard Run/Walk

Measure out a 500-yard course. On the starter's signal, run the distance. You are permitted to walk if necessary, but the idea is to cover the distance as quickly as possible. Record the time in minutes and seconds.

395

Date	SITUPS Aim: ___	PULLUPS Aim: ___	PUSHUPS Aim: ___	LONG JUMP Aim: ___	500-YARD RUN/WALK Aim: ___

Your Age	SITUPS Number of times		PULLUPS Number of times		PUSHUPS Number of times		LONG JUMP Meters (feet/inches)		500-YARD RUN/WALK* Minutes:Seconds	
	Good	Excellent	Good	Excellent	Good	Excellent	Good	Excellent	Good	Excellent
11	41	45	5	6	15	22	1.75 (5' 9")	1.83 (6')	1:50	1:45
12	43	48	5	7	18	24	1.83 (6')	1.90 (6' 3")	1:43	1:37
13	47	50	6	9	20	26	1.96 (6' 5")	2.08 (6' 10")	1:37	1:31
14	48	52	8	10	22	28	2.08 (6' 10")	2.18 (7' 2")	1:31	1:26
15	49	52	10	12	24	30	2.21 (7' 3")	2.32 (7' 7")	1:27	1:23
16	49	52	10	12	27	32	2.29 (7' 6")	2.41 (7' 11")	1:25	1:21

BODY GROWTH CHART

Measure yourself at 3-month intervals and fill in the spaces below.
The numbers refer to the measurement dates.

(1) __ / __ 19 __ (2) __ / __ 19 __ (3) __ / __ 19 __ (4) __ / __ 19 __

HOW TO MEASURE YOUR BODY

Height: barefoot.

Weight: stripped.

Neck: thinnest part.

Chest: across nipples, chest
    expanded.

Waist: thinnest part, stomach
    relaxed, *not* pulled in.

Hips: widest part.

Biceps: around tensed biceps,
    arm bent.

Forearm: thickest part, arm
    straight, fist clenched.

Wrist: thinnest part

Thigh: thickest part at top of leg.

Calf: thickest part.

Ankle: thinnest part.

R Wrist	L Wrist	R Biceps	L Biceps
1 _____	1 _____	1 _____	1 _____
2 _____	2 _____	2 _____	2 _____
3 _____	3 _____	3 _____	3 _____
4 _____	4 _____	4 _____	4 _____

R Forearm	L Forearm	Neck	Chest
1 _____	1 _____	1 _____	1 _____
2 _____	2 _____	2 _____	2 _____
3 _____	3 _____	3 _____	3 _____
4 _____	4 _____	4 _____	4 _____

more . . .

Waist	Hips	R Thigh	L Thigh
1 _____	1 _____	1 _____	1 _____
2 _____	2 _____	2 _____	2 _____
3 _____	3 _____	3 _____	3 _____
4 _____	4 _____	4 _____	4 _____

R Calf	L Calf	R Ankle	L Ankle
1 _____	1 _____	1 _____	1 _____
2 _____	2 _____	2 _____	2 _____
3 _____	3 _____	3 _____	3 _____
4 _____	4 _____	4 _____	4 _____

Height	Weight
1 _____	1 _____
2 _____	2 _____
3 _____	3 _____
4 _____	4 _____

**Resting
Pulse Rate**

1 _____

2 _____

3 _____

4 _____

RELATIVE PHYSICAL FITNESS
VALUES OF SPORTS

SPORT	Legs, hips	Abdomen	Lateral muscles	Arms, shoulders	Back	Endurance	Flexibility	Carryover value
Archery	L	M	M	H	M	L	L	M
Backpacking	H	M	M	H	H	H	M	H
Badminton	M	M	L	M	M	M	M	M
Baseball	M	M	M	M	M	M	M	L
Basketball	H	M	M	H	M	M	M	L
Bicycling	H	L	L	L	L	M	L	H
Bowling	M	L	L	M	L	L	L	H
Camping	M	L	L	M	L	M	L	H
Canoeing	L	M	M	H	M	H	M	H
Climbing, Rock	H	M	M	H	M	H	M	M
Dancing, Folk	H	M	M	L	M	H	M	M
Dancing, Social	H	M	M	L	M	M	M	H
Fencing	M	M	M	H	M	H	M	M
Field Hockey	H	M	M	H	M	H	H	L
Football	H	H	M	H	H	H	M	L
Golf	M	L	M	M	L	L	L	H
Handball	H	M	M	M	M	M	M	M
Hiking	H	M	L	L	M	H	M	H
Horseback Riding	M	L	L	L	M	L	L	H
Orienteering	H	M	L	L	M	H	M	H
Rowing	M	M	M	H	M	H	M	M
Running	H	M	L	L	M	H	M	M
Skating	H	L	L	L	L	H	H	H
Skiing	H	M	M	M	M	H	H	H
Soccer	H	M	M	L	M	H	H	L
Softball	M	M	M	M	M	M	L	L
Swimming	H	M	M	H	M	H	H	H
Tennis	H	M	M	H	M	H	H	H
Volleyball	M	L	M	M	L	L	M	M
Water Polo	H	M	M	H	M	H	H	L
Weight Lifting	H	H	M	H	H	H	M	M
Wrestling	H	H	H	H	H	H	H	L

H—High   M—Medium   L—Low

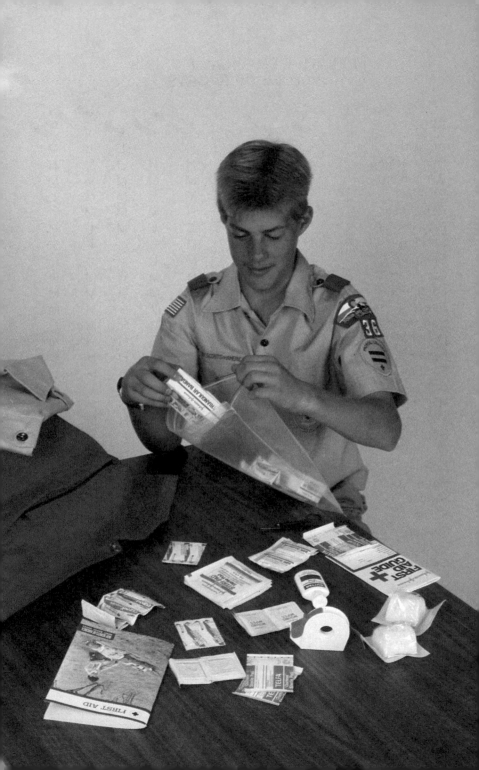

FIRST AID

BE PREPARED FOR ACCIDENTS!

A SCOUT on a campout falls against a rock. He shouts for help. His head is bleeding and his arm is bent at an odd angle.

What do you do?

Walking home from school, you hear the squeal of tires and turn to see an automobile knock a man to the ground. He is unconscious. Blood is spurting from a gash in his leg and you think he isn't breathing.

What do you do?

At home, a small child complains that he feels sick. You see a box of rat poison spilled on the floor and think the child may have eaten some.

What do you do?

What you do is give first aid.

THE BOY SCOUTS OF AMERICA RECOMMENDS:

Treat all blood as if it were contaminated with bloodborne viruses. Do not use bare hands to stop bleeding; always use a protective barrier; always wash exposed skin areas with hot water and soap immediately after treating the victim. The following equipment is to be included in all first aid kits and used when rendering first aid to those in need:

- Latex gloves, to be used when stopping bleeding or dressing wounds
- A mouth-barrier device for rendering rescue breathing or CPR
- Plastic goggles or other eye protection, to prevent a victim's blood from getting into rescuer's eyes in the event of serious arterial bleeding
- Antiseptic, for sterilizing or cleaning exposed skin areas, particularly if there is no soap or water available

---

WHAT IS FIRST AID?

First aid is the first help given to the victim of an accident. There are three primary objectives in giving first aid:

☆ Stop life-threatening dangers.

☆ Keep the victim safe from further harm.

☆ Get proper medical help for the victim.

Take Charge

The scene of an accident can be scary. An injured person may be crying or screaming. The sight of blood might frighten you. Other people may be too stunned to help.

The most important thing you can do is stay *calm*. Focus your attention on the job of making people safe. Act with *confidence,* using the first aid skills you know. *Cheerfulness* will help the victim and the people around you lose their fear.

Approach Carefully.

Keep your own safety and the safety of other rescuers in mind. At the scene of a car accident, watch for other cars on the road. In the backcountry, be aware of falling rocks, slippery footing, steep slopes, and other hazards.

Do First Things First

Here are five vital steps for treating accident victims. Perform them in the order they are given.

1. Treat "hurry cases" immediately. A hurry case is any condition that threatens a victim's life. The most serious are: stopped breathing, no heartbeat, severe bleeding, choking, and poisoning by mouth.

2. Send someone to a phone to call for help. Give full information about your location and the extent of the injuries.

3. Treat *every* accident victim for shock.

4. Examine the victim for other injuries that may require first aid.

5. Plan what to do next. If help is on the way, keep the victim comfortable and watch for any changes in his condition. Where there are no phones, decide on a clear course of action. A victim who can walk alone or with

some support may be able to hike to a road. When injuries are serious, though, it is usually best to send two Scouts for help.

Getting Help

At home, help is often just a phone call away. Most cities have a police or sheriff's office, a rescue squad, a fire department, and a hospital ambulance service. You may be able to reach all those emergency services by dialing **911**. You can also get help by dialing **0** for an operator.

The front pages of your telephone book will tell you the best ways to call for help. Look up the numbers now and write them here. Turn down the corner of the page or put a paper clip on it so you can find it fast.

Emergency Telephone Numbers

Police _____

Fire _____

Ambulance _____

Family doctor _____

Rescue or emergency medical service _____

Poison control center _____

Friendly neighbor _____

Copy the numbers on a card, too, and post it near your telephone. Put another copy in your pocket or billfold and keep it with you at all times. Carry a few "emergency quarters" wherever you go. You may need them to use a pay phone.

When you call for help, say, "I want to report an accident." Then use the three *W*'s: *who, what, where.*

☆ *WHO?* Give your name and telephone number: "This is Scout Joe Brown calling from 555-2222."

☆ *WHAT?* Explain the emergency: "I am reporting an automobile accident. Three people are hurt. One is unconscious."

☆ *WHERE?* "The accident is at the intersection of Highway 2 and Maple Street."

Speak slowly and clearly. Stay on the line until the other party hangs up; they may have important questions for you to answer.

HURRY CASES

Most accidents you come upon will be minor. You will have plenty of time to give first aid treatment.

However, the following five situations, called *hurry cases,* are life-threatening. You must quickly administer the correct first aid. Otherwise, the victim may die.

☆ Stopped breathing   ☆ Choking

☆ No heartbeat   ☆ Poisoning

☆ Severe bleeding

Stopped Breathing

A drowning person is pulled from the water. A man is hauled out of a burning building. A hiker is struck by lightning. A child is pulled off an electrical wire. In each of these accidents, breathing may have stopped.

To save a victim who is not breathing, you must begin first aid immediately! The brain can survive only about 4 minutes without oxygen before suffering serious damage. At normal temperatures, the person cannot live without air for more than 10 or 12 minutes.

Whenever you come upon an accident, find out if the victim is breathing. Is the chest rising and falling? When you place your ear near the mouth and nose, can you hear or feel exhaled air? If not, *immediately* start giving *rescue breathing.*

FIRST AID: *Time is critical! Act quickly!* Position the victim. Place the victim on his back. Tilt his head far back, chin pointing up. Lift with one hand under the chin. With the other hand, press down on the forehead and pinch the nostrils shut with your thumb and forefinger. Then take a deep breath and begin rescue breathing:

☆ *Step 1.* Open your mouth wide and seal it over the victim's mouth. Blow into his mouth to fill his lungs. Look to see if his chest rises. (If the victim is a child, seal your mouth over both the victim's mouth and nose, then blow gently.)

☆ *Step 2.* Remove your mouth and take another deep breath. Watch to see that the victim's chest falls as he exhales.

Repeat steps 1 and 2 every 5 seconds for anyone over 9 years of age, every 3 seconds for anyone 9 or under.

☆ *Check the effect.* If the victim's chest does not rise and fall, no air is reaching his lungs.

RESCUE BREATHING

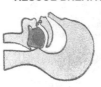

To open airway, place victim face up. Tilt his head far back, chin pointing up. Lift chin with one hand, press forehead with other. Pinch nostrils.

Diagram shows importance of far-back position of head. With victim's head flat on the ground (top), his tongue closes the airway. With his head far back (bottom), airway is fully open.

STEP 1 IN RESCUE BREATHING
Seal your mouth over victim's mouth, using a mouth-barrier device to prevent direct contact with body fluids. Blow into his mouth to fill his lungs. Watch to see that his chest rises as air enters lungs.

STEP 2 IN RESCUE BREATHING
Remove your mouth. Take a deep breath. Watch to see that the victim's chest falls as the air escapes from lungs.

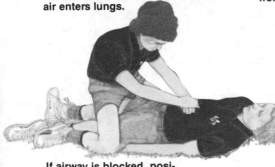

If airway is blocked, position yourself astride the victim's thighs. Place the heel of one hand in the midline between the waist and rib cage and the second on top. Press into abdomen with eight quick inward and upward thrusts.

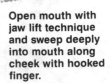

Open mouth with jaw lift technique and sweep deeply into mouth along cheek with hooked finger.

406

- *Reposition his head.* It must be tilted back so that the tongue does not block the airway.
- *Perform the Heimlich maneuver* (see page 416) to remove anything lodged in the throat.

Then quickly resume rescue breathing.

Don't give up! Continue rescue breathing until a doctor or medical technician tells you to stop, or it becomes physically impossible for you to keep going. If the victim resumes breathing and regains a pulse during or following resuscitation, you should place the victim on his or her side, in the recovery position, until help arrives.

Heart Failure

Accidents that cause a person to stop breathing may also stop his heart. With *cardiopulmonary resuscitation (CPR)*, you can provide both oxygen and blood circulation for such a victim. Learning CPR requires careful instruction and practice. You may be able to learn it at Scout meetings. The Red Cross and American Heart Association offer CPR courses, too. Your Scoutmaster can help you find the training you need to master this lifesaving skill.

Heart Attack

Heart attack is the major cause of death in the United States. Exercise, a good diet, and staying away from smoking and drugs will help you avoid danger to your own heart. However, you may have to help someone else who is having a heart attack.

The following are warning signals of heart attack:

⭐ Uncomfortable pressure, squeezing, fullness, or pain in the center of the chest behind the breastbone. The feeling may spread to the shoulders, arms, neck, jaw, and back. It may last 2 minutes or longer, and may come and go. It need not be severe. *Sharp, stabbing twinges of pain usually are not signals of heart attack.*

⭐ Unusual sweating—for instance, perspiring even though a room is cool.

⭐ Nausea—stomach distress with an urge to vomit.

⭐ Shortness of breath.

⭐ A feeling of weakness.

FIRST AID: Have the victim sit or lie down, whichever is more comfortable for him. Get him under medical care as soon as possible. Follow steps for getting help on page 404. Keep watching the victim. CPR may be necessary before medical help arrives.

	Activity
 	Establish unresponsiveness and call out for help. Position the victim (4–10 seconds). **Caution:** If the victim resumes breathing and regains a pulse during or following resuscitation, you should place the victim on his or her side, in the recovery position, until help arrives.
	Open airway. Establish breathlessness (look, listen, feel—3–5 seconds).

Critical Performance	Rationale
Tap, gently shake shoulders and shout: "Are you OK?" Call out "Help." Turn on back if necessary, supporting head and neck. Take adequate time.	One concern about teaching people CPR is the risk of unnecessary resuscitation and possible damage from unnecessarily resuscitating sleepers, fainters, etc. Call for help will summon nearby bystanders. Frequently the victim will be face down. Effective CPR can only be provided with the victim flat on back. The head cannot be above the level of the heart or CPR is ineffective. Accurate diagnosis is important. Four to 10 seconds gives time to do that.
Kneel beside victim's shoulder; upper hand on forehead, lower hand lifting chin. The chin should be lifted so that the teeth are nearly brought together. Avoid completely closing the victim's mouth. Turn your head toward victim's chest with your ear directly over and close to the victim's mouth. Listen and feel for evidence of breathing. Look for respiratory effort (rise and fall of the chest).	Airway must be open to establish breathlessness. Many victims may be making efforts at respiration that are ineffective because of obstruction by the tongue. Hearing and feeling are the only true ways of determining the presence of breathing. If there is chest movement but you cannot feel or hear air, the airway is still obstructed.

Performance Guidelines and Rationale
Single Rescue CPR (Continued)

	Activity
	Two ventilation breaths (3–5 seconds)
	Establish pulselessness (5–10 seconds) Activate the EMS systems

Critical Performance	Rationale
Pinch nostrils with thumb and forefinger of upper hand while maintaining pressure on victim's forehead to keep the head tilted. Open your mouth widely, take a deep breath and make a tight seal. Use a mouthbarrier device to prevent direct contact with body fluids. Breathe into victim's mouth two times with complete refilling of your lungs after each breath. Watch victim's chest rise. (If you cannot give rescue breaths, start first aid for an unconscious choking victim, page 417.)	When you are beginning rescue breathing, it is important to get as much oxygen as possible to the victim. If your rescue breathing is effective, you will: ☆ Feel air going in as you blow ☆ Feel the resistance of the victim's lungs ☆ Feel your own lungs emptying ☆ See the rise and fall of the victim's chest
Place two or three fingers on voice box just below chin. Slide fingers into groove between voice box and muscle, on side next to rescuer. Other hand maintains head tilt. Palpate (feel for) the carotid pulse in the neck.	This activity should take 5 to 10 seconds because it takes time to find the right place, and the pulse itself may be slow or very weak and rapid. The victim's condition must be properly assessed.
Know your local EMS or rescue unit telephone number. Send second rescuer to call.	Notification of the EMS system at this time allows the caller to give complete information about the victim's condition.

Performance Guidelines and Rationale
Single Rescue CPR (Continued)

	Activity
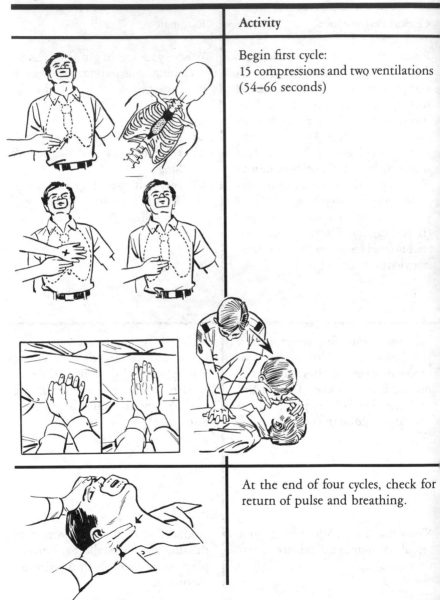	Begin first cycle: 15 compressions and two ventilations (54–66 seconds)
	At the end of four cycles, check for return of pulse and breathing.

Critical Performance	Rationale
To begin first cycle: Move to victim's chest. Run fingers up lower margin of the rib cage and locate sternal notch with middle finger. With index finger on sternum, place heel of hand closest to head on sternum next to, but not covering, index finger. Place second hand on top of first.	Precise hand placement is essential to avoid serious injury.
Position body: Weight is transmitted vertically, elbows should be straight and locked, shoulders over hands.	
Compress smoothly and evenly, keeping fingers off victim's ribs. The rescuer must apply enough force to depress the sternum 1½–2 inches at a rate of 80–100 compressions per minute. Count aloud to establish rhythm; "one-and-two-and-three-and-four-and . . ."	50 percent of compression is downward to empty the heart, 50 percent of compression/relaxation is upward to fill the heart. With each compression, you want to squeeze the heart to increase pressure within the chest so that blood moves to the vital organs.
Ventilate properly: After every 15 compressions, deliver two rescue breaths.	Adequate oxygenation must be maintained.
Take 5 seconds to: Check pulse and breathing. If no pulse, give two breaths and resume compressions. Continue several minutes of compression and breaths before checking pulse again. If there is a pulse but no breathing, apply rescue breathing.	To establish whether there is a spontaneous return of pulse and breathing.

Severe Bleeding [2]

A car crash. A bicycle accident. A careless moment with a knife, an ax, or a power tool. Suddenly there is a victim with blood spurting from a nasty wound.

FIRST AID: Cover the wound with a pad—a bandanna, shirt, or any other cloth—and **press hard!** Stop that blood! Tie the pad firmly in place with a cravat bandage, gauze bandage, or whatever is close at hand. If the pad becomes blood-soaked, don't remove it. Put another pad and bandage on top of the first and continue the pressure. Get medical help.

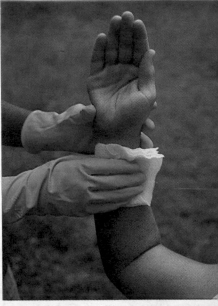

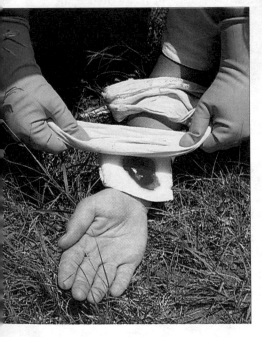

THE BOY SCOUTS OF AMERICA RECOMMENDS:

Treat all blood as if it were contaminated with blood-borne viruses. Do not use bare hands to stop bleeding; always use a protective barrier; always wash exposed skin areas with hot water and soap immediately after treating the victim. The following equipment is to be included in all first aid kits and used when rendering first aid to those in need:

- Latex gloves, to be used when stopping bleeding or dressing wounds
- A mouth-barrier device for rendering rescue breathing or CPR
- Plastic goggles or other eye protection, to prevent a victim's blood from getting into rescuer's eyes in the event of serious arterial bleeding
- Antiseptic, for sterilizing or cleaning exposed skin areas, particularly if there is no soap or water available.

CHAPTER 17

Spurting blood comes from an artery—one of the blood vessels that carry blood from the heart out into the body. Some bleeding from a cut artery can be controlled by pressure.

Pressure on four pressure points—two on each side of the body—can be used to control bleeding of arm and leg. Press the artery against the bone at the pressure point. The effect is like stepping on a water hose.

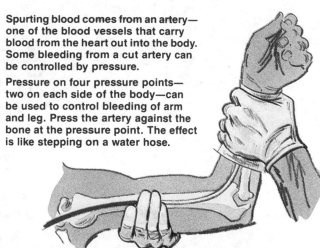

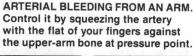

ARTERIAL BLEEDING FROM A LEG. Control it by pressing the artery with the heel of your hand against the pelvic bone at the pressure point.

ARTERIAL BLEEDING FROM AN ARM. Control it by squeezing the artery with the flat of your fingers against the upper-arm bone at pressure point.

CRAVAT BANDAGE

Make a cravat bandage for holding a pad by folding a triangle bandage or Scout neckerchief (1). Fold the point up to the long edge (2). Finish by folding the bottom edge twice to the top edge (3 and 4).

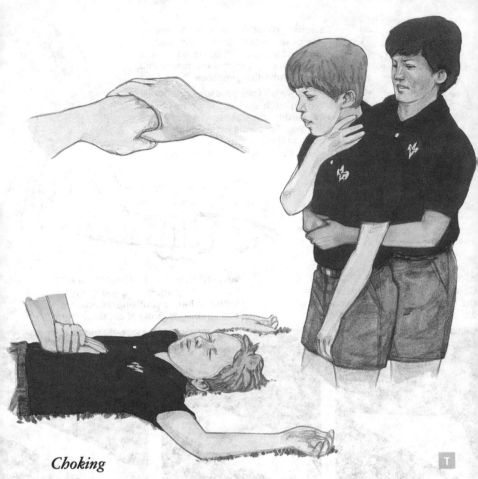

Choking

T

During a meal, a man lurches from his chair and clutches his throat. His face turns red and he cannot breathe. You realize a piece of food is stuck in his throat and rush to his aid by performing the *Heimlich maneuver.*

FIRST AID: Food caught in the throat is like a cork stuck in a plastic bottle. Nothing can get in, but if you squeeze the bottle just right, the cork will fly out.

Step behind the victim and put your arms around his midsection. Clasp your hands together with the knuckle of one thumb just above his navel. With a sharp, inward thrust, drive your hands up under the victim's rib cage. The food should pop loose. If it doesn't, repeat this Heimlich maneuver several more times.

CHAPTER 17

If a choking victim is very large or pregnant, chest thrusts may be more effective. If the victim has lost consciousness, straddle the victim on the floor. Place one hand atop the other between the navel and rib cage. Thrust the heel of your hand sharply inward and upward eight times on the abdomen just below the breastbone. Probe the victim's mouth with a hooked finger. Remove any obstructions, and be ready to start rescue breathing. (Advanced first aid courses will teach you the techniques to use with infants.)

If you ever choke on food and cannot breathe, clutch your throat with your hand. That's the universal sign for choking, and it may bring someone to your aid. You can perform the Heimlich maneuver on yourself by pulling your fist into your upper abdomen. Or you can bend over the back of a chair and force it against your belly.

If you suspect poisoning, call for help immediately.

Poisoning by Mouth

2

One-third of all accidental deaths among children are caused by poisons. Young children will swallow almost anything: fuels, rat poisons, insecticides, battery acid, peeling wall paint, pills from a medicine cabinet, weed killer from garden supplies.

Outdoors, some mushrooms, fungi, berries, and leaves are poisonous if swallowed. Eat no wild plants unless you are very sure they are safe.

FIRST AID: Quickly take any poison containers to the phone, then call a poison control center or emergency medical service and follow their instructions. Treat the victim for shock and check breathing frequently. Do not give anything by mouth unless you have been advised to do so by medical professionals.

Save any containers and vomit. These will help a medic or physician identify the poison and give the right treatment.

SHOCK AND FAINTING

Shock occurs in every accident. It is a sudden lowering of strength caused by pain, fear, and sometimes loss of blood. A shock victim is very weak. His face is pale. His skin becomes cold and clammy. He shivers from chills, and he might vomit.

Don't wait for the symptoms to appear! Quickly treat *every* accident victim for shock. Injury always causes some degree of shock, but the victim may not be affected right away. Prompt first aid may prevent severe shock from setting in.

FIRST AID FOR SHOCK: Have the injured person lie down. Raise his feet 10 to 12 inches. In cool weather, cover him and keep him warm. Place blankets or sleeping bags underneath him as well as on top. If the patient is conscious, let him sip a little water.

Never leave an accident victim alone. Fear and uncertainty may increase shock. Talk to him in a calm voice and assure him he is going to be all right. Even a victim who appears to be unconscious may be able to hear you. Keep letting him know he is not alone.

Treatment of shock ▶

Fainting is a mild form of shock. The victim loses consciousness because too little blood is reaching his brain. Fainting can be caused by fright, bad news, breathing foul air, or standing too long. The victim becomes pale. He may wobble and fall to the ground.

FIRST AID FOR FAINTING: Keep the victim lying down until he recovers. Loosen his collar and raise his feet. If he does not recover right away, treat for shock and get medical help.

If you ever feel faint yourself, sit down and put your head between your knees. Even better, lie down and raise your legs.

OTHER FIRST AID CASES

Cuts and Scratches

Cuts and scratches are *wounds*—openings in the skin. Clean even the smallest wound to remove germs that could cause infection.

FIRST AID FOR SMALL WOUNDS AND SCRATCHES: Clean a wound by washing it with soap and water. At home, use plenty of water right out of the faucet. On a hike or in camp, use water from your canteen or a clear stream. Let the skin around the wound dry, then apply an adhesive bandage. If you don't have a bandage and the wound is small, simply wash it. Any bleeding will stop as soon as the blood clots.

FIRST AID FOR LARGER CUTS: Wash a larger cut with lots of soap and water. Let it dry, then keep dirt out of the wound by covering the injury with a sterile gauze compress. Hold the gauze in place with adhesive tape or a binder. If you don't have a compress, fold a clean piece of cloth into a pad. The binder may be a gauze bandage from a first aid kit.

Or use a triangular bandage or your Scout neckerchief folded into a cravat bandage (see page 415).

If the wound is serious, treat the victim for shock and see that he gets proper medical attention.

Nosebleed

A nosebleed looks bad but is usually not very serious. Most nosebleeds stop themselves in just a few minutes.

FIRST AID: Have the victim sit up and lean forward slightly to prevent blood from draining into his throat. Press the bleeding nostril toward the center. Apply a cool, wet cloth to the nose and face.

Burns, Scalds, and Sunburn T 2

Someone touches a hot coal — result: an ordinary burn. Someone spills boiling water over his foot — result: a scald. Someone falls asleep on the beach after a swim — result: sunburn.

FIRST AID: When a burn covers a large area, you can be certain that shock will set in. Give first aid for shock as well as for the burn.

☆ *First-degree burn.* In minor ⊤ burns and sunburns, the skin gets red. Treat immediately with cool water. Keep the burn under water until there is little or no pain. Then apply a moist dressing, and bandage loosely. Where water is not available, apply a clean, dry dressing.

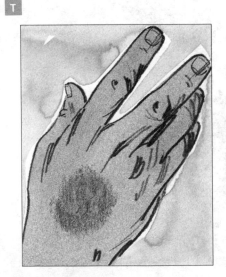

CHAPTER 17

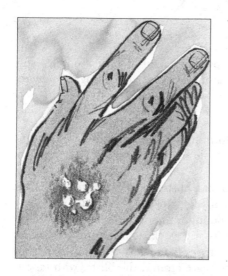

☆ *Second-degree burn.* If blisters form, the burn is more serious. Do not break the blisters — this will compound the injury by causing an open wound. If the blisters are not open, place the injury in cool water until the pain lessens, then apply a moist dressing, and bandage loosely. **Do not** apply creams, ointments, or sprays.

☆ *Third-degree burn.* In the most severe burns, the skin may be burned away. Some flesh will be charred. If many nerve endings are damaged, there may be little pain. **Do not** try to remove any clothing; it may be sticking to the flesh. **Do not** apply creams, ointments, or sprays. Wrap a clean sheet around the victim and, if the weather is cool, cover him with blankets. Rush him to a hospital. His life is at stake.

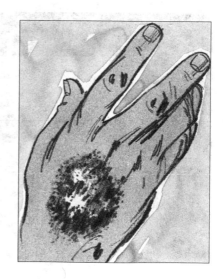

Blisters

Blisters on the foot are most often caused by shoes that don't fit well or are new and stiff. Working without gloves may result in blisters on the hand. Break in your boots by wearing them around home before using them on the trail. A pair of thin inner socks under woolen hiking socks will reduce the friction on your feet.

FIRST AID: If you feel a "hot spot" forming as you walk, stop right away and treat it before it becomes a blister. Moleskin or adhesive tape offers some protection.

Better yet, surround a tender spot or a blister with a *doughnut bandage.* Begin by washing your foot or other affected area with soap and water. Cut a piece of moleskin in the shape of a doughnut and fit the hole around the injury. Shape several more doughnuts and stack them on top of the first. (Instead of moleskin, you can cut a corner off a foam sleeping pad and trim it into a doughnut shape. Hold it in place around the blister with tape.)

When you resume hiking, the doughnut bandage will keep pressure off the blister and probably prevent it from breaking. If you think the blister will break anyway, drain the fluid. Sterilize a pin in the flame of a match. Prick the blister near its edge and press out the liquid. Keep the wound clean with a sterile bandage and protect it from pressure with a doughnut bandage.

Sprained Ankle

It's not unusual to stumble on a hiking trail or playing field. But if your foot twists, the tendons and ligaments of your ankle may stretch too far, resulting in a painful sprained ankle.

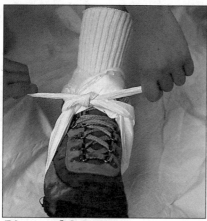

FIRST AID: Do not remove your shoe. It will give your ankle support. For added protection, tie an ankle bandage around the shoe and your injured ankle. If your foot is already bare, lie down. Raise your leg and reduce swelling with cold, wet towels around the ankle. Seek medical care.

Bites and Stings

Insect Bites and Stings

The bites and stings of certain insects, spiders, chiggers, and ticks can be painful. Some may cause infection.

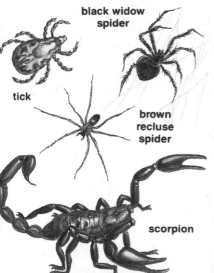

black widow spider

tick

brown recluse spider

scorpion

FIRST AID: Relieve the pain of insect bites or stings with ice water or a cold towel. If the stinger of a bee or wasp is still in the skin, flick it away with your fingernail or the edge of a knife.

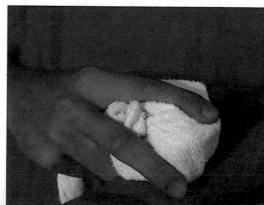

Ticks are small, bloodsucking animals that bury their tiny heads in the skin. Keep them away by wearing long pants and a long-sleeved shirt whenever you travel and camp in tick-infested woodlands and fields. Button your collar and tuck the cuffs of your pants into your boots or socks. Inspect yourself daily, especially the hairy parts of your body, and remove any ticks you find. If a tick has fastened itself to you, grasp it with tweezers and gently pull it away from the skin. Twisting or jerking the tick may cause its head to break off in your skin, so use gentle pressure. Once the tick is gone, wash the area of the bite with soap and water. Calamine lotion may ease any itching.

Chiggers are the almost-invisible relatives of ticks. They burrow into the skin and cause itching and redness. Try not to scratch chigger bites. You may find some relief by covering the bites with calamine lotion or painting them with clear fingernail polish.

Anaphylactic Shock

Some people are very allergic to insect stings and spider bites. If one of these people is bitten or stung, he may develop a dangerous condition called *anaphylactic shock*. It causes the tissues of the throat to swell and block the airway. A victim may have great trouble breathing. People who know they are allergic to stings and bites should carry special "bee-sting kits" containing medicine to treat them in an emergency. The following first aid also is used for the victim of the bite of a black widow spider or brown recluse spider.

FIRST AID: If a victim has no bee-sting kit, here is what you must do:

☆ Send someone to get medical help.

☆ Be sure the victim keeps breathing. Give rescue breathing if needed.

☆ If the bite is on an arm or leg, immediately tie a constricting band above the bite. Use a strip of cloth or your Scout neckerchief folded as a cravat bandage. Tighten it only enough to stop the blood in the skin. You must be able to slide your finger under the band. Keep an eye on the limb. If it swells from the bite, loosen the band.

☆ Keep the arm or leg lower than the body.

☆ Put ice packed in a cloth or a cold compress on the bite.

☆ Treat for shock.

☆ Get the person under medical care very quickly.

Jellyfish Stings

2

The bell-shaped pink jellyfish of cool northern seas and the Portuguese man-of-war of warm southern seas have thousands of stinging cells on their tentacles. When touched, the poisons of those cells cause a sharp, burning pain.

FIRST AID: Wash the affected area with diluted ammonia or rubbing alcohol. Quickly get the victim under medical care. People who are allergic to jellyfish stings may go into deep shock without warning.

Animal Bites

If it breaks the skin, the bite of a dog, cat, rat, or any warm-blooded wild animal is not an ordinary wound. The animal may suffer from *rabies,* a deadly disease carried in its saliva. The only way to learn if an animal is infected is to have it caught and kept under observation. You have three jobs to do:

☆ Give first aid.

☆ Get medical help.

☆ Call the police or rangers to capture the animal.

FIRST AID: Scrub the bite with plenty of soap and water to remove the saliva. Cover the wound with a sterile bandage and get the victim to a doctor.

Leather hiking boots offer some protection from snakes, since snakes rarely strike very high.

Snakebites   T

Both harmless and poisonous snakes may strike when they feel threatened. The bite of a nonpoisonous snake requires only ordinary first aid for small wounds (see page 419). Snakes are not warm-blooded, so they cannot carry rabies.

First aid for the bite of a poisonous snake is more complicated and must begin quickly.

KEEP YOURSELF SAFE AROUND SNAKES

Although poisonous snakes are common in some parts of the country, bites from them are rare. Snakes try to avoid humans, usually striking only when cornered. Few bites result in death.

Still, you must be alert when you walk through areas where snakes may live. Use your hiking stick to poke among the rocks and brush ahead of you. Watch where you put your hands as you climb over rocks and logs or collect firewood. Many snakes are active at night; don't walk through camp barefooted.

Snakes seldom strike very high, so leather hiking boots will offer protection. When swimming or boating in southern states, watch for cottonmouth snakes sunning along the shore or on tree branches overhanging the water. (For more on snakes, see pages 302–305.)

FIRST AID:

☆ Have the victim lie down and rest the bitten part lower than the rest of the body. Keep him calm and quiet.

☆ Put a constricting band 2 to 4 inches above the bite to slow the spread of the venom. Make it just tight enough so it's not too easy to push your fingers between the band and his skin. If the area swells, loosen the band.

☆ Treat the victim for shock.

☆ Get medical help immediately. If you know what kind of snake it was, tell the doctor.

    CHAPTER 17

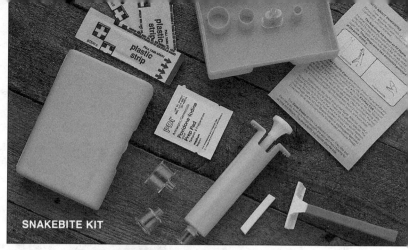

SNAKEBITE KIT

Used immediately, a snakebite kit may remove some venom from a wound. The kit also will lift out insect stingers.

POISONOUS SNAKES

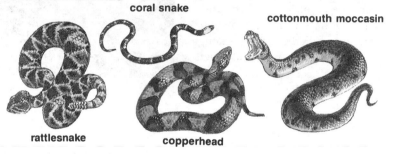

coral snake

cottonmouth moccasin

rattlesnake

copperhead

Something in the Eye

2

Anything in the eye is painful. Sometimes a foreign object may endanger vision.

FIRST AID: Have the person blink his eyes, and tears may flush out the object. If that doesn't work, pull the upper lid down over the lower one. The lower lashes may brush out the speck. Or, if the object is under the lower lid, place your thumb on the skin just below the lid and pull it down gently. Lift out the speck with a corner of a sterile gauze pad or clean handkerchief. If that fails, cover the eye with a gauze pad and get the patient under medical care.

Puncture Wounds

Puncture wounds can be caused by pins, splinters, nails, fishhooks, knife stabs, and gunshots. All are dangerous because they may allow tetanus (lockjaw) germs into a wound that is difficult to clean.

FIRST AID: Take out any foreign matter, then squeeze gently around the wound. Wash with soap and water. Apply a sterile bandage and get to a doctor. A tetanus antitoxin shot may be needed to prevent lockjaw.

If someone has been snagged by a fishhook, cut the line and let a doctor or medic remove the hook from the flesh. In the backcountry, you may have to do the job yourself. First, push the barb out through the skin and snip it off with pliers, wire cutters, or even nail clippers. Then back the barbless hook out of the wound.

Skin Poisoning from Plants

The poison in poison ivy, poison oak, and poison sumac is contained in oily sap throughout the plant. Touching these plants may cause the skin to become red and itchy. Later, blisters may form.

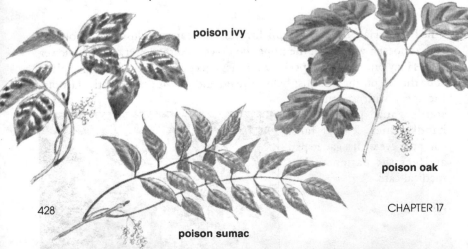

poison ivy

poison oak

poison sumac

CHAPTER 17

FIRST AID: The sap of poisonous plants takes about 20 minutes to bind to the skin. If you think you have touched one, rinse immediately with soap and water if you have it, or water alone. Calamine lotion may relieve itching. Try not to scratch. Remove any lingering sap by laundering clothing that has come in contact with poisonous plants.

Heat Emergencies

Exposure to heat makes the body work to keep itself cool. But sometimes the body's cooling system becomes strained, resulting in *heat exhaustion*. Or it breaks down completely, which is a condition called *heat stroke*.

Common sense will protect you from heat problems. Drink plenty of fluids. Rest in the shade when you feel too warm. If the weather is hot, ease up on hard physical work and play.

Heat Exhaustion
2

Heat exhaustion may affect a person outdoors or in an overheated room. Here are the symptoms:

☆ The victim's face is pale, with cold sweat on the forehead. The whole body may feel cool and clammy from perspiration.

☆ Shallow breathing.

☆ Nausea and vomiting.

☆ Dilated pupils.

☆ Headache and dizziness.

FIRST AID: Move the patient to a cool, shady spot. Place him on his back and raise his feet. Loosen his clothing. Fan him and apply cool, wet cloths. Give him sips of water.

Heat Stroke

Heat stroke is usually caused by exposure to the sun. The victim's body temperature soars, making heat stroke a life-and-death matter. Get medical assistance at once.

☆ The patient's face is like the sun—red and very hot. The skin is often dry, but if the victim has been exercising hard, he may be covered with sweat.

☆ Very small pupils.   ☆ Rapid, strong pulse.

☆ Slow, noisy breathing.   ☆ He may be unconscious.

FIRST AID: Quickly get the victim into a cool, shady spot. Place him on his back with his head and shoulders raised. Undress him immediately, then cool him—especially his head—with water. Cover him with dripping wet towels, shirts, or cloths. Keep the coverings cool by dousing them with water or wringing them in cold water. Be ready at any time to begin rescue breathing.

Cold Emergencies

Frostbite

Someone outdoors in cold weather may complain that his ears, nose, fingers, or feet feel numb. Or you may notice white or grayish-yellow patches on someone's ears, nose, or cheeks—a sure sign of frostbite.

FIRST AID: Move the victim inside a warm tent or building and thaw the frozen area. If an ear or part of the face is frozen, have the person remove a glove and cover the part with his warm hand. Slip a frostbitten hand under the clothing and tuck it beneath an armpit, next to bare skin. Frozen toes? Put the victim's bare feet against the warm skin of your belly or armpit. **Do not** rub or massage frozen skin.

TREATING FROSTBITE

You can also warm a frozen part by holding it in warm — not hot — running water. Or wrap it in a warm blanket. When the area has become warm, have the patient exercise injured fingers or toes. Get him to a doctor.

Hypothermia

When you hear that someone has "died of exposure" or has "frozen to death," the killer may actually have been hypothermia — from *hypo*, meaning "low," and *thermia*, meaning "heat." Hypothermia occurs when the body is losing more heat than it can generate.

A victim of hypothermia begins feeling chilly, tired, and irritable. If he receives no help, he will begin to shiver. Soon his shivering becomes violent. He cannot think clearly enough to take care of himself. He may stumble and fall. If he continues to chill, the shivering will stop and he will be close to death.

Hypothermia is a threat to anyone who is not dressed warmly enough for the air around him. Wind, rain, and exhaustion increase the risk. The temperature doesn't have to be below freezing. A lightly dressed hiker caught in a cold, windy rainstorm is at great risk of hypothermia.

Prevent hypothermia by wearing enough clothing to keep yourself warm and dry. If bad weather catches you in the backcountry, put up your tent and crawl into your sleeping bag. Eat plenty of food and drink lots of fluids. Watch others in your group for signs that they are becoming cold, hungry, and irritable.

FIRST AID: If someone is showing any symptoms of hypothermia, take action right away. Get the victim indoors or put up a tent. Peel off his wet clothes and zip him into a dry sleeping bag. If hypothermia is far advanced, the victim

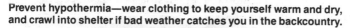
Prevent hypothermia—wear clothing to keep yourself warm and dry, and crawl into shelter if bad weather catches you in the backcountry.

431

won't be able to warm himself. The rescuer must also strip down to his shorts and get into the sleeping bag so that body contact can warm the victim slowly. Give an unconscious patient nothing by mouth. Get a hypothermia victim under medical care.

NOTE: The body temperature of a swimmer drops steadily in water cooler than himself. The shivering that results is the onset of hypothermia. Get out of the water. Cover up. Exercise to get warm.

Closed and Open Fractures

A fall, a violent blow, an automobile accident — these are common causes of *fractures.*

A *closed,* or *simple, fracture* is a broken bone that has not caused an open wound. A victim will complain of pain around the injury. He won't want to move the injured area. A broken arm or leg may look bent or shortened. Swelling may occur, and the victim may suffer from shock.

An *open,* or *compound, fracture* has the same symptoms plus one more — the sharp edges of the broken bone have cut through the flesh and skin.

The great danger in treating fractures is that incorrect handling may turn a closed fracture into an open one, or make an open fracture more serious. Such an injury can cripple the patient or even endanger his life. What you *do* about a fracture is important. What you *don't do* may be even more important.

FIRST AID: These are the *dos* and *don'ts* of first aid for fractures:

☆ **Do** let the patient lie with as little motion as possible right where you found him. Make him comfortable by tucking blankets, sleeping bags, or clothing under and over him.

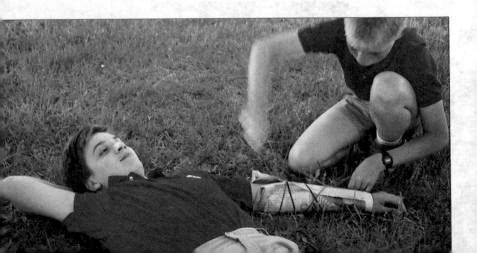

SLINGS

Make a sling from a large triangular bandage or Scout neckerchief, plain or with a "pig's tail"—an overhand knot tied in the large angle of the triangle. Use it to support an injured hand, arm, or shoulder.

Place the bandage over the chest with the "pig's tail" at the elbow of the injured arm and one end over the opposite shoulder. Bring the remaining end up to the other shoulder. Tie the two ends together behind the neck so that the hand is held about 3 inches higher than the elbow.

Overhand knot for "pigs' tail"

☆ **Do** treat "hurry cases"—stopped breathing, no heartbeat, severe bleeding. If blood is spurting from a wound, stop it with hand pressure against a pressure point (see page 415) rather than direct pressure over a broken bone.

☆ **Do** treat for shock.

☆ **Do** call a doctor, rescue squad, or an ambulance immediately.

☆ **Don't** let anyone bundle your patient into a car and rush him to the hospital. That's the easiest way of turning a closed fracture into an open fracture.

☆ **Don't** try to set the bone—that's the doctor's job.

ADDITIONAL FIRST AID: In cases of extreme emergency, you may have to move the patient before medical help arrives. Perhaps the victim is lying on a dark, busy highway or in a cold mountain stream. Follow this do and don't:

☆ **Do** support the broken limb by making it immovable between well-padded splints. **Splint him where he lies!**

☆ **Don't** move the patient before the splinting is complete, unless the patient's location poses an imminent danger to the patient or rescuers.

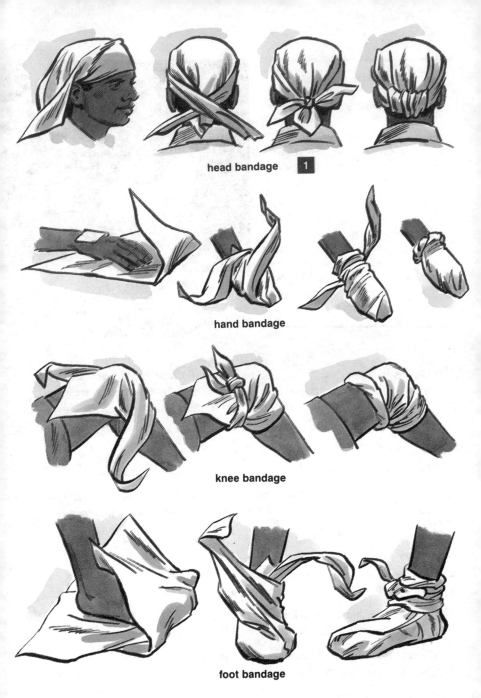

head bandage 1

hand bandage

knee bandage

foot bandage

Collarbone or Shoulder Fracture 1

No splint is necessary. Place the forearm in a sling (see page 433) with the hand raised about 3 inches higher than the elbow. Tie the upper arm against the side of the body with a wide cravat bandage. Make sure the bandage is not so tight that it stops circulation in the arm.

Lower-Arm or Wrist Fracture

Use splints long enough to hold the wrist, lower arm (forearm), and elbow motionless. Place the splinted arm in a sling with the thumb up and the hand slightly higher than the elbow. Use a cravat bandage to tie the upper arm against the side of the body. The body itself will act as a splint, too.

SPLINTS

A splint is any stiff material that can be bound to a fractured limb to prevent the broken bone from moving and tearing the flesh with its sharp edges. It should be longer than the bone on which it is to be used. Pad the splint with soft material.

For splints, use whatever you can find nearby: boards, tent poles, branches, hiking sticks, ski poles, shovel handles, heavy cardboard, chicken wire, folded newspapers, magazines.

For padding, you can use clothing, blankets, pillows, or crumpled paper. Padding makes splints fit better and eases a patient's pain. Bind the splints with triangular bandages, neckerchiefs, roller bandages, strips of cloth, or belts.

Right now — this very minute — look around you. What is within reach that you could use for splints, padding, and binding?

SPLINT MATERIAL

Upper-Arm Fracture

Tie one padded splint to the outside of the upper arm. Place the forearm in a sling, then use a cravat bandage to tie the upper arm against the side of the body.

Lower-Leg Fracture

Apply two splints, each as long as the distance from the middle of the thigh to just past the heel. Place the splints on either side of the injured limb and bind them together with four or more binders.

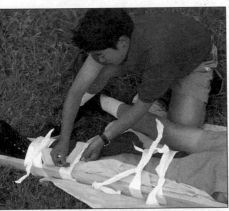

SPLINTING A LOWER-LEG FRACTURE

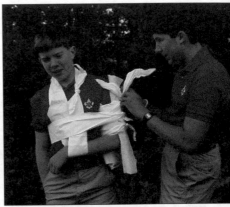

SPLINTING AN UPPER-ARM FRACTURE

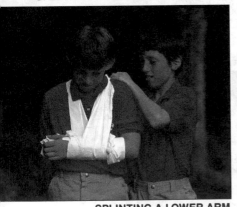

SPLINTING A LOWER-ARM
OR WRIST FRACTURE

SPLINTING A THIGH FRACTURE

Thigh Fracture

Use padded splints, one for outside the leg extending from heel to arm-pit, and one for inside the leg from heel to crotch. Bind the splints together. Use four binders around the splints and leg, and three binders around the upper part of the outside splint and the body.

NOTE: The muscles of the upper leg are strong enough to pull the broken ends of the thighbone into the flesh. For this reason, the first aid described here is early emergency care. The patient should not be moved any great distance without a traction splint. Ambulances carry them, and they can be made by persons with advanced first aid training.

NOTE: All knots should be square knots.

Transportation

Moving an injured person requires great common sense and care. A seriously injured person should be moved by a first-aider only in cases of extreme emergency—and then only after the patient has received first aid and has had possible fractures splinted.

An accident victim suspected of having neck, back, or head injuries should be moved only under the guidance of qualified medical personnel. To transport a person from a smoke-filled room, place the victim on a blanket and drag him out, crawling on your hands and knees (the same way you would enter the room). If there are two rescuers, one person stays outside and calls for help. Unless visibility is fairly good, never enter a smoke-filled room—stay outside and call for help. (For more information on transporting injured persons, see the *First Aid* merit badge pamphlet.)

Assists and Hand Carries

Walking assist. A patient who has suffered a minor accident and feels weak may be assisted to walk. Bring one of his arms over your shoulder and hold onto his wrist. Place your free arm around his waist.

One-person carry. This is best done piggyback. Kneel in front of the patient with your back to his belly. Bring your arms under the patient's knees. Grasp his hands over your chest. Avoid injury to your own back by keeping it straight and lifting with your legs.

WALKING ASSIST

ONE-PERSON CARRY

FOUR-HAND SEAT

TWO-MAN CARRY

Four-handed seat carry. Two first-aiders can transport a conscious patient with this carry. Each bearer grasps his own right wrist with his left hand. The two bearers then lock hands and wrists with each other. The patient sits on their hands and places his arms around their shoulders.

Two-person carry. Use this carry when a patient is unconscious. Bearers kneel on either side of the patient. Each slides one arm under the patient's back, the other under his thighs. The bearers grasp each other's wrists and shoulders and rise from the ground with the patient supported between them.

CHAPTER 17

Stretchers

If a patient must be moved for some distance or his injuries are serious, he should be carried on a stretcher.

Emergency stretchers. Use a not-too-heavy door, a short ladder, a gate, or a sheet of stiff plywood.

Making a stretcher. Start with two poles somewhat longer than the patient is tall. Use strong saplings, tool handles, oars, or tent poles.

Button up two or three Scout shirts or coats and push the poles through the sleeves. Or use blankets, a tent fly, or a sleeping bag with the bottom-corner seams opened. Or lash together three metal pack frames.

MAKING A STRETCHER

Rescues

First aid is something you do after an accident has happened. But sometimes a rescue must be made before any injuries can be treated.

A Building on Fire

Thousands of Americans die each year in fires. You may help prevent some of these deaths by going into action the instant you see a burning building.

☆ *Get the people out!* Yell, bang on the door, ring the bell, set off the alarm. Get them out, but **do not** enter a burning building yourself. You may be overcome by smoke or trapped by flames.

☆ *Call the fire department.*

☆ *Offer your help.* While waiting for the fire engines, figure out if there is anything else you can do—calming frightened victims, for instance, or directing traffic. With a cool head, do what you can.

A Person on Fire

A person's clothing may catch fire from a campfire or from burning oil, kerosene, or gasoline. Instinct tells the victim to run, but that's the worst thing to do. Running doesn't put out the fire—it fans the flames.

Rush up to the victim and tackle him if necessary to get him to the ground. Then slowly roll him over as you beat out the flames with your hands. Take care that your own clothes don't catch fire. If there is a blanket, sleeping bag, or rug handy, wrap it around the victim to smother the flames. Once the fire is out, administer first aid for shock and burns.

Live Wires

After a storm, someone may stumble over a live power line that has been knocked down. A person fixing an electrical outlet may get a shock. Old house wiring may cause an electrical accident. ▶

Rescue from house electrical current. If someone in a house is in contact with a live wire, shut off the current by pulling the main switch, or grab the electric cord where it is not bare or wet and pull it from the socket.

If you don't know where to find the main switch and can't pull the plug, you will have to remove the wire from the victim. To do this, take a dry sheet, dry towel, or other dry cloth, encircle the wire with it, and pull the wire from the victim. Or push it away with a wooden board, a wooden hiking stick, or even a wooden spoon.

If you can't move the wire, use the cloth or a board to move the victim instead. *Do not touch the victim until he and the wire are separated!*

Be very careful if there is water on the floor. It can carry a deadly current from a wire lying in it. Pull the main switch or call the police or a rescue squad.

After the rescue, check the victim for breathing and heartbeat. Be prepared to give rescue breathing or CPR.

Outdoor power line accident. Rescuing a person in contact with a live power line outdoors is extremely dangerous. Do not attempt a rescue yourself. Call the electric company, police, or fire department instead.

Drownings

Water accidents. Scouting will give you chances to become a good swimmer and to learn lifesaving methods. If you ever see someone struggling in the water, make use of what you have learned. Water rescues are explained on pages 237–239. The most important points are these:

☆ First, try to **reach** the victim from shore.

☆ Second, **throw** him a rope, life jacket, or other flotation device.

☆ Third, **go with support**—a boat of some kind or a surfboard.

☆ Only as a last resort should you attempt to rescue someone by swimming out to them, and then *only* if you are a strong swimmer trained in lifesaving.

Ice rescue. Many people drown after falling through ice on lakes, rivers, and streams. Act quickly if you see such an accident, but think clearly! Do not rush out onto the ice—you may break through, too. Instead, figure out a safe way to save the victim.

Try to reach him from shore with a pole, a branch, a coat, or a rope. Tie a loop in the rope for the victim to put his arm through. Use a bowline knot (see page 134–135). Without a loop, he may not be able to hang on. At lakes where there is skating, you might find an emergency ladder. Push it out onto the ice until the victim can reach one end.

If you must go onto the ice yourself, distribute your weight as much as possible over the surface. Lie on your belly and snake out over the ice until you are close enough to throw a rope to the victim or to reach him with a ladder or pole. When he has a firm grasp, slowly pull him out.

If helpers are close, form a human chain (see illustration below). Crawl out onto the ice while one person holds your ankles and another hangs onto his. Grasp the victim by the wrists and scoot back. Even better, reach him with a pole.

Once the victim is ashore, get him into a warm shelter and treat him for hypothermia (see page 431). If he has stopped breathing, start rescue breathing.

You are of no help to an accident victim if you become a victim yourself. Do not attempt to rescue someone from drowning, electrical currents, or other hazardous situations unless you can do it without endangering yourself.

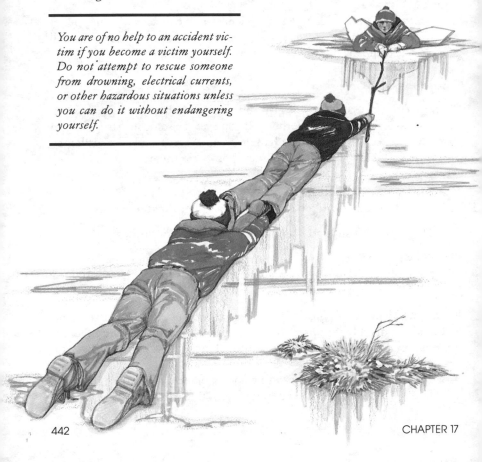

Tornadoes and Floods

Tornadoes. Every spring and summer, sections of the southern and central United States are swept by tornadoes — violent whirlwinds that usually move from southwest to northeast. A tornado can lift houses off the ground and tear up trees. Fortunately, its path is usually only a few hundred feet wide.

Prepare for tornado season by having on hand a battery-powered radio and a flashlight. Decide ahead of time what you will do in case a tornado approaches.

When a tornado forms, television and radio stations will issue warnings. Sirens may sound the alarm. You should seek shelter in a storm cellar or in the corner of a basement nearest the approaching tornado. Where there is no basement or cellar, crouch low in an interior bathroom or closet.

If you are caught in the open, move quickly at right angles out of the path of the tornado. But if you can't get to safety, lie down in the nearest ditch, ravine, or other depression. Don't stay in a car — get out and get down.

Floods. The thaws of early spring can bring destruction to river valleys. Heavy rains or warm weather melting the snow upstream may force rivers to rise above their banks. Usually, there is plenty of warning before real danger develops. You may be able to aid authorities by helping people move out of their homes and reach higher ground.

On Scout trips, choose campsites well above streams and dry washes where your tents will be safe if flooding occurs during the night. Don't try to cross flooded streams. Their swift currents are strong enough to knock you down.

SIGNALS AND DISTRESS CODES

SILENT SCOUT SIGNALS

THERE are times when a Scout leader wants the members of a troop or patrol to join a formation or move in a certain direction. Instead of shouting, the leader may use hand and arm signals.

Troop Signals

Attention. When a leader makes the Scout sign and holds it high, you know that you are to do the same and come to quiet attention.

Single rank (troop line). The leader extends both arms parallel to the line he wants formed. Patrols fall in line with the patrol leaders centered in front of their patrols.

Council or U (horseshoe). The leader raises both arms 45 degrees from the sides. Scouts form a semicircle with each patrol leader to the right of his patrol.

Troop circle. The leader raises both arms 45 degrees, then swings them from front to rear and back several times. Patrols form a complete circle around him.

ATTENTION

SINGLE RANK

COUNCIL

TROOP CIRCLE

CLOSE COLUMNS

PARALLEL FILE

CHAPTER 18

DISMISSAL

Close columns. The leader extends both arms forward, bent at the elbows, with hands fisted. Scouts fall in patrol lines, with patrol leaders at their far right.

Parallel file (relay file). The leader extends both arms forward at shoulder height. Patrol leaders take positions two paces apart. Their Scouts fall in behind them.

Dismissal. The leader swings both arms in a crossed-front position.

Patrol Signals

On a hike or while stalking animals, your patrol leader can use silent signals to tell you what he wants you to do.

Move forward. The patrol leader raises his right arm and swings it forward.

Hurry! The patrol leader quickly moves his right fist up and down.

Halt! The patrol leader raises his right fist up high.

Spread out. The patrol leader swings his arms out to the sides.

Assemble. The patrol leader swings his raised arm in a wide circle.

MOVE FORWARD

HALT!

ASSEMBLE

HURRY!

SPREAD OUT

SIGN LANGUAGE FOR
HEARING-IMPAIRED PEOPLE

People who cannot hear can communicate with each other—and with others who know the method—by forming symbols with their hands and fingers. Many things and ideas can be described with a single sign. Others, including names of people and places, are spelled out with the letters of the manual alphabet.

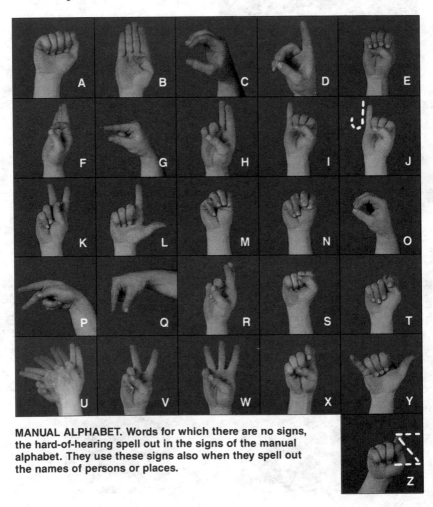

MANUAL ALPHABET. Words for which there are no signs, the hard-of-hearing spell out in the signs of the manual alphabet. They use these signs also when they spell out the names of persons or places.

THE SCOUT LAW IN SIGN LANGUAGE

THE   SCOUT   LAW

A   SCOUT   IS

TRUSTWORTHY   LOYAL   HELPFUL

FRIENDLY   COURTEOUS   KIND

OBEDIENT   CHEERFUL   THRIFTY

BRAVE   CLEAN   REVERENT

SIGNAL AND DISTRESS CODES

449

BRAILLE

    Blind people can read and write by using the *braille system*. It was invented in 1824 by a 15-year-old blind French student, Louis Braille.

    Braille is a system of raised dots for touch reading and writing. The system is based on an arrangement of six dots. Each cluster of six dots is called a *braille cell*. The dots in a cell are numbered 1-2-3 down the left side and 4-5-6 down the right.

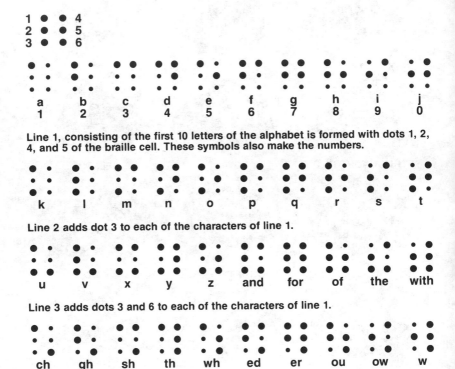

Line 1, consisting of the first 10 letters of the alphabet is formed with dots 1, 2, 4, and 5 of the braille cell. These symbols also make the numbers.

Line 2 adds dot 3 to each of the characters of line 1.

Line 3 adds dots 3 and 6 to each of the characters of line 1.

Line 4 adds dot 6 to each of the characters of line 1.

Line 5 uses dots 2, 3, 5, and 6. These are mostly punctuation characters.

Courtesy of American Federation for the Blind

CHAPTER 18

SIGNAL CODES

Before the development of telephones and two-way radios, signal codes allowed people to communicate over long distances. Telegraph operators used Morse code to send messages across the nation. Sailors relied upon Morse code and the semaphore code to pass information between ships at sea.

Many Scouts have learned one or both of these codes. While you may find few practical uses for either code, you can have fun communicating from one hilltop to another or across a lake. Write out messages in Morse code when you want them read only by another Scout.

Semaphore code. Semaphore requires two flags. Send messages by snapping the flags into the positions that indicate the letters of the alphabet (see the illustrations on page 453).

Morse code. This code of dots and dashes was invented by Samuel Morse in 1835 for use with telegraphs. Use it to send messages with a light (a flashlight or a mirror reflecting the sun), with sound (whistle or buzzer), a ham radio, or a single flag. Swing the flag to the right for a dot, to the left for a dash.

INTERNATIONAL MORSE CODE

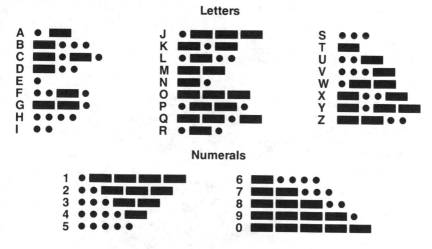

PROCEDURE SIGNALS

Used by Sender (Letters with line over them are sent as one letter.)

MORSE	SEMAPHORE	MEANING	EXPLANATION
$\overline{AAAA}$	Attention (flags swung overhead)	Attention	I have a message for you. Are you ready?
8 E's	8 E's	Error	I made a mistake. I will repeat beginning with last word that I sent correctly.
Front or pause	front (flags down)	End of word	End of word. More coming. (Front with flags; pause in other methods.)
$\overline{AAA}$	AAA	Period	End of sentence. More coming. (Punctuation is usually spelled out in long messages.)
$\overline{AR}$	AR	End of message	That's all for now. Did you get it?

Used by Receiver (Letters with line over them are sent as one letter.)

MORSE	SEMAPHORE	MEANING	EXPLANATION
K	K	Go ahead	I am ready to receive. Start sending.
$\overline{IMI}$	IMI	Repeat sign	Please send again; I missed it.
T	C	Word received	I understood word. (To be sent upon receipt of each word; not used in telegraph and radio receiving.)
R	R	Message received	I got it OK.

MORSE CODE TRAINER

You can make a training kit from a buzzer, pieces of tin can, screws, spool, and wire.

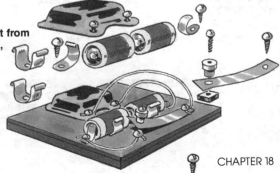

CHAPTER 18

SEMAPHORE CODE

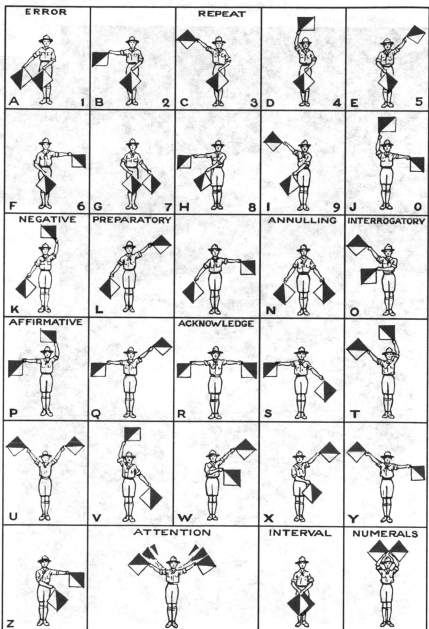

From the 1911 *Handbook for Boys.*

SIGNAL AND DISTRESS CODES

Boys' Life also is available in a Braille edition for readers with visual impairments.

Flag signaling with Morse code uses one flag. Semaphore requires two.

DISTRESS SIGNALS

If you are ever completely lost, stay put and wait for rescuers to find you. Their job will be easier if you make yourself very visible. Use a distress signal to attract attention. To catch a rescuer's eye, a signal must somehow disturb the usual appearance or sound of an area.

☆ Fly a brightly colored flag, sleeping bag, or blanket from a tree.

☆ Use the universal distress signal, which is any kind of signal repeated three times: three shouts, three blasts of a whistle, three gunshots, three columns of smoke.

☆ Sweep the horizon with a mirror or a bright can lid. An airplane pilot may see the flash of reflected sunlight, even if the day is a little hazy.

☆ If you can see someone in the distance, send the *S-O-S* Morse code distress call (three dots, three dashes, three dots). Send the code with a flag, a shirt on a pole, or a flashlight, lantern, mirror, bugle, whistle, or radio.

☆ Set up the appropriate ground-to-air signal as shown. Make it in an open area near camp. Tramp out the shape in snow or sand, line up rocks, or use parts of tents, ground cloths, and clothing. Once in place, these signals will work even if you are asleep or ill. Remove all trace of your signals when you no longer need them.

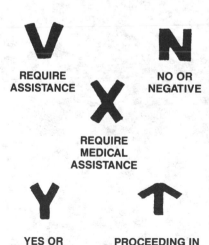

V
REQUIRE
ASSISTANCE

N
NO OR
NEGATIVE

X
REQUIRE
MEDICAL
ASSISTANCE

Y
YES OR
AFFIRMATIVE

↑
PROCEEDING IN
THIS DIRECTION

SIGNAL AND DISTRESS CODES

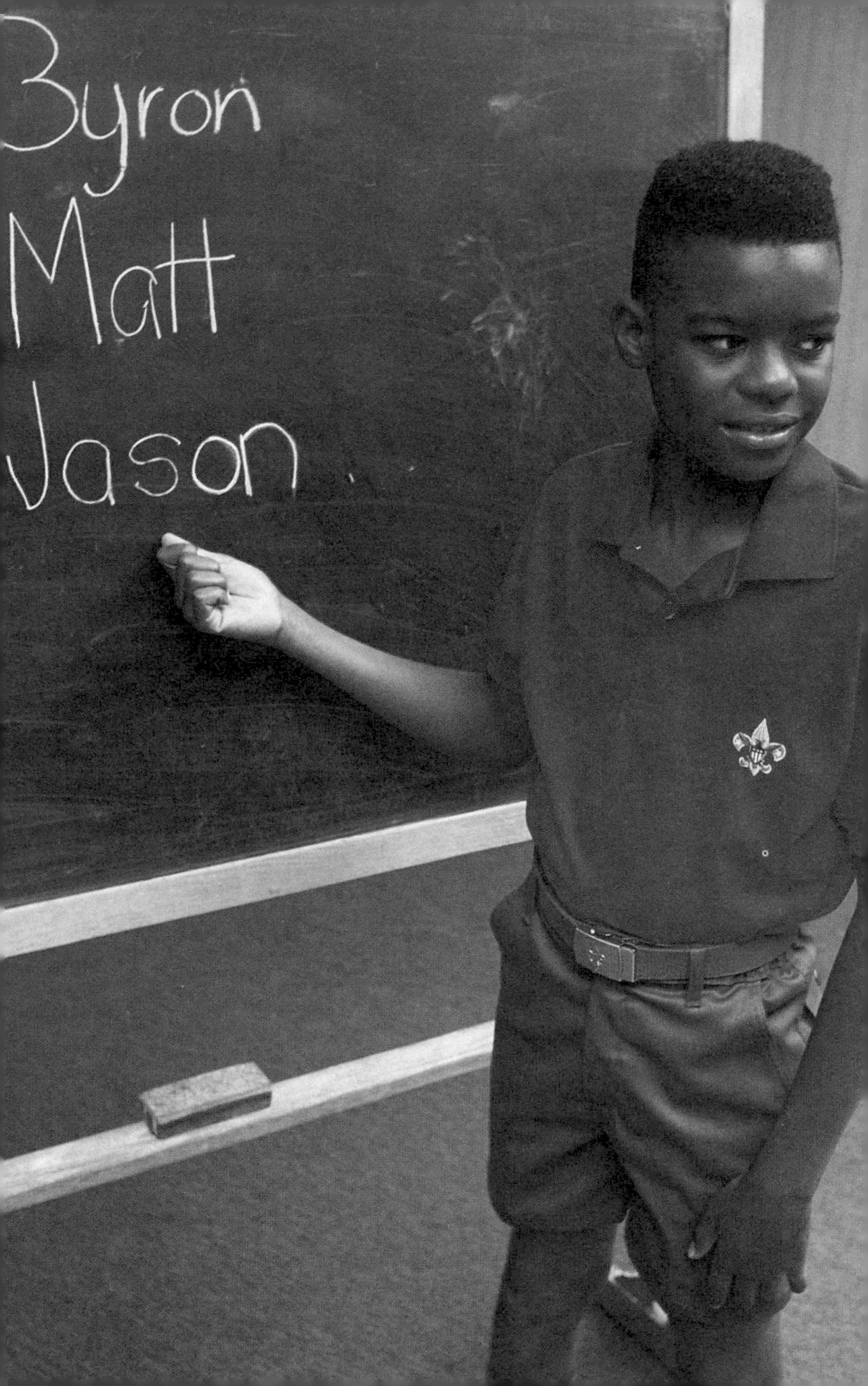
Byron
Matt
Jason

DEMOCRACY

1

D O you like to get together with your friends? Do you read all sorts of books and newspapers? Do you live in a home no one can enter unless they are invited? Those are your rights. You can also believe in any religion you want. You can write and say what you wish without fear of arrest. You can travel freely.

The rights you have are the same rights shared by everyone in our nation. They are freedoms that protect each person's opportunity to have a happy, productive, and safe life.

Americans have had these rights for more than 200 years. These rights are so much a part of everyday life in our nation that you may take them for granted. You might think that people have always enjoyed such freedoms, but they have not. Rarely in human history have the rights of every person been so respected.

Our nation sprang forth out of a desire for freedom. The colonists who settled the eastern coast of North America were ruled by the British government. It was a government that limited some of the freedoms the colonists believed they should have. For example, the Americans had to let British soldiers stay in their homes. They had to obey British laws and pay British taxes even though they had no legal way to make changes when they felt those laws and taxes were unfair.

The colonists decided they would be better off if they formed their own nation and governed themselves. In 1776, they declared their independence from Great Britain. The 13 colonies became the first 13 states, and the United States of America was born.

The British did not want such valuable colonies to slip out of their control. They sent armies to put down the rebellion. The Revolutionary War dragged on for 8 bitter years. Many American and British lives were lost before a treaty was signed in 1783. It signaled the end of the war and Great Britain's recognition of the United States as an independent nation.

Representatives of the 13 states met to write the Constitution — the blueprint for building the government of the United States. The form of government outlined in the Constitution is a *democracy*. *Demos* means "the people"; *cracy* means "power." In a democracy, every citizen has an equal say in the decisions of the government.

Even in the 1700s, there were too many people to meet together every time a law had to be made. Such "absolute" democracy works in a small group such as your Scout patrol, but not in a nation where people are spread across many states.

The Constitution solves that problem by making our democracy the "representative" kind. All adult citizens can vote for officials who will represent them in the government. A country ruled in this way is called a "republic."

The Constitution was signed by delegates to the Constitutional Convention in Philadelphia on September 17, 1787. This painting of the historic event hangs in the national Capitol.

CHAPTER 19

The Constitution also spells out the freedoms shared by every American. Some of the most important are explained in the first 10 amendments to the Constitution—the Bill of Rights.

The writers of the Constitution could not have imagined the kind of world that would exist 200 years in the future. But they were wise enough to design a government that could meet the needs of a growing, changing nation.

During the last two centuries, the strength of the Constitution has been tested many times. One of the most difficult issues was the question of slavery. When the Constitution was written, some people believed slaves did not have the same rights as free Americans. Many others thought slavery was wrong and that the Constitution should protect all people regardless of their race.

The argument became so bitter that in 1861 the states supporting slavery tried to break away and form their own country. Citizens of the other states fought against them in order to hold the nation together.

The nation was strong enough to withstand the Civil War, and the states were still united when the fighting ended. Constitutional liberties had been extended to all people. But those bloody years of war will always be a dark reminder that our freedoms have a high price. Throughout our history, hundreds of thousands of Americans have paid that price by sacrificing their lives to defend the Constitution and our nation.

There are times when America must have good soldiers. Our country also needs good teachers, engineers, scientists, writers, bus drivers, farmers, and merchants. America relies on capable coaches, pilots, computer programmers, and park and forest rangers. It depends on people willing to protect the environment, care for the sick, shelter the homeless, and defend those in trouble with the law.

A strong democracy also must have informed citizens. Voters must understand the candidates and the issues in order to make wise choices. They must take the time to be sure their representatives in the government are acting in a responsible, ethical manner.

Finally, our nation needs young people like you who are doing something good with their lives. You are the future of the country, but you can contribute to the good of the nation right now. When you do your best in school and in Scouting, keep yourself fit, and work hard for the good of others in your family and community, you are strengthening the fabric of America. Make the most of yourself and you will become the kind of citizen our nation must have. That is what it means to be an American. That is the high goal the Constitution sets for us all.

THE AMERICAN'S CREED

In the words of William Tyler Page, *The American's Creed* sums up the ideals for which our nation stands. It points out the rights of all Americans and our duty to keep America great.

I believe in the United States of America . . .

Covering more than 3½ million square miles of land, the United States of America is a nation rich in natural resources. We can also count as a resource the millions of citizens who call America home. Each of us can contribute in our own way to making life in our country good for ourselves and everyone else.

. . . as a government of the people, by the people, for the people; . . .

Our government is made up *of* all of us. Decisions are made *by* us through those we elect to office. The rights of the Constitution are *for* each and every one of us. The Declaration of Independence states that "all men are created equal." It doesn't matter where we live, how much money we have, the color of our skin, whether we are male or female, or the nature of our beliefs; we are all equal under the law.

. . . whose just powers are derived from the consent of the governed; a democracy in a Republic; . . .

It is our duty to vote in elections to select those who will represent our views in the government. To vote wisely, we must spend time learning about the candidates and the issues on which they will make decisions.

. . . a sovereign Nation of many sovereign States, . . .

Our national government headquarters is in the city of Washington in the District of Columbia. Congress makes federal laws, the Supreme Court interprets them, and the executive branch under the leadership of the president carries them out. In addition, 50 separate state governments enact laws to suit conditions in their sovereign states. "Sovereign" means each state controls its own affairs.

. . . a perfect Union, one and inseparable; . . .

Maintaining a union of 50 states has never been easy. There are still many problems that face us. But if we work toward solutions and keep as a goal the shining vision of a perfect nation, we can continue to make our country the best place possible for all of us.

. . . established upon those principles of freedom, equality, justice, and humanity for which American patriots sacrificed their lives and fortunes.

Freedom. Equality. Justice. Humanity. We want every person on Earth to share those rights. To that end, many Americans have shared their wealth, their skills, their wisdom, and some have even sacrificed their lives. Their willingness to die for basic human rights should make us all more determined to live for those high ideals.

I therefore believe it is my duty to my country to love it; . . .

America is your country. Its soil feeds you. Its laws protect you and give you "the right to life, liberty, and the pursuit of happiness." Show your love for America with actions that make it a better country for you and for all citizens.

. . . to support its Constitution; . . .

The United States Constitution protects your rights as an American. By supporting the Constitution, you help preserve these rights. Support all the same rights for others, even when you do not agree with their actions.

. . . to obey its laws; . . .

Written by our representatives, the laws of our country, states, and communities govern much of what we do every day. By obeying laws, you strengthen them and maintain the protection they afford. By learning about laws and seeking to improve them through Constitutional processes, you help keep your government responsive to the needs of its citizens.

. . . to respect its flag; . . .

The flag is the symbol of our country. When we show it our respect, we are showing our respect and love for all that is America — our land, our people, our way of life.

. . . and to defend it against all enemies.

America relies on its citizens to keep it safe. The men and women of the armed forces stand ready to defend the nation against threats from beyond our borders. But ignorance, prejudice, and apathy are enemies of our country, too. Do your part to defeat those threats by working hard at school. Defend the rights of others. Make your neighborhood, state, and nation good places in which to live.

KNOW OUR COUNTRY'S GREATS

American history is full of dignity and heroism. Most of America's greats — pioneers, parents, Scoutmasters, teachers, and millions of others — make their contributions in quiet ways.

Some individuals have had the opportunity to perform deeds that changed our country and the world. Some did it by their statesmanship, others by their educational skills. Some with their books, others by their inventions. Some with speeches, others by sacrificing their lives.

Many of those we remember found fame with the support of many whose names are long forgotten. Great coaches win only with the help of fine players. Generals gain fame only if they are leading dedicated soldiers.

You will find some of America's best-known greats pictured on pages 462–463. They represent not just the achievements of individual citizens, but also how the lives of all Americans are important to the United States of America.

ALBERT EINSTEIN

DANIEL BOONE

Susan Brownell Anthony	*Alexander Graham Bell*
Daniel Boone	*Mark Twain*
Thomas Alva Edison	*Albert Einstein*
Dwight David Eisenhower	*Benjamin Franklin*
John Muir	*Matthew Henson*
Martin Luther King, Jr.	*Robert E. Lee*
Sacajawea	*Chief Plenty Coups*
Walter Reed	*Henry David Thoreau*
Eleanor Roosevelt	*Padre Junipero Serra*
Harriet Tubman	*Whitney Young, Jr.*
Jim Thorpe	*I. M. Pei*

FAMOUS SAYINGS

Many Americans are known by their deeds. Others are remembered not only for what they did, but also for what they said. Our national heritage is enriched by their sayings. Here are a few. Find out the background of those who said them.

"Ask not what your country can do for you—ask what you can do for your country."

John F. Kennedy

"Dost thou love life? Then do not squander time, for that is the stuff life is made of."

Benjamin Franklin

"Labor to keep alive in your breast that little spark of celestial fire—conscience."

George Washington

"A candle loses nothing of its light by lighting another candle."

James Keller

"The only way to have a friend is to be one."

Ralph Waldo Emerson

"The only thing we have to fear is fear itself."

Franklin D. Roosevelt

"Give me liberty, or give me death!"

Patrick Henry

"Always do right. This will gratify some people, and astonish the rest."

Mark Twain

"Injustice anywhere is a threat to justice everywhere."

Martin Luther King, Jr.

"Men, their rights and nothing more. Women, their rights and nothing less."

Susan B. Anthony

"Liberty is the only thing you cannot have unless you are willing to give it to others."

William Allen White

"As I would not be a slave, so I would not be a master. This expresses my idea of democracy. Whatever differs from this, to the extent of the difference, is no democracy."

Abraham Lincoln

"If a man does not keep pace with his companions, perhaps it is because he hears a different drummer. Let him step to the music he hears, however measured or far away."

Henry David Thoreau

KNOW AMERICA'S PAST

The history of our country is alive with the deeds and words of many men and women. It is also full of places and things, each of them with a story to tell.

On these pages and the next are pictures of places and things that have special meaning to Americans. How many places and things can you name? Do you know why they are famous? What is their importance to our history?

Minuteman Statue

Wright brothers' airplane

Spirit of St. Louis

Indian village

Pony Express

Oregon Trail

Old Ironsides

Tomb of the Unknown Soldier

USS Arizona *monument at Pearl Harbor*

Yellowstone National Park (the world's first)

Liberty Bell

Spacecraft on the moon

Driving the "Golden Spike"

Ellis Island

Appomattox Courthouse

Statue of Liberty

Civil rights marches

KNOW THE PLEDGE OF ALLEGIANCE

The Pledge of Allegiance to the Flag
of the United States of America

I pledge allegiance to the flag of the United States of America and to the Republic for which it stands, one Nation under God, indivisible, with liberty and justice for all.

The Meaning of the Pledge of Allegiance

When you pledge allegiance to your flag, you promise loyalty and devotion to your nation. Each word has a deep meaning.

I pledge allegiance . . . I promise to be true

. . . *to the flag* . . . to the symbol of our country

. . . *of the United States of America* . . . a country made up of 50 states and several territories, each with certain rights of its own

. . . *and to the Republic* . . . a country where the people elect representatives from among themselves to make laws for them

. . . *for which it stands,* . . . the flag represents the country

. . . *one Nation under God,* . . . a country whose people are free to believe in God

. . . *indivisible,* . . . the country cannot be split into parts

. . . *with liberty and justice* . . . with freedom and fairness

. . . *for all.* For every person in the country.

KNOW OUR COUNTRY'S FLAG

The United States flag is far more than the red, white, and blue cloth of which it is made. As the living symbol of America, it stands for the past, present, and future of our country. It symbolizes our people, our land, and our way of life.

The flag represents the men and women who built America. It reminds us of the native Americans who inhabited the continent for thousands of years, of Pilgrims finding a place to worship their God in their own way, of pioneers building homes in a new land, of Washington leading a young nation, of Lincoln holding that nation together, of Martin Luther King Jr.'s dream of justice and equality for all, and of the men and women of all races and beliefs who fought and died for our country.

Respect the flag and the ideals it represents by handling it, displaying it, folding it, and saluting it in the right way.

The History of the Flag—Old Glory

The flag of the United States of America has 13 stripes—7 red and 6 white—and 50 white stars on a blue field. The stripes remind us of the 13 original colonies that gained us our liberty. The stars represent the 50 states bound together as one country.

The flag of today evolved out of many earlier flags raised over American soil in days gone by. For several centuries after European explorers first sailed to North America, the flags of Spain, France, Holland, Sweden, and England flew over different parts of the continent. A British flag known as the Red Ensign waved over the American colonies from 1707 until the beginning of the Revolutionary War.

When the Revolution started in 1775, the colonies wanted a flag of their own. That new flag, the Grand Union, was raised over George Washington's headquarters outside Boston on January 1, 1776.

On June 14 of the following year, the Continental Congress meeting in Philadelphia chose a design for the first official flag of the United States of America. Today we celebrate June 14 as Flag Day.

When two more states joined the Union in 1795, the American flag gained 2 stars and 2 stripes, bringing to 15 the total of each. That Star-Spangled Banner flew above Fort McHenry during the British bombardment in 1814, inspiring Francis Scott Key to write our national anthem.

As more states joined the United States, Americans realized the flag would become an awkward shape if additional stripes were sewn to it. Congress restored the design to the original 13 stripes, and decided that a star would be added to the blue field for each new state. The 50th star—for Hawaii—was added on July 4, 1960.

The Red Ensign was the merchant flag of Great Britain. It was red with a union in the upper inner corner combining the cross of St. George (red on white), patron of England, with the diagonal cross (white on blue) of St. Andrew, patron of Scotland.

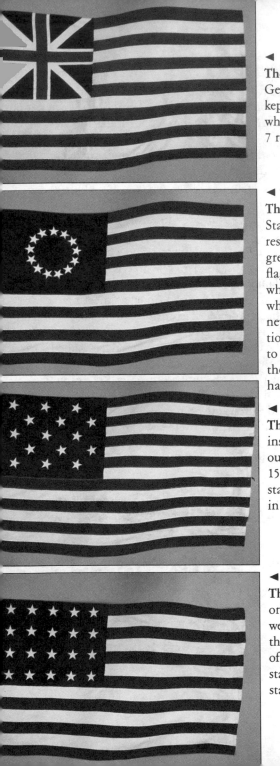

◄

The Grand Union flag raised over George Washington's headquarters kept the union of the British flag. Six white stripes broke the red field into 7 red stripes—13 in all.

◄

The first official flag of the United States of America was created by a resolution of the Continental Congress in 1777. It specified "that the flag...be 13 stripes alternate red and white; that the union be 13 stars, white in a blue field, representing a new constellation." Since the resolution did not tell how the stars were to be arranged, flag makers grouped them in different ways: in rows, in a half circle, in a full circle.

◄

The Star-Spangled Banner of 1814 inspired Francis Scott Key to write our national anthem. The flag had 15 stripes and 15 stars. The 2 new stars and stripes had been added in 1795.

◄

The Flag of 1818 returned to the original 13 stripes. Five more stars were added, for a total of 20. From that time to the present, the number of stripes has remained the same. A star has been added for each new state.

Respecting the Flag

The United States Flag Code adopted by Congress provides the rules for honoring and displaying the flag. The code states: "The flag represents a living country and is itself considered a living thing." Give it your full respect.

The following is an interpretation of the parts of the flag code you should know as a Scout:

When to Fly the Flag

The flag of the United States may be flown every day when weather permits. If made of weather-resistant material, a flag may be flown in any weather. Although the custom of flying the flag only from sunrise to sunset is generally practiced, there is no law prohibiting the flag being flown both day and night. The flag should especially be flown on all national and state holidays, and on other special days designated by the president of the United States.

Raising and Lowering the Flag

Show joy by flying the flag at full-staff. Raise it briskly and lower it slowly.

Indicate sorrow and mourning by flying the flag at half-staff. Raise it first to the top of the flagpole, hold it for an instant, then lower it to half-staff (one-half the distance between the top and the bottom of the pole). To take it down, first raise it to the peak, then lower it slowly. On Memorial Day, fly the flag at half-staff until noon, then raise it to full-staff.

Raising the flag. It takes two persons to raise, lower, and fold the flag correctly. For raising, one holds the folded flag to prevent it from touching the ground. The other attaches the flag to the flag line (halyard) and then raises the flag briskly, keeping the line taut. When the flag has left the arms of the first person and is flowing freely, he steps back and comes to a salute while the other person fastens the halyard to the cleat on the flagpole.

◄ **UNFASTENING THE HALYARD**

► **RAISING THE FLAG**

Lowering the flag. One person unfastens the halyard from the cleat and slowly lowers the flag while the other salutes. When the flag is within reach, the second person drops his salute and gathers the flag into his arms. The first person removes the flag from the halyard and ties the halyard to the cleat.

Folding the flag. Begin by folding the flag lengthwise in halves, then in quarters with the blue field on the outside. Then, while one person holds the flag by the blue field, the other makes a triangular fold in the opposite end and continues folding the flag in triangles until only the blue field is showing.

FOLD INTO HALVES

FOLD INTO QUARTERS

FOLD IN TRIANGULAR FOLDS

Greeting the Flag

When you are wearing your Scout uniform with or without a cap, greet the flag with a Scout salute. Do this whenever you see it being hoisted or lowered, when you pass it, or when it passes you. Give the Scout salute when you recite the Pledge of Allegiance, too.

►

When you are not in uniform, use the civilian salute. Greet the flag by placing your right hand over your heart. If you are wearing a hat, remove it and hold it in your right hand over your heart.

Carrying the Flag

Always carry the flag aloft and free, never flat or horizontally.

When the flag is carried alone, there should be an honor guard to the left of it or one on each side of it. Carried with other flags, the United States flag should be in front of the others or to the right if the flags are arranged in a line.

▼ Never dip the flag of the United States in salute to any person or thing.

International usage forbids the display of the flag of one nation above that of another nation in time of peace. Flags of other nations must be flown from separate flagpoles of equal height, and all flags should be approximately equal in size with the United States flag.

◄

Displaying the Flag

You may have a chance to put the flag on display. Here are the basic rules you should follow:

☆ When flags are displayed at different heights, the United States flag flies higher than all the others. It is hoisted first and lowered last.

☆ When flags are displayed at equal heights, the United States flag is either in front of or farthest to the right of the other flags.

▶

☆ When the flag is displayed flat against a wall, horizontally or vertically, the blue union should be at the top, *at the flag's own right* (to the left as you look at it).

◄

☆ In a church, synagogue, temple, or auditorium, the flag on a staff is placed to the clergy's or speaker's right.

▶

DEMOCRACY

☆ When displayed from a staff that projects from a window or from the front of a building, the flag goes to the peak of the staff, except when displayed at half-staff.

☆ Across a street, hang the flag vertically with the union to the north in an east-west street, to the east in a north-south street.

☆ When displayed on an automobile, the staff should be firmly clamped to the right front fender. It should not be draped on or over any part of the car.

☆ The flag is never flown upside down except as a distress signal to call for help.

Care of the Flag

Never let the American flag touch the ground, the floor, or water. Place nothing on it. Never use the flag as drapery—use red, white, and blue bunting instead.

Clean the flag if it becomes soiled. Mend it if it is torn. When worn beyond repair, destroy it in a dignified way, preferably by burning.

KNOW OUR NATIONAL ANTHEM

During the War of 1812, the British fleet attacked U.S. Fort McHenry near Baltimore. A young lawyer named Francis Scott Key watched the bombing that lasted through the night. He did not know if the American soldiers could withstand the assault. As morning came, he gazed toward the fort and wondered:

O say can you see, by the dawn's early light,
What so proudly we hail'd at the twilight's last gleaming,
Whose broad stripes and bright stars through the perilous fight
O'er the ramparts we watched, were so gallantly streaming?

The bombardment ended at 8 a.m., September 14, 1814. The smoke cleared and Key saw that the flag was still flying over the fort. That day he wrote down the feelings he had during the night and the hope he felt for his country's future. Soon the words were being sung throughout the country. What Francis Scott Key had written became our national anthem.

> O say can you see ~~the~~ by the dawn's early light,
> What so proudly we hail'd at the twilight's last gleaming,
> Whose broad stripes & bright stars through the perilous fight
> O'er the ramparts we watch'd, were so gallantly streaming?
>   And the rocket's red glare, the bomb bursting in air,
>   Gave proof through the night that our flag was still there,
> O say does that star spangled banner yet wave
> O'er the land of the free & the home of the brave?

To get the full meaning of every line that Key wrote, read them in his own handwriting above. Study them carefully. Then try to express them in your own words.

Whenever you hear our national anthem played or sung, show your respect by standing up. Salute if you are in uniform. Place your right hand over your heart if you are in civilian clothes. Think of your own future under the Star-Spangled Banner.

Know Your Local Flag

Find the flag of your state, commonwealth, territory, or island possession.

ALABAMA

ALASKA

AMERICAN SAMOA

ARIZONA

ARKANSAS

CALIFORNIA

COLORADO

CONNECTICUT

DELAWARE

DISTRICT OF COLUMBIA

FLORIDA

GEORGIA

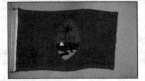

GUAM

HAWAII

IDAHO

ILLINOIS

INDIANA

IOWA

CHAPTER 19

KANSAS

KENTUCKY

LOUISIANA

MAINE

MARYLAND

MASSACHUSETTS

MICHIGAN

MINNESOTA

MISSISSIPPI

MISSOURI

MONTANA

NEBRASKA

NEVADA

NEW HAMPSHIRE

NEW JERSEY

NEW MEXICO

NEW YORK

NORTH CAROLINA

NORTH DAKOTA

OHIO

OKLAHOMA

OREGON

PENNSYLVANIA

PUERTO RICO

RHODE ISLAND

SOUTH CAROLINA

SOUTH DAKOTA

TENNESSEE

TEXAS

UTAH

VERMONT

VIRGINIA

VIRGIN ISLANDS

WASHINGTON

WEST VIRGINIA

WISCONSIN

WYOMING

BILL OF RIGHTS

Congress of the United States, begun and held at the City of New York, on Wednesday, the fourth of March, one thousand seven hundred and eighty nine.

The Conventions of a number of the States, having, at the time of their adopting the Constitution, expressed a desire, in order to prevent misconstruction or abuse of its powers, that further declaratory and restrictive clauses should be added: And as extending the ground of public confidence in the Government, will best insure the beneficent ends of its institution:

Resolved, by the SENATE and HOUSE OF REPRESENTATIVES of the UNITED STATES OF AMERICA in Congress assembled, two thirds of both Houses concurring. That the following Articles be proposed to the Legislatures of the several States, as Amendments to the Constitution of the United States; all, or any of which articles, when ratified by three fourths of the said Legislatures, to be valid to all intents and purposes, as part of the said Constitution, viz.

Articles in addition to, and Amendment of the Constitution of the United States of America, proposed by Congress, and ratified by the Legislatures of the several States, pursuant to the fifth Article of the Original Constitution.

ARTICLE THE FIRST . . . After the first enumeration required by the first Article of the Constitution, there shall be one Representative for every thirty thousand, until the number shall amount to one hundred, after which, the proportion shall be so regulated by Congress, that there shall be not less than one hundred Representatives, nor less than one Representative for every forty thousand persons, until the number of Representatives shall amount to two hundred, after which, the proportion shall be so regulated by Congress, that there shall not be less than two hundred Representatives, nor more than one Representative for every fifty thousand persons. [Not Ratified]

ARTICLE THE SECOND . . . No law, varying the compensation for the services of the Senators and Representatives, shall take effect, until and election of Representatives shall have intervened. [Not Ratified]

First Amendment

ARTICLE THE THIRD . . . Congress shall make no law respecting an establishment of religion, or prohibiting the free exercise thereof; or abridging the freedom of speech, or of the press; or the right of the people peaceably to assemble, and to petition the Government for a redress of grievances.

Second Amendment

ARTICLE THE FOURTH . . . A well regulated Militia, being necessary to the security of a free State, the right of the people to keep and bear Arms, shall not be infringed.

Third Amendment

ARTICLE THE FIFTH . . . No Soldier shall, in time of peace, be quartered in any house, without the consent of the owner, nor in time of war, but in a manner to be prescribed by law.

Fourth Amendment

ARTICLE THE SIXTH . . . The right of the people to be secure in their persons, houses, papers, and effects, against unreasonable searches and seizures, shall not be violated, and no Warrants shall issue but upon probable cause, supported by oath or affirmation, and particularly describing the place to be searched, and the persons or things to be seized.

Fifth Amendment

ARTICLE THE SEVENTH . . . No person shall be held to answer for a capital, or otherwise infamous crime, unless on a presentment or indictment of a grand jury, except in cases arising in the land or Naval forces, or in the Militia, when in actual service in time of War or public danger; nor shall any person be subject for the same offense to be twice put in jeopardy of life or limb; nor shall be compelled in any criminal case, to be a witness against himself, nor be deprived of life, liberty, or property, without due process of law; nor shall private property be taken for public use without just compensation.

Sixth Amendment

ARTICLE THE EIGHTH . . . In all criminal prosecutions, the accused shall enjoy the right to a speedy and public trial by an impartial jury of the State and district wherein the crime shall have been committed, which district shall have been previously ascertained by law, and to be informed of the nature and cause of the accusation; to be confronted with the witnesses against him; to have compulsory process for obtaining witnesses in his favor, and to have the assistance of counsel for his defense.

Seventh Amendment

ARTICLE THE NINTH . . . In suits at common law, where the value in controversy shall exceed twenty dollars, the right of trial by jury shall be preserved, and no fact, tried by a jury, shall be otherwise re-examined in any Court of the United States, than according to the rules of the common law.

Eighth Amendment

ARTICLE THE TENTH . . . Excessive bail shall not be required, nor excessive fines imposed, nor cruel and unusual punishments inflicted.

Ninth Amendment

ARTICLE THE ELEVENTH . . . the enumeration in the Constitution of certain rights, shall not be construed to deny or disparage others retained by the people.

Tenth Amendment

ARTICLE THE TWELFTH . . . The powers not delegated to the United States by the Constitution, nor prohibited by it to the States, are reserved to the States respectively, or to the people.

COMMUNITY

WHAT IS YOUR COMMUNITY?

HISTORY is full of stories of a person setting out alone to climb a mountain or explore unknown territory. Alone, men and women have made great scientific discoveries, written books that changed the world, and stood up for their beliefs. Their successes show us how much one person is able to do.

Yet over the centuries, most humans have chosen to live and work in the company of others. We enjoy being with other people. We learn from each other's experiences. Because there is strength in numbers, we can solve problems together that are too difficult for any one of us alone. When we care for one another and share our knowledge and resources, our small groups become communities.

A community could be a row of brick homes on a city street or a few farmhouses surrounded by fields of corn. It might be a circle of mud huts on the plains of Africa, a pueblo in New Mexico or Arizona, or apartments in a tall building. What really matters is how people feel about their community. If they take pride in their neighborhood and work to make it happy, healthy, and full of life, then it will be.

WHAT A COMMUNITY GIVES YOU

Do you cheer for a sports team in your town? Are you pleased when your school band marches in a parade? Are you proud of the troop number on the sleeve of your Scout uniform shirt? That's because you know you belong. You are a part of that team, that school, and that troop.

You probably feel the same way about the community in which you live. You are proud to say, "I am from that place." You can boast about your neighborhood, and rightly so. It is your home. It gives you an identity. It also provides the support, safety, and services you need.

Support. At a Scouting awards ceremony, you've known the joy of having your friends and family watch you receive a new badge. If you play on a ball team, you know how good it feels to have the home fans cheer you on. When you do your best in school, your neighbors may give you a pat on the back to let you know that you are making your community better for everyone.

People in a community support each other through the bad times as well as the good. Perhaps you have known of a family whose home was damaged by fire. Right away, neighbors brought over food, blankets, spare clothing, and used furniture. Some people may have pitched in to repair the smoky rooms, or they might have raised money to help the family get started again. That's what a community can do.

Safety. People who care about their neighbors and the places where they live want to keep their community safe. You can help in small ways—shoveling snow from sidewalks, sweeping glass out of the street, reporting a downed stop sign or a broken street light. With your knowledge of first aid, you are always ready to assist injured persons. You can also support the police, fire departments, and rescue squads which handle more serious safety matters. They are part of your community, too.

Services. If there were no communities and your family lived by itself, you would need to find your own food and water every day. At night you could burn a candle or a lantern, but there would probably be no other light. If you became sick, you would have to heal yourself. But because we have communities, water is as close as the nearest faucet. Lights come on at the flip of a switch. When you're injured or ill, help is available at clinics and hospitals.

Fresh water, power, medical attention, and dozens of other services exist because of your community. By sharing the work and cost involved, you and your neighbors provide yourselves and your community with the necessities of life.

CHAPTER 20

WHAT YOU CAN GIVE YOUR COMMUNITY

Scouts can do a lot to support their community, keep it safe, and volunteer their own services. A good way to start is by getting to know your neighborhood.

Know Your Community

Many American towns and cities are hundreds of years old. They may have grown up near rivers and harbors where ships could dock. Or they might have been built along the trails and railroad lines that crossed the continent in the last century.

Some communities rely on farming to produce income for people. For others, a major business may be shipping, tourism, mining, or a large factory. Today there are even cities whose wealth lies in computers and space travel. In addition to these basic industries, people need grocery stores, banks, schools, and places of worship. Together, all of these businesses and services form a network that gives a community shape and character.

Why is your hometown located where it is? Who started it? What are its main industries? You can find some of the answers just by looking around. Most libraries have information about local history. There may be museums

Study a city map to learn more about your community and your neighborhood.

or monuments honoring local historical events. Ask people who have lived in your neighborhood for a long time to share their memories of what your community was like in years gone by.

You can also discover a great deal about your city or town by studying a map. Street maps are available at your local chamber of commerce, city hall, tourist information center, or library. Most urban maps are drawn with north at the top, just like the topographic maps you use in the backcountry. And like those wilderness maps, a city map gives clues about the lay of the land. Do the streets curve around hills and along shorelines? Can you find bridges over rivers and streams?

On the map, pinpoint the location of your house. Find nearby schools, stores, churches, synagogues, and parks. Spot the locations of your troop meetings and the homes of others in your Scout patrol. Trace the routes you travel to school and on troop outings.

You should know your neighborhood well enough to give useful directions to a visitor who needs help in finding his way. By developing a sense of place, you will also increase your own feeling of belonging to your community.

Know Your Neighbors

Your neighbors are the people who live in houses near yours, on farms down the road, or in apartments in the same building. You see them working and playing in their yards, going to the store, and coming home in the evening. Take time to introduce yourself. Explain that you are a neighbor and a Scout. You want to let them know who you are, and you would be pleased to learn about them.

When you know your neighbors, you become surrounded by the most exciting of all community resources. Your neighbors have all lived different lives. Every one of them has an interesting story to tell or a skill to teach. As you learn from your neighbors and offer them what you know, you will be reminded that community is not just a row of houses or a faceless apartment building. It is the unified strength of people sharing with one another.

There are some special kinds of neighbors you won't want to overlook.

Senior citizens. Older Americans are very valuable members of any community. They can draw on many decades of experience to help solve local problems. They might be retired, so they often have more time to devote to their neighborhood. Because their own families may be far away, senior citizens appreciate the friendship of neighbors, especially of young people like you.

Special populations. Each of us must overcome challenges in our lives. Perhaps you or another Scout in your troop gets around in a wheelchair or with crutches. A few of your neighbors may experience impaired hearing or a loss of sight. Some people must adjust to developmental disabilities, as well.

We all wish we could have perfect physical health and mental awareness. However, illnesses and accidents can leave people of any age with impairments and disabilities. Someone in your family may have faced physical or mental limitations since birth.

While they may have special ways of overcoming certain conditions, people with disabilities are members of communities just like anyone else. They have much to offer. Be sensitive to their needs, but then look beyond their limitations and get to know the people they really are.

Ethnic groups. Eveyone has an ethnic background. For native Americans, that means being part of the tribes that lived in North America before European explorers arrived. The ethnic origins of everyone else lie outside the borders

of the United States. Your parents, grandparents, or other ancestors may have come from Africa, Asia, Europe, South America, or another part of the globe. Perhaps your family arrived in America hundreds of years ago. Maybe you've lived in the United States only a few months.

Americans try hard to make our nation a place where people of all backgrounds and races can live and succeed together. At the same time, we take great pride in our ethnic roots. Ethnic songs, clothing, languages, foods, and religious beliefs help give us each a special connection with our past. Ethnic festivals and holidays let us celebrate our own heritage and share in those of our neighbors.

Watch for posters in store windows telling of local celebrations and festivals. Read the newspapers for announcements of special events. You can have a good time learning about other cultures. By accepting the differences among us, you will realize the wonderful variety and strength that different ethnic groups can bring to a community.

Learn about community services by taking a patrol outing to a fire station.

How Your Community Is Run

A big city usually has a large full-time government. In a small town, officials may be men and women who serve without pay. In either case, a city council and a mayor, city manager, or tribal leader are elected by the people of the community to run the local government. One important job of that government is providing good services such as schools, fire and police protection, repair of streets and sewers, public transportation, and other community needs.

Services cost money. A single family could not afford to buy its own telephone company, pave its own street, hire police officers, and build a dam to make electricity. Instead, the cost of these needs is shared by everyone in a community. The utilities are often owned by the community itself—by you and all your neighbors. Money to pay for them comes from monthly rates and sometimes from taxes. That way, everybody pays a little in order to receive a lot.

Plan a patrol outing to visit a fire department, police station, sewage treatment plant, utility, or other community service. Call in advance to set up the visit. Officials will be happy to show you around and let you see your community services at work.

Get to Know the Leaders of Your Community

City council meetings are usually open to the public. The same is true of county, state, and federal sessions of elective bodies. By watching a meeting, you can see how decisions affecting the public are made. That is one of the ways you and other citizens can decide if officials are making the choices you want them to make. Talk with your Scoutmaster about taking the troop to see a government meeting.

You can also visit directly with many local leaders. Write or call their offices for an appointment. Public officials are busy, but they often make time to talk with the people they represent. Before you go, write down the questions you would like to have them answer. Perhaps you are interested in how a mayor does his or her job. Maybe you have seen a problem in your neighborhood that you feel a city council member should know about, or you want to suggest a solution. By answering your questions and by being supportive of your interests, community leaders are helping to ensure a better community tomorrow.

Volunteer Organizations

A mayor or city council member may tell you that government cannot provide every service a community needs. That is where volunteer organizations step in—special groups of people who donate time and energy to get things done. A good example is the parent-teacher organization your parents or guardian may attend. They aren't paid to go. However, they know that teachers and parents working together can make your school a good place for you to learn.

Your Scout troop wouldn't exist without volunteers. Volunteers organize and run it. They find funding to pay for tents and cooking gear. On their own time, Scout leaders receive training, hold troop meetings, and go with you on campouts.

Scouts help their community by conducting "Scouting for Food" Good Turns. Scouts go door to door to collect canned goods for donation to local food banks.

Many churches, temples, and synagogues help with community needs. So do volunteer fundraising organizations such as the United Way. Block-watch and neighborhood crime-stopper groups do much to increase the safety of homes and businesses. In some towns, even the fire department is made up of people who have other jobs but are ready at a moment's notice to fight a fire.

You could be a volunteer, too. Perhaps you could help an organization at your school that tells students about the dangers of drug abuse and drunken driving. Or you and your friends could volunteer to spend one Saturday each month collecting food and used clothing for homeless people.

Other Community Resources

Every time you run across a playground, visit a museum or a zoo, or read a book in a library, you are using community resources. The same is true for the hiking trails, beaches, and picnic areas you enjoy in your city parks. The quality of life in a community depends on more than the utilities and

Mark your property with a driver's license number.

services that heat our homes and keep the lights burning. We also need places to relax. We need places that fill our minds with new ideas.

Like utilities, these public resources have a price tag. Some are funded with tax money or depend on volunteer help. Your community may have privately owned theaters, concert halls, and sports fields, which are usually supported by admission fees.

But these resources need more than money. A library without readers has no purpose. A zoo without visitors won't stay open long. A concert hall without an audience is doomed to close. Help keep community resources full of life by using them. Guard them against vandalism. When windows are broken or slogans are painted on walls, money must be spent to make repairs. Your community may lose some of its resources if maintenance costs are too high. That would mean fewer opportunities for everyone.

Solving Community Problems

Communities are always changing, and with change come many challenges. As you gain a greater understanding of the ways in which your community operates, you can take a larger role in solving its problems. Finding solutions often begins by seeing problems clearly.

◀ LIBRARY

▼ CITY PARK

▼ ZOO

Recognize the problem. On its monthly campouts, a Scout patrol was always sure to pick up litter and leave every campsite clean. But near their homes, the Scouts saw lots of trash on city streets. There were piles of rubbish in vacant lots. The Scouts were upset that not everyone had pride in their neighborhood. And they knew it was an awful waste to use all of that metal, glass, and paper just once and then throw it away.

Get the facts. Some people might think that there is nothing they can do about a community problem, but not these Scouts. They began reading about trash and asking questions. They learned that it takes a lot of energy and raw materials to make glass, cans, and paper products. If we throw them away after one use, then we have to cut more trees and use more resources to make new paper and containers.

The Scouts also found out that glass, metal, and newspapers can be used over and over. It's called *recycling*. In fact, there was a place in their city that paid a few cents a pound for trash that could be recycled.

Think of solutions. The Scouts talked with their families and Scoutmaster. What could they do to solve the problem? Perhaps they could each save their own family's trash and take it to the recycling center. Better yet, instead of each family taking its own trash, they might set one Saturday a month when one of the parents would drive everyone's trash to the center.

What was really needed, though, was a way to encourage the whole neighborhood to recycle. The Scouts met with the owner of the recycling company, who suggested that the Scouts set up a collection point in an empty lot. They could build bins where anybody could leave recyclable trash. If the Scouts

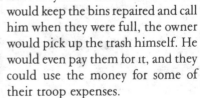

would keep the bins repaired and call him when they were full, the owner would pick up the trash himself. He would even pay them for it, and they could use the money for some of their troop expenses.

By acting on a problem they saw in their community, these Scouts found a solution that benefited everyone. It helped them realize they had the power to make things better, and that they are important members of their community.

Above: Helping earthquake victims. *Right:* The 1984 Olympic Games in Los Angeles. ▶

WORLD COMMUNITY

From the moon, the earth looks like a glowing blue marble floating in the blackness of space. If we could see our world from that far away, the differences between people and between nations would seem very small. Scouting is a growing, worldwide youth movement of more than 16 million members in 150 countries and territories. Each nation has its own national organization that develops a program and structure to meet the needs of its members relative to their own culture and society. Even though the details of Scouting differ from country to country, there are things common to Scouts everywhere such as duty to God and country, a universal three-finger Scout sign, and the basic idea of the Good Turn. We are all members of one world community.

We think of people in other lands differently when we realize they are our neighbors. We see examples of international cooperation every 4 years during the Olympic Games. Athletes from around the world gather to compete in a spirit of friendship and trust. Scouts from many countries gather every 4 years to share the spirit of Scouting at world jamborees. We see a feeling of world community whenever drought, flood, or famine threaten some part of the globe, and other regions with plenty of food respond with supplies and medical aid for the stricken people.

Many problems today are so great they cannot be solved by one country. Throughout the world, Scouts are active in local community improvement projects dealing with hunger, disease, environmental pollution, illiteracy, and drug abuse, to name a few.

The search for solutions to these problems will continue. In fact, someday you may have some of the answers. You can begin by learning all you can about people around the world. The World Crest, an emblem of the World Organization of the Scout Movement, may be worn by all registered youth and adult members of the Boy Scouts of America as a symbol of their membership in a worldwide Scouting brotherhood.

FAMILY

FAMILY. That's one of the best words we know. It means belonging, support, and love. For many Scouts, a family is made up of parents, brothers, and sisters all under the same roof. There may even be grandparents sharing the home, and cousins, aunts, and uncles living nearby.

But there are other kinds of families, too. Perhaps you live in a family with a single parent, or share time with a father and mother who live in different places. Grandparents and other relatives may live far away—even in other countries. Maybe your family has no parents at all, but instead is made up of relatives or guardians who want the best for you.

Two parents, one, or none—what makes a family is not the number of people in it or whether they are related. It is the way they care for each other and share their lives with each other.

The family is where learning begins. How did you learn to speak? By imitating words you heard in your family. Much of what you know and who you are comes to you from long ago, passed down through the generations by your family. The language you speak, foods you eat, holidays you celebrate, and values you hold are all reflections of the people with whom you live.

Our families provide us with shelter, clothing, and food. They should accept us for what we are and help us become the best people we can. When we are with our families, we want to feel safe. We want to belong.

No family is perfect. There may be times when you feel that others in your family don't understand you. You may disagree with some of their ways of doing things. As you grow older, you want to develop more independence. All of the changes you are going through can cause strain at home. But you can make the most of family life. That takes work, especially on your part. It begins by learning how to listen.

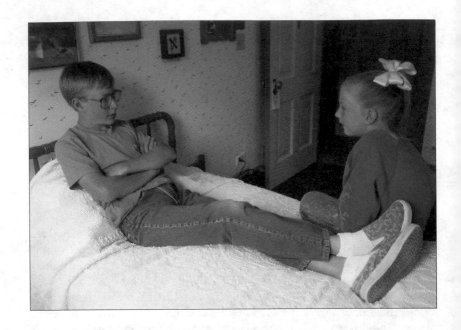

LISTENING

We are so eager to say what we think that we don't always listen carefully. For instance, your little sister may just be learning how to kick a soccer ball. When you come home from school, she can hardly wait to tell you about it. At first you think that's boring—kicking a ball is no big deal for you. But then you stop and listen, because you realize she is seeking your support and wants to share her excitement with you. So you go outside with her and kick the ball back and forth. It's fun, and you can give her a few pointers on playing the game. By taking the time to listen, you are building her confidence and strengthening the bonds in the family.

Listening is just as important when someone is angry. Perhaps your father is angry with you because he thinks your room is a mess. Instead of getting mad yourself, wait until both of you are calm, and then look for a solution. Is there really a problem with your room? Then maybe you do need to talk about ways you can do better. On the other hand, he may have been tired or upset about something else and snapped at you. That can happen to anyone. By listening rather than returning his anger, you are helping to improve the situation.

THE FAMILY COUNCIL

Many families use a family council so that everyone can share in making decisions. They may talk around the dinner table during meals, or set a special time each week when they can sit down together. A family council can even be a single parent and an only child talking with each other.

The council is a good time to discuss family rules. For instance, your parent or guardian may expect you to be home at a certain time. If you will be late, how will you contact them? What will happen if you break their trust by not calling?

By having rules that set clear, reasonable limits, your family gives you the freedom to explore, but not to go too far. When you respect the rules, you prove that you are a reliable member of the family. Your parents may respond to your maturity by having greater trust in you.

A family council is a good way for all family members to share in decision making.

A family council is an opportunity for you to share problems of your own. You might be having difficulty with a subject in school, or you don't understand why your friends are acting a certain way. The adults in your family and your older brothers and sisters have a lot of experience with life. It's easy to share the good times with them. They may be even more helpful and supportive when times are not so good.

FAMILY JOBS

On a patrol campout, you're always ready to jump right in and help with the camp chores. It's fun to set up tents, cook meals, and leave a clean campsite. Doing your part goes a long way in making the outing a success.

The same is true at home. A lot of work must be done to keep a household running smoothly. The more you help out, the better. Offer to take on those tasks you can handle. Ask family members to show you the right way to do different chores. You can learn a lot that way.

Here are some suggestions:

☆ Keep your room neat.

☆ Do your own laundry.

☆ Care for younger children.

☆ Mow the lawn.

☆ Set the table.

☆ Help with cooking.

☆ Care for family pets.

☆ Wash dishes.

☆ Shop for groceries.

Doing your share of the work at home will do much more than please your family. If you learn to make a meal at home, cooking it in camp will be easy. Learn to wash your clothes and you'll be a step closer to being on your own. Of course, you don't have to wait to be asked to do family jobs. Look around for what needs to be done and then just do it.

TAKING CARE OF YOURSELF WHEN YOU ARE ALONE

Discuss with your family what you should do when you must be home alone. That may happen once in awhile when your parents or guardian are gone for an evening. If they work, you may be alone every day after school.

Make a list of emergency phone numbers and tape it near the telephone (see page 403). Then add the following:

Mother at work _____   Nearest relative _____

Father at work _____   Neighbor _____

Family friend _____

The list will give you plenty of trusted people to call if you need help.

Ask your parent or guardian what you should do if someone knocks on your door and wants to come in while you are alone. It's usually best to ask the visitor to wait outside. Then call one of the numbers on your list and ask for instructions.

Decide how you should answer if a stranger calls on the phone. A good response is this: "My parents can't come to the phone right now. Would you like to leave your name and a message?"

Your parent or guardian may establish other rules you are to follow when you are in the house by yourself. They may ask that you not invite friends over during those hours, or that you call before you go somewhere else.

CARING FOR YOUNGER CHILDREN

One of your most important family jobs could be looking after little brothers and sisters. Perhaps you will be asked to take care of other children in the neighborhood, too.

Younger children look up to you. They admire what you can do. You have a responsibility to set a good example for them. Let them know you appreciate them.

Before you take charge of young children, learn the following:

☆ Know where the parents can be reached.

☆ Know a neighbor who can lend a hand if you need it.

☆ Have emergency phone numbers handy in case of illness or accident.

☆ Ask what the children are allowed to eat.

☆ Ask when the children are to go to bed.

☆ Ask about any guidelines concerning the television, stereo, or radio.

While children are in your care, remember these rules:

☆ Keep children out of danger areas.

☆ Occupy the children's time with worthwhile activities such as reading.

☆ After the children are in bed, check every half hour to be sure they are all right.

☆ Lock outside doors. Don't open a door for anyone unless you know the person.

☆ Don't invite your friends over or allow them in; they may distract you from looking after the children.

☆ Stay awake until the parents return.

506

TELEVISION

Television offers us entertainment and many opportunities for learning. Coverage of sporting events lets us feel as though we are sitting in the stands. News programs keep us in touch with our nation and the world.

But television is a tool that must be used wisely. It can take up tremendous amounts of time. Researchers estimate that before graduating from high school, the average American watches 18,000 hours of programs. That's more than 2 years of a young life spent sitting in front of a television.

Many families look through program listings at the beginning of the week and pick a few good programs they want to watch. Otherwise, they leave the television off. They have much more time for playing sports, reading, learning music, helping neighbors, working on Scout projects, and enjoying each other.

In addition to filling so many hours, television programs and commercials often present an unrealistic view of life. This is true of many movies, too. Actors neatly solve all their problems by the end of each show. They frequently use violence to settle differences with others. Smoking, drinking, and illegal drug use are sometimes shown as being glamorous.

None of those are realistic values. Solving real problems takes a lot of hard work. Hitting or shooting real people causes pain and death, not peace. Tobacco, alcohol, and drug abuse make real people ill and dependent, not attractive and strong.

When you do watch television, talk with your family about what you are seeing. Do you agree with the

With your family, select television programs and then discuss what you watched.

way the actors are treating one another? Could the story really happen that way? By discussing programs, you can better separate the fantasies of television from the realities of life.

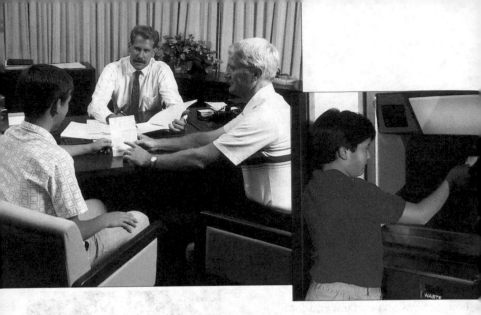

FAMILY FINANCES

A family is like a small business with money coming in and money going out. Expenses include housing, food, clothing, transportation, and education. In many families, money to cover those costs is earned by parents or guardians. Sometimes one parent works at home taking care of children during the day while the other goes to an office or factory, or into the fields.

You might be interested in learning where your family's money comes from and where it goes. See if your father, mother, or family head will let you visit them where they work. Learn what they do during the day. Perhaps they will talk with you about home finances. They might explain what it costs to run a household.

One of your most important jobs for the next few years is to stay in school and get a good education. No one expects you to have much money for paying family bills. But by knowing a little bit about what those expenses are and how they are paid, you can understand the importance of your parents' work. You will also have greater appreciation for the clothing, food, and other necessities your family provides for you.

If you have an allowance or a part-time job, you can cover some of your own expenses. School supplies, Scout dues, and your share of food money for campouts are costs you might be able to pay yourself. Get in the habit of putting some of your money into savings. Even if you have only a small amount to deposit each month, your savings will grow.

CHAPTER 21

HOME SAFETY

As a Scout, you can help make your home safe for everyone. First, make sure there is a list of emergency contact numbers near the telephone. Then safety-inspect your home. Tell your family about any health or safety hazards you see, and correct as many as you can.

Falls

Falls happen more often than any other home accidents.

☆ Remove clutter and toys from floors and stairs. Store tools and toys where they belong.

☆ Repair weak or broken stair railings.

☆ Put nonslip backing on throw rugs and mats.

☆ Use nonskid strips in bathtubs and showers for safe footing.

☆ See that electrical cords, wires, ropes, and hoses are placed where no one can trip over them.

☆ Use a sturdy stepladder when you want to reach an object on a high shelf.

Find ways to make your home safe, such as installing no-slip pads on stairs.

Fires

Fires rank right behind falls as causes of home accidents.

Sit down with your family and talk about how each of you will get out of the house in case of a fire. Locate at least two routes of escape from each part of the house, then decide where you will meet once you are outside. A neighbor's porch would be fine, or a nearby street corner. That way, you will all know when everyone is safely out of the house. Finally, remind everyone that their safety is much more important than trying to save possessions. Things can be replaced, but people can't. If your house is on fire, **GET OUT!**

Protect your home from fire by doing the following:

☆ Place matches out of the reach of children.

☆ Keep papers and trash away from stoves and heaters.

☆ Replace frayed electrical wires and broken plugs.

☆ Keep a spark-catching screen in front of a fireplace that has a fire burning in it.

☆ Check the location of fire extinguishers, and be sure they are fully charged.

☆ Test smoke detectors and replace dead batteries.

☆ Piles of oily rags may spontaneously catch fire. Wrap oily rags in aluminum foil to keep air away from them, and get rid of them.

Wounds

Accidents causing wounds happen most often in the kitchen, garage, and workshop.

☆ Store all knives and other sharp tools where children cannot reach them.

☆ Get rid of broken glass safely. Remove the bigger pieces with a broom and dustpan, then carefully wipe up tiny splinters with a wet, crumpled paper towel.

Poisons

Most poisonings in the home happen to children who are not being watched.

☆ Store poisonous substances in clearly marked containers.

☆ Place poison containers and all medicines, cleaning items, and pesticides where children cannot get at them.

☆ Learn the location of the nearest poison control center and keep its number near the telephone.

HOME EMERGENCIES

Medical Emergency

Stay calm when an accident happens. Use the first aid you have learned as a Scout (see pages 401–443). If the injury is serious, give first aid and call for help, using the emergency phone numbers you listed on page 403.

Fire Emergency

Follow your family escape plan to get out of the house and meet at your chosen location. Then call the fire department.

Utility Emergencies

Be prepared for problems with utilities by learning how to

☆ Turn off the main water supply.

☆ Shut off electrical power.

☆ Close the main gas line if your home has one.

If the emergency is a broken water pipe, an electrical wire shorting out, or the smell of gas, simply shut off the water, power, or gas for the whole house. Then call the utility company for help. If the problem is with your telephone, call from a neighbor's house or from the nearest public phone.

Know where your water main valve is and how to turn it off.

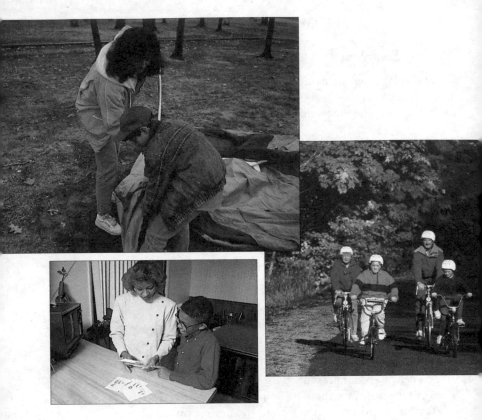

TIME TOGETHER

The demands of school, homework, friends, Scouting, and religious activities may fill most of your days and evenings. Older family members often have jobs and projects of their own. Even though you all live in the same house, you and others in your family may be rushing past one another with hardly a word.

Make a real effort to spend time together. On a weekend while helping with family chores, you can work alongside your parents and talk. Share with them what you are doing in school and in Scouting. Let them enjoy your excitement about life.

Go on walks as a family. Try bicycling together, or having picnics. Go together to visit exhibits, libraries, and museums. In fact, almost everything is better if you share it with the people you love.

Your Family and Scouting

When you join the Boy Scouts, your whole family becomes part of the Scouting family. Your relatives may attend special Scout gatherings, and they may even lend a hand in running the troop. Scout meetings, hikes, and campouts take you away from your house, but you bring home what you learn in your patrol and troop. You can share your new knowledge and enthusiasm with others in your family. Everyone wants you to have all the fun that Scouting has to offer. They want to see you reach the Scouting goals you set for yourself. By helping you, each of them receives some of the excitement and satisfaction of Scouting.

CHAPTER **22**

PERSONAL DEVELOPMENT

M ANY Scouts enjoy music. Perhaps you are able to play a trumpet, strum a guitar, or sing a song. You may like sports, too. Can you kick a soccer ball and run a good race? When you throw a baseball, is it right on target?

Every young person has many talents. You may be able to draw faces, airplanes, buildings, and cars. Math and science may seem easy to you. Maybe you have a knack for telling a funny story. At troop meetings, Scouts may respect you as a leader or as a good listener. Perhaps you are very gentle with animals and like to care for them.

You are a collection of wonderful abilities and ideas. Your skills and interests are your possibilities. They are hints of what you can become.

In addition to the gifts you have today, you also own the past. As a member of the human family, the history of all people is your history as well. The centuries of discovery, invention, and learning all belong to you. You can draw on that knowledge and wisdom any time you want it.

And the future is yours, too. Your curiosity and your ideas will make a difference. The world needs what you have to offer. It needs you to make the most of your skills. To do that, you must be open to the joy of learning.

WHY LEARN?

Four Scouts on a hike were talking about strength. They each tried to name the most powerful force on earth. One said a hurricane. The second thought of a blizzard at the North Pole. The third suggested an atomic bomb.

"It's not any of those," the last Scout said. "I think the force with the most power is knowing how to learn." He went on to explain that with knowledge he could find shelter in a hurricane, and that made him stronger than the wind. He would know how to stay warm, and that would let him defeat any blizzard. With knowledge he could make an atomic bomb, but he could also take one apart and get rid of it.

Knowing how to learn gives you the power to deal with change. Later in your life you may hold jobs that today don't even exist. You will be faced with exciting opportunities and challenges. Knowledge is your key to the future. If you know how to learn and are willing to try out new ideas, you will be ready for almost anything.

HOW TO GATHER INFORMATION

Detectives love mysteries. Anything you don't understand is a mystery just waiting to be solved. For instance, you may not know how to bake bread on a campout. It's a mystery to you. You could decide to go without bread, or wait until someone else makes the dough and bakes it. If you want to get to the bottom of a mystery, you need some clues. Every detective knows that. Some ways to find them are

☆ Looking and listening

☆ Asking

☆ Reading and writing

☆ Doing and teaching

Looking and Listening

Use your eyes and ears to scoop up clues wherever you go. Watch a neighbor plant a garden. Study the way a window washer ties a safety rope around his waist. Figure out how your school bus driver shifts gears.

Learning by observing is especially important when you are hiking and camping. You can only make sense out of a map if you are aware of landmarks around you. When you notice changes in the clouds, you can pitch your tent before a storm breaks. Sit quietly in the woods and you will see and hear wildlife that otherwise stays hidden.

Practice using your other senses, too. The smell of rain, the taste of a huckleberry, and the feel of the bark on a tree can deepen your enjoyment of adventures and teach you much about the outdoors.

Asking

"Can you show me how this works?" "Would you tell me why this happens?" "Is there a better way to get this done?"

When you are curious about something, ask. People are almost always willing to share what they know. Teachers, pilots, Scoutmasters, farmers—whenever you have a question for anybody, go ahead and ask. Be polite. If someone is busy, you may need to arrange a time when he or she can talk with you. But there are no silly questions. No questions are too simple. Questions are stepping stones to knowledge. Unless you ask, you may never know.

Reading

Strap yourself into the pilot's seat of a bright red rocket and feel its engines blast you through space. Or hoist the anchor of a creaky wooden ship and cross the Atlantic with Columbus. Smell the salt of the sea and hear the canvas sails flapping in the breeze. Later you can shrink yourself to the size of a red blood cell and swim through the arteries and veins of the human body. Or you might become a giant and stride across the land with long, thundering steps.

Through the magic of reading, you can do almost anything. A book is a flying carpet, a time machine, a looking glass. Open a book and go off with explorers. Spend time with adventurers, heroes, and villains. Travel to the far corners of the world, to the inside of an atom, and to the most distant stars. Do you know what people ate a thousand years ago? What makes a computer work? How you can become a better Scout? Books will give you the answers.

Books are loaded with ideas. The *Boy Scout Handbook* is a good example. The pages you are reading right now contain the combined knowledge of more than 80 years of Scouting experience. In your hands you are holding hundreds of nights of camping, thousands of miles on the trail, and the skills of millions of Scouts before you.

School and public libraries are full of books as exciting as the *Boy Scout Handbook*. Librarians will show you how to find books about subjects you like—just ask. They can also explain how you may use library films, recordings, and other forms of stored information. Find out about getting a borrower's card so you can take books home with you.

Read the books you like to someone else. Read to your parents or guardian, your brothers and sisters, and your friends. Perhaps you know of elderly neighbors who would love to hear a story. Reading out loud is a generous act of sharing. If there are younger children in your family, encourage them to read to you. That's a fine way to help them improve their own reading skills.

Reading is a window through which you can see into the past and the future. It is a doorway to discovery and adventure. Read, read, and read some more. It will expand your mind, entertain you, and fill your mind with new ideas.

Writing

When explorers go into new territory, they write their observations in a journal. That's how they remember the important things they have seen. Scientists make notes of their discoveries. Sailors keep records by writing in a ship's log. Some Scout patrols have a trip log in which they write accounts of all their hikes and campouts.

Try keeping a journal of your own. Get a notebook and write a little every day about what you have done and seen. Write about school or your travels around the neighborhood. Make drawings. Include photos, stories you have cut from newspapers, baseball cards, and anything else that's important. No one but you ever has to read your journal, though you may want to share it with family and friends. Some people write in journals every day for many years. But even if you write just once in a while, putting your words on paper will give you a fresh view of your world.

Learning by Doing

There's a good chance you already know how to ride a bicycle. Do you remember how you learned? Perhaps you saw somebody else riding and thought you would like to do that, too. So you climbed on a bike, started pedaling, and fell over. You got back on and probably fell over again.

You kept at it, though, and slowly figured out how to ride. Today, riding may be so easy that you've forgotten it was ever difficult.

Much of learning is like that. You try something and grasp a small piece of it. You try again and understand a little more. The key is to learn from your successes *and* your mistakes. When you master a skill that way, you can use it for the rest of your life. You own it. It's yours.

Learning by Teaching

Scouts have many opportunities to share their knowledge with others. For instance, you might show your patrol how to use a compass. Once they have the idea, give them the compass and let them try it. They may make mistakes, but that's all right. Encourage them to keep trying. Be ready to give guidance when they are really stuck. They will remember the skill much better if they learn on their own rather than having you do all the work for them.

Teaching is good for the teacher, too. As you share a skill, you'll find yourself thinking very carefully about how you do it. Helping someone else learn will polish your own understanding of what you know.

HAVE INITIATIVE

Reading about rocket ships and sailboats is exciting. Going out and having adventures of your own is even better.

Develop the habit of seizing opportunities. Plan patrol hikes and head for the hills whenever you can. Paddle a canoe, sharpen a knife, and sleep under the stars. Catch a fish, repair an eroded meadow, cook a meal over a camping stove, and hike in the rain.

See new places, too. Explore neighborhood parks, city museums, and zoos. Visit factories and public utilities. Your travels as a Scout may take you to a high-adventure base far from home, or even across the ocean to a world jamboree.

Meet people. Greet neighbors down the street and Scouts from other troops. Visit with new students at school and hikers you meet on the trail. Who are they? What do they do? Everyone has a story. Listen, learn, and discover.

Look for chances to increase your knowledge. Teachers and books have much to give you. Develop good study habits and then use them.

The hardest part of seizing opportunities may be simply getting started. But once you've laced up your hiking boots and are standing at the beginning of a trail, nothing can hold you back. Once you've said hello to someone and been greeted with a smile, the tough part of making a new friend is over. And once you've opened a book and started reading, the words will seem to flow.

A patrol hike is a good way to meet people and make new friends while on the trail.

To complete big projects, you may need to reach for small goals along the way. Scouts who hike the 2,000 miles of the Appalachian Trail from Maine to Georgia don't do it all in one day. Each morning during school vacations for a total of 5 months they set out to walk about 12 miles. Each night they camp near the trail.

Twelve miles may not seem like much when there are 2,000 miles to cover. But 12 miles every day carries Scouts over mountains, through valleys, and past sparkling lakes. Late one afternoon, they come to a windy mountaintop that is the end of the trail. By setting reasonable goals for each day of hiking and then sticking to their plan, they can walk down the entire Appalachian mountain range.

You can meet many challenges that way. Map out a route to reach your goal. Determine what small steps will take you there. Then go for it.

But nothing will happen unless you make it happen. You've got to get up out of the chair, turn off the TV, and get going. Open a book and see what it says. Open your mind and see what you can put into it. Open your heart and let other people come inside.

MAKING THE MOST OF LIFE

A Scout patrol camping in the mountains was hit by a cold, wet storm. Even though they had snug tents and warm sleeping bags, some of the Scouts began to complain. They were sure the storm was ruining their trek, and they wished they had never come.

But another Scout thought it was terrific fun to be face to face with a mountain storm. He loved to hear thunder crashing down the long valleys. He saw the beauty of a forest full of mist. He knew that bad weather would put his camping skills to the test, and he welcomed the chance to improve.

"I always hope for the best, prepare for the worst, and accept whatever comes my way," he told the others. "And then I have fun no matter what." With a smile on his face, he had a fine campout.

Rain falls on everyone. There is not much you can do about that. But you can decide to see storms as opportunities rather than obstacles. You can choose to make the most of a situation rather than giving up and wishing you were somewhere else.

Overcoming tough times builds your ability to meet future challenges. Not long after that stormy campout, the same Scout took over his older sister's newspaper delivery route for a few weeks. The route was long, and there were lots of papers. He finished the route so late the first evening that he came home discouraged. He wasn't sure he could handle the work until his sister returned.

But then he thought back to the trip in the mountains. He had met a challenge then and came out just fine. If he could do that, surely he could succeed with this route. The next night he made a game out of tossing the papers on the porches. He began having a good time, and the work went quickly. He was pleased that he was meeting another challenge head-on.

Challenges are great teachers when you let them be. If you want to see life as full of opportunity and excitement, it will be. The choice is up to you.

SELF-RELIANCE

As a Scout, you learn how to cook camp meals for yourself. You can pitch a tent and get your bed ready for the night. You know ways to care for your clothing and gear.

You can do those things at home, too. Helping with the cooking is really not much different in your own kitchen than it is in camp. The same goes for taking care of your clothes, making your bed, and keeping your part of the house neat.

The time you spend outdoors studying animals, finding your way, and working with other Scouts can increase your patience and concentration at home and in school. When you lead a patrol on a hike, you are also learning to be a leader in your family and your community.

Many of Scouting's skills improve your ability to take care of yourself rather than depending on someone else to do things for you. Scouting teaches independence. By knowing what to do, you develop trust in your own abilities. You have the quiet confidence that you will do your best no matter what happens. That's what self-reliance is all about.

GOOD JUDGMENT

Each of us knows someone who often does the right thing at the right time. Your patrol leader might be that kind of person. He comes up with fresh ideas at meetings. He gives you a hand with Scout skills when you need a little help, and leaves you alone when you want to do them yourself. He always seems to be looking out for the safety and well-being of others, both in the patrol and beyond the troop. Some people would say he is using common sense. Others might call it wisdom. What they are really talking about is good judgment.

Good judgment is the ability to make wise decisions even under difficult conditions. You don't need great knowledge in order to use good judgment. You just have to do your best with what you already know.

"Good judgment," says an old Scoutmaster, "comes from having lived through lots of bad judgment." Your patrol leader didn't become wise without making a lot of little errors. But he doesn't let them discourage him. Instead, he learns all he can from each failure and then moves on. He knows that he can often learn more from his mistakes than from his greatest successes.

If you look at the end of a log, you will see a series of rings expanding out from the center. Every ring represents a period of growth. Together, they made the tree strong and helped it withstand the worst storms.

Your experiences, both good and bad, are like those rings. Each adds a little bit to your wisdom and to the strength of your judgment. Good judgment can't be taught, but through the gathering of many experiences, it can be learned.

Choosing Friends

Part of good judgment is choosing friends. You spend a lot of time with the people you enjoy. You learn from them, have fun with them, and want them to like you.

Hang on to friends who have attitudes and values you admire. Seek out those with healthy interests. Share adventures with people who want to make the most of themselves.

However, don't limit your opportunity to meet someone new just because he or she is not exactly like your other friends. Differences of race, culture, and language can be the basis of many close bonds. Some people are shy, so it may be up to you to open the door to friendship. Visit with them at school. Invite them to join in with Scouting events, ball games, and neighborhood activities. You will be surprised how eagerly others respond to your offers of friendship.

Peer Pressure

The language you and your friends use is a clue to how you think about the world. Swear words, dirty jokes, and crude talk often are used as weapons to hurt other people. Clean language is a mark of intelligence, kindness, and respect for other people.

Once in a while, you may discover that some of the people you know are using tobacco, alcohol, or illegal drugs. They may pressure you to use them, too. However, you know that real friends would not want you to do things that could harm your health or cloud your mind. If smoking, drinking, or drugs are a part of your circle of friends, you may need to find new friends who are more interested in making the most of their lives. Don't worry, they are out there. Look around and you will find them.

SEXUAL RESPONSIBILITY

As you grow into manhood, your friendships will change. People around you are also changing. Girls you know are becoming young women. They are growing both physically and emotionally. Your relationships with them will become closer and more meaningful to you and to them.

You are maturing sexually, too. As a young man, you are capable of becoming a father. That is a profound responsibility with powerful consequences in your life and the lives of others. It is a responsibility that requires your very best judgment.

Sex is not the most important or most grown-up part of a relationship. Having sex is never a test of maturity. True manliness comes from accepting the responsibility for your actions toward others and yourself in the following ways:

☆ *Your responsibility to women.* Whenever you like someone, you want the best for that person. A healthy relationship is supportive and equal. You owe it to the women in your life to keep their best interests in mind. You can have a terrific time together enjoying life and growing emotionally. However, the difficulties created by a pregnancy can be enormous. Don't burden yourself and someone you care for with a child neither of you is ready to bear.

☆ *Your responsibility to children.* When you are fully grown and have become secure in yourself and in your relationship with another person, the two of you may decide to marry and have a child. That is a wonderful choice full of challenges and rewards. By waiting until you are thoroughly prepared to be parents, you can give your own child a close, loving family in which to grow.

☆ *Your responsibility to your beliefs.* For the followers of most religions, sex should take place only between married couples. To do otherwise may cause feelings of guilt and loss. Abstinence until marriage is a very wise course of action.

☆ *Your responsibility to yourself.* An understanding of wholesome sexual behavior can bring you lifelong happiness. Irresponsibility or ignorance, however, can cause a lifetime of regret. AIDS and venereal diseases spread by sexual contact may undermine your health and that of others. Having a baby before you are ready may drastically limit your future chances for education, occupations, and travel.

You owe it to yourself to enter adulthood without burdens. You owe it to yourself to enrich your life by learning what is right. Your religious leaders can give you moral guidance. Your parents or guardian or a sex education teacher should give you the facts about sex that you must know.

Learn by asking, remember? If you have questions about growing up, about relationships, sex, or making good decisions, ask. Talk with your parents, religious leaders, teachers, or Scoutmaster. They have experienced much of life, and they are interested in what is best for you. Let them know your concerns.

CHILD ABUSE

Most relationships with others can be warm and open. That is because they are built on trust. A pat on the back, a hug of encouragement, or a firm handshake are ways we can show someone we care about them.

However, it is a sad fact that some adults use their size and power over children to abuse them. You need to know about child abuse so that you will understand what to do if you are ever threatened. You may also be able to help stop the abuse of a friend.

The following are the four kinds of child abuse you may encounter:

Neglect. Parents or guardians abuse by neglect if they willingly choose not to provide their children with the food, clothing, shelter, and care needed for a healthy life. Neglect is often caused by adults who are dependent on alcohol or drugs.

Emotional abuse. Children are emotionally abused when they are repeatedly told that they are no good or that they will never amount to anything. Lasting harm is done if children begin to believe those falsehoods.

Physical abuse. Physical abuse occurs when excessive force is used to punish a child. It may result in bruises, burns, cuts, broken bones, and sometimes death.

Sexual abuse. Any sexual activity between an adult and a child is sexual abuse. So is forced sexual activity between an older or larger youth and a smaller or weaker child. Many people think sexual abuse happens only to girls, but they are wrong. Boys may also be victims of molesters.

What You Can Do

If you think you have been a victim of child abuse, you may want to talk with an adult you feel you can trust. Also, every state has a child abuse hotline you can call for help.

Be aware of the ways you treat people younger or smaller than yourself. Every child deserves respect. Serve as a good role model whenever you are in position of responsibility—for example, as a babysitter, a patrol leader, or someday as a parent. Sometimes it may seem easy to respond to the poor behavior of others by name-calling or physical force, but you should always use other methods to resolve conflicts. Talk with your Scoutmaster and parents about better ways to lead.

Protecting Yourself from Sexual Abuse

Most sexual abuse can be prevented if young people know and follow these three R's:

☆ Recognize   ☆ Resist   ☆ Report

Recognize. Recognizing a situation that may become sexual abuse can help you get away before you are in serious danger. An adult attempting sexual abuse may begin touching you in ways that are confusing. He or she may try to touch your groin area and pretend it was an accident. You may be asked to pose for photographs in your underwear or swimming suit, and then in no clothing at all.

Some adults or older youths may try to use your normal curiosity about sex as an opportunity to attempt sexual abuse. Sex is a normal bodily function that you need to understand. If anyone makes it seem dirty or secretive, you should be very cautious.

People who sexually abuse young people are called child molesters. A child molester may be anyone. Most often, the molester is known by his or her victim. The molester may be a member of the family, a schoolteacher, religious leader, or youth group leader. By knowing how a child molester operates, you can recognize what is happening regardless of who that person is.

Resist. Molesters look for victims who do not know enough to resist the abuse. You have the right to control your body. Anytime a person does something to your body that makes you feel bad or you know is wrong, you have the right to stop them even if you must be rude. You should be ready to run, scream, or make a scene in public in order to protect yourself. When faced with resistance, most molesters will stop.

Report. Anytime you feel that a person has tried to molest you or someone you know, you must report it. Talk to a trusted adult or call a child abuse hotline. Child abuse is an adult-size problem. By talking about it with adults you respect, you can let them solve it.

BE PREPARED FOR LIFE

You may have grandparents who seem very young. With bright eyes and a quick step, they enjoy outdoor activities, hard work, and a good life. You may also know younger people, even people your own age, who seem tired, bored, and just plain old. All they want to do is sit in front of the television and watch other people having fun.

Decide right now to put a Keep Off! sign on the rocking chair. Life is bursting with opportunities. The wise physical fitness habits you are developing now will keep your body in good shape through the decades to come. Just as important are habits to keep your mind alert, fresh, and healthy. A lifetime of reading, learning, and trying out new ideas does for your mind what exercise and sports do for your body. It's up to you to make the most of every moment of every day. You can jump at life, celebrate it, and live it well. You have one chance at this lifetime — one precious, golden opportunity. Savor every moment. Do nothing that is not of value. Live every second to the fullest.

Patrols and troops are the building blocks of the Scouting movement. When you join, you become part of a nationwide network of young people who are making the Scout program a big part of their lives.

Campouts, hikes, service projects, meetings, a week at summer camp— the great adventures of Scouting are high on the list of what your patrol and troop can do. But nothing will happen without you. Turn the page to discover how your energy, cheerfulness, and enthusiasm will bring your patrol and troop to life.

YOUR SCOUT PATROL AND TROOP

A S a Scout, there are times when you are on your own. You set personal goals and strive to reach them. You learn skills at your own speed and decide how hard you want to work to master all that a Scout can know.

As a member of a patrol, you are no longer alone. You can pour your energy into patrol efforts and turn exciting plans into action. With a patrol, you can head for the hills for hiking and camping. You will be able to achieve much more than you would by yourself.

Your troop is even larger. With the strength of many patrols, a troop is a community of Scouts. It has the size and leadership to undertake large projects and adventures. The troop acts as a framework within which you can develop as a Scout and a leader.

YOUR SCOUT PATROL

A patrol is a team of good friends working together to make things happen. Because all of you are different, you each have much to share with the others. At meetings, you can teach each other the skills you know. In camp, you can help one another set up tents, cook meals, and do cleanup. As friends, you look out for one another. Let others know when an unsafe situation develops. Cheer them up when they are down. Congratulate them when they do well. Friendship, fun, adventure — that's what a Scout patrol is all about.

The New Scout Patrol

The New Scout Patrol is a special group for boys who are just becoming Scouts. They are helped by a troop guide — an older Scout chosen on the basis of his experience, maturity, and willingness to work with younger Scouts. An assistant Scoutmaster is also assigned to the patrol to give it the support and leadership it deserves.

Supported by the troop guide and assistant Scoutmaster, a new Scout patrol operates much like the other patrols in the troop. The members elect their own patrol leader, plan activities, and take part in troop meetings and outings.

The Scouts of a new Scout patrol also spend plenty of time learning the skills that will help them enjoy outdoor adventures and take advantage of plenty of Scouting opportunities. Before long, a member in a new Scout patrol will discover that he is passing many of the requirements for the ranks of Tenderfoot, Second Class, and First Class.

When a Scout has earned the First Class badge or has entered the seventh grade, he can move into one of the troop's patrols for experienced and older

Scouts, or get involved with the Venture program. There he can put his new knowledge to use in many different ways.

Experienced Scout Patrols

Scouts who have entered at least the seventh grade or who hold the rank of First Class or higher may become members of patrols for experienced Scouts. Those older Scouts who have not yet reached First Class may continue to complete the requirements for that rank. Scouts holding the First Class award may work on the merit badges and service projects that lead to the ranks of Star, Life, and Eagle.

Many troops also include Venture activities in their programs for older Scouts. As a member of a Venture crew, you'll find a whole world of fresh opportunities opening before you. The excitement, challenge, and adventure of the Venture program gives you every reason to stay active in your troop and use your Scouting know-how.

Patrol flag and emblem. Many patrols are named after animals. Perhaps you are a member of the Wolf Patrol, or you might be one of the Hawks, Bears, or Owls. Some patrols name themselves for trees (the Pine Tree Patrol) or a person (the Daniel Boone Patrol).

Each patrol has a flag with an emblem representing its name. You may have a chance to help make a flag for your patrol and carry it at troop meetings and on campouts. You can also wear your patrol's emblem on your right sleeve.

Some Scouts paint or stencil a patrol emblem on their camping gear. You can practice drawing the emblem with a few quick lines so you can add it to your signature when you sign your name as a Scout. It's the sign of your own patrol, the one you are helping grow into the best it can be.

Patrol call. Every patrol has a call, too. If your patrol is named for an animal, use its sound—the howl of a wolf, for example, or the hoot of an owl. Patrols not named for animals may also use an animal's call.

Sound your call each time your patrol wins a contest at a troop meeting. Patrol cooks can use the call on campouts to let everyone know dinner is ready. Your patrol leader makes the call when he wants the patrol to gather. Members of the patrol will understand, but others may think they are just hearing the natural sounds of the woods.

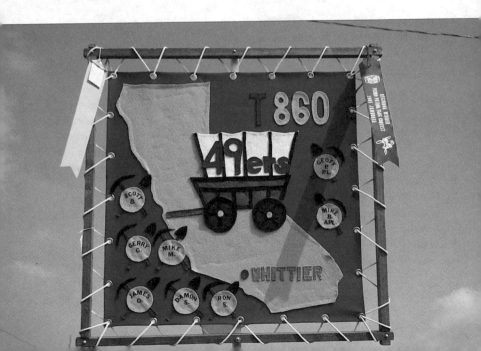

Your patrol leader. Each patrol elects a Scout from among its members to be patrol leader. It is an important position with much responsibility. You will want to choose someone you respect and whose leadership you will follow. A patrol leader must have the energy and will to help you bring out the best in your patrol.

Your patrol leader is in charge of the patrol at troop meetings and during outdoor adventures. He suggests Good Turns and service projects, and then encourages the patrol to pitch in. When spirits are low, he is the one who says, "Come on, let's go!" and starts off. Working with the Scoutmaster, your patrol leader thinks of ways everyone in the patrol can make progress in Scouting, complete special projects, and be somebody.

There are plenty of jobs to go around in a patrol. To help him fulfill his duties, a patrol leader picks another Scout to be assistant patrol leader. The assistant leads the patrol whenever the patrol leader is absent.

Your patrol leader will give everyone in the patrol jobs that will make things happen. He may ask a Scout who writes well to keep a journal of patrol adventures. He might show another Scout how to repair and store patrol camping gear. He could ask you to help him come up with menus for a campout, songs and stunts for a campfire, or information on conservation projects for the whole patrol.

A good patrol leader lets others share the duties of leadership. He may leave it up to you to find the route on a hike, to be head cook in camp, or to teach other Scouts how to use a backpacking stove. By sharing leadership with all of you, your patrol leader allows you to learn what it means to be in charge. Someday when you have enough experience and have displayed your maturity and wisdom, the other Scouts may choose you to be the leader of a patrol.

All of you in a patrol will want to support your patrol leader through thick and thin. At times you may not want to go along with patrol plans. Rainy weather may dampen a hike, or work on a service project may be harder than you had expected. But remember that Scouting is based on cheerful cooperation. Sometimes you may need to put aside your own comforts if it will benefit the patrol. A "sunshine Scout" who only shows up when the sun is shining isn't of much value to a patrol. It's the "all-weather Scout" who makes a patrol hum and who gets the most fun out of Scouting. When you and the rest of your patrol go all out to overcome hurdles, the rewards and the satisfaction are great.

Patrol meetings. Patrols are such a key part of Scouting that a portion of troop meetings is set aside for each patrol to meet by itself. A patrol may also hold meetings of its own in the home of one of its Scouts or at a special patrol meeting place.

During patrol meetings, Scouts help one another understand Scouting skills. You can plan campouts, hikes, canoe trips, bicycle adventures, and dozens of other patrol activities. As the plans develop, each of you will take responsibility for getting everything ready.

Patrol activities. A patrol is fueled by real adventures. Some are indoor activities, such as making camp equipment, fixing up a patrol meeting place, and practicing first aid and knot tying.

Your patrol will also have plenty of outdoor fun. With your Scoutmaster's approval, you can head out on day hikes and overnight campouts. Your patrol leader may have the training and experience to lead those outings on his own, or your patrol may be accompanied by several troop leaders or parents of patrol members.

Hikes and camping trips are the high points of the patrol's activities. Those are the times you can put your Scouting knowledge to good use. Away from home and school, you have time to focus on your friendships with other Scouts and on your enjoyment of the outdoors. Patrol spirit reaches its peak as you make camp together, cook your meals, and enjoy evenings under the stars. On patrol treks, all of you are close to the true heart of Scouting.

YOUR SCOUT TROOP

No patrol stands alone. Each is part of a troop made up of a number of patrols. You can think of the patrols as the building blocks of the troop. The stronger and more active the patrols, the better the troop.

Your troop leaders. The *Scoutmaster* is the adult leader of your troop. He is dedicated to bringing learning, adventure, and good times to you and other Scouts. He is present at every troop meeting and goes on most hikes and camping trips. Patrol leaders look to him for guidance. You will come to know him as a wise friend to whom you can always turn for advice.

A Scoutmaster is not paid for the time he gives to Scouting. He sees the value of the Scout program, and he wants to have a hand in making it available to you and other boys in your neighborhood. You can let your Scoutmaster know you appreciate his efforts by doing everything possible to make your patrol and your troop a real success.

Assistant Scoutmasters are adults who help your Scoutmaster. Sometimes they take charge of the troop. Assistant Scoutmasters are also assigned to new Scout patrols, and one is in charge of the Venture crew for older Scouts. Like every Scoutmaster, assistant Scoutmasters volunteer their time to see that a troop's program is strong, interesting, and of value.

Your *senior patrol leader* is an experienced older Scout who is elected by all the Scouts in the troop to help all the patrols succeed. He may conduct the troop meetings. *Junior assistant Scoutmasters* and other older Scouts may help the senior patrol leader prepare and carry out troop activities. Each of these important offices is held by a young man who has had plenty of Scout training.

Your Scoutmaster works with a troop committee to promote the troop's welfare.

Backing up all of these leaders is the *troop committee*. The committee is a group of people who are responsible for the troop's welfare and who stand ready to help it. Behind the troop committee, in turn, is a troop's *chartered organization* — the church or synagogue, school, or service club that has accepted the Scouting program as one of its ways of helping youth.

The patrol leaders' council. The activities of your troop are planned by a *patrol leaders' council* made up of your patrol leaders, senior patrol leader, and Scoutmaster. Other troop leaders may attend if their help is needed.

The patrol leaders' council meets each month to discuss upcoming meetings, hikes, and campouts for the whole troop. Your patrol leader shares with the council ideas that come from you and other Scouts in your patrol. Together, the members of the patrol leaders' council consider the suggestions and needs of all the Scouts, then come up with a troop plan for the next 4 weeks and the rest of the year.

Troop meetings. When you go to a weekly troop meeting, you can expect 90 minutes packed with activities. Often, there will be games that improve your Scouting know-how. Demonstrations and contests put on by patrols will help you learn new skills. During part of a meeting, patrols and Venture crews may meet on their own. There will be plenty of fun and good fellowship, too, in the form of songs, stunts, and ceremonies.

Not every troop meeting is held at the same place or at the usual time. Now and then a troop may hold its weekly meeting at a fire station or police headquarters so that you can learn firsthand how your town is protected. Another time you may gather at a local pool and try to pass some of the swimming requirements for a rank or merit badge. Or the troop might go to city hall to see your government in action.

Troop hikes and camps. A strong Scout troop has a vigorous outdoor program. Once a month throughout the year, your troop will set off on a hike or an overnight campout. On most troop outings you will hike and camp with your patrol. Troop activities provide an opportunity for you to see how well you are mastering outdoor skills and how effectively your patrol works together.

Your patrol is only as good as its members are willing to make it. Likewise, the success of your troop depends upon the energy of each Scout wearing the troop's number on his sleeve. You can keep your troop exciting and alive by coming to meetings on time. Join in every activity with enthusiasm and good cheer. Show up for troop hikes no matter what the weather. Make it your goal to become one of your troop's best all-around Scouts.

Remember that everything that happens in the patrol and in the troop happens because you and others like you are proud to be Scouts. You *are* your patrol and your troop. They are a reflection of you as a Scout. The more you give of yourself to Scouting, the more Scouting will give to you.

YOUR DISTRICT AND COUNCIL

The area in which your troop is located is called a district. In a large city, a district could be one or more neighborhoods. In rural areas, it could take in several counties.

A number of districts make up a council. At the council office, a full-time staff of trained people helps every troop have a successful program. They provide training for Scoutmasters and their assistants, troop committee members, and others associated with Scouting. Training for older Scouts is available at troop junior leader training, junior leader training conferences, and national junior leader instructor camps.

District and council activities. Many districts and councils hold camporees—a chance for all the troops in an area to camp together. Through contests and games, Scouts get to know each other. Each troop can show off its camping ability, and Scouts can learn Scouting skills from the patrols of other troops.

Some councils also put on big shows called Scoutoramas, expos, circuses, or see'n'dos. Troops gather to demonstrate Scouting skills for the public to see.

The biggest and best council activity each year is summer camp held on the council's own property. You probably will be invited to go to summer camp with your troop. Surrounded by open country, you can spend a week or more learning and using Scout skills. A trained camp staff will provide all the instruction and leadership you need. Many camps offer swimming, boating, canoeing, and plenty of other water activities. Most also give you chances for hiking, camp cooking, nature study, and more.

CHAPTER 23

BADGES AND INSIGNIA

The badges on your uniform show how far you have advanced in your Scout life.

Identification. The first badges you wear will indicate the patrol, troop, and council to which you belong.

Badges of rank. Tenderfoot, Second Class, First Class, Star, Life, Eagle — the ranks of Scouting offer every Scout chances to learn, to do, and to succeed.

The first three ranks will give you a solid background in camping, hiking, and other important Scouting skills. The merit badges leading to the higher ranks help you explore your interests in many different areas. Wear your badge of rank on your left pocket and your merit badges on a merit badge sash.

Badges of office. Someday your fellow Scouts may recognize your Scouting skills, leadership ability, and maturity by selecting you to be their patrol leader. That's a high honor. Wear the patrol leader's badge on your sleeve with pride.

Activities. Each time you take part in Scout summer camp, big service projects, and unusual outdoor adventures, you may receive a colorful patch to wear on your right pocket. That temporary insignia will show others what you have done. It will remind you of the good times you have had.

BE PREPARED · DO A GOOD TURN DAILY

GOD AND COUNTRY

On MY HONOR

I WILL DO MY BEST

TO DO MY DUTY

TO GOD AND MY COUNTRY

TO OBEY THE SCOUT LAW

TO HELP OTHER PEOPLE

TO KEEP MYSELF PHYSICALLY ST

AT ALL TIMES MENTALLY AWAKE AND

MORALLY STRAIGHT

TROOP 2

BE PREPARED

TO THE GLO·Y OF GOD AND ✠
IN LIVING TRIBUTE TO TROOP 2 AND
SCOUTMASTER SEYMOUR F. WEEKS
ON THE OCCASION OF THE
FIFTIETH ANNIVERSARY OF THE TROOP
1916   1966

CHAPTER 24

THE SPIRIT OF SCOUTING

I T is easy to join a Scout troop, but it is not so easy to live up to the ideals of Scouting. For that, you need courage and determination.

In some ways, Scouting is like a game with rules you must follow to be a member of the team. The rules of Scouting are found in the Scout Oath, Scout Law, Scout motto, and Scout slogan. It is by following these rules that you can become a true Scout.

Scout Oath

On my honor I will do my best
To do my duty to God and my country
and to obey the Scout Law;
To help other people at all times;
To keep myself physically strong,
mentally awake, and morally straight.

THE MEANING OF THE SCOUT OATH

Before you pledge yourself to any oath or promise, you must know what it means. The paragraphs that follow will help you understand the meaning of the Scout Oath.

On my honor . . .

By giving your word, you are promising to make every effort to live by the high ideals of the Scout Oath. Your success is a measure of your honor. As a Scout, you must hold your honor sacred.

. . . I will do my best . . .

You have many talents, skills, and interests. Do your best with them, and use them for good purposes. Don't be satisfied with less than your best effort even when less is required of you. Measure your achievements against your own high standards, not against the performance of others. As a Scout and throughout your life, you will have opportunities to learn and to help many people. You will also be faced with challenges that may severely test you. Use your abilities to do your very best. That is what Scouting requires.

. . . To do my duty to God . . .

Your family and religious leaders teach you to know and love God and the ways in which God can be served. As a Scout, you do your duty to God by following the wisdom of those teachings in your daily life, and by respecting the rights of others to have their own religious beliefs.

. . . and my country . . .

As you study our country's history, you learn about the men and women who toiled to make America great. Most contributed in quiet ways. Others sacrificed their lives for our country. All of them did their part to build the nation we have today. Help keep the United States strong by obeying its laws. Learn about our system of government and your role as a citizen and future voter. Do all you can to help your family and neighbors live happy, productive lives. The land itself is an important part of our national heritage. Work for the conservation of our natural resources. Teach others respect for the land. Your efforts really will make a difference.

. . . and to obey the Scout Law; . . .

The twelve points of the Scout Law are the rules of Scouting. They are also rules you can apply to your whole life. The Scout Law sets forth ideals to live up to. By using the Scout Law as a guide, you will know you are always doing your best. Others will respect you for the way you live. Most importantly, you will respect yourself.

. . . To help other people at all times; . . .

There are many people who need you. Your young shoulders can help them carry their burdens. A cheerful smile and a helpful hand will make life easier for many who need assistance. By helping whenever aid is needed and by doing a Good Turn daily, you prove yourself a Scout. You are doing your part to make this a better world.

. . . To keep myself physically strong, . . .

Take care of your body. Protect it and develop it so that it will serve you well for an entire lifetime. That means eating nutritious foods and being active to build strength and endurance. It also means avoiding drugs, alcohol, tobacco, and any other practices that can destroy your health.

. . . mentally awake, . . .

Develop your mind. Strive to increase your knowledge and make the greatest use of your abilities. Be curious about the world around you. Learn all you can both in class and beyond school. With an open attitude and the willingness to ask questions, you will get the most out of your life.

. . . and morally straight.

To be a person of strong character, guide your life with honesty, purity, and justice. Respect and defend the rights of all people. Your relationships with others should be honest and open. Be clean in your speech and actions, and faithful in your religious beliefs. The values you follow as a Scout will help you become virtuous and self-reliant.

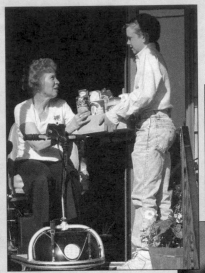

SCOUT LAW

The Scout Law is the foundation upon which the entire Scouting movement is built. The points of the Scout Law are a guide by which every Scout tries to live.

The Scout Law is a statement of facts:

"A Scout is trustworthy . . . loyal . . . helpful . . . friendly . . . courteous . . . kind . . . obedient . . . cheerful . . . thrifty . . . brave . . . clean . . . reverent."

By doing all you can to live up to the Scout Law, you are a Scout. If you should *willfully* break the Scout Law, you violate the spirit of Scouting.

The ideals of the Scout Law are very high. Strive to live by them, and you will excel on your own and as a part of your Scout troop, community, and nation.

The Meaning of the Points of the Scout Law

Each point of the Scout Law is expressed in a single word rich with meaning. You should understand that meaning so well that you can explain it in your own words. What follows will help you reach that understanding.

A Scout is TRUSTWORTHY. *A Scout tells the truth. He keeps his promises. Honesty is a part of his code of conduct. People can always depend on him.*

Your parents, teachers, and friends know that as a Scout you tell the truth and keep your promises. When your parents or guardian ask you to do something, they know you will do it. When your troop has a meeting, your leaders know you will be there. When you have said that you are going on a patrol campout, the other Scouts know you will be on time. People can depend upon you to do your best in every situation.

There will be times when your judgment fails and you make mistakes. Everyone does. Your baseball may smash a window. You may misread your map and come home late from a hike. If you quickly admit what you have done and make good on any damage, others will soon forget the incident. By learning from those mistakes, you can do better in the future.

A reputation for being trustworthy is important to you now and in years to come. It can help you get and keep jobs. Others will depend on your word. You prove you can be responsible with money. Trustworthiness will help you make and maintain good friendships.

You must also have trust in yourself. You are your own best judge. You know when you have done right and wrong. Live in such a way that you respect yourself, and others will respect you, too.

A Scout is LOYAL. *A Scout is true to his family, friends, Scout leaders, school, nation, and world community.*

Loyalty starts at home. You show your loyalty by being the kind of person your family can trust and respect. Let them know through your actions that you appreciate what they do for you.

A chain is only as strong as its weakest link. The success of your patrol and your troop depends on the loyalty of each Scout in it—in the way you support your leaders and pitch in with the team, and in the way you act as a Scout.

Express your loyalty to the United States by respecting our flag and our government, and by participating in the democratic process. Another part of loyalty is seeing where things can be made better and then working toward that ideal. Our form of government allows each of us to voice our concerns and work within the system to make changes. Give real meaning to your loyalty by helping make our communities, states, and nation a reflection of the best America can be.

A Scout is HELPFUL. *A Scout is concerned about other people. He willingly volunteers to help others without expecting payment or reward.*

In pledging yourself to the Scout Oath, you promised "to help other people at all times." The Scout motto asks you to Be Prepared. The Scout slogan reminds you to Do a Good Turn Daily. These three ideals work together: you *promise* to help, you *can* help because you have learned how, and you *do* help because you care about all people.

As a Scout, prepare yourself to be helpful, then look for ways to help. Learn first aid, and you are ready to assist someone who is hurt. Know about your town, and you can help a stranger find the way.

A Scout's willingness to help is evidence of his attitude toward life. He wants the best for everyone, and acts to make that happen. A Scout may work for pay, but he does not expect to receive money for being helpful. A Good Turn done in the hope of getting a tip is not a Good Turn at all.

A Scout is FRIENDLY. *A Scout is a friend to all. He is a brother to other Scouts and all the people of the world. He seeks to understand others. He respects those with ideas and customs that are different from his own.*

Friendship is like a mirror. When you have a smile on your face as you greet someone, you are more likely to receive a smile in return. If you are willing to be a good friend, you will find that others enjoy being with you.

The moment you become a Scout, you join a brotherhood of friends that circles the world. Those in it are of different countries and colors and creeds, but they are all brother Scouts. They live up to Scout Oaths and Laws just as you do.

Making a friend is fairly easy if you are friendly yourself. Keeping a friend is more difficult. Every person is an individual with his or her own ideas and ways of doing things. To be a real friend you must accept other people as they are, show interest in them, and respect their differences.

Accept who *you* are, too. You don't have to be just like everyone else. Real friends will respect the beliefs, interests, and skills that make you unique.

A Scout is COURTEOUS. *A Scout is polite to everyone regardless of age or position. He knows that good manners make it easier for people to get along together.*

This is another way of saying, "A Scout is a gentleman." Good manners show that you respect the feelings and needs of others. Open a door for someone. Offer your seat on a bus to an elderly person, a pregnant woman, or someone carrying a baby. Rise from your chair when a guest enters the room. Help your parents be seated at the family table. Greet others with a firm, sincere handshake. Say "please" and "thank-you" or "pardon me" and "sorry" whenever they are needed. Do your share of family chores in a pleasant way. The courtesy you practice as a Scout will stay with you throughout your life.

A Scout is KIND. *A Scout understands there is strength in being gentle. He treats others as he wants to be treated. Without good reason, he does not harm or kill any living thing.*

There is nothing weak about being kind. In fact, kindness is a sign of true strength. To be kind you must look beyond yourself to the needs of others. Take time to listen to the thoughts of other people. Imagine what it would be like if you were in someone else's place.

It is not difficult to be kind to those in need and those who cannot defend themselves. What may be harder is being kind to people you don't know or don't understand, and to people with whom you disagree. We live in a world that has more than its share of anger, fear, and war. Extending kindness to those around you and having compassion for all people is a good antidote to the poisons of hatred and violence.

Kindness is not limited to the ways we feel about people. Be kind to pets and wildlife. Develop a positive land ethic that respects the earth. Help protect our natural resources by practicing no-trace methods of hiking and camping.

A Scout is OBEDIENT. *A Scout follows the rules of his family, school, religion, and troop. He obeys the laws of his community and country. If he thinks these rules and laws are unfair, he tries to have them changed in an orderly manner rather than disobey them.*

Obedience begins in your home. Your family cares for you and wants you to be safe. Cheerfully follow any rules your family has set for you.

There are others besides family members to whom you owe obedience. When teachers give you homework, it is usually because the assignments will help you learn. When an employer gives you an order, it is usually for the good of the business. And when your Scout leader asks you to do a job, it is because your efforts will help your patrol and troop. Being obedient also means following city, state, and national laws.

However, obeying must be guided by judgment. If someone orders you to cheat, steal, or do something else that you know is wrong, you have to say no. Obedience is based on trust. Those who give you orders trust that you will do what they ask. But you must also trust your own beliefs and obey your conscience when you know you are right.

A Scout is CHEERFUL. *A Scout looks for the bright side of life. He cheerfully does tasks that come his way. He tries to make others happy.*

Some people grumble when they are losing a game. On a campout, they become angry if the weather turns bad or the trail is long and dusty. Others are always cheerful. With a sense of joy and adventure, they jump at every opportunity life presents. Their good spirits make everything easier for them, their friends, and their families.

Adversity is a tremendous teacher. Even though it may test the limits of your cheerfulness, the way to become a top-notch camper is to get outdoors, rain or shine, do your best every time, and be willing to learn from your mistakes.

The same is true off the trail. You can become a good athlete by playing against those who are better. You will become a better student by realizing your studies are a chance for discovery. And you will become a finer person if you approach all you do with energy and good cheer.

A Scout is THRIFTY. *A Scout works to pay his way and to help others. He saves for the future. He protects and conserves natural resources. He carefully uses time and property.*

Paying your way with money you have earned gives you independence and pride. When you dig into your own pockets to buy clothing, your Scout uniform, or your camp equipment, you learn the real value of those items. You will be sure to take good care of them.

Save some of your earnings in a bank account. Even if you have only a dollar or two to put aside each month, the habit of saving regularly is very important. Share with others, too. Volunteering your time and energy is just as valuable as giving money.

As a camper and backpacker, you will learn that you can live very well with no more possessions than the clothes you are wearing and the gear in your pack. As a Scout, you will also see that practicing conservation is a sign of thrift. Protect and conserve the earth's natural resources — its soil, water, forests, wilderness areas, and wildlife. Recycle papers, glass, and metal used in your home and community. Waste is an enemy of thrift. When you act to stop it, you are doing your part to keep the earth beautiful.

A Scout is BRAVE. *A Scout can face danger even if he is afraid. He has the courage to stand for what he thinks is right even if others laugh at him or threaten him.*

Since 1910 when Scouting came to America, thousands of Honor Medals have been awarded to Scouts who saved lives at the risk of their own. They proved themselves ready when emergencies arose. They may have been afraid, but they each went to the aid of someone in serious trouble. Once they reached the victims, they had the skills to make successful rescues.

ADOPT A HIGHWAY
LITTER CONTROL
NEXT 2 MILES
BOY SCOUT TROOP 79
LAFAYETTE

Lifesaving is not the only test of bravery. You are brave every time you do what is right in spite of what others might say. You are brave when you speak the truth and when you admit a mistake and apologize for it. You are brave when you refuse to let alcohol, tobacco, or drugs become a part of your life. And you show true courage when you defend the rights of others.

A Scout is CLEAN. *A Scout keeps his body and mind fit and clean. He chooses the company of those who live by these same ideals. He helps keep his home and community clean.*

You never need to be ashamed of dirt that will wash off. If you play hard and work hard you can't help getting dirty. But when the game is over or the work is done, that kind of dirt disappears with soap and water.

There's another kind of dirt that won't come off by washing. It is the kind that shows up in foul language and harmful thoughts.

Swear words, profanity, and dirty stories are weapons that ridicule other people and hurt their feelings. The same is true of racial slurs and jokes making fun of ethnic groups or people with physical or mental limitations. A Scout knows there is no kindness or honor in such mean-spirited behavior. He avoids it in his own words and deeds. He defends those who are targets of insults.

A Scout is REVERENT. *A Scout is reverent toward God. He is faithful in his religious duties. He respects the beliefs of others.*

The word *reverence* refers to a profound respect for God. The wonders of the world remind us of our God's creative power. We find it in the tiny lines of a leaf and the great mysteries of the universe. It exists in the kindness of people and in the teachings of our families and religious leaders.

We show our reverence by living our lives according to the ideals of our beliefs. The Scout benediction is "May the Great Master of all Scouts be with us until we meet again."

The United States Constitution gives each of us complete freedom to believe and worship as we wish without fear of punishment. All your life, you will encounter people who hold different religious beliefs or even none at all. It is your duty to respect and defend the rights of others whose beliefs may differ from yours.

SCOUT MOTTO

Be Prepared. That's the motto of the Boy Scouts.

Someone once asked Baden-Powell, the founder of Scouting, "Be prepared for what?" "Why," said Baden-Powell, "for any old thing." The Scout motto means that you are always ready in mind and body to do your duty and to face danger, if necessary, to help others.

The more Scouting skills you have, the better able you are to live up to the motto. When someone has an accident, you are prepared because of your first aid training. Because of lifesaving instruction, you can save a child who has fallen into the water. If a building catches fire, you are ready to help because you have practiced what to do. Proper training prepares you to do your best in the face of any emergency.

But Baden-Powell wasn't thinking just of being prepared for accidents. His idea was that every Scout should prepare himself to become a useful citizen and to give happiness to other people. He wanted each Scout to be prepared to work for all the good things that life has to offer and to face with a strong heart whatever may lie ahead.

Be prepared *for life* — to live happily and without regret, knowing that you have done your best. That's what the Scout motto means.

562

SCOUT SLOGAN

Do a Good Turn Daily. This is the slogan of the Boy Scouts. Some Good Turns are big—saving a human life . . . rescue work in floods . . . service in hurricane-stricken areas . . . recycling community trash . . . working with your patrol on a backcountry conservation project.

But Good Turns are more often small, thoughtful acts—helping a child cross the street . . . doing the shopping for an elderly neighbor . . . cutting back brush blocking a street sign . . . making a new student feel at ease in your school.

A Good Turn is more than simple good manners. It is an extra act of kindness. Answering the question of a driver about reaching an address is not really a Good Turn. That is common courtesy. But if you take time to draw a map for him or to lead him to his destination, that extra effort makes it a Good Turn.

SIGNS OF A SCOUT

When you become a Scout, use the Scout sign, salute, and handclasp to show that you belong to the world brotherhood of Scouting. And, of course, you can wear the Scout badge and the Scout uniform.

Scout sign. The Scout sign marks you as a Scout everywhere in the world. Give it each time you recite the Scout Oath and Law. Held high, the Scout sign is a signal for attention. When a Scout leader raises his hand in the Scout sign, all Scouts should also make the sign and come to silent attention.

To give the Scout sign, cover the nail of the little finger of your right hand with your right thumb. Then raise your right hand, palm forward, with the three middle fingers upward. Those three fingers stand for the three parts of the Scout Oath. Your thumb and little finger touch to represent the bond that unites all Scouts.

Scout salute. The Scout salute signifies respect. Use it to salute the flag of the United States of America. As a sign of courtesy, you may also salute a Scout leader or another Scout.

To give the Scout salute, form the Scout sign with your right hand. Bring that hand smartly up to your head until your forefinger touches the edge of your hat or your forehead above the right eye.

Scout handclasp. The Scout handclasp is a token of friendship. That is why it is made with the left hand, the hand nearest your heart. Give the Scout handclasp by extending your left hand to another Scout and firmly grasping his hand.

Scout badge. The shape of the complete Scout badge, which is also on the First Class badge of rank, was adapted from the north point of an old mariner's compass. The design is often called a *trefoil*—a flower with three leaves.

It is also known by its French name, *fleur-de-lis*—lily or iris flower. The shape resembles an arrowhead.

With slight changes, the trefoil badge is used by Scouts around the world.

The *trefoil* means that a Scout can point the right way in life as truly as a compass can in the field.

The *three points,* like the fingers of the Scout sign, stand for the three parts of the Scout Oath: duty to God and country, duty to others, and duty to self.

The *two stars* symbolize truth and knowledge, and the outdoors in Scouting.

The *eagle with the shield* stands for freedom and a Scout's readiness to defend that freedom.

The *scroll* with the Scout motto is turned up at the ends. It is a hint that a Scout smiles as he does his duty.

The *knot* at the bottom of the scroll is a reminder to Do a Good Turn Daily.

The field uniform consists of a shirt, shorts or trousers, socks, a belt, and a cap or broad-brimmed hat.

Scout uniform. Wearing a uniform is part of the thrill of being a Scout. Put on your uniform and you feel ready for hiking, camping, and other Scout activities. By dressing alike, you and all other Scouts show that you are equals in the spirit of brotherhood and that you stand for certain ideals.

Wear your uniform proudly. It is a steady reminder to you and to others that a Scout is a person who can be trusted to lend a hand when help is needed. Dressed as a Scout, you want to act as a Scout.

The parts of a uniform. The Scout uniform consists of a cap or a broad-brim hat, a shirt, trousers or shorts, a belt, socks, and shoes or hiking boots. For cold weather, your troop will prefer the long-sleeve shirt with trousers. The favorite summer uniform is the short-sleeve shirt and shorts. Scouts involved in conservation projects may wear work pants or jeans with their Scout shirts.

Scouts throughout the world are recognized by their neckerchiefs. Each troop chooses its own color.

Uniforms build team spirit in your patrol and troop. The color and design of the Scout uniform make it the ideal clothing for many outdoor adventures.

The activities uniform consists of a knit shirt (red for Boy Scouts, maroon for Venture crews, tan for Varsity teams), Boy Scout shorts, and Boy Scout socks.

How to wear a neckerchief. Roll the long edge of the neckerchief to about 6 inches from the tip. Place the neckerchief smoothly around your neck. Lay it over or under your collar, depending on the custom of your troop, and hold it in place with a slide. Troop custom will also decide whether you tie the ends of the neckerchief with a slipknot or square knot, or leave them free. Scout bolo ties may be worn under an open collar.

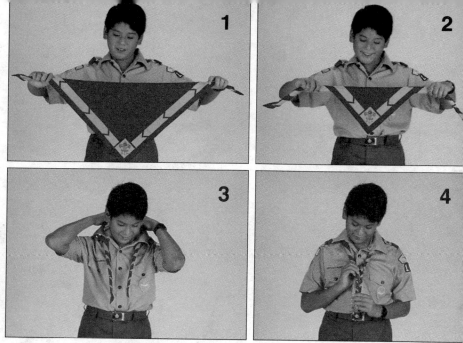

HOW TO WEAR A NECKERCHIEF. (1) Hold the long end of the neckerchief, and (2) roll the long edge to about 6 inches from the tip. (3) Place the neckerchief smoothly under your collar, or turn your collar under if your troop wears the neckerchief over the collar. (4) Hold the neckerchief in place with a slide. Tie the ends with a slipknot if that is your troop's custom.

How to get a uniform. The moment you join a troop and have been registered as a Scout, you can get a uniform from the nearest Scouting equipment distributor. Your Scoutmaster will know the location. There you can buy your uniform, community strip or council shoulder insignia, troop numeral, and patrol medallion. If you need help finding money for a uniform, your Scoutmaster may suggest ways you can earn it. Your troop may also be able to let you use uniforms that older Scouts have outgrown.

Wearing your Scout uniform. Wear your complete uniform proudly and correctly at all Scouting events:

☆ At patrol and troop meetings, hikes, camps, and rallies.

☆ When you appear before a board of review or a court of honor.

☆ When you take part in Scout service projects in your community and in the backcountry.

☆ During Scouting Anniversary Week in February.

SUMMER CAMP AND CAMPOREES

THE very first Scout summer camp was held in 1907. Lord Baden-Powell, the founder of Scouting, brought together a group of 22 Scouts on Brownsea Island off the coast of England. They were divided into four patrols—the Wolves, Bulls, Curlews, and Ravens. They set up their tents and cooking areas, then devoted 7 days to woodcraft, lifesaving, nature observation, and the other skills of Scouting. Around evening campfires they told stories, sang songs, and performed skits. When it was over, the Scouts agreed that their summer camp had been a complete success.

Today's camporees and summer camps are just as exciting as that first one on Brownsea Island. You can spend your days hiking, swimming, mastering Scout skills, and learning about nature. You'll have plenty of chances to pass requirements for badges. You can get to know Scouts from other areas.

Summer camp is the high point of the year for many troops. It lets Scouts devote their full time to living the Scouting life. As with other kinds of Scout camping, you will learn much about the importance of low-impact methods. Always pick up litter, dispose of ashes, and leave your campsites in better condition than you found them

CAMPOREE CAMPING

A camporee is usually a weekend of fun, fellowship, and Scouting activities shared by two or more troops camping together. It's a perfect opportunity for your patrol to show its skill as you make camp, prepare your meals, and take part in camporee activities. You can also share good times and fresh ideas with Scouts from other troops. What are they cooking for meals? How do they set up their dining fly? Can they show you how to lash together a signal tower or how to paddle a canoe?

Perhaps your patrol will lay out an orienteering course where every Scout can practice using a map and compass. A knot rack helps everyone learn to handle rope. An obstacle course can give you a real workout. Camporee games may require the members of your patrol to cooperate with each other in order to reach a goal. Some games can't be won unless all the patrols pool their efforts and work as one big group.

Camporees are always great fun. They are also a perfect way for a patrol to get ready for summer camp.

SUMMER CAMP

Most councils have a special camp where Scouts can enjoy a full week or more of Scouting. Some council camps lie in deep forests or at the base of high, windy peaks. Others are tucked back in the woods along rivers and lakes. A few are located in the desert or along a seashore. Scout camps come in many shapes and sizes, but they all share one thing in common — they offer as much adventure and excitement as a Scout can have anywhere.

Summer camp is a terrific place to work on many Scouting skills. Your own troop leaders will be there to help you as much as they can. A camp staff of experienced older Scouts and adults will give you a helping hand whenever you need it. You can form new friendships with Scouts from other troops and learn how they do things in their patrols.

Morning in Summer Camp

You'll want to get an early start for a day packed with activity. Breakfast is the first order of business. In some camps, each patrol cooks its meals over stoves or a campfire, and everyone takes a turn as the chef. Perhaps pancakes will become your specialty. Can you flip a flapjack in the air?

Other camps have a dining hall where you will eat most of your meals. That leaves plenty of time for all that a summer camp has to offer. Here's a small sampling of what you will find:

☆ Nature hikes with instructors who really know their stuff.

☆ Map and compass courses.

☆ A wood yard for practicing wise use of knives, saws, and axes.

☆ Archery and rifle ranges.

☆ Conservation projects, meadow repair, trail maintenance, and erosion control.

☆ Instruction in the best no-trace methods of backcountry travel.

☆ Ropes courses that test your balance, fitness, and ability to solve problems.

☆ Swimming pools, lakes, and streams.

☆ Crafts areas.

Afternoon

After you chow down on a tasty lunch, you still have half the day to get back into camp activities. A hot afternoon is a good time to go to the swimming pool or lake. You'll follow the Scout Safe Swim Defense method whenever you are in the water. If you don't know how to swim, staff instructors will help you learn. Strong swimmers can learn lifesaving. You can also get a feel for canoeing and rowing, and maybe windsurfing and sailing.

Evening

Supper is over and the dishes have been washed and put away. As darkness falls, you can gather for an evening around the campfire. Your patrol may do a skit. Perhaps you'll lead the group in a song or tell a story. As the fire burns down to embers, your Scoutmaster may talk with you about the importance of what you are doing in camp. He knows that these experiences will stay with you for many years to come.

Then to bed. Sleep fast and well. Early the next morning, you'll be ready to plunge into another day of summer camp adventures.

NATIONAL HIGH-ADVENTURE BASES

For real excitement beyond your council, it's hard to beat the national high-adventure bases of the Boy Scouts of America. Designed for older Boy Scouts and Explorers, each base offers the training, equipment, and support you need to set out on wilderness treks that challenge your skills, strength, and willpower.

Philmont Scout Ranch. Explore the rugged high country of northern New Mexico on a backpacking trek, as a member of a conservation crew, or on an advanced wilderness adventure. Covering more than 137,000 acres of mountains, forests, prairies, and streams, Philmont is an inspiring backpacker's paradise. Staffed camps in the backcountry offer program opportunities including rock climbing, blackpowder rifle shooting, living history, horseback riding, archaeology, conservation, and many others.

▼

▲

Florida National High Adventure Sea Base. During voyages aboard watercraft and sailboats, you can explore the clear waters of the Florida Keys and Bahamas. Snorkel and scuba dive amid pillars of coral surrounded by brilliantly colored tropical fish. Explore a primitive island, search for the wreckage of old ships, cast your bait for sailfish in the Gulf Stream waters, practice windsurfing, and study the marine life of North America's only living coral reef.

Northern Tier National High Adventure Programs. The Sioux and Chippewa once traveled this northern lake country. French-Canadian trappers followed, their canoes heavily laden with furs. Headquartered in the beautiful Lake Superior-Quetico Provincial Park boundary waters of Minnesota and Ontario, and in northern Wisconsin, the Northern Tier offers wilderness canoeing expeditions and programs featuring sailing, fishing, and winter camping.

▼

575

CHAPTER 25

SUMMER CAMP AND CAMPOREES

577

THE STORY OF A GOOD TURN

HOW good must a Good Turn be to be *good?* The answer is best given by telling you the story of how Scouting came to America. It shows that it isn't the size of the Good Turn that counts. What is important is the spirit with which a Scout does a Good Turn.

GOOD TURN TO AN AMERICAN

One day in 1909 in London, England, an American visitor, William D. Boyce, lost his way in a dense fog. He stopped under a street lamp and tried to figure out where he was. A boy approached him and asked if he could be of help.

"You certainly can," said Boyce. He told the boy that he wanted to find a certain business office in the center of the city.

"I'll take you there," said the boy.

When they got to the destination, Mr. Boyce reached into his pocket for a tip. But the boy stopped him.

"No thank you, sir. I am a Scout. I won't take anything for helping."

"A Scout? And what might that be?" asked Boyce.

The boy told the American about himself and his brother Scouts. Boyce became very interested. After finishing his errand, he had the boy take him to the British Scouting office.

At the office, Boyce met Lord Robert Baden-Powell, the famous British general who had founded the Scouting movement in Great Britain. Boyce was so impressed with what he learned that he decided to bring Scouting home with him.

On February 8, 1910, Boyce and a group of outstanding leaders founded the Boy Scouts of America. From that day forth, Scouts have celebrated February 8 as the birthday of Scouting in the United States.

What happened to the boy who helped Mr. Boyce find his way in the fog? No one knows. He had neither asked for money nor given his name, but he will never be forgotten. His Good Turn helped bring the Scouting movement to our country.

In the British Scout Training Center at Gilwell Park, England, Scouts from the United States erected a statue of an American buffalo in honor of this unknown Scout. *One* Good Turn to *one* man became a Good Turn to millions of American boys. Such is the power of a Good Turn.

On a foggy day in 1909, a British Boy Scout guided an American businessman, William D. Boyce, to his destination and refused a tip for his Good Turn. Impressed with the boy's spirit, Mr. Boyce brought Scouting to the United States.

THE FOUNDER OF SCOUTING

The man who started the Scouting movement, Robert Baden-Powell, spent much of his life serving in the British cavalry. He received his early military training in India, then served in Africa. At the turn of the century he was an officer in the war between Britain and the descendants of Dutch settlers, the Boers, in South Africa. He gained world fame during the war by defending the town of Mafeking against a force of Boer soldiers. He stood fast for 217 days until another British army group broke through the enemy lines and lifted the siege.

Baden-Powell came home to England as the best-known hero of the Boer War. He decided to use his fame to help British boys become better men. He based his ideas for a boys' organization on his own experiences as a youngster in England and as a soldier in India and Africa. In 1907 he invited a group of boys to attend the world's first Boy Scout camp on the English island of Brownsea. The success of the camp led him to write a book he called *Scouting for Boys.* It was an instant best-seller. Boys by the thousands bought it and decided to become Scouts. Scouting spread like wildfire throughout England and, before long, around the world.

ERNEST THOMPSON SETON

DANIEL CARTER BEARD

JAMES E. WEST

EARLY DAYS IN AMERICA

Among the founders of the Boy Scouts of America, Ernest Thompson
Seton and Daniel Carter Beard were skilled at living outdoors. Both had written books about camping and nature study, and both had developed their
own outdoor programs for young people. Seton became the first Chief Scout
of the Boy Scouts of America. Beard served as the National Commissioner.

James E. West, a young Washington lawyer, became the first Chief Scout
Executive of the young organization. His own childhood had been difficult.
His father had died before he was born. His mother passed away when he was
7 years old, and West was raised in an orphanage. He suffered from an illness
that made it difficult for him to walk. Despite these hardships, he put all his
ambition, ability, and energy into becoming a lawyer. He succeeded and then
dedicated himself to helping all children — healthy, sick, and disabled — to
have a better life. James West gave the Boy Scouts of America 32 years of strong,
wise leadership. His efforts helped build Scouting into the largest organization for boys in the country.

CHAPTER 26

THE FIRST HANDBOOK

The boys joining the new Boy Scouts of America needed a manual of their own. Published in 1911, the BSA's *Handbook for Boys* was an American version of Baden-Powell's *Scouting for Boys*.
It was packed with information about hiking and camping, forming patrols, and having fun in the outdoors. The book also described activities for Scout troops and listed the requirements for Scout ranks and merit badges.

The Scout handbook has been revised 10 times to include the latest developments in Scouting and outdoor adventures. Since 1911, more than 33 million copies of the *Boy Scout Handbook* have been printed. That makes it one of the most popular American books of all time.

BOYS' LIFE

When he became Chief Scout Executive, James West felt that the Boy Scouts of America needed a magazine. Scouts reading a good publication could share the best Scouting had to offer. In 1912, Mr. West and the BSA national office began printing a magazine they called *Boys' Life.* Today, more than 2,000,000 Scouts receive *Boys' Life* every month. Each issue is filled with terrific stories, camping hints, and Scout projects. James West's good idea has become a very important part of Scouting.

BOY SCOUT SERVICE

Service to others has been a vital part of Scouting since its beginning. Individual Scouts have done millions of Good Turns of all descriptions. Patrols and troops have organized to carry out worthwhile projects for their communities. They have gathered food and clothing for needy neighbors, built playgrounds, and repaired parks and public buildings. In times of emergency, they have assisted fire and police departments, aided in the evacuation of flood victims, and cleaned up after storms.

Service on a national scale started when the United States became involved in World War I. Boy Scouts throughout the country sold bonds to raise money for the war effort. They collected recyclable paper and metal. Their efforts showed the public an important side of the Scouting program. The Congress of the United States signaled its support by granting a charter to the Boy Scouts of America.

Scouts today carry on this tradition of service in their homes, communities, and nation. In recent years, Scout service has led to more active roles in caring for the land. Scouts not only enjoy going outdoors for adventures, they also see themselves as good stewards of the land, working with park and forest rangers to complete a wide variety of conservation and restoration projects.

THE FIRST WORLD JAMBOREE

By 1920, Scouting had spread around the world. To strengthen this world brotherhood, Baden-Powell invited Scouts from all nations to a world jamboree in London. He wanted young people from many countries to camp together, share their skills, and develop friendships.

The first jamboree was such a success that Scouting's leaders promoted the idea of more worldwide gatherings. With the exception of the World War II years, world jamborees have been held every 4 years.

Since 1937, the Boy Scouts of America has held one national jamboree between every two world jamborees. As many as 50,000 Scouts have attended each gathering.

▼ 1989 NATIONAL JAMBOREE

▲ 1920 WORLD JAMBOREE

▲ CUB SCOUTING

EXPLORING ▶

THE GROWTH OF SCOUTING

Through the years, the Boy Scouts of America has continued to grow. To serve the special needs and interests of Scouts, the BSA has developed a variety of programs.

Sea Scouting began in 1912 as a branch of Scouting for older boys. Eventually it became Senior Scouting, which proved to be very popular. Today, Exploring is the program for young men and women in the Boy Scouts of America.

The Lone Scouts of America merged with the BSA in 1924. An organization for boys who lived in sparsely populated areas of the country, the Lone Scouts had been founded by William Boyce.

In 1930, a younger-boy program, first called Cubbing but now known as Cub Scouting, began drawing boys from age 8 and up into the movement. Tiger Cubs, BSA, was added in 1982 to serve boys younger than 8 and their families. Varsity Scouting, added more recently, rounds out the program of the Boy Scouts of America.

From its beginning with a Good Turn by an unknown Scout, to the present with millions of Scouts across the nation, the Boy Scouts of America has had a colorful, exciting, and important history. Now that you are a Scout, what does the future hold for the organization? Well, that depends on you. Like that British Scout on a foggy London street, you never know when a simple act of kindness can have far-reaching effects on another person, an entire organization, or even the world.

TRAIL TO EAGLE

BE PREPARED

BSA

AMERICA

The long trail to Eagle, Scouting's highest rank, is full of opportunities for you to learn, to lead, to listen, and to teach. By setting goals for yourself and then working to reach them, you can gain valuable knowledge and experience in many fields. It takes determination and effort, but the rewards are great. This next *Handbook* section discusses the challenges and the recognition that await you along the trail to Eagle.

ADVANCEMENT IN SCOUTING

W HEN Baden-Powell started the Scouting movement, he felt that any Scout who took the time and trouble to master skills should be rewarded for his effort. He gave to each Scout who passed certain tests a badge to wear on his uniform. It recognized the importance of what the Scout had done and let others know of his achievement. That is how the badge system started in Scouting.

Scout advancement is designed to let you move ahead in your own way and at your own speed. Rather than competing against others, you challenge yourself to reach goals and then go as far as your ambition will carry you. Your rate of advancement depends upon your interest, effort, and ability.

The Scouting advancement program provides a forward-moving series of tests. To complete each rank, you must master certain Scout skills. You must be active in your patrol and troop, for that is where you can learn and teach those skills. By your actions, you must show that you are trying to live up to the ideals of the Scout Oath and Scout Law.

Once you have completed the requirements for a new rank, meet with your Scoutmaster for a conference. When he is satisfied with your progress, he will arrange for a board of review.

SCOUTMASTER CONFERENCE

Over the months and years that you are a Scout, you will have no difficulty seeing yourself becoming taller and heavier. But you are also growing in ways you may not be able to see. The thoughts and attitudes you are developing will help determine the kind of adult you will become.

Your Scoutmaster wants to give you plenty of opportunities for growth. When you join a troop and as you complete the requirements for each rank, he will sit down with you for a friendly visit. Those conferences will help your Scoutmaster get to know you better. He will gain a clearer idea of what you can contribute to your patrol and troop. He may also discover new ways that he can bring you the best that Scouting has to offer.

Each Scoutmaster conference is also an opportunity for you to learn more about your Scoutmaster and what he expects of you. This is a good time to bring up any concerns you have about the troop, and to discuss anything you don't understand about the Scout program.

Setting a Goal for Yourself

During each conference, your Scoutmaster will ask you to decide on a new goal you want to achieve. He will encourage you to think up your own goal, one that will challenge you without being out of reach.

If your goal is to become a better leader, your Scoutmaster may suggest ways you can develop as a leader in the troop. If you have your eye on earning a higher rank, he may give you suggestions that will help you prepare to meet the requirements.

If you enjoy the outdoors, you may set a goal of helping your patrol complete a conservation project. It might involve erosion control, building bird-houses, clearing fallen trees from trails, or helping a park or forest ranger study the movements of wildlife.

You may have goals outside of Scouting, too. Suppose you are good at sports — baseball, for instance. Your goal might be to organize some ball games for youngsters in your neighborhood. Since you know all the rules, you could plan to be the umpire.

Maybe you like to do crafts such as woodworking. Your goal could be to build a candle stand for use at troop ceremonies, or to repair chairs for your neighborhood day-care center.

These are only a few examples, but you get the idea. Things don't just happen. You need to set a goal, then work hard to reach it.

BOARD OF REVIEW

A Scoutmaster conference takes place each time you complete the requirements for a new rank. At the end of the conference, your Scoutmaster will schedule a board of review.

The board of review is conducted by adult troop leaders interested in your progress as a Scout. They want to make sure you really have completed the requirements for a rank. They may also be able to suggest ways you can get more out of Scouting.

The troop or team committee is the board that will review you for Tenderfoot, Second Class, First Class, Star, and Life ranks. Your council will conduct a special Eagle Scout review to consider you for Scouting's highest rank.

When board of review members are satisfied that you have completed the requirements, they will send an advancement report to your local council service center. For the Eagle Scout Award, a special application will be forwarded by your council for certification by the BSA national office. Soon after the board of review, you will receive your new badge at a troop ceremony.

UPWARD TO EAGLE

The requirements for the ranks of Star, Life, and Eagle are quite a bit different from those you must fulfill to earn Scouting's other badges of rank. Each of the higher ranks requires that you

☆ Earn a certain number of merit badges.

☆ Accept a position of responsibility in your troop.

☆ Be of service.

Merit badges. Earning a merit badge is like having an admission ticket to explore an exciting subject. Some badges cover areas you may already know about, while others will be fresh discoveries. You will find the descriptions of them on pages 599–608.

Positions of responsibility. You may seek some of your troop's positions of responsibility while other opportunities seek you.

If you have certain interests, you may offer to be troop scribe, quartermaster, librarian, or chaplain aide. You may become den chief of a Cub Scout den. At some point, the Scouts in your patrol may elect you patrol leader, or you may become your troop's senior patrol leader.

Star and Life service projects. Service to others is important. The service projects for the ranks of Star and Life require you to give at least 6 hours of service. You can complete this requirement on your own, or do it along with others in your patrol or troop. The project must be approved by your Scoutmaster before you start.

Eagle service project. There is a major difference between the service projects for Star and Life, and the one you will complete for Eagle. In the first two, you can be a follower. For Eagle, you must be a leader. You must plan, develop, and give leadership to others in a project of help to any religious group, school, or community. There are some limitations. Work involving council property or done in conjunction with other Scouting activities is not acceptable for an Eagle service project. In addition, your project may not be performed for a business, be of a commercial nature, or be a fund-raiser except for securing materials or supplies needed to carry out your project. Your project idea must be approved by your Scoutmaster, by your troop committee, and by your council or district before you begin.

An Eagle project will take many more hours of planning and effort than projects for Star and Life. You must use the *Eagle Scout Service Project Workbook* to plan, receive the necessary approvals, and report the results of your project. Here are a few service projects Scouts have done to fulfill their Eagle requirement:

☆ Organized a bicycle safety campaign. Trained fellow Scouts as inspectors and judges. Ran a bike rodeo that included a bicycle safety check and a contest promoting safe riding.

☆ Trained fellow students as audiovisual aides for their school. Arranged for more than 200 hours of audiovisual work.

☆ Set up a used-toy collection and repair service within the troop. Gave the toys to a school for children with disabilities.

☆ Prepared plans for a footbridge on a trail in a national forest. Worked with rangers to learn the skills necessary to build the structure. Gathered materials and tools, then directed a Scout work group to do the construction.

All these projects required the help of others. In every case, the Eagle candidate planned the project, lined up the help he needed, and led the effort.

STAR RANK

Date/Leader's
Initials

1. Be active in your troop and patrol for at least 4 months as a First Class Scout.   2-9   Rmn

2. Demonstrate Scout spirit by living the Scout Oath (Promise) and Scout Law in your everyday life.   2-19   Rm

3. Earn six merit badges including any four from the required list for Eagle.

Emer- prep	merit badge* 1-5-93 Rm
Swimming	merit badge* 1-5-98 Rm
First Aid	merit badge* 12-97 Rm
Enviornm Science	merit badge* 2-19-98 Rm
Pioneering	merit badge 8-97 Rm
Wood Carving	merit badge 8-97 Rm

4. While a First Class Scout, take part in service projects totaling at least 6 hours of work. These projects must be approved by your Scoutmaster.   2-19   Rm

5. While a First Class Scout, serve actively 4 months in one or more of the following positions of responsibility (or carry out a Scout-master-assigned leadership project to help the troop):
   Boy Scout troop. Patrol leader, assistant senior patrol leader, senior patrol leader, troop guide, den chief, scribe, librarian, quartermaster, junior assistant Scoutmaster, chaplain aide, instructor, crew chief
   Varsity Scout team. Captain, cocaptain, program manager, squad leader, team secretary, librarian, quartermaster, chaplain aide, instructor, den chief

   Asst. Patrol Leader   2-19-98 Rm

6. Take part in a Scoutmaster conference.   2-19-98 Rm

Became a Star Scout on 2 / 19 / 19 98   Rm

Board of review initials

*The required list for Eagle has 15 merit badges in 12 categories. Any of the 15 may be used for this requirement.

LIFE RANK

Date/Leader's
Initials

1. Be active in your troop and patrol for at least 6 months as a Star Scout. _____ _____

2. Demonstrate Scout spirit by living the Scout Oath (Promise) and Scout Law in your everyday life. _____ _____

3. Earn five more merit badges (so that you have 11 in all), including any three more from the required list for Eagle.

_____ merit badge*   ____ ____

_____ merit badge*   ____ ____

_____ merit badge*   ____ ____

_____Trv clL____+ r a n s_____ merit badge   ____ ____

_____ merit badge   ____ ____

4. While a Star Scout, take part in service projects totaling at least 6 hours of work. These projects must be approved by your Scoutmaster.   ____ ____

5. While a Star Scout, serve actively for 6 months in one or more of the positions of responsibility listed in requirement 5 for Star Scout (or carry out a Scoutmaster-assigned leadership project to help the troop).

_____   ____ ____

_____   ____ ____

6. Take part in a Scoutmaster conference.   ____ ____

Became a Life Scout on _____ / _____ / 19 ____ _____

Board of review initials

*The required list for Eagle has 15 merit badges in 12 categories. Any of the 15 may be used for this requirement.

EAGLE RANK

NOTE: If you have a permanent physical or mental disability you may become an Eagle Scout by qualifying for as many required merit badges as you can and qualifying for alternate merit badges for the rest. If you seek to become an Eagle under this procedure, you must submit a special application to your council service center. Your application must be approved by your council committee for advancement BEFORE YOU CAN WORK ON ALTERNATIVE MERIT BADGES.

Date/Leader's
Initials

1. Be active in your troop and patrol for at least 6 months as a Life Scout.   ____ ____

2. Demonstrate Scout spirit by living the Scout Oath (Promise) and Scout Law in your everyday life.   ____ ____

3. Earn a total of 21 merit badges (10 more than you already have), including the following: (a) First Aid, (b) Citizenship in the Community, (c) Citizenship in the Nation, (d) Citizenship in the

World, (e) Communications, (f) Safety, (g) Emergency Prepared-
ness OR Lifesaving, (h) Environmental Science, (i) Personal
Management, (j) Personal Fitness OR Swimming OR Sports, (k)
Camping, and (l) Family Life.*

	merit badge		
	merit badge		
	merit badge		
	merit badge		
	merit badge		
	merit badge		
	merit badge		
	merit badge		
	merit badge		
	merit badge		

4. While a Life Scout, serve actively for a period of 6 months in one
    or more of the following positions of responsibility:
    Boy Scout troop. Patrol leader, assistant senior patrol leader,
    senior patrol leader, troop guide, den chief, scribe, librarian, quar-
    termaster, junior assistant Scoutmaster, chaplain aide, instructor,
    crew chief
    Varsity Scout team. Captain, cocaptain, program manager,
    squad leader, team secretary, librarian, quartermaster, chaplain
    aide, instructor, den chief

5. While a Life Scout, plan, develop, and give leadership to others in
    a service project helpful to any religious institution, any school, or
    your community. The project idea must be approved by your
    Scoutmaster and troop committee and approved by the council
    or district before you start. You must use the *Eagle Scout Service
    Project Workbook* in meeting this requirement.

6. Take part in a Scoutmaster conference.

Became an Eagle Scout on _____ / _____ / 19 ____ _____
Board of review initials

*You must choose only one merit badge listed in items *g* and *j*. If you have earned more
than one of the badges listed in items *g* and *j*, choose one and list the remaining badges
to make your total of 21.

EAGLE PALMS

After becoming an Eagle Scout, you may earn palms by completing the following requirements:

1. Be active in your troop and patrol for at least 3 months after
    becoming an Eagle Scout or after award of last palm.

2. Demonstrate Scout spirit by living the Scout Oath (Promise)
    and Scout Law in your everyday life.

3. Make a satisfactory effort to develop and demonstrate leadership ability. _____ _____

4. Earn five additional merit badges beyond those required for Eagle or last palm.* _____ _____

5. Take part in a Scoutmaster conference. _____ _____

Bronze palm

_____ merit badge _____ _____
_____ merit badge _____ _____
_____ merit badge _____ _____
_____ merit badge _____ _____
_____ merit badge _____ _____

Bronze palm earned on _____ / _____ /19____ _____
Board of review initials

Gold palm earned on _____ / _____ /19____ _____
Board of review initials

Silver palm earned on _____ / _____ /19____ _____
Board of review initials

You may wear only the proper combination of palms for the number of merit badges you earned beyond the rank of Eagle. The Bronze Palm represents five merit badges, the Gold Palm 10, and the Silver Palm 15.

*Merit badges earned any time since becoming a Boy Scout may be used to meet this requirement.

ADVANCEMENT FOR LONE SCOUTS

Lone Scouts are not generally registered with a Boy Scout troop and must rely on their lone friend and counselor for leadership and guidance. They cannot be expected to meet the specific advancement requirements in the same way a member of a troop does.

The Boy Scouts of America allows the Lone Scout's friend and counselor to suggest alternative requirements. This is important, since a boy cannot meet all the advancement requirements by reason of not being in a troop or patrol.

All such alternative requirements should be equal to the replaced requirement and be approved by the local council advancement committee. Any unequal or dissimilar requirement should be allowed only in extreme circumstances or when such like requirements could not be met without extreme hazard or hardship.

MERIT BADGES

Merit badges are a part of Scouting for two reasons. First, they encourage you to increase your skill in things you like to do. Second, they challenge you to try out new activities that may result in fresh interests or hobbies. One of these may even start you on the path to a career.

Picking a Merit Badge

Check the complete list of merit badges on pages 599–608 and choose a subject you like. If it is a badge that is required for the Eagle rank, you will find the requirements on pages 609–623. If not, you can find out how to earn the badge by reading the *Boy Scout Requirements* booklet. You may be able to borrow the booklet from your patrol or troop library.

Ask your Scoutmaster for the name of the person who is serving as counselor for the badge you want to earn. The merit badge counselor knows the subject well and is interested in helping Scouts learn all they can about it.

Earning a Merit Badge

These are the steps:

☆ Get a signed merit badge form from your Scoutmaster and find a buddy to accompany you at each meeting with a merit badge counselor. Your buddy can be another Scout, or be a parent or guardian, brother or sister, relative or friend.

☆ Get the merit badge pamphlet on your subject. Your patrol or troop may have one you can borrow. So may your library. You may also purchase one from your local council service center.

☆ Contact the merit badge counselor and explain that you would like to earn the badge. Along with your buddy, meet with the counselor and discuss how you can get the most out of the time you spend working on the badge.

☆ Learn and do the things that the pamphlet explains. Go as far as you can to fulfill the requirements on your own.

☆ When you are ready, you and your buddy make another appointment with your counselor. He will spend time with you going over the important points of the subject. A good counselor will also help you see beyond the requirements and discover ways to continue learning about the subject. If he is satisfied that you have completed the requirements, he will sign your merit badge form. If not, he will explain what you still must do.

☆ Give the signed form to your Scoutmaster. He will get the badge for you and present it to you during a troop ceremony.

CHAPTER 27

HOW TO WEAR MERIT BADGES

Up to six merit badges may be worn on the right sleeve of the long-sleeve shirt starting 3 inches from the bottom edge of the cuff in rows of two. No merit badges may be worn on the short-sleeve shirt. Merit badges also are worn on the merit badge sash.

AMERICAN BUSINESS
helps you understand the
free enterprise system.

AMERICAN CULTURES
is about customs
and traditions of others.

AMERICAN HERITAGE
helps you enjoy
our country's history.

AMERICAN LABOR
represents the work
force of our nation.

ANIMAL SCIENCE
leads you to explore farm
and animal production.

ARCHERY
helps you develop
skills for safe
and accurate shooting.

ARCHITECTURE
is the art and
science of planning
homes and buildings.

ART
can reflect the real
world or the world
of your imagination.

ASTRONOMY
is the study of
the universe.

ATHLETICS
tests your skill in
track and field.

ATOMIC ENERGY
is power for
many uses.

AUTO MECHANICS
helps you extend the life
of your car.

AVIATION
makes the world
a neighborhood for
business and pleasure.

BACKPACKING
is being ready
for outdoor adventures.

BASKETRY
is an ancient art
and skill in a
world of machines.

BIRD STUDY
can be fun for as
long as you live
wherever you live.

BUGLING
can make you the
man of the hour as
you sound the calls.

CAMPING
experience makes
outdoor living a
lot more fun.

CANOEING
can take you to
faraway places.

CHEMISTRY
is a part of the nature
of things; how they work
and what they do.

CINEMATOGRAPHY
lets you tell your
story on film.

CHAPTER 27

*CITIZENSHIP
IN THE COMMUNITY*
is where you work
with your neighbors.

*CITIZENSHIP
IN THE NATION*
is a birthright that is
yours to use wisely.

*CITIZENSHIP
IN THE WORLD*
helps you know that you
are a world citizen, too.

COIN COLLECTING
is a special interest that
can last a lifetime.

COLLECTIONS
play a major role
in career choices or
become lifetime hobbies.

COMMUNICATIONS
is how to get your
message to others.

COMPUTERS
make it possible to
condense and control
facts and figures.

COOKING
can be fun for the Scout
who learns how to
make tasty meals.

CYCLING
for fun and
transportation puts
you in the driver's
seat for safety.

DENTISTRY
shows you how to
care for your teeth.

*DISABILITIES
AWARENESS*
helps you know about
and work with
disabled persons.

DOG CARE
shows that a dog
deserves a master
who knows dogs.

DRAFTING
is the way we
transfer ideas about
making things.

ELECTRICITY
is an invisible force
that powers our
lights and appliances.

ELECTRONICS
applies magic to
electricity in doing
specialized work.

*EMERGENCY
PREPAREDNESS*
helps you to know
how to help
in times of trouble.

ENERGY
needs to be
conserved to keep
the world going.

ENGINEERING
is designing and
building the world's
largest structures.

*ENVIRONMENTAL
SCIENCE*
helps you know
the world around you.

FAMILY LIFE
allows us to touch
others' lives so that
everyone grows stronger.

FARM MECHANICS
helps you to know
how to care
for equipment.

FINGERPRINTING
is a natural means
of identification.
Prints are unique.

FIRE SAFETY
teaches fire prevention
and rescue.

FIRST AID
helps a Scout meet
serious emergencies.

CHAPTER 27

*FISH AND WILDLIFE
MANAGEMENT*
helps conserve our
outdoor friends.

FISHING
is always fun
because excitement
may hit at any time.

FORESTRY
helps us make the
best use of our
trees for many uses.

GARDENING
your own vegetables
can be done
almost anywhere.

GENEALOGY
helps you trace
your ancestry.

GEOLOGY
is for anyone who
wants to find out
about the earth's features.

GOLF
is the only game
where you are
your own "official."

GRAPHIC ARTS
is the way to spread
ideas and images.

HIKING
the trails of
adventure and fun.

HOME REPAIRS
will always require a
handyman around
the house.

HORSEMANSHIP
involves learning
how to ride and
care for horses.

INDIAN LORE
is the story
of our native
Americans.

INSECT STUDY
is about the familiar
and strange insects
that live near us.

JOURNALISM
searches for
stories that the public
should know about.

LANDSCAPE
ARCHITECTURE
visualizes and plans
for pleasing scenes.

LAW
helps you to know your
rights and responsibilities
as a citizen.

LEATHERWORK
skill helps you make
many useful things.

LIFESAVING
skills help you
make water rescues.

MAMMAL STUDY
helps you get to know
more outdoor friends.

MEDICINE
examines the history
and the practice of the
healing arts.

METALWORK
is using metals
to make useful
articles and tools.

MODEL DESIGN
AND BUILDING
includes land, air, space,
and water vehicles.

MOTORBOATING
can place you at
controls of excitement.

MUSIC
may be your thing
if you play an instrument
and can read music.

NATURE
helps you understand
the world around you.

OCEANOGRAPHY
takes you deep
into ocean life
and movement.

ORIENTEERING
is a fast-moving
sport with compass
in hand.

PAINTING
preserves and beautifies
the surface of things.

PERSONAL FITNESS
is a debt you owe
to yourself, your
mind and body.

*PERSONAL
MANAGEMENT*
helps you use your time
and money wisely.

PETS,
other than dogs,
require their own special
care from their owners.

PHOTOGRAPHY
is a skill in handling
equipment, and an
art in stopping time.

PIONEERING
makes use of primitive
building materials.

PLANT SCIENCE
helps you know
how plants
produce food.

PLUMBING
brings water in and
takes waste out
of our buildings.

POTTERY
provides the bowls, dishes,
and jars that
we use every day.

PUBLIC HEALTH
is guarded
by government
and informed citizens.

PUBLIC SPEAKING
helps you tell
your story to others.

PULP AND PAPER
provides us with
many things we
use every day.

RADIO
is a worldwide
hobby of operators,
young and old.

RAILROADING
hauls the freight and
captures the interest
of model builders.

READING
for fun and information
can give you a lifetime
of adventure.

*REPTILE AND
AMPHIBIAN STUDY*
is fascinating for some and
frightening for others.

RIFLE SHOOTING
trains your eye
and mind.

ROWING
a boat, so that it does
what you want it
to do, is fun.

SAFETY
first is the smart
way of doing
things anytime.

SALESMANSHIP
says opportunity
hides in every
selling situation.

SCHOLARSHIP
makes the best of
time and talent;
you have both.

SCULPTURE
is art in the
round or in relief,
and it is your creation.

SHOTGUN SHOOTING
is the big bang
in marksmanship.

SKATING
is fun and helps
keep you in shape.

SKIING
makes us think
snow even when
it's summertime.

SMALL-BOAT SAILING
can thrill you as
you try to catch
up with the wind.

SOIL AND WATER
CONSERVATION
must be followed,
or our future will be sad.

SPACE EXPLORATION
is exploring the
last frontier.

SPORTS
can last a lifetime
and help keep you
in good condition.

STAMP COLLECTING
helps you become
a better citizen.

SURVEYING
marks the boundaries
of land sections.

SWIMMING
is one of the
sports to enjoy
throughout your lifetime.

TEXTILE
includes natural and
synthetic fibers
for many uses.

THEATER
can be a way to
understand another person
by playing a role.

TRAFFIC SAFETY
is important in
your everyday life.

*TRUCK
TRANSPORTATION*
moves the country's
goods.

VETERINARY MEDICINE
can lead you into
a career of animal care.

WATER SKIING
is as exciting
as it looks;
learn the fundamentals.

WEATHER
forecasting isn't perfect,
but it's getting
better every day.

WHITEWATER
is excitement
with safety.

*WILDERNESS
SURVIVAL*
skills are important
to every outdoor activity.

WOOD CARVING
is creative expression
in design and form.

WOODWORK
is for carpenters,
cabinetmakers, and
home handymen.

CHAPTER 27

MERIT BADGE REQUIREMENTS
FOR BADGES REQUIRED FOR EAGLE

Camping

1. Make a layout of a typical patrol campsite. Show cooking spots, dining fly, latrine, and at least three two-man tents. Explain how and why weather, season, and water supply are considered when choosing a site. Explain what care to take with regard to safe water, sanitary facilities, and emergencies.
2. Make a written plan for getting to and from a camping spot on foot or by vehicle.
3. Make a chart showing how a typical patrol is organized for an overnight campout. List assignments for each member.
4. Prepare a list of clothing you would need for an overnight campout in:
   (a) Summer
   (b) Winter
   Discuss the kinds of footwear for different kinds of weather. Explain care of the feet.
5. Describe four kinds of tents. Cite their good and bad points.
6. Prepare for an overnight campout with your patrol by doing the following:*
   (a) Make a checklist of personal and patrol gear that will be needed.
   (b) Prepare a camp menu that is right for the time of year. Give recipes. Make a food list for your patrol. List foods you can get from your grocery store. Supplies should be lightweight, though some canned foods may be used. Plan two breakfasts, three lunches, and two suppers.
   (c) Pack your own gear and your share of the patrol gear and food for proper carrying. Protect it against bad weather. Show that your pack is right for getting what's needed first, and that it has been assembled properly for comfort, weight, balance, size, and neatness. Explain how the

rest of the patrol gear and food is divided among members.
   (d) Show the right way to pack your full gear on a pack frame. Use a diamond hitch or other good hitch.
7. Complete the following while on an overnight campout:
   (a) Present yourself with your pack for inspection. Be correctly clothed and equipped for an overnight camping trip.
   (b) Working with another Scout, pitch a two-man tent. Consider weather and terrain. On this campsite, where allowed, make a latrine for your patrol. (Where not allowed, as in state parks, etc., describe how to build it.)
   (c) Make a comfortable ground bed. Use it for 2 nights. Use ground cloth and padding of clothing, pack, grass, leaves, or straw.
   (d) Where it's allowed, build up a fireplace area of nonburnable soil. Show proper use of woods tools in getting and preparing fuel for a cooking fire. Show how you would get, prepare, and protect your wood on a rainy day. Show how you would prepare a meal properly when it's raining.
   (e) Build three kinds of top-of-the-ground fires. Use charcoal for one. Show how to put out a fire properly. (Where open fires cannot be used, show how to build the fires, but don't light them.)
   (f) Show the right way to protect your camp, including food and gear, against animals, insects, and wet or bad weather. Discuss how you would protect yourself against all kinds of weather if caught out on the trail with only a pocketknife.
   (g) Strike camp. Fold or roll your tent for packing. Pack all gear. Leave a clean camp. Show the right way to get rid of garbage and rubbish.
8. Show experience in camping by doing the following:
   (a) Camp out a total of at least 20 days and 20 nights. Sleep each night under the sky or under a tent you have pitched. (You may use a week of summer camp as a part of the 20 days and 20 nights.)

*May be part of a troop trip.

(b) On one of these camping trips, hike 1½ miles or more each way to and from your campsite. Pack your own gear plus your share of patrol gear and food.

(c) Serve as one of the cooks for your patrol for at least five meals prepared in camp.

9. Discuss how the things you did to earn this badge have taught you personal health and safety, survival, public health, conservation, and good citizenship.

Citizenship in the Community

1. Describe your community to your counselor giving:
   (a) Short history
   (b) Cultures and ethnic groups
   (c) Major places of employment
   What is the future of your community?

2. Mark or point out on a map of your community the following:
   (a) Chief government buildings
   (b) Fire station, police station, and hospital nearest your home
   (c) Schools, churches, and synagogues near your home
   (d) Main highways to neighboring cities and towns
   (e) Nearest railroads and bus stations and airport, if any
   (f) Chief industries or other major places of employment
   (g) Historical and other interesting points

3. Do the following:
   (a) Chart the organization of your local or state government. Show the top offices and tell which are elected or appointed.
   (b) Name the political parties in your community government and list four persons active in the politics of your community and what positions they hold.

4. Attend ONE:
   (a) County or parish board meeting
   (b) City council meeting
   (c) School board meeting
   (d) Municipal, county, or state court session

5. After visiting the governmental meeting, obtain a copy of that body's published

budget. Review the major sources of income and expenses for its operation with your counselor.

6. List the services your community provides to the citizens in return for the taxes paid by you and your parents.

7. Select a city, county, or school problem or issue under consideration from the local newspaper or news broadcast and write a letter expressing your views to the mayor, administrator, or school board president. Show this letter and any response to your counselor.

8. List and describe the work of five volunteer organizations through which people in your community work together for the good of your community.

9. Tell how to report an accident or an emergency in your community.

10. List five ways you can demonstrate good citizenship in your community, religious institution, school, or Scouting unit.

Citizenship in the Nation

1. After reading, discuss with your counselor the following documents:
   (a) Declaration of Independence
   (b) Preamble to the Constitution
   (c) Constitution
   (d) Bill of Rights
   (e) Amendments to the Constitution

2. Name the three branches of government and explain their functions. Explain the checks and balances on each branch of government.

3. Outline the relationships between state and federal governments.

4. Do ONE of the following:
   (a) Visit the National Capitol.
   (b) Visit your state capitol.
   (c) Tour a federal installation.
   Explain your experiences to your counselor.

5. Name your two senators and the congressman from your congressional district. Write a letter to one of these elected officials on a national issue sharing your view with him or her. Show your letter and any response to your counselor.

6. What are five important functions of your national government? Explain how these functions affect your family and local community.
7. Discuss the main ways by which our federal government is financed.

Citizenship in the World

1. Answer the following:
   (a) What is citizenship? How does one become a citizen in the United States? How does one become a citizen in other countries?
   (b) What rights, duties, and obligations does an American citizenship entail? How are these similar to or different from the way citizenship is experienced in two other countries?
2. Do the following:
   (a) Discuss the concept of national interest.
   (b) Explain how a country's security, economy, and values relate to its national interest.
3. Explain ONE of the following to your counselor:
   (a) How communications and transportation have changed relationships between countries
   (b) How changing national interests, democratic values, and global economic partnerships are affecting the relationships between countries
4. Do the following:
   (a) Tell how the geography, natural resources, and climate of a country affect its economy.
   (b) Using a map of the world, select two countries. Describe how geography, natural resources, and climate are important in defining each country's national interest. Explain how these interests affect relations with at least two other countries.
5. Do the following:
   (a) Explain international law and how it differs from national law. What role does international law perform in the international system? Describe how international law can be used as a tool for conflict resolution.

(b) Select TWO of the following global issues and explain how they have been affected by international agreements and treaties:
(1) Environmentalism
(2) Terrorism
(3) International trade
(4) Communications
(5) Transportation
(6) Famine relief
(7) Disease control
(8) International sports
(c) Select TWO of the following organizations and describe their role in the international system:
(1) The United Nations
(2) The World Court
(3) World Organization of the Scout Movement
(4) The World Health Organization
(5) Amnesty International
(6) The International Red Cross
(7) Americas Watch
(8) CARE
6. Do the following:
   (a) Explain to your counselor what is meant by
   (1) International trade agreement
   (2) Foreign exchange
   (3) Balance of payments
   (4) Tariffs
   (5) Free trade
   (b) Explain how world trade and global competition affect the economy of your state and your community.
   (c) (1) Locate the listing of foreign currency exchange rates in the financial section of a newspaper. Select three major foreign currencies and explain the rates of exchange between these currencies and the American dollar.
   (2) Select a foreign currency and price a product in that currency. Explain how fluctuations in currency exchange rates affect the price of that product if you are exporting it from the United States. Explain how fluctuations in currency exchange rates affect the price of that product if you are importing it into the United States.
7. Do the following:
   (a) Discuss the differences between constitutional and non-constitutional governments.

(b) Name at least five different types of government currently in power in the world.

(c) Show on a world map countries that use each of these five different forms of government.

8. Do the following:

(a) Explain how a government is represented abroad. How is the United States government accredited to international organizations?

(b) Describe the roles of the following in the conduct of foreign relations:

(1) Ambassador

(2) Consul

(3) United States Information Agency

(4) Agency for International Development

(5) Foreign Commercial Service

(c) Explain the purpose of a passport and visa for international travel.

9. Do ONE of the following:

(a) Attend a world jamboree.

(b) Take part in an international event in your area.

(c) Visit with a foreign exchange student and discuss his or her country and customs.

(d) Study a foreign language for a year.

(e) Write an embassy or consulate for material about its country and discuss the material with your counselor.

(f) Examine a particular international issue and give a brief oral presentation and a written report to your counselor.

Communications

1. Develop a plan to teach a skill. Have it approved by your counselor. Then, create and make teaching aids. Carry out your plan. With the counselor, check to see if the learner has learned.

2. Pick an item or product. It may be real or imagined. Build a sales plan based on its good points. Try to "sell" the counselor on buying it from you. Talk with the counselor about how well you did in telling about the item and the wisdom of buying it.

3. Show how you would make a telephone call inviting someone who is an expert (in the field of your choice) to give a demonstration on their skill to your unit.

4. Do the following:

(a) Write a 5-minute speech. Give it at a meeting of a group.

(b) Show how to introduce a guest speaker.

5. Attend a town meeting where two or three points of view are being given. Record what you hear. Make a report from your notes. Tell your troop or patrol what you think you heard.

6. Plan a troop court of honor or campfire program. Give it to the patrol leaders' council for approval. Write the script. Prepare the program for reproduction. Act as master of ceremonies.

7. Prepare an autobiographical résumé that you would use in applying for a job.

8. Check careers in the field of communications. Prepare a statement on the one you like. Talk it over with your counselor.

Emergency Preparedness

1. Earn First Aid merit badge.

2. Do the following:

(a) Tell what you would do to prevent injury and possible loss of life to yourself and others in each of the following emergencies: fire or explosion at home and in a public building, car stalled in blizzard or desert, motor vehicle accident, mountain accident, food poisoning, boating accident, search for lost person, lost or marooned group, gas leak, earthquake, flood, tornado or hurricane, atomic emergency, and avalanche (snow or rock).

(b) Show that you know what to do in at least TWO of the above.

3. Show how you could safely save a person from the following:

(a) Touching a live electric wire

(b) A room with carbon monoxide or other fumes or smoke

(c) Clothes on fire

(d) Drowning using nonswimming rescues (including ice accidents).

4. Tell the things a group of Scouts should be prepared to do, the training needed, and the safety precautions to be taken for the following emergency service:
(a) Crowd and traffic control
(b) Messenger service and communication
(c) Collection and distribution services
(d) Group feeding, shelter, and sanitation.

5. Take part in an emergency service project, either real or a practice drill.

6. Show three ways of attracting and communicating with rescue planes.

7. With another person, show a good way to move an injured person out of a remote and rugged area, conserving the energy of the rescuers.

8. Do the following:
(a) Prepare a written plan for mobilizing your troop when needed to do emergency service. If there is a plan, explain it. Tell your part in making it work.
(b) Take part in at least one troop mobilization. Describe your part.
(c) Show the personal "emergency pack" which you have prepared to be ready for a mobilization call. Show a family kit (suitcase or box) for use by your family in case an emergency evacuation is needed. Explain the need.

9. Show proper use of ropes and lines for rescue work by doing the following:
(a) Tie knots for joining lines. Tie knots for shortening or adjusting lines. Tie knots for lashings.
(b) Lower a person from a height sufficient to show how.
(c) Coil and accurately throw light and heavy 50-foot heaving lines.

Environmental Science

1. Explain the meaning of the following: ecology, biosphere, ecosystem, plant succession, limiting factor. Give an example of each.

2. With the help of your counselor, pick an area of 10 acres* for study.

3. Visit the area four times for 2 hours each time. Do this at different times on one day a week for a month, or if at camp, on four different days of the week at different times of the day.
(a) Record the temperature, rain, and wind.
(b) List the animals you saw. Tell what they were doing.
(c) List the plants you saw.
(d) Name the kinds of rocks and soil.

4. Write about your study in 500 words or more showing:
(a) How the climate, topography, and geology have influenced the number and kinds of plants and animals.
(b) How the living and nonliving elements are interrelated.
(c) Why it is important that people understand this.

5. With your counselor, plan and carry out a project in ONE of the following:
(a) The effect of water-holding capacity of soil on plant life. The relation of plant cover to runoff. How both are related to the water and oxygen cycles.
(b) The influence of land plant life on temperature, light intensity, wind velocity, and humidity. The influence of water plant life on the water environment. How both land and water plants affect animal life.

6. Make a report, in the form of a short talk to a Scout group, on what you did in requirement 5.

7. Show you understand the following:
(a) The causes of water pollution. Tell what it does to rivers and lakes.
(b) The causes of land pollution. Tell what it does to the environment.
(c) The causes of air pollution. Tell what it does to the environment.
(d) How some chemicals get into the tissues of animals miles from where they were used.

8. Describe what you and others can do to help solve a local problem of air pollution, water pollution, or litter.

9. Describe the duties of three positions in environmental science.

*City Scouts may pick an area in a large park, if a better place is not available.

Family Life

1. Prepare an outline and discuss with your merit badge counselor what a family is and how the actions of one member can affect other members.

2. List 10 reasons why you are important to your family. Review these points with your parents or guardians and with your merit badge counselor.

3. Prepare a list of your regular home duties or chores (at least five) and do them for 90 days. Keep a record of how often you do each of them.

4. With the approval of your parents/guardians and your merit badge counselor, decide on and carry out a project that you would do around the house that would benefit the family. Submit a report to your merit badge counselor outlining how the project benefited the family.

5. Plan and carry out a project that involves the participation of your family. After carrying out the project, discuss the following with your merit badge counselor:
(a) The objective or goal of the project
(b) How individual members of your family participated
(c) The results of the project

6. Do the following:
(a) Discuss with your merit badge counselor how to plan and carry out a family discussion.
(b) After this discussion, plan and carry out a family discussion to include the following subjects:
(1) How to avoid the use of drugs and drug abuse
(2) Understanding the growing-up process, how the body changes, and making responsible decisions dealing with sex
(3) Personal and family finances

First Aid

1. Satisfy your counselor that you have current knowledge of all first aid requirements for Tenderfoot, Second Class, and First Class ranks.

2. Do the following:
(a) Explain how you would obtain emergency medical assistance from your home, on a wilderness camping trip, and during an activity on open water.
(b) Prepare a first aid kit for your home. Display and discuss its contents with your counselor.

3. Do the following:
(a) Explain what action you should take for someone who shows signs of a heart attack.
(b) Identify the conditions that must exist before performing CPR on a person.
(c) Demonstrate proper technique in performing CPR on an adult manikin for 3 minutes.
(d) Show the steps that need to be taken for someone suffering from a severe laceration on the leg and on the wrist. Tell the dangers in the use of a tourniquet and the conditions under which its use is justified.
(e) Explain when a bee sting could be life threatening and what action should be taken for prevention and for first aid.
(f) Explain the symptoms of heat stroke and what action needs to be taken for first aid and for prevention.

4. Do the following:
(a) Describe the signs of a broken bone. Show first aid procedures for handling fractures, including open (compound) fractures of the forearm, wrist, upper leg, and lower leg using improvised materials.
(b) Describe the symptoms and possible complications and demonstrate proper procedures for treating suspected injuries to the back, neck, and head. Explain what measures can be taken to reduce the possibility of further complicating these injuries.

5. Describe the symptoms, proper first aid procedures, and possible prevention measures for the following conditions:

(a) Hypothermia
(b) Convulsions
(c) Frostbite
(d) Bruises, strains, sprains
(e) Burns
(f) Abdominal pain
(g) Broken, chipped, or loosened tooth
(h) Knocked out tooth
(i) Muscle cramps

6. Do the following:
(a) If a sick or injured person must be moved, tell how you would determine the best method.
(b) With helpers under your supervision, improvise a stretcher and move a presumably unconscious person.

7. Teach another Scout a first aid skill selected by your counselor.

Lifesaving

1. Before doing requirements 2–15
(a) Earn the Swimming merit badge.
(b) Swim 400 yards.

2. Explain
(a) Safe Swim Defense and Safety Afloat
(b) The order of methods in water rescue

3. Show reaching rescues using such things as arms, legs, branches, sticks, towels, shirts, paddles, and poles.

4. Show rescues using items that can be thrown, such as lines, ring buoys, rescue bags, and free-floating supports.

5. Show or explain the use of rowboats, canoes, and other small craft in making rescues.

6. With a helper and a practice victim, show a line rescue both as tender and as rescuer. Perform the rescue with the practice victim approximately thirty feet from the tender. Use a 100-foot length of ⁵⁄₁₆-inch line.

7. Show that you can remove street clothes* on shore (except underwear or swim trunks) in 20 seconds or less. Explain the importance of disrobing before a swimming rescue.

8. Explain the importance of avoiding contact with a victim; explain "lead" and

"wait" tactics; and explain why equipment should be used in a swimming rescue.

9. Swim 30 feet and make the correct approach to a tired swimmer. Move him 30 feet to safety using the following:
(a) Underarm swim-along
(b) Two-person assist

10. Make rescues on a practice victim 30 feet from shore, using the correct entry and a strong approach stoke, and bringing the victim back to pier or poolside, using
(a) A rescue tube or torpedo buoy
(b) A shirt, towel, or other equipment
(c) A front approach and wrist tow
(d) A rear approach and single armpit tow
(e) A rear approach and single armpit tow, changing to the cross-chest carry
Discuss the different methods for removing a victim from the water. Choose the appropriate method for your situation. Remove the practice victim from the water and place in position for resuscitation.

11. Show in deep water your defense against grasps by blocking and escaping. Free yourself from a wrist hold, rear head-hold, and a front head-hold.

12. Make four surface dives in 8 to 10 feet of water. Retrieve an object on each of the first three dives. Bring up a 10-pound weight on the fourth dive.

13. Show search techniques as part of a lost-swimmer drill. Discuss search techniques using mask, fins, and snorkel (not scuba).

14. Do the following:
(a) Identify the conditions that must exist before performing CPR on a person, and explain how such conditions are recognized.
(b) Demonstrate proper technique for performing CPR on an adult mannequin for at least 3 minutes.

15. Demonstrate proper management of a spinal injury by
(a) Explaining the signs and symptoms of a spinal injury
(b) Supporting a faceup victim in calm, shallow water
(c) Turning a person from a facedown to a faceup position while maintaining support

*"Street clothes" means low shoes, socks, underwear (or trunks), pants, belt, and long-sleeve shirt. A jacket, sweater, or sweatshirt also may be worn.

Personal Fitness

If meeting any of the requirements for this merit badge is against the Scout's religious convictions, it does not have to be done if the boy's parents and the proper church officials state in writing that

- To do so would be against religious convictions.
- The parents accept full responsibility for anything that might happen because of such exemption. They release the Boy Scouts of America from any responsibility.

1. (a) Before you try to meet any other requirements, have your physician give you a thorough examination. He or she is to use the Scout medical examination form. Describe the examination. Tell what questions you were asked about health. Tell what recommendations your doctor made. Report what you have done about them. Explain the following:
   (1) Why physical exams are important
   (2) Why preventative habits are important in maintaining good health
   (3) Diseases that can be prevented and how
   (4) The seven warning signs of cancer
   (b) Have an examination made by your dentist. Get a statement saying that your teeth have been checked and cared for. Tell how to care for your teeth.

2. Explain to your merit badge counselor verbally or in writing what personal fitness means to you, including
   (a) Components of personal fitness.
   (b) Reasons for being fit in all components.
   (c) What it means to be mentally healthy.
   (d) What it means to be physically healthy and fit.
   (e) What it means to be socially healthy. Discuss several healthy social traits.
   (f) What you can do to prevent social, emotional, or mental problems.

3. From the *Personal Fitness* merit badge pamphlet, answer the questions titled "Evaluating Your Personal Fitness" and list several signs of poor personal fitness. Describe your activity in the eight areas listed.

4. With your counselor answer and discuss the following questions:
   (a) Are you free from all curable diseases? Are you living in such a way that your risk of preventable diseases is minimized?
   (b) Are you immunized and vaccinated according to the advice of your family and school physicians?
   (c) Do you understand the meaning of a nutritious diet and know why it is important for you? Does your diet include foods from all food groups?
   (d) Is your body weight and composition what you would like it to be and do you know how to modify it safely through exercise, diet, and behavior modification?
   (e) Do you carry out daily activities without noticeable effort? Do you have extra energy for other activities?
   (f) Are you free from habits relating to nutrition and the use of alcohol, tobacco, drugs, and other practices that could be harmful to your health?
   (g) Do you participate in a regular exercise program or recreational activities?
   (h) Do you sleep well at night and wake up feeling refreshed and energized for the new day?
   (i) Are you actively involved in the religious organization of your choice and do you participate in their youth activities?
   (j) Do you spend quality time with your family and friends in social and recreational activities?
   (k) Do you support family activities and efforts to maintain a good home life?

5. Explain the following about physical fitness:
   (a) The components of physical fitness
   (b) Your weakest and strongest component of physical fitness
   (c) The need to have a balance in all four components of physical fitness
   (d) How the components of personal fitness relate to the Scout Laws and Scout Oath

6. Explain the following about nutrition:
   (a) The importance of good nutrition
   (b) What good nutrition means to you
   (c) How good nutrition is related to the other components of personal fitness
   (d) The three components of a sound weight (fat) control program

7. From the *Personal Fitness* merit badge pamphlet, perform the physical fitness test (chapter 8) with your patrol leader,

Scoutmaster, parent, or adviser before doing the next two requirements. Be evaluated above the 50th percentile in the aerobic endurance test, flexibility test, and muscular strength test.

Aerobic Endurance Test

There are several tests that can be used. They are the 9- or 12-minute run and the 1- or 1½-mile run. In the timed run, the objective is to run as far as you can in the allotted time (9 or 12 minutes). In the distance run, the objective is to run the given distance (1 or 1½ miles) in the shortest time. Walking is permitted but the Scouts should not stop. If they need to stop running, they should walk until they can continue to run.

Flexibility Test

By using the sit-and-reach test, boys should remove their shoes and sit down facing the sit-and-reach box with knees fully extended and flat on the floor with feet up against the end of the board. The arms are extended forward with the hands placed on top of each other with palms down. The boy bends at the hips and reaches forward along the measuring scale four times. Record the farthest reach.

Muscular Strength Test

Using timed sit-ups, the boy lies on his back with his knees flexed, feet on the floor, and heels 12 to 18 inches from the buttocks. The arms are crossed on the chest with the hands on the opposite shoulders. The feet are held by partners to keep them in touch with the floor. The boy curls to the sitting position until the elbows touch the thighs. Arms must remain on the chest and the chin remains tucked on the chest. The number of sit-ups that the boy can correctly do in 60 seconds is the score.

8. Outline a 4-week physical fitness program using the results of your physical fitness tests. Use the guidelines in chapter 8 to write your program. Use exercises to develop aerobic endurance, upper body muscular strength, and flexibility of the lower back and legs. Have the program approved by your Scoutmaster or adviser and your parents.

(a) Fulfill requirement 1 for this merit badge.

(b) Complete one of the four aerobic endurance tests, the flexibility test, the muscular strength and endurance test, and the body composition measurements.

(c) Fill in your results on the record sheet and chart your percentile ranks for each test (using the norms found in the appendix) on the progress chart.

(d) Determine the types of exercises you want or need to do, the amount of time you have to exercise, and the equipment or facilities that are available for your use.

(e) If muscular strength exercises are to be a part of your program, determine how many push-ups and pull-ups you can do.

(f) Use the guidelines discussed in the text concerning cardiovascular endurance, flexibility, and muscular strength and endurance to determine the frequency, intensity, and duration of your exercises.

(g) Write your exercise program out for each day of the week on a sheet of paper. Have it approved by your adviser or Scoutmaster and parents.

(h) Retest yourself after 2 full weeks of exercising. Also retest for the number of pull-ups and push-ups you can do. Record the results of this test on the record sheet and graph the percentile ranks on the progress chart.

(i) Retest yourself after another 2 full weeks of exercising and record your results on the record sheet and progress chart.

9. Carry out the physical fitness program you wrote in requirement 7. Keep a log of all your exercises (i.e., how long you exercised; how far you ran, swam, or biked; how many exercises you did; your exercise heart rate; etc.). Test yourself again after two weeks of exercise on the information sheets provided in this book. Compare improvements. Describe your experience.

10. Describe your long-term plans regarding your personal fitness.

Personal Management

1. Talk over with parents or guardian how family funds are spent to meet day-to-day and long-term needs. Tell how you can help with the family budget.

2. Make a budget for yourself for 90 days. Keep a record of income and expenses for that period. Review it and report.

3. Help to choose and buy family groceries for 1 month. Make a report of what you learned.
4. Explain the possible use, advantages, and risks in using $100 in each of the following ways. Tell how it might help you and others.
   (a) Hide it in a mattress.
   (b) Put it into a savings account at a bank or savings and loan association. (Explain the difference.)
   (c) Buy a bicycle.
   (d) Open a checking account.
   (e) Buy a U.S. Savings Bond.
   (f) Buy a power mower or paint sprayer.
   (g) Invest in a mutual fund.
   (h) Start a life insurance policy.
   (i) Buy fishing gear.
   (j) Buy common stock.
5. Talk about things you would like to do within the next 90 days. Tell how you plan to get these done. After 90 days, tell what you did. Tell how you did them.
6. Tell how important credit and installment buying are to our economy and the individual and the family. Visit an officer of a bank or credit department of a store. Find out and tell what you must do to establish a "good credit rating." Tell what it means to you now and in the future.
7. Check out jobs or career opportunities through interviews or reading. Tell what the "next step" would be to prepare yourself for one of these careers.

Safety

1. Prepare a notebook to include:
   (a) Newspaper and other stories showing common kinds and causes of accidents in the home.
   (b) Newspaper and other stories showing common kinds of crimes against families like yours.
   (c) Facts you have obtained concerning the frequency of accidents and of crimes involving families in your locality.
   (d) A paragraph or more written by you explaining how your family life could be changed by serious fire, accident, or crime.
   (e) A list of safe practices and safety

devices currently used in your home and automobile.
2. Do the following:
   (a) Using a safety checklist approved by your counselor, make an inspection of your home. Explain the hazards found and how they can be corrected.
   (b) Review or develop your family's plan of escape in case of fire in your home.
3. Do the following:
   (a) Discuss with your counselor how you contribute to the safety of yourself, your family, and your community.
   (b) Show your family members how to protect themselves and your home from accidents, fire, theft, robbery, and assault.
4. Show your family exits you would use from different public buildings (such as church, theater, municipal building, library, supermarket, shopping center) in the event of an emergency. Teach your family what to do in the event of a panic.
5. Make a plan for accident prevention programs for five family activities outside the home (such as church, theater, picnic, beach, travel). Each plan should include an analysis of possible hazards, proposed action to correct hazards, and reasons for the correction you propose.
6. Plan and complete a safety project approved by your counselor in your home, school, church, or community.

Sports

1. Explain sportsmanship. Tell why it is important. Give several examples of good sportsmanship in sports. Relate at least one of these to everyday citizenship off the sports field.
2. Take part for one full season as a member of an organized team in ONE of the following sports: baseball, basketball, bowling, cross country, diving, fencing, field hockey, football, golf, gymnastics, ice hockey, lacrosse, rugby, skating (ice or roller), soccer, softball, swimming, team handball, tennis, track and field, volleyball, water polo, and wrestling. (Or any other recognized team sport approved in

advance by your counselor, except boxing and karate.)

3. Take part in ONE of the following sports on a competitive basis in two organized meets or tournaments: archery, badminton, bait or fly casting, bowling, canoeing, cycling, diving, fencing, fishing, golf, gymnastics, handball, horsemanship, horseshoes, judo, orienteering, paddleball, rifle or shotgun shooting, sailing, skating (ice or roller), skiing, swimming, table tennis, tennis, track and field, waterskiing, and wrestling. (Or any other recognized sport approved in advance by your counselor, except boxing and karate.)*

4. Make a set of training rules for the sports you picked. Tell why these rules are important. Follow these rules. Design exercises for these sports. Keep a record of how you do in these sports for one season. Show how you have improved.

5. Show proper techniques in your two picked sports.

6. Explain the attributes of a good team leader and a good team player.

7. Draw diagrams of the playing areas for your two sports.

8. Explain the rules and etiquette for your two sports. List the equipment needed. Describe the protective equipment. Tell why it is needed. Tell what it does.

*This cannot be the same sport used to meet requirement 2.

Swimming

1. Successfully complete the BSA swimmer test. Explain how the Safe Swim Defense plan is used to protect Scout troops and other groups when they are swimming.

2. Swim continuously for 150 yards using the following strokes in good form and in a strong manner: sidestroke for 50 yards, elementary backstroke for 50 yards, front crawl or trudgen for 25 yards, and either the breaststroke or back crawl for 25 yards.

3. In water over your head, but not to exceed 10 feet, do each of the following:

(a) Use the feetfirst method of surface diving and bring an object up from the bottom.

(b) Do a headfirst surface dive, pike, or tuck, and bring the object up again.

(c) Do a headfirst surface dive to a depth of at least 5 feet and swim underwater for 3 strokes. Come to the surface, take a breath, and repeat the sequence twice.

4. In water at least 8 feet deep, show a headfirst dive from a dock or pool deck. Show a long shallow dive, also from the dock or pool deck. If a low board (not to exceed 40 inches above water at least 9 feet deep) is available, show a plain front dive.

5. Enter water over your head wearing clothes (shoes and socks, underwear or swim trunks, long pants, belt, long-sleeved shirt). Remove the shoes and socks. Inflate the shirt and show that you can float using the shirt for support. Remove the pants and use them for support while floating. Swim 50 yards using inflated clothing for support. **(Note:** If the bottom surface of the swimming area is dark or objects can not be seen easily, practice removing shoes and socks in neck-deep water, then leave shoes and socks on land or in a protected area to prevent loss, and demonstrate the above.)

6. Do the following:

(a) Float faceup in a resting position as nearly motionless as possible for at least a minute.

(b) While wearing a properly fitted personal flotation device (PFD), demonstrate the "HELP" and "huddle" positions. Explain their purpose.

(c) In warm water (at least 70°F or 21°C), show survival floating. If water is cooler than 70°F, discuss the purpose, technique, and limitations of survival floating.

7. Do the following:

(a) Demonstrate rescuing a person from water by reaching with an arm or leg, by reaching with a suitable object, and by throwing lines and objects.

(b) Explain why swimming rescues should not be attempted when a reaching or throwing assist or boat rescue can be done instead. Explain why and how a person making a swimming rescue should avoid contact with the victim.

SCOUTING OPPORTUNITIES

POSITIONS OF RESPONSIBILITY

MOST boys who have had a happy Boy Scouting experience want to help the younger boys who are following in their footsteps have just as much Scouting fun as they had. You can be a great influence in the lives of this next generation of Scouts by offering your services to your troop for leadership in troop activities or by serving in one of the positions of responsibility illustrated by the badges below.

If you have shown that you are a real leader, the Scouts in your patrol may choose you as patrol leader. Or you may be elected the senior patrol leader.

DEN CHIEF

WEBELOS
DEN CHIEF

SPECIAL OPPORTUNITIES

Below are some of the awards you can earn. Requirements are outlined in *Boy Scout Requirements* or on the application forms.

Snorkeling, BSA. You can earn this award by completing the requirements on the application form.

Mile Swim, BSA. You can earn this award by completing the requirements outlined in the *Swimming* merit badge pamphlet, including swimming 1 mile.

BSA Lifeguard. If you hold the Swimming, Lifesaving, and Rowing merit badges you can earn this badge. You do it by meeting the further tests outlined on the application form.

Hornaday Award and badge. These awards go to Scouts who have done exceptional and distinguished service in conservation. If you desire to make an extra effort toward saving our natural resources, aim for this award. Get an application for it at your local council service center.

World Conservation Award. You can get this by earning Environmental Science, Citizenship in the World, and either Soil and Water Conservation or Fish and Wildlife Management merit badges.

WORLD CONSERVATION AWARD

PAUL BUNYAN WOODSMAN

DEN CHIEF SERVICE AWARD

Interpreter. To earn an interpreter strip, you must be able to carry on a conversation in a foreign language or in sign language, write a letter in the foreign language (not required for signing), and translate orally and in writing.

50-Miler Award. You earn this award by taking part in a troop event involving a wilderness trip. You go on foot, by canoe, or by boat. The trip must cover 50 consecutive miles over at least 5 consecutive days. On the trail you must do service projects to improve the environment.

WORLD CREST

Historic Trails Award. For this award, you must work with other members of your troop to locate a historic trail or site. You must also find out about its significance. You must then hike to camp 2 days and 1 night along the trail or near the site. You finish the tests by working with a group of adults. You help them mark and restore the trail or site.

Paul Bunyan Woodsman. If you like axmanship, this award is for you. You must have earned the Totin' Chip and helped a Scout to earn his. You must show your skill with a three-quarter ax or a saw and do a forestry job. You must also teach other Scouts how to use woods tools.

Den Chief Service Award. A special recognition given to den chiefs who complete certain service and training requirements.

World Crest. This crest may be worn by all members as an expression of world brotherhood.

RELIGIOUS EMBLEMS

"A Scout is reverent." All Scouts show this by being faithful in their duty to God. Some go further and give special service. This may qualify them for a religious emblem. Such an emblem is not a Scouting award. It is conferred on a Scout by his religious leader. Each faith has its own requirements for earning its emblem. Listed below are the emblems and where to find out about them. Before writing, check with your religious leader.

Ad Altare Dei. Roman Catholic—local council service center or diocesan Scout office.

Alpha Omega. Eastern Orthodox—PRAY, Box 6900, St. Louis, MO 63123.

Ararat. Armenian—Youth Director, Diocese of the Armenian Church of America, 630 Second Avenue, New York, NY 10016.

Bog I Ojczyzna. Polish National Catholic—Mr. Arthur Wyglon, 115 Heather Hill Drive, West Seneca, NY 14224.

God and Country. Baptist—local council service center or PRAY, Box 6900, St. Louis, MO 63123.

God and Country. Episcopal—local council service center or PRAY, Box 6900, St. Louis, MO 63123.

God and Country. First Church of Christ, Scientist—PRAY, Box 6900, St. Louis, MO 63123.

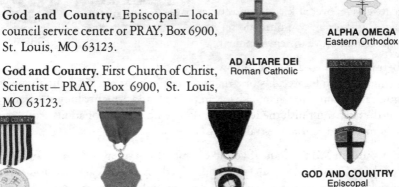

AD ALTARE DEI
Roman Catholic

ALPHA OMEGA
Eastern Orthodox

GOD AND COUNTRY
Episcopal

GOD AND COUNTRY
Moravian

IN THE NAME OF GOD
Islamic

GOD AND COUNTRY
Baptist

GOD AND COUNTRY
Protestant

GOD AND COUNTRY
First Church of Christ, Scientist

GOOD LIFE
Zoroastrian

GOD AND THE SALVATION ARMY
The Salvation Army

LIGHT IS LIFE
stern Rite Catholic

LIGHT OF GOD
Association of Unity Churches

LIVING FAITH
Lutheran

BOG I OJCZYZNA
Polish National Catholic

LIAHONA
Reorganized Church of Jesus Christ
of Latter Day Saints

ARARAT
Armenian

RELIGION IN LIFE
Unitarian Universalist

NER TAMID
Jewish

God and Country. Moravian—The Moravian Church, Drawer Y, Winston-Salem, NC 27108.

God and Country. Protestant—local council service center or PRAY, Box 6900, St. Louis, MO 63123.

God and The Salvation Army. The Salvation Army, 120 West 14th Street, New York, NY 10011.

Good Life. Zoroastrian—Zoroastrian Association, c/o Fred Morris, 117 Madie Avenue, Spotswood, NJ 08884.

Good Servant. Churches of Christ—Members of Churches of Christ for Scouting, ACU Station, Box 7618, Abilene, TX 79699.

In the Name of God. Islamic—Islamic Committee on Scouting, 130 East 40th Street, Fifth Floor, New York, NY 10016.

Liahona. Reorganized Church of Jesus Christ of Latter Day Saints, Director of Scouting, The Auditorium, Box 1059, Independence, MO 64051-0559.

Light Is Life. Eastern Rite Catholic—local council service center.

Light of God. Association of Unity Churches, P.O. Box 610, Lee's Summit, MO 64063.

Living Faith. Lutheran—local council service center or PRAY, Box 6900, St. Louis, MO 63123.

ON MY HONOR
Church of Jesus Christ
of Latter-day Saints

THE OPEN WORD
General Church of the
New Jerusalem

SANGHA
Buddhist

GOD AND COUNTRY
Presbyterian

GOD AND COUNTRY
Methodist

UNITY OF MANKIND
Baha'i

GOD AND COUNTRY
Disciples of Christ

Ner Tamid. Jewish – local council service center or PRAY, Box 6900, St. Louis, MO 63123.

On My Honor. Church of Jesus Christ of Latter-day Saints, Church Distribution Center, 1999 West 1700 South, Salt Lake City, UT 84104.

Religion in Life. Unitarian Universalist or members of other liberal groups – Unitarian Universalist Association, 25 Beacon Street, Boston, MA 02150.

Sangha. Buddhist – Buddhist Churches of America, National Headquarters, 1710 Octavia Street, San Francisco, CA 94109.

Spirit of Truth. Religious Society of Friends (Quakers) – Friends Committee on Scouting, 85 Willbrook Road, Cromwell, CT 06416.

The Open Word. General Church of the New Jerusalem, Chairman, Boy Scout Relations Committee, General Church of the New Jerusalem, P.O. Box 278, Bryn Athyn, PA 19009.

Unity of Mankind. Baha'i – Baha'i Committee on Scouting, Baha'i National Center, Wilmette, IL 60091.

CHAPTER 28

MORE OPPORTUNITIES

Order of the Arrow. This is a national brotherhood of Scout campers. The honor of becoming a member of the Order of the Arrow is one that you cannot set out to earn on your own. This honor is bestowed on a Scout by the members of his troop. This is done when he has proved himself worthy of receiving it. He must be an outstanding Scout and an unselfish camper.

Alpha Phi Omega (APO). APO is a national college service fraternity active on many campuses. The fraternity is based on the principles of the Scout Oath and Law. APO's service program includes many opportunities for its members to continue their Scouting involvement through college connections. Many chapters are coeducational. For more information, contact the Alpha Phi Omega National Office, 400 Mainmark Building, 1627 Main Street, Kansas City, MO 64108.

National Eagle Scout Association (NESA). NESA is a fellowship of men who have achieved the Eagle Scout Award. Membership applications are available at your local council service center.

Exploring. When you have completed the eighth grade and are at least 14 years of age, or are 15 years of age or older, you may join an Explorer post. As an Explorer, you are a member of the Boy Scouts of America. You may also be in a Scout troop. Explorer posts often do some form of career exploration. Young women as well as young men may become Explorers.

HONOR MEDAL

HEROISM AWARD

MEDAL OF MERIT

LIFESAVING AWARDS

The National Court of Honor makes awards for rare Scoutlike action and for saving life.

Honor Medal. The highest special award in Scouting is the gold Honor Medal for saving life. This is awarded by the National Court of Honor. It is given to Scouts and Scouters who show heroism, resourcefulness, and skill by saving or trying to save life at the great risk of their own. In rare cases it is awarded with crossed palms.

Heroism Award. Awarded for heroic action where there is minimum risk to self.

Medal of Merit. The Medal of Merit is awarded by the National Court of Honor. It is given to Scouts who put into practice the skills and ideals of Scouting by doing some great act of service. This act need not necessarily be a rescue or involve risk to self.

ORGAN DONOR AWARENESS

A good idea for a service project is to help educate others in your community about the need for organ donation. The Boy Scouts of America did this on a nationwide basis as a Presidential Good Turn in 1986.

Because of advances in science, medicine, and surgery, it is possible to transplant numerous organs and tissues from one human to another with satisfactory results. About 50,000 people in the United States each year benefit from transplants. Thousands still wait for the miracle to happen that will keep them alive or improve the quality of their lives. A corneal transplant can return sight to a blind person. A skin transplant can speed the recovery of a burn victim. A bone transplant can enable a person confined to a wheelchair to walk again. A liver transplant can save a life. But there are not enough donors for the thousands of Americans who would benefit from an organ or tissue transplant.

Becoming an organ donor is easy. Complete a donor card and carry it with you at all times. Inform your family that you want to be a donor if the occasion arises. Organs and tissue are not removed without written approval of your next of kin. You may wish to have a family talk about organ and tissue donation.

To learn more about the need for and the process of organ and tissue donation, contact local donor organizations.

HIGH ADVENTURE
AND SPORTS

AS you become older, you want adventures that really test your Scouting know-how and increase your confidence. How about long treks in the backcountry, on wild rivers, and over the open road? Would you like to be part of a top-notch team playing softball, basketball, or any of a dozen other sports?

Those are just a few of the challenges you'll find in the Venture and Varsity program for older Scouts. This section of the *Boy Scout Handbook* tells you all about it.

VENTURE PROGRAM

HIGH ADVENTURE EMPHASIS

HOW would you like to become an expert winter camper, or set out on a 10-day backpacking trek across a rugged mountain range? Imagine guiding a whitewater canoe through the roaring rapids of a wilderness river, or using your mountaineering skills to rappel down the face of a sheer cliff.

Scouts in a Venture crew do all this and more. You can choose from among dozens of outdoor adventures. Your First Class skills give you the background you need to get started. Activities leading up to ultimate adventures will teach you everything else you must know to have safe, exciting experiences in the outdoors.

For example, one Venture crew selected a 500-mile bicycle trek as an ultimate adventure. Several months before the big trip, they began using their weekly meetings to learn all they could about bicycling. They invited a local bike mechanic to show them how to take apart a bicycle, lubricate it, adjust the gears, and fix flat tires. The mechanic also stressed how important it is for everyone to wear a safety helmet as they ride, and to obey all traffic laws.

An assistant Scoutmaster helped the crew find information about making bicycle saddlebags, or *panniers,* in which the Scouts could carry their camping gear. The Scouts also decided just what camping gear they would need during the long ride, and how to divide up group equipment.

On the weekends leading up to the ultimate adventure, the Venture crew members set out on bike rides of 40 miles or more. They also went on one overnight bike-hike so that they could test out their camping gear and be sure they were carrying just what they needed.

As the weeks of preparation went by, every Scout in the crew felt he was becoming a strong, experienced cyclist. One night the crew looked over the maps and made final decisions on the route of their 500-mile journey. They knew they were ready for the ultimate adventure.

Five hundred miles on a bicycle! As they made the long ride, they explored backroads far from home, camped each night in a different park, saw plenty of fresh sights, and met new people. They put many of their Scouting skills to good use—route finding, outdoor cooking, camping, and safe bicycling, to name a few. If an emergency had arisen along the way, the Scouts were prepared to handle that, too.

The Venture crew members returned home happy and full of new confidence. They had lots of stories to tell about their travels, but they were also eager to decide what their next ultimate adventure would be. Among their ultimate adventure options were snow camping, fishing, survival, and orienteering.

SPORTS EMPHASIS

While the Venture program can focus on ultimate adventures relating to the outdoors, it also gives older Scouts the chance to get involved in sports. A Venture crew may form to play volleyball, basketball, softball, or soccer. Other sports available to a team may include bowling, shooting, tennis, golf, racquetball, and swimming.

Venture crew members will devote much of their weekly meeting time to practicing the skills of a sport. They may invite experts from outside the troop to help them learn all they can and to help coach them in a sport. Referees who officiate local high school games could meet with a Venture crew interested in basketball and help them understand the rules of the game. The team might visit a nearby college athletic department, watch a practice, and talk with coaches and players. Under the guidance of their own crew chief and assistant Scoutmaster, Venture crew members practice their sport and become a close-knit squad. When they are ready, a team may challenge a Venture crew from another troop or participate in organized community leagues.

VENTURE CREW LEADERSHIP

The members of a Venture crew select a crew chief to represent them at the patrol leaders' council. He takes the leadership role of the crew and assigns tasks and duties that will help make the activity a reality. Crew members elect a crew chief each time they begin working toward a new ultimate adventure or sport.

An assistant Scoutmaster is assigned to each Venture crew by the Scoutmaster. His duties include working with the Venture crew chief to develop an outstanding program. He will advise the crew on where they can locate resources for each program, and help them find the outside experts they need to instruct them in Venture skills.

Older boys (13 and older) who have not been Scouts before are welcome to join troops with Venture programs. They must fulfill the basic joining requirements, but can then go directly into a Venture crew. An assistant Scoutmaster will meet with the parents of older Scouts who are new members of the troop and help them understand what the Venture program is all about.

VENTURE LETTER

Scouts in the Venture program may earn a letter "V" to be sewn on a Scout jacket or on the bottom of a merit badge sash. At the completion of each sports season or ultimate adventure, each Scout will receive a medallion that may be worn on the letter.

Requirements for earning the letter are

Date/assistant
Scoutmaster's initials

1. Be a registered troop member. _____ _____

2. While a crew member, actively participate in or accomplish at least one ultimate adventure/recognized sport (to the satisfaction of your assistant Scoutmaster). _____ _____

3. Have an attendance record at crew meetings and activity meetings/practice sessions of at least 75 percent for 3 consecutive months. _____ _____

4. Satisfy the assistant Scoutmaster that you know and live by the Scout Oath and Law. _____ _____

ABOUT THE VENTURE PROGRAM

The Venture program is a part of the regular troop, just as the new Scout patrol is a part of the troop. Older Scouts involved in the Venture program are encouraged to participate in campouts, service projects, camporees, and other troop activities. Venture members should continue to interact with other Scouts in the troop and serve in troop leadership roles.

Older Scouts are free to move back and forth between high adventure and sports opportunities. For example, they may decide they would like to do the Venture activity leading to an ultimate adventure in snow camping. For several weeks they learn all about snow camping. They make equipment, go on weekend campouts, then plan and complete an ultimate adventure by snow camping for a week in a remote area.

Those Scouts may next choose to form a team and spend several months becoming a well-trained volleyball squad. When they are ready, they may challenge Venture crews from other troops to a series of games, or they might represent their own troop in a city league.

As an older Scout, you may take advantage of any of the offerings of the Venture program. You will need to work hard to make the programs successful, but if you are willing to try, there is no limit to what you can accomplish.

Coed Activities

Venture program may be coeducational. Girls may take part in the Venture program as guests of Scouts in the crew. They may participate in meetings, team practices and games, and high-adventure preparations and activities. They may not register in the troop and cannot earn Scout badges of rank or hold offices in the troop.

VARSITY SCOUTING

VARSITY Scout teams are intended for young men who are at least 14 but not yet 18 years old and are available through organizations chartered by the Boy Scouts of America to deliver the Varsity Scout program. The Varsity Scout program is designed around five program fields of emphasis.

The name of the program is Varsity Scouting. Youth participants are known as Varsity Scouts. The adult leader of a group of Varsity Scouts is the Varsity Scout Coach. The basic unit of youth members is the Varsity Scout team. The youth leader of the team is the Varsity Scout captain. His associate or assistant leaders are called cocaptains. Smaller subdivisons of the team are called squads. The youth leader of a squad is the Varsity Scout squad leader. Youth who have responsibility for each of the five program fields of emphasis are called program managers.

LEADERS

We all know that the Scouting movement would not go very far without leaders. This goes for Varsity Scouting just as for Cub Scouting, Boy Scouting, and Exploring. Throughout Scouting, adults and youth work together as leaders so that the best possible Scouting experience happens for those who participate. In Varsity Scouting there are many leaders—about one leader for every two or three Varsity Scouts. Starting at the team level, here are some of the most important Varsity Scout leaders:

☆ *Team captain.* He's the youth leader of the team—really runs things (calls the signals). When he needs assistants, they are called cocaptains.

☆ *Program managers.* There are five program managers for every team — regardless of the number of boys in the team. Each manager is in charge of one of the five program fields of emphasis in Varsity Scouting — advancement, high adventure/sports, personal development, service, and special programs and events.

☆ *Squad leader.* In large teams with eight or more boys, the group is divided into squads with four to eight boys all working under a squad leader. Some teams find it helpful to have a team secretary, some need a treasurer, some a quartermaster, etc. These are positions of responsibility that teams can have if they need them.

PROGRAM FIELDS OF EMPHASIS

First and foremost, Varsity Scouting is a program of activities — things you can do that influence your thinking, attitudes, and behavior. Day-to-day programming for Varsity Scouting provides activities in all of the five program fields of emphasis. Each Varsity Scout is expected to participate regularly in each field.

Individualized Scout Advancement

As you enter Varsity Scouting, your status in the Scout advancement program is assessed by you, your Varsity Scout captain, and your Varsity

Scout Coach. Then a plan of action is custom-made for you, leading to your qualification for the Eagle Scout rank, or Eagle palm if you are already an Eagle Scout. Activities are arranged with these goals in mind. In addition, you may pursue and achieve other Scout awards and recognitions. The Varsity Scout team's *advancement manager* is responsible for coordinating advancement activities, personally encouraging each Varsity Scout to advance, and stimulating interest and enthusiasm for advancement work.

High-Adventure/Sports Activities

An important feature of Varsity Scout programming is the inclusion of challenging activities that require planning, resourcefulness, skills, and abilities. These activities are featured in the Venture (high-adventure) and Varsity (sports) pamphlets. Other high-adventure/sports activities could include the following:

☆ Experiences at national high-adventure bases (Philmont, Florida Sea Base, etc.)

☆ Camping experiences while on fishing, mountain climbing, wilderness backpacking expeditions, etc., with emphasis on practical application and development of basic camping techniques

☆ Noncamping educational, cultural, touring, or recreational activities

☆ Intercultural or international exchange or reciprocal visits

☆ Project COPE

Coordinating high-adventure and sports activities and promoting the participation and enthusiasm of each Varsity Scout are the chief responsibilities of the Varsity Scout team's *high-adventure/sports manager.*

VARSITY SCOUTING

Personal Development Programs

Serious, organized, and individualized effort is made to promote the Varsity Scout's personal growth and development in the areas of

☆ Spirituality

☆ Leadership abilities

☆ Citizenship

☆ Social and cultural attributes

☆ Physical fitness

The Varsity Scout team's *personal development manager* assists each member of the team in selecting and participating in activities from all five areas.

Service

As a Varsity Scout you can participate in group service projects for the benefit of your church, community, needy individuals, and worthwhile activities. In addition, you think up, plan, and conduct such service projects on

your own initiative. You are expected to continue the habit started in Scouting of doing a Good Turn daily, making it a constant ingredient in your life.

Assisting each Varsity Scout in developing a service-oriented way of life and coordinating all Varsity Scout group and individual service projects are responsibilities of the Varsity Scout team's *service manager.*

Special Programs and Events

Providing time, ways and means, and encouragement to participate in special programs and events is an important feature of Varsity Scouting. These special events are of three types: national Scouting activities; regional, area, council, and district events; and activities done by your team.

Some of the national programs, events, and organizations available to and particularly appropriate for you as a Varsity Scout are

☆ Order of the Arrow (OA)

☆ National Eagle Scout Association (NESA)

☆ National and world jamborees

☆ National scholarship awards for Scouts sponsored by industry

☆ Save Our American Resources (SOAR) projects

There are many others. The Varsity Scout team's *special programs and events manager* has the responsibility to coordinate participation in these events.

Varsity Scout Letter

By participating actively in all phases of Varsity Scouting, you can qualify for the Varsity Scout letter. The requirements are

Date/assistant
Scoutmaster's initials

1. Be a registered Varsity Scout team member. _____ _____

2. While a team member, actively participate in or accomplish at least one recognized Varsity or Venture program to the satisfaction of your Varsity Scout Coach. _____ _____

3. Have an attendance record at team meetings and practice sessions of at least 75 percent for 3 consecutive months. _____ _____

4. Satisfy the Varsity Scout Coach that you know and live by the Scout Oath and Law. _____ _____

Medallions can be inserted into the "V" letter to denote the specific ultimate adventure or sport that has been completed. The letter can be worn on the Varsity Scout blaze jacket or the bottom front of the merit badge sash.

Meetings

Varsity Scouts generally meet once a week for 1½ to 2 hours. Varsity Scout meetings are of two types—the team meeting and the team activity.

The team meeting is primarily a business meeting for reports, checkups, and planning. The team captain presides over the team meeting. The specific agenda for each team meeting is arranged by the team leaders. Typically, the meeting has a short opening ceremony, followed by a brief welcome and general announcements or explanations. Next, each of the five program managers conducts business related to his assignment (advancement, personal develop-

With the completion of team business, if time permits, the meeting may break into smaller groups, such as squads or more informal groups of young men working together on specific service projects or advancement.

Frequently, a short appropriate inspirational or motivational message is given by the Coach or a visiting dignitary during the meeting. This is known as the Coach's Corner.

The second type of meeting, the activity meeting, is primarily a planned activity session. The team carries out, either as a complete group or in smaller groups (squads), a planned activity that was selected from any of the five program fields of emphasis. The appropriate program manager conducts the activity meeting.

Uniform

The Varsity Scout uniform is the field uniform of the Boy Scouts of America with distinctive blaze-colored shoulder loops and a "Varsity" identification strip above the right pocket. There is also an activities uniform available for teams. This uniform consists of a tan knit shirt, Boy Scout shorts, and Boy Scout socks.

The official Varsity Scout uniform should be worn to formal Scouting activities such as courts of honor, recognition dinners, or similar functions.

No badges of office, special recognition, or rank may be worn on the activities uniform. The activities uniform is designed to be worn at events and functions where there will be a high level of physical activity.

CREDITS

Illustrations

Don Adair—pages vii–ix, 372–73, 586–87

Ron Adair—pages 18–19, 532–33, 630–31

Frank Bolle—pages 38, 72, 73, 86, 87, 91, 200, 242, 288, 289, 290, 408, 410, 412, 434, 449, 452

Howard Chandler Christy (courtesy Archives of the Capitol)—page 458

Jim Darnell and Randy Fisher—pages 562–63

Robert Depew—pages 31, 34, 40, 60, 70, 87, 88, 95, 112, 114, 115, 119, 121, 122, 125, 127, 149, 154, 170, 171, 191, 216, 232, 233, 234, 235, 236, 238, 319, 329, 349, 350, 359

Randy Fisher—pages 580–81

Joseph Forte—pages 50, 72, 83, 119 (bottom), 151, 155, 352, 415, 420, 421, 433.

Fred Henley—pages 462–63, 464–65, 479

Taylor Oughton—pages 251–57, 260–77, 291–317, 321–23, 325–27, 330–31, 333–39, 341–45, 352, 423, 427, 428

Joel Snyder—pages 39, 141, 142, 143, 144, 145, 148, 167, 168, 198, 199, 203, 204, 205, 206, 208, 243, 354–55, 364–65, 368, 406, 442, 492–93

Other artwork by Bernard Barton, and G. Don Ray

Photographs

Amateur Athletic Foundation of Los Angeles—page 499 (right)

American Red Cross—page 499 (left)

Eric Bakke—pages 6 (top left, top right), 9, 41, 44 (bottom), 48 (top), 49, 57, 59, 99 (bottom right), 108, 109 (top), 110, 113, 114, 172, 187, 195 (top, center), 224 (top), 430, 431, 446, 447 (top), 502, 503, 522

Barclay Bollas—page 575 (top right)

Jack Brown—pages 348, 477 (center)

Darrell Byers—pages 40, 73 (bottom), 74 (top), 75 (top), 78, 82, 93 (top), 102 (top), 104, 150, 160 (top), 163, 169, 175, 177 (bottom), 196, 202 (bottom), 210, 225, 374, 379, 393 (top), 394, 395, 396, 404 (top left, bottom right), 491, 497 (right), 504 (right), 505, 517 (bottom), 519, 520, 592, 635

Phil Davis—pages 575 (bottom right), 576 (bottom right)

Richard DeWeese—pages 28–29, 31, 34, 36, 51, 53, 54, 64, 77 (top), 80, 94, 162 (bottom), 218–19, 427 (top), 435

W. B. Hamilton, USGS Photo Library, Denver, Colo.—page 26 (bottom left)

Vince Heptig—pages 576 (lower left), 577 (top)

R. D. Jarrett, USGS Photo Library, Denver, Colo.—page 443 (right)

Carolyn Kohls—page 425

Kevin Kolczynski—pages 3 (center right, right), 5, 6 (bottom left), 8, 93 (bottom), 95, 99 (top), 103, 106, 124 (top), 125, 160 (bottom), 174 (left), 186 (top), 207 (bottom), 227 (top left, bottom), 230 (top left), 231 (top left, bottom left), 237, 238, 239, 346, 384, 389, 392, 393 (bottom), 418, 433, 476 (top), 497 (top), 521, 524, 527, 536 (top right), 543 (bottom)

Doug Knutson—pages 32, 33, 35, 43 (bottom), 48 (bottom), 88, 99 (bottom left), 109 (bottom), 118, 162 (inset), 164, 202 (top), 367, 385, 386, 387, 390, 415, 432, 436 (bottom left), 469, 476 (bottom), 490, 497 (bottom left), 504 (bottom left), 509, 510, 513, 543 (top left)

Chris Michaels—pages 6 (left), 20, 24, 26 (top left), 30, 56, 102 (bottom), 124 (bottom), 126 (bottom), 158, 173 (top right), 178, 184 (top), 189, 207 (top), 208, 214 (bottom right), 222, 224 (bottom left), 244, 245, 284 (bottom), 371, 378, 382, 383, 417, 422, 423 (bottom), 426, 427 (bottom), 428, 438 (top left), 456, 474, 477 (top, bottom), 486, 489, 498, 506, 507, 508, 526, 528, 529, 545 (bottom left), 546 (right), 552 (center, bottom left, bottom right), 559 (top left, top right), 560 (left), 632

National Aeronautics and Space Adminis-
tration—pages 360, 467 (center left)
National Air and Space Museum—page 467
(bottom left)
National Severe Storm Laboratory—page
443 (left)
National Weather Service—page 443
New York Public Library Schomburg
Center—page 466 (right)
Brian Payne—pages 536 (left), 537 (top left,
top right), 545 (top right), 559 (center
left), 560 (top), 575 (bottom left), 576
(top), 577 (inset)
Randy Piland—pages 11, 17, 23 (bottom),
26 (top), 44 (top), 65 (bottom), 66, 67, 71
(top right, bottom right), 75 (bottom),89,
176, 242, 447 (all at bottom), 454(top left,

bottom), 455, 494, 516, 517 (top)
J. G. Rosenbaum, USGS Photo Library,
Denver, Colo.—page 258
Dr. Edward S. Ross—page 249
Tuservices—page 440
U.S. Department of the Interior/Robert
Pankey—page 467 (top left)
USS *Arizona* National Monument—page
467 (top right)
Paul Williams—page 98
Doug Wilson—pages 3 (left), 69, 177 (top),
224 (bottom), 226, 227 (top), 366, 403,
423 (top), 436, 438 (top right, bottom
right), 439, 473, 495, 496 (bottom), 500,
511, 512 (right), 525, 531, 534, 539
(right), 552 (top left, top right), 572 (top
left), 590, 591

A special task force of Scoutmasters reviewed the manuscript for this tenth edition of the *Boy Scout Handbook*. The Boy Scouts of America is grateful to these men for their insights and comments. The Scoutmasters are William Balfrey, Seaside Park, New Jersey; Michael Bernhardt, Hockessin, Delaware; George W. Bunnell, Jr., Hamden, Connecticut; Russell B. DeVore, Bloomsburg, Pennsylvania; Erland C. Hedblom, Brunswick, Maine; Craig L. Henderson, Elmira, New York; Robert F. Knapp, Pittsburgh, Pennsylvania; Robert C. Lohnes, Whitestone, New York; Frank P. Macaluso, Brooklyn, New York; John F. Rauber, Dansville, New York; Philander M. Wiggins, Sr., Baltimore, Maryland; Stanley J. Zabawa, Middletown, New Jersey; Henry T. Armstrong, Augusta, Georgia; Robert Burke, Winter Park, Florida; Charles Call, Merritt Island, Florida; Daniel M. Fendley, Monroe, Georgia; James A. Hardin, Nashville, Tennessee; John B. Kinney, Burlington, North Carolina; Aaron K. Lyle III, Roanoke, Virginia; David L. Nunn, Williamsburg, Virginia; Robert Pope, McNeill, Mississippi; Larry M. Reid, Spanish Fort, Alabama; James Y. Robinson, Hilton Head, South Carolina; Edgar Shults, Sr., Dyersburg, Tennessee; Richard O. Smith, Columbus, Georgia; Ray T. Throckmorton, Brentwood, Tennessee; Larry E. Warlick, High Point, North Carolina; John Wiggins, Miami, Florida; Jerry D. Brewster, Jr., Mayfield Heights, Ohio; Lester Brown, Danville, Illinois; Charles R. Greenwood, New Cumberland, West Virginia; Robert D. Koenig, Middleton, Wisconsin; Glenn D. Miller, Washington, West Virginia; Henry M. Newcome, Bowling Green, Ohio; Peter Probst, Franklin, Wisconsin; Dee Slate, Peters, Michigan; Albin Sporny, Jr., Glenwood, Illinois; John C. Valdez, Indianapolis, Indiana; Milan Vosvick, Jr., Wheeling, West Virginia; Phil Washington, Southfield, Michigan; Larry A. Weaver, Marion, Indiana; Ron Begeman, Mayview, Missouri; Chuck Biskner, Ames, Iowa; Reid A. Christopherson, Sioux Falls, South Dakota; Tom Dobelbower, Topeka, Kansas; Ted Fahs, Chesterfield, Missouri; Dave Henning, Cottage Grove, Minnesota; David C. Lunning, Jr., O'Fallon, Illinois; Thomas J. Noakes, Denver, Colorado; Matt Paloma, Jr., Gering, Nebraska; John Phipps, Iowa City, Iowa; James Arnold, Lubbock, Texas; Joe Bicik, Plano, Texas; Jim Bryant, Hewitt, Texas; James E. Farley, Edmond, Oklahoma; James D. McClure, Albuquerque, New Mexico; Louis Rodrigue, Kenner, Louisiana; George William Shaffer, Tulsa, Oklahoma; Raul Torres, San Benito, Texas; Joseph Bertola, Apple Valley, California; John R. Black, Idaho Falls, Idaho; Charles Ingelbrigtsen, San Jose, California; Hugh Garrett Jacobs, Hayden Lake, Idaho; Wayne Joffs, Salt Lake City, Utah; Crissman R. Lawrence, Phoenix, Arizona; Charles Marr, Redwood City, California; James H. Milham, Las Vegas, Nevada; Dick Phillips, Astoria, Oregon; and Charles Snedeker, El Toro, California.

INDEX

A tradition of excitement and challenge:

Original edition, 1910

First edition, 1911

Second edition, 1915

Third edition, 1927

Fourth edition, 1940

Fifth edition, 1948

Sixth edition, 1959

Seventh edition, 1965

Eighth edition, 1972

Ninth edition, 1979

Tenth edition, 1990

The latest *Boy Scout Handbook* continues the tradition of guidebooks to terrific adventures, the best way to enjoy the outdoors and gain lifetime skills.